Alf Martensson's Book of
FURNITURE MAKING

Alf Martensson's Book of
FURNITURE MAKING

COLLINS

Managing editor	Wendy Martensson
Editor	Pamela Tubby
Technical editor	Alison Louw
Assistant editor	David Parker
Design	Flax + Kingsnorth Zena Flax, Carole Hay, Linda Murphy, Colin Stone
Photography	Chris Overton
Illustration	Terry Allen Designs Limited Lyn Brooks, Roger Courthold, Robert Stoneman

© Alf Martensson, 1979, 1983

First published in paperback (metricated) in 1983

First published in hardback
as *The Book of Furniture Making* in 1979
Reprinted 1980, 1982

Published by William Collins Sons & Co Ltd
London · Glasgow · Sydney
Auckland · Johannesburg

Printed in Spain

ISBN 0 00 411781 6

How to use
Alf Martensson's Book of
FURNITURE
MAKING

In this book we have tried to overcome the limitation of most books on woodworking by showing specific instructions for actual projects as well as general woodworking techniques. And to make the projects section and the techniques section work together, we have included frequent cross references from one section to the other to help illustrate points.

Before starting a project, read through the instructions at least twice to get a good, overall impression of the work involved. If there are unfamiliar techniques follow the cross references and read the appropriate techniques pages.

Notice that the shopping list includes all the items you will need to make the project with the exception of things like sandpaper and glue which you may already have on hand. It is a good idea to have all the materials together before you start so that you will have no interruptions when you work. Make a copy of the shopping list and take it with you when buying wood or hardware. Notice that the wood lengths shown already allow for about ten per cent waste, so don't add anything to the lengths given.

For most projects you can use readily available standard softwood sections. We have also specified standard 1220×2440mm sheets of plywood or chipboard throughout.

Since large sheets are difficult to transport and to cut up accurately, it is a good idea to find a wood supplier who will cut it up for you. Take the cutting lists and diagrams with you and make sure to take a tape measure and try square to check the work. Remember that the success of any project depends very much on accurate cutting.

Keep in mind that all the project instructions can be varied where necessary to suit specific needs and personal tastes.

Please note that the metric sizes of some materials vary from country to country, and indeed, from supplier to supplier. Thus, 19mm plywood, converted from $\frac{3}{4}$in, may be 18, 19, or even 20mm. Check all supplies carefully and if necessary adapt the instructions.

CONTENTS

KITCHEN AND DINING PROJECTS

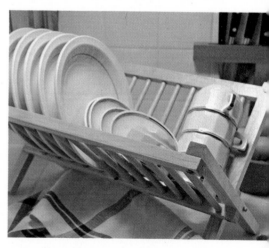
Cutting board

Country kitchen

Kitchen work island

Dining chair

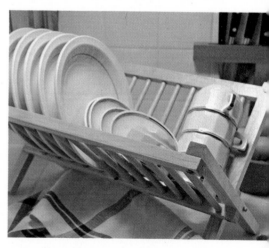
Standing dishrack

Slat unit

Town kitchen

A custom made kitchen is special not only because it can be made to fit the exact measurements of a room, but also because it can be designed to reflect your taste. This chapter has instructions for two complete kitchens which use inexpensive materials and which will give you a lot of good design ideas. The section also includes a classic pine dining table, an elegant beech and cork gate leg table with matching chairs, a kitchen work island and an array of smaller projects like dishracks, cutting boards and storage racks.

Country kitchen

Gate leg table

Town kitchen

Trivets

Welsh dresser

Pine dining table

TRIVETS

Teak trivet

These trivets look best made in a dark hardwood such as teak or mahogany. As an alternative, use softwood stained a dark tone.

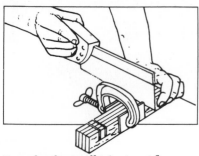

To make the small trivet, cut four 12 × 40mm teak strips, 150mm long. Clamp them together and mark a 12mm wide slot about 40mm from each end. Hold a 12mm strip against the marks to check the slot width. Cut within the

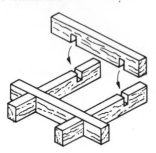

waste area to half the depth and use a chisel to clear out the waste.

Make sure that the pieces fit snugly together without glue.

Finish the trivet by rubbing in two coats of linseed or teak oil.

Follow the same procedure for making the larger 225mm square trivet which requires 14 strips of teak 12 × 40mm long. Take extra care when marking and cutting as the slots must line up exactly for all the pieces to fit together without breaking.

Plywood trivet

To make this trivet you will need a 175 × 325mm piece of 12mm plywood and two of 25mm diameter dowel, 200mm long. Cut the plywood into seven 45mm wide strips each 175mm long. To drill the

holes for the dowels, use a 25mm bit. The holes should be centred 40mm from each end. Clamp the pieces to the bench with waste underneath. Use a centre punch to mark the exact location then drill the two holes all the way through. Make sure that you hold the drill vertical.

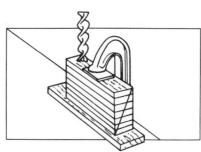

Before unclamping, mark a diagonal line down one edge as shown so that the pieces can be reassembled in the same order. Sand all the pieces including the dowel.

Then push the plywood pieces onto the dowels and space them out evenly. Add glue or small pins from underneath if the pieces fit loosely. Finish the trivet either with clear polyurethane or, as here, with a teak shade polyurethane stain.

CUTTING BOARDS

Plywood end grain chopping board

This unusual 240mm square chopping board is made up of strips of birch plywood turned on edge and glued together like the coffee tables on page 166. It is best to use a fairly thick plywood, at least 19mm, so you will need fewer strips. From a piece of 19mm plywood, 350 × 890mm, cut about twenty strips 40mm wide and 350mm long. Glue the pieces together with waterproof resin glue making sure that the edges line up. As you glue each piece on, secure it with two 25mm pins. This keeps the pieces from sliding when clamped together.

After clamping, use a block plane or belt sander to smooth the surface. Finally mark a diamond shape on the board using a mitre square (page 193) or a 45° triangle. Saw carefully along the lines and then sand the edges well.

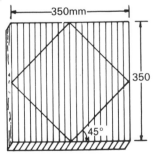

Seal the board by applying several coats of polyurethane. It may be necessary to re-seal the board from time to time to keep it waterproof.

Oval meat platter

Make a board about 300 × 500 × 25mm thick by gluing up smaller boards if necessary. Use teak, mahogany, cherry or, as shown here, American black walnut. Plane and sand the board before marking out the oval shape. If you have difficulty in drawing an oval, start with a rectangle and draw a semi-circle at either end. Cut out the oval with a sabre or coping saw. Then smooth out the curve using a file or rasp, checking often by eye that the curve is regular and smooth on both ends of the board.

The groove which catches the meat juices can be cut out with a gouge, but only by someone with a steady

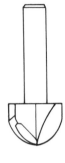

and experienced hand. It is far easier to use a router with a core box cutter. Set the guide designed to follow curves so that the groove is cut about 25mm from the edge of the board (page 216).

Finishing the board

Scrape the board with a cabinet scraper (page 205) and sand the groove and edges carefully. After the final sanding wipe the surface with a damp cloth to raise the grain and then sand again. Finally apply one or two coats of salad oil or olive oil.

Pine board with dowel insets

By simply insetting a few ordinary dowels in a pine board, you can make a novel and beautifully decorated chopping board.

Make sure the drill bit matches the diameter of the dowel exactly by first drilling a trial hole in a piece of waste wood. Dowels vary slightly in diameter so it may be necessary to reject any which are smaller than the sizes required.

Use a pine board about 225 × 375mm at least 25mm thick. Start with the largest diameter dowel. Drill a hole about 20mm deep making sure not to go all the way through the board. Cut off a length of dowel just slightly longer than the hole is deep and glue it in place.

After the glue sets, plane the dowel flush using a block plane.

Continue drilling holes and setting in dowels of various sizes in the four corners until you build up a pleasing pattern.

PINE DINING TABLE

This elegant dining table is simple and straightforward in its design and it would look equally good in a traditional or in a modern setting. The top is made from pine boards glued together to make up a smooth surface. If you use butt joints they must be well made, close fitting and joined with a resin glue to hold firmly. However, to be sure the joints won't open up when the wood expands or contracts it is better to reinforce the joints with dowel pegs as explained in the instructions below.

Assembling the rails and legs

CUTTING LIST
38 × 100mm
    2 pieces 1625mm long, for rails
    2 pieces 540mm long, for rails
75 × 75mm
    4 pieces 725mm long, for legs

After cutting and squaring the legs and rails, make dowel joints for the leg to rail connections. Use two 100mm long dowel pegs for each joint and space them about 55mm apart (page232). Be careful to mark all the pieces and joints in turn as each one is drilled so that they will be assembled in the correct order.

After drilling all the dowel holes, sand the pieces so that the edges are gently rounded. A useful trick furniture makers use is to bevel the front edge of the rail ends and also the edges of the legs with a block plane. This tends to make any errors in alignment between the rail and the leg less obvious.

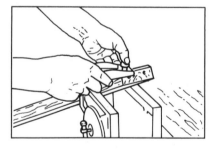

Join each long rail to its two legs, allow the glue to set and then join the assembled pair with the short rails. The joints shouldn't need clamping, but because of the size of the framework it is advisable to use

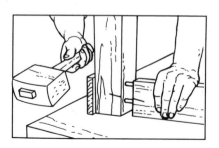

clamps to hold the final assembly together until the glue sets.

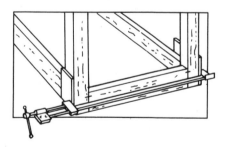

Making the top

CUTTING LIST
25 × 150mm
    5 pieces 1900mm long
    (to be trimmed)

Start by laying the five boards on the bench and selecting the best face. Try various combinations of boards to get the most pleasing grain patterns on the top. Arrange the boards so that the end grains alternate to minimize warping.

Mark the boards as shown to remember the order. Then check that matching boards are straight and true by holding them together in pairs to check for gaps. Thin boards tend to slide a little under clamping pressure so, to hold them in place and to strengthen the joint, add four short dowel pegs along each joint (page 232). Lay the clamps on the bench or on sawhorses, add glue and join up the boards according to the markings.

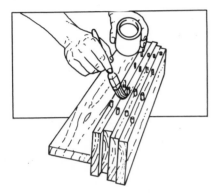

Remember to alternate the clamps over and under the boards to prevent the top from arching up or down (page 231). As an alternative to using bar clamps, make your own clamping jig (page 203). Be sure to protect the work with pieces of waste wood so that the clamps do not mar the edges.

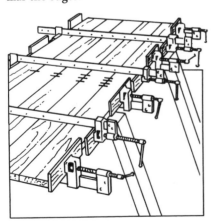

Using a damp rag, wipe up any glue that squeezes out of the joints. When the glue has set, remove the clamps and clean up the top with a plane or a power sander to make it smooth and even. Finally, trim the top to length and finish sanding it smooth. Use a sanding block, block plane or router to round the edges so that they feel smooth to the touch.

SHOPPING LIST
to make a standard size table, 725 × 1800mm to seat 8

softwood	10.5m of 25 × 150mm (choose straight clear pieces) 5m of 38 × 100mm 3.5m of 75 × 75mm
hardware	30 no.8 round head screws, 19mm long 10 metal shrinkage brackets with slotted holes
plus	1m of 10mm diameter dowel for pegs, cut into 16 pieces 40mm long, 1.8m of 12mm diameter dowel for pegs; cut into 16 pieces 100mm long clear polyurethane

As an alternative, make a top out of 25 × 50mm lengths of pine, glued and pinned in the same way as the plywood table on page 166. Mixing dark stain with the glue emphasizes the thin lines of the boards and adds an elegant touch to the table.

Final assembly

Carefully lay the top face down on a blanket on the bench or on the floor and centre the leg assembly to even the overhang on all sides. Then mark the holes for the brackets and drill the screw holes carefully to avoid going straight through the top. Fit a depth stop to the drill to be sure you don't drill too deep. Three shrinkage brackets per side and two per end is about right. Use the slot which allows the screw to move across the boards as the table top will expand and contract with the seasons (page 220). Then turn the table over and inspect the top for marks and scratches. Carefully sand these smooth before you apply the first coat of polyurethane.

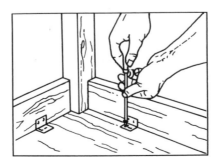

Finishing the table

Sanding is all important for a good finish. Start with medium paper (80 to 100 grit) and finish with fine (about 150 grit). An orbital sander makes the job easier but sometimes leaves small circular marks on the surface. Sanding by hand still achieves the best results. Before applying the first coat of thinned polyurethane, wipe the top with a damp rag to raise the grain. Allow to dry and sand smooth. Apply three or four coats, sanding with very fine paper or fine steel wool between each application (page 248).

DISHRACKS

Hanging dishrack

Making the shelves

CUTTING LIST
19 × 19mm
    15 pieces
    220mm long, for top shelf
    13 pieces
    245mm long, for middle shelf
    3 pieces
    270mm long, for bottom shelf
19 × 38mm
    2 pieces
    155mm long, for top shelf
    2 pieces
    180mm long, for middle shelf
    2 pieces
    205mm long, for bottom shelf
    6 pieces
    600mm long, two for each shelf

Start by making the top shelf. Join
the two 155mm lengths of
19 × 38mm between the 600mm
lengths with one 60mm long dowel
peg per corner. Clamp the pieces
together and drill through from the
outside. Then simply tap the pegs
into the glued hole and cut the dowel
off flush. One dowel per joint is
enough because the nailed strips will
make the shelf more secure.

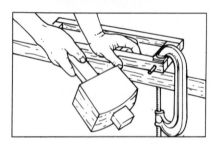

Glue and nail the 220mm lengths to
the frame. Use a piece of waste wood
as a spacer, leaving a 25mm space
between the strips. Set the nails and
fill the holes.

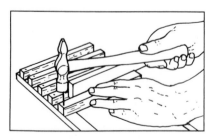

The other two shelves are made in
exactly the same way except that the
spacing between the nailed strips
should be increased to 35mm to hold
larger plates.

SHOPPING LIST	
softwood	12.2m of 19 × 19mm / 6.7m of 19 × 38mm / 1.5m of 25 × 50mm
dowel	1m of 6mm diameter for pegs
hardware	24 no.6 countersunk brass screws, 32mm long
	12 no.6 brass screw cup washers
	about 100 finishing nails or panel pins, 25mm long
	2 brass mirror brackets with 19mm screws
plus	wood filler / clear polyurethane

Assembling the dishrack

CUTTING LIST
25 × 50mm   2 pieces 710mm long
19 × 38mm   6 pieces 250mm long

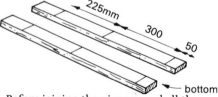

Before joining the pieces, sand all the
shelves well, then mark the two
25 × 50mm pieces as shown to judge
the location of the shelves. Attach
the 25 × 50mm to the back of each
shelf first with a pin to hold it
temporarily, then with two 32mm
screws per joint. Notice the wood
blocks under the shorter shelves to
help support them.

To attach the diagonal bracing, first
hold one 250mm piece in place and
mark the angle to be sawn. Then cut
six identical pieces and screw them
in place to the 25 × 50mm and to the
shelf using one 32mm screw with a
screw cup washer.

Finish with three coats of clear
polyurethane and attach the mirror
brackets to hang the dishrack.

SHOPPING LIST	
softwood	3.7m of 19 × 38mm
dowel	5.2m of 10mm diameter
hardware	8 no.6 countersunk brass screws, 25mm long
	8 no.6 countersunk brass screw cup washers

Standing dishrack

CUTTING LIST
19 × 38mm
    4 pieces 448 mm long
    4 pieces 300mm long
10mm dowel
    26 pieces 175mm long
    2 pieces 75mm long

Begin by marking one of the 448mm lengths into fourteen equal 32mm spaces. Mark along the narrow edge starting 32mm from the end. Transfer the marks to the other three lengths with a try square. Then use a centre punch or nail to mark the thirteen centres for the dowels on each strip.

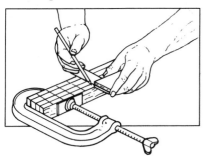

Drill thirteen 10mm diameter holes in each strip, using a depth stop to make the holes 20mm deep (page 195). Before inserting the dowels, taper the ends slightly with sandpaper so that they will fit into the holes more easily. Add a drop of glue to each hole and tap thirteen dowels into the holes of one strip. Then fit the second strip onto the dowels by tapping lightly with a mallet. Repeat this procedure with the second pair of 448mm lengths and the remaining thirteen dowels to make the two sides of the dishrack.

Then simply screw the 300mm lengths to the frames and join the two assemblies by slotting them together and drilling and installing the 75mm lengths of dowel through each pair of legs to allow the dishrack to be folded flat when not in use.

Cutlery stand

A flower pot is perfect for drying and storing everyday cutlery. Make this stand for a 125mm pot by dowel jointing four pieces of 25 × 50mm together; two pieces should be 100mm long and two 190mm long. Clamp the four pieces together to drill the holes and tap in 75mm long 6mm diameter dowel pegs, two per corner. Instead of cutting the dowels off flush, leave the ends sticking out about 3mm as a decorative feature. Mark and cut a circular shape along the inside to fit the diameter of the flower pot. For the legs, cut four pieces of 32 or 38mm diameter dowelling, long enough to allow the base of the flower pot to hang clear of the worktop. Attach the legs by dowel jointing from the top. Sand smooth and finish with at least two coats of clear polyurethane.

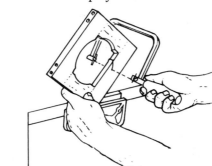

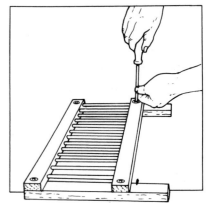

COUNTRY KITCHEN

Having a brand new kitchen installed can be an expensive business and may come at a time when there is a lot of other building and decorating work to pay for. At first glance this kitchen looks much too complicated, but if you examine each component on its own, you will see that it is not as difficult as it looks.

The small alcove in the corner was used to advantage by filling it with a full height spice rack large enough to hold a collection of cookbooks too. Adapt the basic instructions on page 116 for making the unit using plywood or chipboard. Then paint the shelf to give a touch of bright colour to the kitchen.

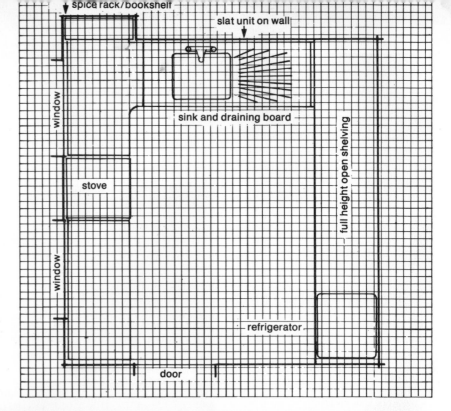

spice rack/bookshelf

slat unit on wall

window

sink and draining board

stove

full height open shelving

window

refrigerator

door

Measuring and planning

Kitchens differ very much from house to house. The size and shape vary as do the number of appliances and the location of plumbing, windows, doors, and so on. As a result, specific measurements of units are not given here. Make up your own cutting and order lists, starting by drawing a plan of your kitchen to scale on graph paper with each square representing, say, a 100mm area of floor space. Locate the stove, sink, refrigerator and any other appliances where you want them and then determine the lengths of the units in between, allowing 25mm clearance on each side of the appliances.

The best way to plan each unit is to divide it up into several subdivisions about 450mm wide and then leave any remaining space for things like tray storage, towel rails or broom closets.

Large department stores and specialist suppliers sell many handy kitchen gadgets such as pull-out towel rails, plastic-coated wire baskets, door-mounted bins and the like which you can incorporate into your unit design. Other accessories such as a pull-out ironing board and extension tables can also be fitted into your cabinets.

Choosing materials

The insides of the cabinets should be easy to clean so the best material to use is plastic laminate-covered chipboard which is both inexpensive, good looking and washable. It is available in several colours from larger suppliers in standard 1220 × 2440mm sheets or in handy lengths of varying width. The 525mm width is ideal for these units. Alternatively, use an inexpensive grade of plywood and finish it with several coats of polyurethane to make it washable.

The front edges can be treated in several ways. For laminate-covered chipboard apply matching iron-on edging (page 267), or cover as shown by gluing and nailing on dark-stained strips of pine.

The backs of the units can be of ordinary hardboard or thin plywood. The main function of the back, besides keeping out the dust, is to stabilize the cabinets and to keep them square.

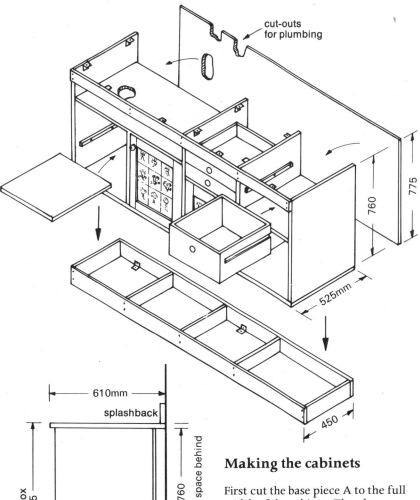

cut-outs for plumbing

775

760

525mm

450

610mm

splashback

approx 915

760

60 mm space behind

125

locating bracket

Making the cabinets

First cut the base piece A to the full width of the cabinet. Then lay out the 450mm divisions separated by the thickness of the dividing panels. Make the base piece A and all the dividers 525mm from front to back. Since the worktop will be 610mm wide, this allows a 25mm overhang at the front and a 60mm clear space at the back for the plumbing.

Cut the 525mm wide dividers 760mm long, then lay base and dividers on edge on the floor to assemble them.

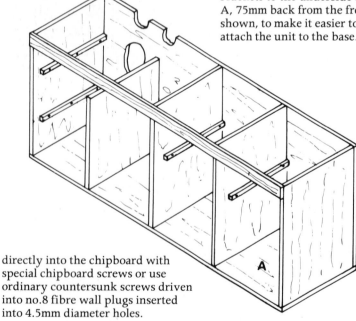

Notice that the divider under the sink has been cut off to accommodate a panel fitted under the sink.

First put in two or three 38mm pins hammered from the outside to hold the pieces until the screws are added. Then add three 38mm no.8 screws at each joint, either screw

directly into the chipboard with special chipboard screws or use ordinary countersunk screws driven into no.8 fibre wall plugs inserted into 4.5mm diameter holes.

Installing the units

First place the base in its exact location 60mm out from the wall. Then, using a spirit level, check to make sure it is completely level both along the length and also across the width. Most often the floor will not be quite level so wedge the base with scraps of hardboard to get it firm and level,

Then glue and nail the 775mm high panel to the back with 19mm pins. It is best to nail along the bottom edge first, then nail into each divider in turn making sure that each one is absolutely square with the base.

Cut out the fascia piece, 60mm wide and about 19mm thick, and screw it to the top front. Counterbore the screws, then hide them with plugs for pine fascias as here, or with plastic screw covers to match the plastic laminate surface.

Locate 450 × 525mm shelves within the cabinets, supporting them on 25 × 25mm battens screwed to the sides. Make the separate 450mm wide base out of 125mm wide boards nailed together.

Finally screw metal shrinkage brackets flush with the top edges of the dividing panels and the fascia. Also add two or three locating brackets to the underside of the base A, 75mm back from the front edge as shown, to make it easier to locate and attach the unit to the base.

and then attach it to the floor with a few metal brackets to fix the cabinet permanently in place and keep it level.

Place the unit on top of the base, sliding it back so that the brackets locate on the front. Finally screw these brackets to the base to fix the cabinet firmly in position.

Making the doors

The doors are a 25 × 50mm pine frame dowel jointed and fitted with a 6.5mm plywood panel. These panels are covered with an attractive gift wrapping paper printed with a William Morris tile design. Glue the paper to the plywood with a rubber-based cement and give it two coats of polyurethane to make it water-proof.

The panels can be covered with any attractive paper, as they have been here, or with a washable wallpaper, sturdy fabric or even with cane which is available in sheet form (page 70). You could also paint the panels or use plastic laminate.

Measure each opening to get the exact size for each door, allowing about 3mm for clearance. Then cut and join the 25 × 50mm pieces (page 232). The centre panel can be located either in grooves or rabbets cut into the frame. Or, to make it very easy, the panel can simply be screwed to the back of the frame with brass screws and matching cup washers.

Fit two small brass hinges and a knob to each door before hanging it in its opening. Then fit small magnetic stops behind each door.

Making the drawers

These consist of 25 × 125mm pine boards with 6.5mm plywood bases set into grooves. These exposed corner box joints were machine cut but can be hand cut (page 237).

It is very convenient to have most of the top drawers quite shallow for cutlery and the like, but a few deeper drawers are also useful. Make the sides for the deep drawers by gluing two boards together.

The worktops

In the kitchen shown here, the work-tops have been made quite easily by laminating 38 × 38mm strips of pine together. To do this, just follow the instructions given on page 12 for making the pine dining table.

As an alternative, you can buy a ready-made counter top and have it cut to the required length. A maple butcherblock top, like the one used as the work surface on the kitchen island on page 24, would be ideal.

You could also, if you prefer, make the counter tops with a chipboard or plywood base and cover them with a plastic laminate as shown on page 46. There are many possibilities and you can select the one that best suits your decorative scheme and your budget.

Make the 100mm high splashback from the same materials as the worktop. It is useful and hygienic, preventing food from falling behind the cabinets

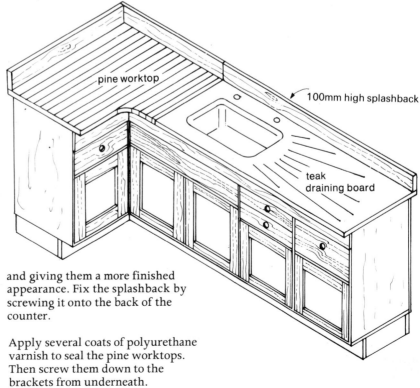

and giving them a more finished appearance. Fix the splashback by screwing it onto the back of the counter.

Apply several coats of polyurethane varnish to seal the pine worktops. Then screw them down to the brackets from underneath.

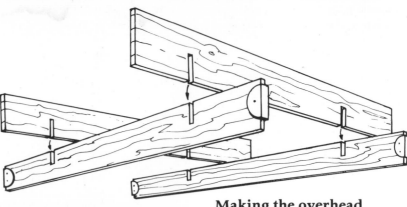

Kitchen storage

The conventional approach to storage in kitchen design is to enclose everything in cabinets; cooking utensils, groceries, pots and pans and the like. But today, many kitchen implements are so colourful and attractive that they can be used to decorate the kitchen. This makes the job of designing your kitchen much easier because, instead of the standard wall-hung cabinets, you can build attractive open storage units to keep everything within easy reach and on show.

The overhead pot hanger is a great idea. Instead of searching for a pan in a cabinet and having to move everything to get it, you just reach up to get the one you want off its hook. The simple slat unit not only holds all the bits and pieces but can also be used to cover any ugly pipes on the wall. The hooks are very easy to make from wire coathangers using the method shown on page 23.

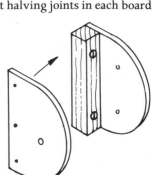

Making the overhead pot hanger

Cut four 25 × 200mm pine boards so that one pair spans the full length of the kitchen in one direction and the other pair spans the room in the other direction.

They should be located about 450mm out from each wall and placed high enough so that the pots and pans will be above head height but low enough to be within reach.

Cut halving joints in each board,

Left:
Instead of the usual stainless steel draining board, make one out of solid teak boards glued together with waterproof glue. Because it contains natural oil which repels water, teak is the ideal wood to use for this purpose. If maintained by regular oiling it will look like new for many years. Cut a hole for your sink with a sabre or coping saw and then cut the 6mm deep grooves of the draining board using a router fitted with a core box cutter. Mount the draining board at a slight angle for easy drainage.

Right:
This slat wall unit is a wonderful way of hanging up everything in the kitchen from scissors, to colanders and pot lids. Adapt the instruction on page 22 to make a slat unit that fills the whole wall. It becomes the focal point of the kitchen when hung with brightly coloured and useful kitchen items.

450mm from the end, then attach the boards to the wall with the home-made brackets painted to match the spice shelf.

Make the brackets from two pieces of shaped 6.5mm plywood sandwiched around a 25 × 25mm strip. Screw the 25 × 25mm board to the wall with two no.10 screws, adding wall plugs into masonry walls. Then attach the 25 × 200mm boards with 19mm brass screws from both sides.

Making the open shelving unit

The sturdy uprights are made from 4mm thick hardboard which is nailed around 50 × 50mm sections of softwood. They are deep enough to allow the shelving unit to incorporate a dishwasher, washing machine, dryer or, as here, a refrigerator.

For the uprights, cut standard 1220 × 2440mm sheets of hardboard in half to make two pieces 600 × 2400mm. Glue and nail them to three 50 × 50mm lengths. Cover the front edge with a 50mm wide piece of teak or stained pine. Place the uprights on a base as for the kitchen units.

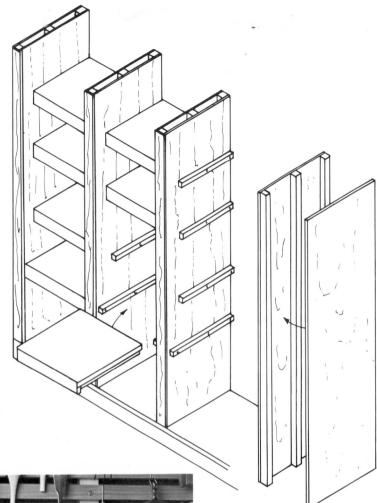

The 560mm wide shelves, supported on 25 × 25mm battens screwed to the uprights, are made as shown from chipboard and strips of 25 × 25mm so that they will slide onto and thereby hide the supporting battens.

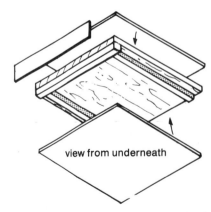

view from underneath

Cover the top, front and bottom of each shelf with white plastic laminate to create an attractive contrast to the dark uprights and to make the shelving unit easier to keep clean. To keep the structure rigid, nail 1200 × 2440mm sheets of hard-board to the back of the uprights.

KITCHEN STORAGE RACKS

Here are three useful storage racks which are very easy to make. The slat unit allows you to hang within arm's reach all the everyday utensils which tend to clutter up kitchen drawers. It is a useful rack not only for the kitchen, but for a workroom or study and it is so simple to make that you can easily adapt the instructions to make the rack to any size required. The towel rack holds aluminium foil and plastic bags as well as paper towels. Finally, the knife rack makes ingenious use of slotted dowels to hold both the handle and blade of each knife.

Slat unit

The instructions here are for a rack 600 × 800mm, but it can be made to fit any space or to cover a wall, as it is on page 21.

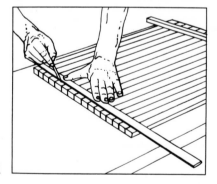

Start by lining up sixteen 600mm slats on the workbench. Draw a light line across each end about 20mm from the edges as a guide for the screw holes.

Then drill a clearance hole centred on the marked line at each end of the sixteen slats to take the no.8 screws.

To assemble the unit, screw on the first and last slats to align with the top and bottom of the 800mm uprights. Check that these are square before

CUTTING LIST
19 × 38mm
  18 pieces 600mm long
  2 pieces 800mm long, for uprights
  2 pieces 830mm long, for surround

SHOPPING LIST	
softwood	about 16m of 19 × 38mm
hardware	2 no.10 round head brass screws, 38mm long 40 no.8 countersunk screws, 32mm long 40 no.8 brass screw cup washers 8 finishing nails or panel pins, 32mm long 2 brass mirror brackets with 19mm screws
plus	clear polyurethane

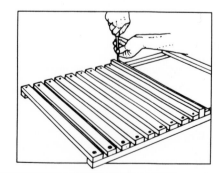

Knife rack

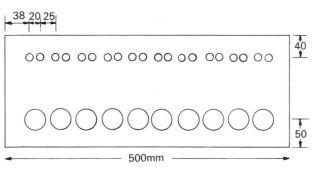

Mark and drill the backing board. The 12mm dowels are mounted in pairs centred 20mm apart There is a 25mm space between the centres of each pair of dowels. Centre the 38mm dowel holes directly below each pair of 12mm dowels. Drill both the 12mm and 38mm holes 15mm deep. It is best to use an electric drill fitted with a depth stop and mounted in a drill stand so that the holes are straight.

Mount the 38mm dowel in the vice, cut a groove 25mm deep in one end and use a bench hook to cut off a 50mm length. Return the dowel to the vice, cut another groove, then cut off the next piece. Repeat, to make ten pieces each with a slot in one end.

Glue all the dowels in place. Finally, drill a small hole in each corner to attach the knife rack to the wall and then seal with polyurethane.

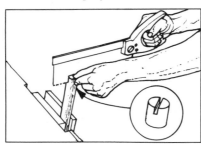

SHOPPING LIST

softwood	500mm of 25 × 200mm
dowel	1.8m of 12mm diameter, cut into 20 pieces 65mm long 600mm of 38mm diameter
hardware	4 no.8 countersunk brass screws, 50mm long 4 no.8 brass screw cup washers
plus	clear polyurethane

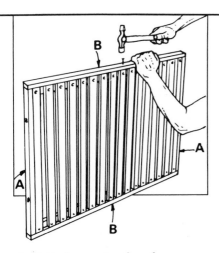

gluing and screwing the other fourteen slats in place using a spare slat on edge as a spacer. The spacing may not work out exactly, so space the last few slats out evenly by eye.

Screw the surround in place using the four remaining 19 × 38mm strips. Start with the two 600mm pieces A on top and bottom. Hold them in place temporarily with pins and add two screws and washers per side. Then nail one 830mm long strip B to each side. Finish with one or two coats of polyurethane. Finally, screw the mirror brackets to the back of each upright. Attach the slat unit to the wall with the two round head screws.

Make simple hooks from wire coathangers. Straighten the wire and with a strong pair of pliers, bend each piece to form a hook.

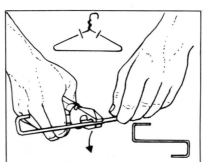

Towel holder

SHOPPING LIST

softwood	1.5m of 25 × 150mm cut into 2 pieces 320mm and 2 pieces 425mm long
plywood	2 pieces 145 × 380mm, 12mm thick
dowel	1m of 25mm diameter, cut into 3 pieces 315mm long
hardware	2 no.8 round head brass screws, 38mm long 16 finishing nails or panel pins, 38mm long 12 finishing nails or panel pins, 19mm long 2 brass mirror brackets with screws

Cut the 27mm wide diagonal slots in the two plywood pieces. Use a sabre or coping saw and sand the edges smooth. The glue and nail the plywood to each 425mm piece of softwood, leaving an equal space at top and bottom. Use six 19mm pins per side.

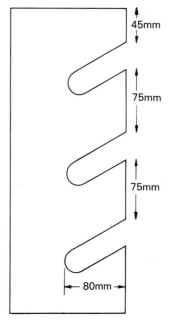

Finally glue and nail the top and bottom 320mm pieces between the sides using four 38mm pins per joint.

Seal with two coats of polyurethane, attach the mirror brackets and hang the holder. Push the three 315mm long dowels through the rolls of paper towel or aluminium foil and drop them in place in the diagonal slots.

KITCHEN WORK ISLAND

If your kitchen is large enough to have a central work island, this is a wonderful project to make for your home. The easiest thing to do is to buy a maple or beech butcherblock chopping board, 750 × 1200mm to use as the top, and to make the base yourself. Alternatively, you can make the top out of 50mm thick maple, beech or pine following the instructions on page 12 for the pine table. The base is made from maple to match the worktop but the project is designed to use standard sections so that you can make it out of a more easily available softwood. The rails are connected to the legs using old-fashioned metal corner brackets which are very easy to fit and which are extremely sturdy. These are available from large hardware suppliers or from mail order firms specializing in woodworking supplies.

Preparing the legs and rails

CUTTING LIST
75 × 75mm
    4 pieces 870mm long,
    for legs A
38 × 150mm
    1 piece 1010mm long,
    for rail B
38 × 100mm
    3 pieces 1010mm long,
    for rails C
    4 pieces 560mm long,
    for rails D
    2 pieces 634mm long,
    for drawer supports E

Cut the pieces to length and as usual, make sure that the ends are square. This is particularly important for legs and rails because the rails must connect squarely with the legs and the legs must be square so that they will stand firmly on the floor.

Then prepare all the pieces by rounding the edges using a plane or rasp. If you have a router, use a 6mm or 10mm radius rounding-over bit. Rounding all the edges of the legs will make them look more graceful, despite the fact that they are quite heavy.

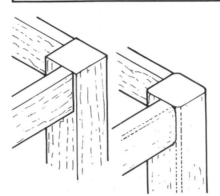

You should also round the four outside edges of the rails. By rounding the edges at the ends, the connection between the rails and the legs need not be precise. This is a trick that professional furniture makers often use to mask slight errors in alignment at joints and it makes the joint look more attractive, as shown left.

To connect the metal corner brackets to the legs, first drill the holes for the threaded bolt supplied with each →

bracket. The bolt goes into the leg at a 45° angle, so to make the drilling easier, make the jig shown below to hold the leg.

Drill two 45° holes in each leg, the first 40mm down from the top and the second 200mm up from the bottom, to take the brackets for the upper and lower rails.

The metal corner bracket has two flanges which fit into shallow slots cut into the inside of the rails. Determine the position of the groove by holding the bracket against the rails and legs.

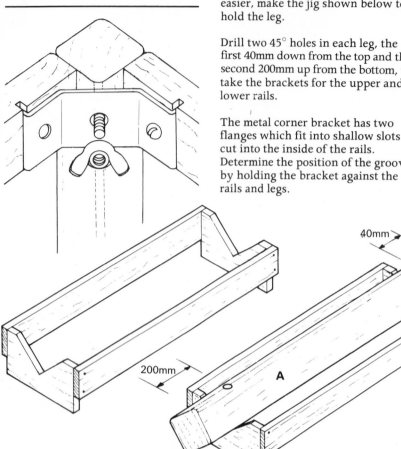

40mm

200mm

A

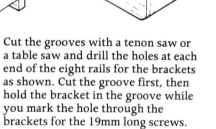

Cut the grooves with a tenon saw or a table saw and drill the holes at each end of the eight rails for the brackets as shown. Cut the groove first, then hold the bracket in the groove while you mark the hole through the brackets for the 19mm long screws. Put the legs and rails aside for assembly.

Making the drawer

CUTTING LIST
19 × 100mm   4 pieces 500mm long, for sides F
19 × 125mm   1 piece 550mm long, for front G
12 × 25mm   2 pieces 500mm long, for runners H

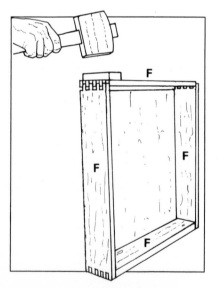

F
F
F
F

Cut F and G, then cut finger joints in the sides (page 237) and cut 6.5 × 6.5mm grooves to hold the bottom.

Glue three sides together, then trim the bottom to size. Slide the bottom into the groove with a little glue to keep it firm and then add the final side.

The drawer is supported by battens which slide in grooves cut in the sides. Cut the 10mm deep grooves using a plough plane or a router, then try the battens in the grooves to make sure they slide smoothly. The grooves can be cut before or after assembly.

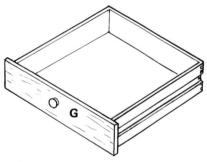

G

Shape the edges of the drawer front G with an appropriate router bit (page 216), or simply round them with a plane. Screw the wooden knob on to the drawer front from behind with a 32mm long screw before screwing the front to the drawer from inside with the six brass screws, lining up the bottom edges.

100mm

B

Assembling the top rails

CUTTING LIST
25 × 25mm
   2 pieces 860mm long

First cut a 100mm deep opening as shown in the centre of the front rail B to take the drawer. Measure the width of the drawer and add 2mm for clearance to get the width of the opening. Use a sabre saw to make the cuts and then clean up the edges with a block plane.

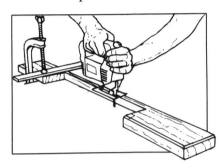

Assemble the rail structure by dowel jointing the two drawer supports E to the front rail B and the back rail C. Use two 10mm diameter dowel pegs, 50mm long, per joint and place the supports E so that they are exactly the same distance apart as the opening cut in B.

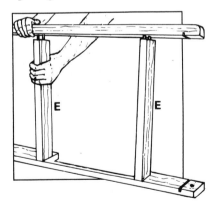

Attach the shrinkage brackets which will hold down the top and then

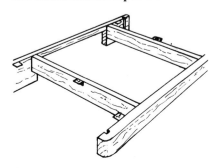

connect the rail structure and the two end rails D to the legs by screwing through the brackets at each corner.

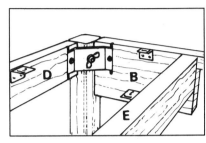

Connect the two 12 × 25mm runners H to the drawer supports E. Locate them carefully so that the grooves will match, leaving the bottom edge flush with the bottom edge of the front rail B. First pin the runners in place, then try the drawer to make sure you have it right before attaching the runners with three 19mm no.6 screws to each batten.

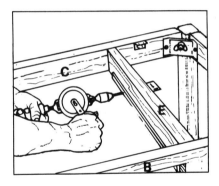

Before attaching the lower rails, two C and two D in exactly the same way, glue and screw a 25 × 25mm batten to the inside of each long rail C with four 32mm long no.8 screws per batten. Place it 40mm down from the top edge as shown.

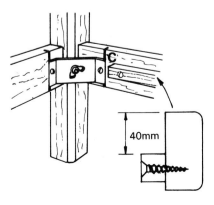

40mm

Assembling the slat structure

CUTTING LIST
25 × 25mm
   2 pieces 1m long

Determine the length of the twelve 19 × 75mm slats by measuring the inside distance between the longer rails C at the bottom. Then cut the twelve slats and sand them, rounding the edges slightly before assembly.

Assemble the slat structure by gluing and screwing the 25 × 25mm battens across the ends of the twelve slats. Lay the first and last battens on the bench and attach them flush with the ends using one 32mm no.8 screw per end. Then continue attaching the successive slats, spacing them about 12 mm apart. Before the glue sets, place the whole assembly between the lower rails, resting it on the battens which you attached earlier.

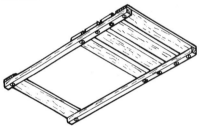

Final assembly and finishing

Prepare the 750 × 1200mm top by sanding it well. Round the corners and edges with a router or plane. Then screw the top to the brackets from underneath with 19mm round head screws. Make sure to use the correct slot to allow the solid wood top to expand and contract across the width with changes in the atmosphere.

The base structure should be given several protective coats of clear polyurethane, or if you prefer a more natural look, wipe on several coats of teak oil allowing the oil to penetrate into the wood between coats.

Teak oil will not be suitable for the chopping board top since it will be used to prepare food. It can either be left unfinished or given a light coat of salad or olive oil just as you would finish a wooden salad bowl. You will probably wipe and scrub the top continuously so you should renew the oil once in a while to keep the wood in good condition.

GATE LEG TABLE

Everyone occasionally needs an extra table for dinner parties, as a work desk or even as a sideboard to hold serving dishes. This fold-away design serves the purpose well and conveniently extends when you need extra seating in the dining area. You can use the table with only one leaf extended to seat two or three people, or fully extended to seat six people very comfortably. Folded flat against the wall, the table only takes up a 150mm depth of floor space. It is not at all difficult to make the table. It is made with a dark cork inlay in each leaf which complements the solid beech surround. Cork is not as durable as say a painted or veneered panel but if you buy cork which has been factory sealed it should serve very well. And it does make the table extremely attractive. Notice that the table is designed to be made using

standard planed sections such as 25 × 50mm, 25 × 75mm and 25 × 150mm, so you can use pine or Douglas fir boards instead of beech, dowel jointing them together to make the table top, as shown on page 12. To make the construction easier, you could use a sheet of 19mm veneered blockboard to make the leaves and the underframe of the table. Refer to the instructions for the chest of drawers on page 64 before cutting up the blockboard. If you use a veneered panel, keep in mind that all the pieces will need matching iron-on veneer edging.

SHOPPING LIST	
hardwood or softwood	2.7m of 25 × 150mm / 4m of 25 × 125mm 8m of 25 × 75mm / 5.5m of 25 × 50mm 6m of 10 × 10mm
plywood	2 pieces 460 × 820mm, 6.5mm thick (to be trimmed)
dowel	1.8m of 10mm diameter for pegs
hardware	12 no.10 countersunk steel screws, 38mm long 8 no.10 countersunk steel screws, 19mm long 35 no.4 countersunk steel screws, 19mm long 25 no.6 countersunk steel screws, 15mm long six 60mm brass butt hinges with 15mm screws about 10 finishing nails or panel pins, 19mm long
plus	about 1.5 sq metre of cork tiles, 3mm thick (presealed) contact adhesive clear polyurethane or wax

Making the table frame

CUTTING LIST
25 × 150mm
   1 piece 1020mm long A
   2 pieces 705mm long B
25 × 125mm
   2 pieces 930mm long C
25 × 75mm
   2 pieces 930mm long D

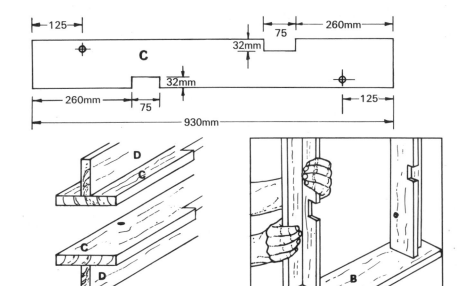

Cut the pieces accurately to length and check that they are square. Before joining them, it is a good idea to sand the pieces well at this stage rather than waiting until the table is assembled.

Start by preparing the T-sections which form the cross rails of the table to hold the fold-out legs. The leg frames will be attached to the rails at the top and bottom by a 10mm dowel peg which allows the leg to pivot.

The other vertical of the leg frame will fit into a cut-out in the rail when the table is folded flat. Before making the T-sections, drill the 10mm diameter holes and cut the slots in pieces C exactly as shown. It is best to clamp them together as you saw and drill so that they will be identical.

Then make two T-sections by gluing C and D together in pairs. Clamp them well until the glue sets, then add four 38mm screws to each T-section to reinforce the glued joint. Counterbore the screws carefully by drilling a 10mm diameter hole about 10mm deep.

Afterwards fill the hole with matching plugs cut from a scrap of beech with a plug cutter fitted into an electric drill.

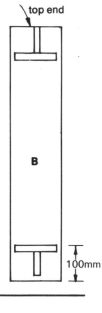

Dowel joint the T-sections to pieces B. Drill so that the holes line up and extend 15mm into pieces B. Then glue the 32mm dowels into the ends of the T-sections before joining the pieces together and clamping across until the glue sets.

Making the fold-out leg structure

CUTTING LIST
25 × 50mm:
   2 pieces 695mm long E
   2 pieces 525mm long F,
   (to be trimmed)
   4 pieces 460mm long G

Cut the pieces to exact length and sand them, rounding the edges. Then dowel joint the pieces together into two identical frames using two 50mm long dowel pegs per joint. Ensure that leg E extends exactly 100mm below F as shown.

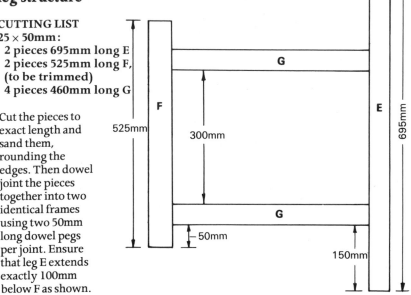

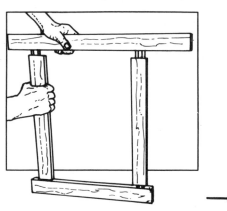

Assembling the table frame

Add the leg frames to the T-sections. Trim the top of F, then place each frame in position with the short leg F centred over the pivot hole already drilled. Hold it there while you extend the hole into the legs, drilling through the 10mm hole already drilled. Then add a little glue to the hole in the leg just before you tap the dowel in place. The dowel is now glued to

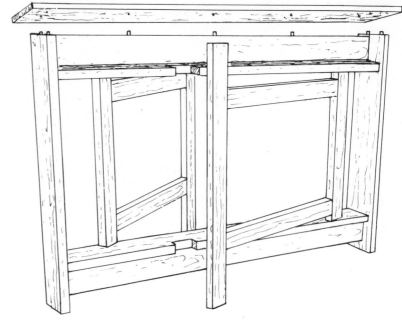

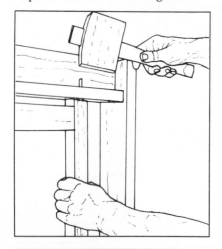

the legs while it remains free to rotate in the cross rail.

Check to make sure that the other leg E fits the slot cut for it, when the leg is folded flat. If not, enlarge the slot to correct it.

To complete the table frame, drill the dowel holes in top piece A and in the top of the ends B and the T-section. Allow a 25mm overhang at each end, but do not attach the top A until later when it has been joined to the table leaves.

Making the table leaves

CUTTING LIST

25 × 125mm
    4 pieces 460mm long H
25 × 75mm
    4 pieces 1020mm long I
    2 pieces 560mm long J
25 × 50mm
    2 pieces 75mm long K
10 × 10mm
    4 pieces 460mm long
    4 pieces 915mm long
    (to be trimmed)

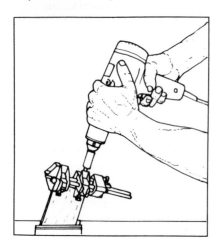

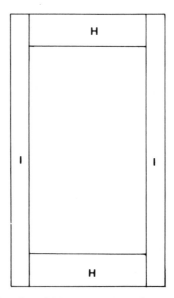

First dowel joint pieces H and I together using a dowelling jig, if possible, to drill two 10mm holes in each connection. Use 100mm long dowel pegs to make the joint very strong.

After making the two frames, glue and screw the 10 × 10mm battens to the inside edges to form a ledge to support the plywood panel. Use 19mm no.4 screws spaced about 225mm

apart making sure the battens are flush with the bottom edge. It is easier if you first glue and pin the battens to hold them in position before you add the screws in previously drilled holes.

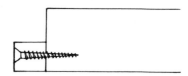

Before gluing the cork to the plywood, trim the plywood pieces so that they fit into the openings exactly. Trim with a plane or saw until they just drop into place and mark them so that each one will match its opening.

Then glue the cork to the plywood panel with contact adhesive. Make

30

sure to cut the cork pieces so that they form a regular pattern. The cork tiles are usually 300 × 300mm so you have to cut them to fit either to make a staggered or symmetrical layout as shown.

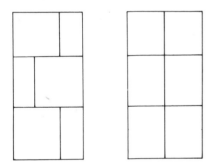

Cut the cork to leave about 6mm overhanging on all four sides so that you can trim it off neatly with a sharp trimming knife after gluing down.

Add glue to the 10 × 10mm battens around the opening. Then lay the plywood panels in the opening, screwing them carefully from underneath with 15mm screws. Be careful not to drill or screw straight through the top of the table as you work.

To reinforce the panel, especially so that the leg doesn't push against the panel itself, screw the

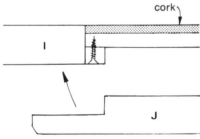

cross pieces J to the frame after first cutting a rabbet at the ends. Use two 19mm no.10 screws per end.

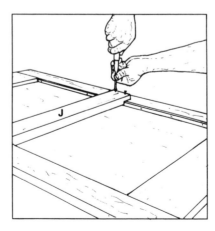

To attach the folding leaves to the table, place piece A on the floor or bench and then attach three brass butt hinges per side. There is no need to set these into the wood. With the leaves butting against the top A, simply lay each hinge in

position, mark the screw holes, drill the screw clearance holes and attach the hinges.

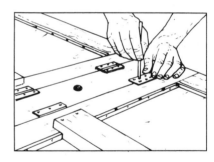

Finally, attach the top A with the leaves attached to the underframe and the dowels already glued in position. If you have trouble lining up the dowels with the holes, it may be just as easy to turn the whole table upside down and screw straight through the T-section with long screws into the top A. With the table fully opened, mark the location of the fold-out support E on the cross piece J. Then glue and screw one small stop K to each cross piece using two 38mm no.10 screws. These will act as stops for the fold-out legs.

Finishing the table

The best finish for the table is clear polyurethane which will seal both the wood and the cork tiles.

DINING CHAIRS

This dining chair is both elegant and comfortable. The upholstered back, which is very easy to make, is tilted at just the right angle so that it supports your lower back when you are sitting upright and yet allows you to lean back and lounge comfortably.

The design works beautifully as an armchair too. The chair with arms is exactly the same design, but with the front legs made longer to take the extra rail and arm.

The small details on these chairs are a very important part of the design. All the pieces have rounded edges, easily done with a router or hand plane, to soften the look and feel of the wood.

These chairs are made of beech which has been left completely natural. Alternatively, before upholstering the seat and back, you can finish the wood with two or three thinned coats of clear polyurethane.

Notice that all the components, except seat and back, are standard 25×75mm sections so you can make the chairs just as easily using good quality pine or Douglas fir. You could even use good quality birch plywood, 19mm thick and paint the chairs, filling the end grain with wood filler before priming.

But, if possible, use a soft-toned

SHOPPING LIST
to make one chair without arms

hardwood (beech or similar)	about 4.6m of 25 × 75mm (approx. 20 × 70mm finished size) Note: Allow an extra 3m of 25 × 75mm for the chair with arms
softwood	2.5m of 19 × 19mm battens
plywood	460 × 900mm, 6.5mm thick
dowel	about 1m of 10mm diameter for pegs
hardware	10 no.8 countersunk steel screws, 32mm long 4 no.8 countersunk brass screws, 19mm long 4 no.8 brass screw cup washers 20 finishing nails or panel pins, 19mm long
plus	foam rubber: 1 firm piece 425 × 425mm, 50mm thick 1 soft piece 200 × 425mm, 25mm thick 600mm upholstery fabric, 1.2m wide fabric adhesive

hardwood, like beech, and choose an upholstery fabric that complements the colour of the wood. The difference in price and labour is well worth the effort and the chairs will be more hard wearing.
All connections are dowel jointed so that the construction is kept simple. Read page 232 on making dowel joints before starting work and, if possible, invest in a dowelling jig which makes the job so much easier and quicker and the joints much more accurate.

Making the dining chair

CUTTING LIST
25 × 75mm
    2 pieces 470mm long,
    front legs A
    2 pieces 800mm long,
    back legs B
    2 pieces 380mm long,
    side rails C
    2 pieces 430mm long,
    cross rails D

First cut all the pieces to exact length and make sure they are perfectly

square. If all the pieces are correct, the assembly is really quite straightforward.

Next, mark the best face and edge in preparation for marking and drilling the dowel joints.

Use a dowelling jig if possible to drill the holes for the 10mm dowel pegs. Use 50mm long dowels for the end frames and 32mm long dowels to connect the cross rails D. Two dowels per joint makes a very strong connection, but all the dowels must be tight fitting for the joint to be successful. Notice that the front legs extend 10mm above the rails C, and that the two cross rails D are set in 6mm from the edge of the legs.

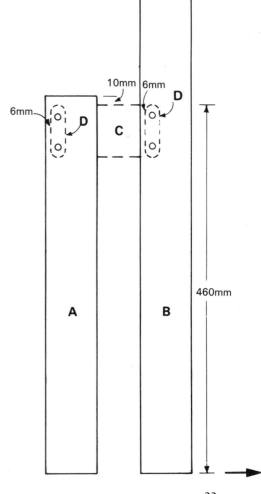

After drilling the dowel holes, round the edges of the rails C and D. Use a router fitted with a 6mm or 10mm radius rounding-over bit to make all the edges uniform.

Alternatively, use a plane first to round the edges roughly and then finish with a fine file or coarse sandpaper. This is an important step so take time to do it carefully and evenly.

Notice that the legs are rounded at the top and bottom to give the chair a more delicate look. These details are not just frills; the difference would be really noticeable if the ends were left square and the design would be less graceful.

Before starting assembly, cut the top of the back legs at an angle using a saw and then plane off to a smooth finish. Round the edges slightly with sandpaper.

It is a good idea to sand all the pieces at this stage because it is much easier to do now with the chair in pieces than after assembly. Sand the wood first with medium and then with fine paper. Assemble the chair carefully so that the pieces are not scratched or marked and check for any flaws before applying a finish.

Preparing the seat and back

CUTTING LIST
plywood
    1 piece 425 × 425mm, for seat
    2 pieces 200 × 425mm, for back
19 × 19mm
    2 pieces 425mm long, for seat
    2 pieces 460mm long, for back
    (to be trimmed)
    2 pieces 200mm long, for back

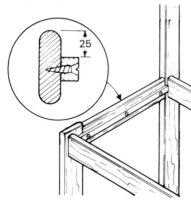

Assembling the frame

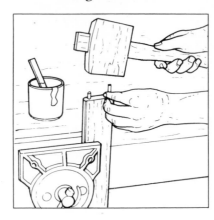

Start by gluing the dowel pegs to the rails. Use a powder resin glue mixed with water if possible, because it will fill any gaps caused by imperfect drilling. If such a glue is not available, then white woodworking glue will do.

Make the side frame by gluing the side rail C to the legs. Clamp it until

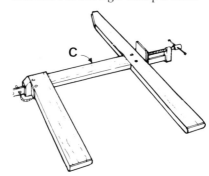

First glue and screw the 425mm long battens to the insides of the side rails C with 32mm screws, using three screws per batten.

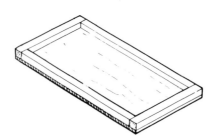

Then prepare the backrest by gluing and pinning the remaining four 19 × 19mm battens to the 200 × 425mm plywood. Attach the 200mm battens to the sides. Trim the 460mm long battens to fit in between as shown, then add these, using five or six pins per batten. Put these pieces aside until later, when you are ready to do the upholstery.

the glue sets. Continue by adding the front and back rails D.

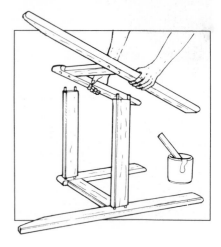

Lay one frame on the bench, add glue to the dowel pegs and then place the other frame in position before tapping it home with a soft-faced hammer or a mallet against a piece of soft wood.

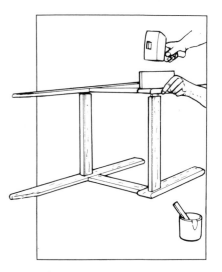

Clamp across the rails with light pressure until the glue has set. Keep a moist cloth handy to wipe off any excess glue during assembly.

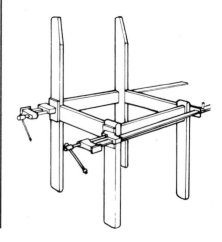

The design of the arm of the chair is a particularly pleasing detail. Not only is it an elegant, sculptured joint, but it provides good support and feels really nice to touch.

Upholstering the chair

This is the easiest part of the project. Start with the seat. Cut a piece of fabric 600 × 600mm, paying particular attention to the direction of the pattern so as to position it attractively. Lay the 50mm thick foam and the 425 × 425mm plywood panel on the fabric, leaving an equal overlap on all sides. Then fold up and wrap the fabric tightly over the plywood base, folding the corners neatly so the fabric does not bunch up.

Fasten the fabric in place with fabric adhesive spread on the plywood, then reinforce it with staples or with small pins. Allow the glue to dry and just drop the upholstered seat in position on the battens in the chair frames.

Upholster the back in the same way, starting by laying the foam on the plywood piece. On top of this place a 360 × 600mm piece of fabric, turn over and secure it as before.

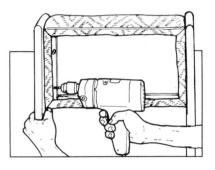

To attach the back, position it at an angle between the uprights so that it lines up with the angle cut at the top of the leg. The top of the fabric should be placed just below the top

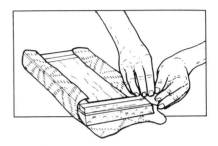

of the upright. Drill and screw through the battens to attach the back to the leg. Use two 32mm screws per side.

Finally, wrap a 250 × 460mm piece of fabric over the remaining piece of plywood and attach this to cover the back of the chair. Use four 19mm brass screws with cup washers for a neat finish.

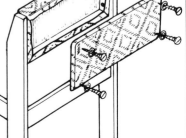

Making the armchair

CUTTING LIST
25 × 75mm
2 pieces 685mm long, front legs AA
2 pieces 800mm long, back legs B
2 pieces 380mm long, side rails C
2 pieces 430mm long, cross rails D
2 pieces 380mm long, top rails E
2 pieces 490mm long, armrest F

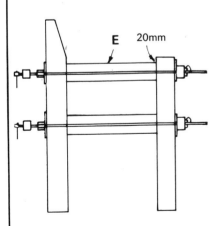

Follow the same procedure as for the dining chair, cutting the wood to length, drilling holes for the dowel joints, rounding the edges and assembling the side frames. Notice that the extra rail E on each side frame has only one rounded edge. The top edge is left square to take the armrest.

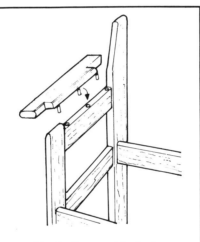

Assemble the frame with the two cross rails D, cut notches in the armrest to go around the legs and neatly round the edges at the notches. Then attach the armrests with three dowel pegs and clamp down until the glue sets. If you want to apply a finish of any kind, do it now.

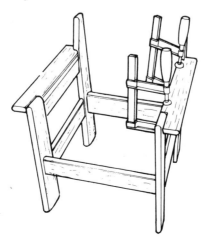

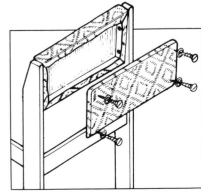

WELSH DRESSER

Making a Welsh dresser is a major project involving a lot of material, time and patience. But it is a beautiful and useful piece of furniture, well worth the time and effort that goes into making it. To make the instructions easier to follow, they are divided into two main parts – one for the base unit and one for the top section. These can be made as separate pieces of furniture and used as a sideboard and shelf unit.

Most of the connections are dowel joints and wherever possible, these are through dowels (page 232). Much of the cabinet construction is quite easy once the gluing up is done. However, the drawer support is more complicated and, like all drawer work, it requires accuracy in cutting and care in assembly. A few bar clamps will help a great deal with the assembly.

The edges, shelves, counters and drawers have been decorated by cutting a profile with a router. This is not essential as the edges would also look very good if they were simply rounded or bevelled with a block plane.

Similarly, the arches in the front and top can be cut easily using a sabre saw or, with a little more work, using a coping saw.

The lower unit

Gluing up the main panels

CUTTING LIST
25 × 150mm
  3 pieces 2m long, top A
  3 pieces 1.8m long, base shelf B
  3 pieces 1.75m long, sides C
  3 pieces 1.2m long, dividers D
25 × 100mm
  1 piece 1735mm long, base rail E
25 × 50mm
  1 piece 1735mm long, back rail E′

Refer to the techniques sections on edge joints (page 231) and clamping (page 202) before starting work. The widest panel is approximately

SHOPPING LIST	
softwood (choose clear pieces of wood)	2.1m of 25 × 225mm / 2.4m of 25 × 200mm / 34m of 25 × 150mm
	1.8m of 25 × 125mm / 5.5m of 25 × 100mm / 2.7m of 25 × 75mm
	10m of 25 × 50mm / 1m of 25 × 25mm
	21 boards of knotty pine tongue-and-grooved cladding, 2.4m long
birch plywood	1 × 1.2m, 12mm thick
	0.6 × 1.2m, 4mm thick
dowel	2.4m of 10mm diameter for pegs
hardware	10 no.8 countersunk steel screws, 57mm long
	12 no.8 countersunk steel screws, 38mm long
	84 no.8 countersunk steel screws, 32mm long
	6 no.8 round head screws, 32mm long
	54 no.8 round head screws, 19mm long
	17 shrinkage brackets
	5 brass drawer pulls with 12mm brass screws
	2 straight metal brackets, 50mm long with 19mm screws
	about 200 finishing nails or panel pins, 19mm long
plus	3.6m of 25mm scotia moulding / 6m of 12 × 25mm beading / clear polyurethane

450mm wide so you will not need very long clamps.

All the edge joints are reinforced with 10mm dowel pegs, 40mm long. These help strengthen the joint and also make it easier to glue up. Using the dowel pegs will also ensure that the boards do not separate when the wood 'moves'. Refer to the techniques section on dowel joints (page 232) for full instructions on marking and drilling.

Start with the top A. Select three matching, clear 2m long boards. Check the edges to make sure they are straight and square. Arrange the boards so that the end grain alternates from board to board. Mark and drill each one for five

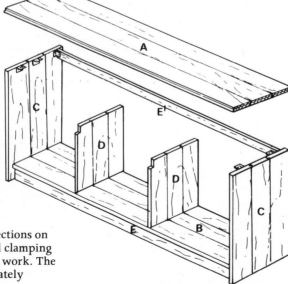

dowel pegs, then apply the glue and clamp using about five clamps, three below and two above the boards to prevent bowing. Remember to protect the edges of the boards from the clamps by using strips of wood on each side.

Use white woodworking glue which takes about 60 minutes to set. While the glue is setting, prepare the next three boards for the base shelf B. After 60 minutes take out the first panel and clamp up the next. Then continue with panels C and D.

The next step is to trim all the panels to length. Refer to the list below for the exact lengths. To cut each panel, start by squaring off one end with a try square as near to the end as possible. Cut off the waste with a handsaw, portable circular saw or table saw. Measure and mark the exact length required and then trim the other end. Then, if necessary, trim one long edge, either with a plane or a circular saw. Repeat this procedure for all the panels.

TRIMMING LIST for panels
1 piece 440 × 1825mm A
1 piece 415 × 1735mm B
2 pieces 425 × 815mm C
2 pieces 400 × 560mm D

Notice that two of the panels are cut in half to get two sides C and two dividers D. Cut the two 815mm side panels C now, but don't trim the dividers D until later in the project.

Making the drawer supports

This is the complicated part of the job, involving cutting and joining many small pieces accurately. Make the front framework first, then the shelf framework and finally, join them together.

Front framework

CUTTING LIST
25 × 125mm
 1 piece 1735mm F
25 × 75mm
 2 pieces 130mm G
25 × 50mm
 4 pieces 130mm H
 1 piece 1735mm I

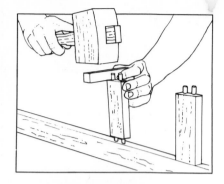

First draw the arches on the 25 × 125mm F, and cut out the shapes with a sabre saw or a coping saw. The best way is to make a template out of cardboard. Draw out the width of the arch and the centre line. Draw

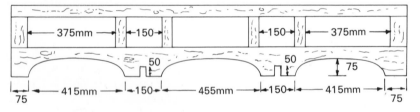

half the arch, fold the paper in half and cut out the shape. Save the template to use for the top of the dresser.

Notice that the central arch is slightly wider than the other two. Simply draw one side, then move the template along to draw the other side. Also cut out the two small notches 50mm deep as shown so that the dividers D will fit snugly into the slots later.

Next set out the dimensions for the drawer openings along the 25 × 125mm F and the 25 × 50mm I. It is easiest to clamp them together and mark the location of the short uprights across both at the same time, using a try square.

To mark the centres for the 10mm diameter 50mm long dowel pegs, clamp each of the uprights H and G to the 25 × 125mm F so that they line up exactly with the marks. Then mark the centres for the two dowel pegs in each joint first with a try square and then with a marking gauge.

Mark the joints along F and then along the 25 × 50mm I. Keep track of which joint is which by numbering all the pieces and joints. After

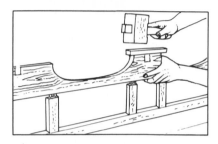

drilling the holes and gluing the pegs into the short uprights H and G, join them to the 25 × 50mm I. Then join the 25 × 125mm F to the other ends.

One or two dowels may not match up exactly. If the dowel cannot be forced in with light clamping, cut the peg off flush and re-drill the hole for a new peg.

Shelf framework

CUTTING LIST
25 × 50mm
 2 pieces
 1735mm long J
 4 pieces
 375mm long K
25 × 75mm
 4 pieces
 285mm long L
 2 pieces
 375mm long M
25 × 100mm
 2 pieces
 285mm long N

The drawer shelf support is a rectangular framework which is screwed together. Start by laying the two 25 × 50mm pieces J on the bench and, using the front framework just completed, transfer the spacing of the 25 × 75mm and 25 × 50mm uprights G and H onto them taking care to mark them accurately.

Then, using these marks, glue and screw the two 25 × 75mm pieces M to the 25 × 50mm pieces J with the 32mm no.8 countersunk screws. The gap between the pieces J should be

38

exactly 285mm, so that the pieces L and N fit snugly in between. Use two pieces L as spacers.

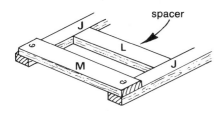

Continue by gluing and screwing the four 25 × 50mm pieces K in place, then turn the frame over and glue and screw first the end 25 × 100mm pieces N in place and then the four central 25 × 75mm pieces L, using two 32mm screws per piece. Allow an equal amount of overhang on each side.

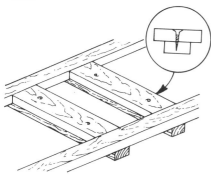

These instructions make the construction sound much more complicated than it really is. Study the drawings carefully and think how the pieces function. The assembly will be quite clear if you realize that the shorter and wider pieces L and N form a shelf to support the drawers, and pieces K and M guide the drawers.

Assembly of base unit

Before joining the pieces, shape the edges of the base B as shown and round the edges of sides C. Use a block plane or a router fitted with a rounding-over bit as shown.

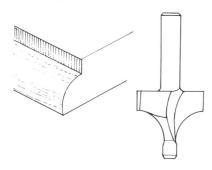

Before assembling, screw one 25 × 25mm batten, 355mm long onto

Joining the front and back

To join these two assemblies, first clamp and glue them together. Then screw from the back of the 25 × 50mm piece J, into the front F

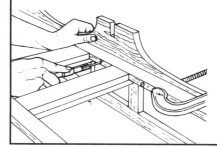

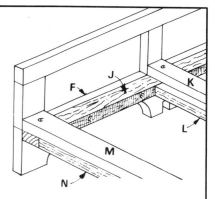

with 57mm screws. Make sure to keep the top edges of F and J exactly flush so that the drawers will slide in smoothly.

the inside of each of the sides C as shown, the top edge of the batten located 95mm from the base of C and the end 12mm from the back edge. To prevent the sides C from splitting use 32mm round head screws, placed in slots in the batten so they are free to move sideways slightly as C expands and contracts.

Then connect the drawer assembly to the sides so that it is set 20mm back from the front edge of the sides C as shown, leaving a 10mm to 15mm gap at the back.

It is important to dowel joint only the front framework (pieces F, G, I) to the sides C. The shelf framework is connected with one metal shrinkage bracket per side and 19mm screws.

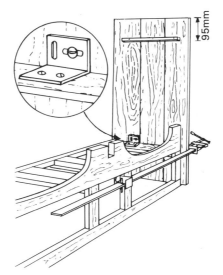

Then attach the base shelf B to the battens from underneath using three 38mm screws. Set the shelf B 10mm in from the back edge of the side C to allow space for the backing. Attach the base rail E to the shelf B and to

the sides C, using five shrinkage brackets.

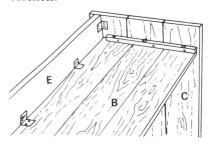

Determine the length of the dividers D by measuring the distance between the base shelf B and the shelf frame above. Then cut the dividers D to size and cut a rounded notch in the top edge as shown to fit into the notch cut in the front F. Slide them in place and through dowel from underneath and on top. Round the corners near the joint.

Finally before attaching the top, attach the back rail E' with a bracket at each end. Then attach eight shrinkage brackets to the top edges; two to each end of C and two to the sides I and E'. Screw down the top to the brackets from underneath. Then apply the backing boards.

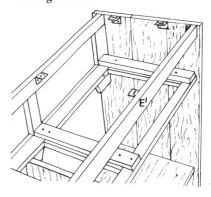

Making the drawers

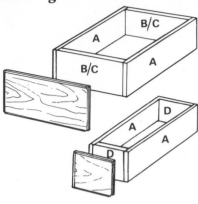

CUTTING LIST
25 × 150mm
   3 pieces 395mm long, for fronts
   2 pieces 170mm long, for fronts
12mm plywood
   10 pieces 125 × 380mm A
   4 pieces 125 × 348mm B
   2 pieces 125 × 406mm C,
   for centre drawer
   (to be trimmed)
   4 pieces 123 × 125mm D
4mm plywood
   The 1 × 1.2m piece should be large
   enough for all the drawer
   bottoms. Cut to exact sizes
   either to fit into grooves or onto
   battens when the drawers are
   completed.

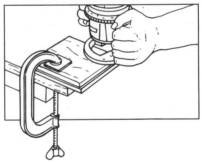

Make the drawer sides out of 12mm plywood, cutting the pieces as shown from a 1.0 × 1.2m piece. It is advisable to measure the openings in the front panel first to double check the dimensions. Subtract 26mm from the centre opening to get the exact size of pieces C. If any of the measurements are out, adjust the drawer sizes accordingly. To fit the 4mm plywood drawer bottoms in place, either cut grooves with a table saw or router, or attach 12 × 12mm battens flush with the bottom edge.

Join the pieces by using two 32mm countersunk screws and wall plugs in each corner.

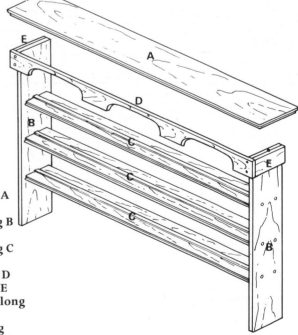

Shape the edges of the drawer fronts with a router or by hand.

After sanding the fronts, attach the drawer pulls and screw the drawer fronts to the plywood from the back using four 32mm screws per drawer. Allow equal overhang on the sides and top and bottom. Finally, test the drawers. It is usually necessary to plane off an edge or two before achieving a good, smooth fit.

The top unit

The top shelving unit is much easier to make than the base unit. It simply consists of three shelves, two uprights and a capping piece.

CUTTING LIST
25 × 225mm
   1 piece 1840mm long A
25 × 200mm
   2 pieces 1200mm long B
25 × 150mm
   3 pieces 1735mm long C
25 × 100mm
   1 piece 1820mm long D
   2 pieces 195mm long E
scotia 2 pieces 1733mm long
12 × 25mm beading
   3 pieces 1733mm long

Before joining the pieces, shape the edges of the shelves C as for the base unit and round off the front edges of the uprights B.

Join the shelves to the uprights by through dowelling. First mark the shelf locations on the insides of the uprights with a try square. To help in drilling straight through for the dowels, clamp two battens to one upright so the shelf fits snugly in between. Set the shelves 10mm in from the back of the upright B to allow for the tongue-and-grooved panelling.

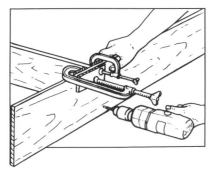

Insert and trim the dowels, allowing the glue to set on one side before continuing with the other upright.

To assemble the top, first glue and clamp the short 25 × 100mm pieces E to the sides of the uprights, flush with the top edge. Then, after cutting the arches using the same template as before, attach the front piece D by through dowelling into the uprights.

Shape the edges of the top A as before on three sides and attach it, shaped edge downward, by screwing or through dowelling to the uprights; aligning back edges.

Finally, pin the beading to the shelves to form stops for standing up plates. Also glue and pin one of the scotia pieces to the underside of the top A, 10mm from the back edge. This will conceal the edges of the backing panel.

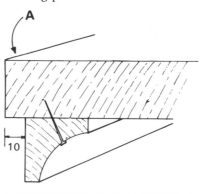

Applying the backing

The 2.4 m boards of knotty pine have to be cut to fit the exact size required. Start with the top unit. Lay it face down and measure from the underside of the top A to the bottom of the uprights B. Subtract 3mm to allow clearance, then cut all the boards and pin them in place, slotting the tongues into the grooves. Remember to put the V-groove down towards the front of the dresser.

Joining the two units

Stand the top on the base, adjusting it until the uprights are in line. Then screw on the 50mm long straight brackets with the 19mm screws. Using brackets like this allows the units to be taken apart and moved easily. If the top unit doesn't stay level on the base, it may be necessary to add a hidden dowel under each upright. But, remember not to glue the dowel so the pieces can be taken apart if necessary. Finally, pin the last scotia piece to the top of the base unit to hide the panel edges along the front.

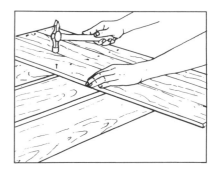

Put two pins into each shelf and one into the back of the scotia. It may be necessary to trim a little bit off the width of the last board to make it fit in.

Now do the same for the base unit. Measure from the underside of the top A to the underside of the base shelf B, cut the boards and nail them in place with two pins per end.

Finishing

Sand the dresser thoroughly and finish it first with a thinned coat and then two full coats of clear polyurethane. If you don't want the surface to be shiny, use a matt finish for the final coat. Rub down between coats with very fine sandpaper or with fine steel wool.

Renew the finish every six months or so by applying a coat of furniture wax.

DIRECTOR'S CHAIR

Folding director's chairs are remarkably comfortable and will serve equally well as dining or utility chairs. This chair is made from 19mm birch plywood and 32mm diameter dowel. The only awkward part in making the chair is drilling the dowel holes. Make sure that the drill bit matches the diameter of the dowels well. It is better if the dowels are not too tight a fit so that they can rotate in their holes as the chair is folded up. Fixed joints are locked with small screws.

SHOPPING LIST	
birch plywood	600 × 850mm, 19mm thick
dowel	about 3.6 m of 32mm diameter / 250mm of 10mm diameter
hardware	4 no.4 countersunk brass screws, 25mm long
plus	1.5 m of 400mm wide deck chair canvas available from large department stores in various patterns and colours strong thread to match

Preparing the pieces

CUTTING LIST
plywood
   4 pieces 60 × 705mm, for diagonals A
   2 pieces 60 × 685mm, for fronts B
   2 pieces 60 × 815mm, for backs C
32mm dowel
   6 pieces 520mm long
   2 pieces 75mm long
10mm dowel
   4 pieces 45mm long

First cut the plywood into eight 60mm wide strips. With a table saw this is only a few minutes work, but it can also be done quite easily with a circular saw fitted with a rip fence (page 208).

After cutting the plywood pieces and dowels to exact lengths, prepare

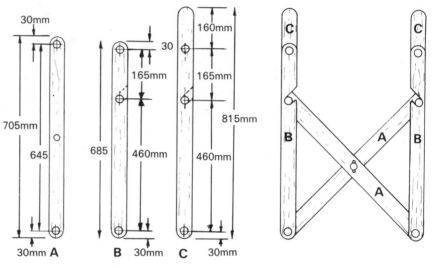

the plywood strips by carefully marking the centres for the 32mm diameter holes. Also mark and round the ends to a 60mm diameter. It is best to use a compass for marking the holes so that the rounded end will be concentric with the dowel hole.

Drill the holes in the plywood strips before cutting the rounded ends with a coping saw or sabre saw. Make sure not to drill straight through from one side. Turn the piece over and finish the hole from the other side to prevent the wood

from splitting. Cut the diagonal slots into the middle holes on B and C.

Before assembling, sand the pieces well, rounding all the edges and making them smooth and even. Whatever the kind of finish you want to give the chair, it will be easier to varnish or paint the pieces now before they are assembled. However, be careful not to get too much varnish or paint in the holes or the dowels will be too tight fitting and the chair will not fold up as easily as it should.

Assembling the diagonals

Putting the pieces together can be like putting up a deck chair – it would be almost comical if it wasn't so frustrating. Do it carefully, step by step, and don't worry if the pieces collapse just as you are about to add the finishing touches.

Start by attaching two 32mm dowels to two of the pieces A to make a rectangle.

Now add dowels to a third piece A, and join it to the rectangle at the centre with a 75mm length of 32mm dowel locked by a 10mm cross dowel

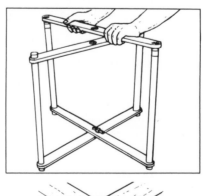

on both sides. Add the last piece A, again attaching it at the centre pivot with the short dowels.

Before continuing, tap the 32mm dowels into their final positions leaving 25mm or 45mm protruding as shown.

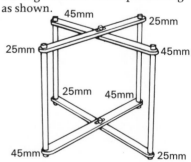

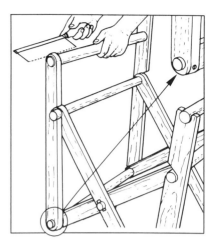

If you prefer, you can also flatten the tops of pieces B by sawing off the top then sanding them smooth to make the armrest more comfortable. Give the chair a final touch up coat of polyurethane or paint if it is needed once this is done.

Making the fabric seat and back

Cut the fabric into two lengths; 660mm for the seat and 610mm for the back. To make the seat, hold the fabric stretched in place over the dowels to determine exactly where to fold it over, then sew two lines of close machine stitching, 12mm apart to make the channel at either end to take the dowel. The seams must be strong, so make sure to use small stitches and strong thread. Add a line of fabric adhesive between the two rows of stitching to reinforce the seams.

seat

To sew the back, make a 65mm hem on the two long 610mm edges. Then fold the fabric in half lengthwise with the right sides facing, to make a piece 135 × 610mm. Make a seam, 25mm in from each end, then after turning right sides out, make 'pockets' by sewing a seam 90mm from either end to fit over the back piece.

back

To fit the seat, free one end of both dowels of the seat so that you can slide the fabric over them. The back piece is simply pulled down over the tops of the plywood pieces C.

Adding the front and back pieces

Now it will be quite straightforward to attach the other pieces. Start by joining one front B to one back C with a 32mm dowel placed through the top holes, leaving 6mm protruding at each end. Notice that the diagonal slots should face the same way. Then join to the already assembled

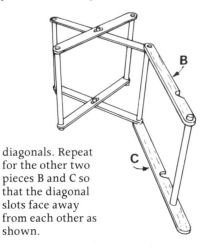

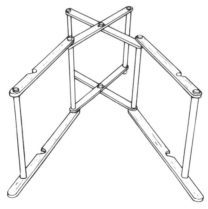

diagonals. Repeat for the other two pieces B and C so that the diagonal slots face away from each other as shown.

Now stand the chair up with the dowels in the slots and add the finishing touches before sewing and fitting the fabric seat and back. It will probably be necessary to tap the pieces with a mallet here and there to make sure the dowels extend the correct amount. Add four 25mm countersunk brass screws at the bottom through the edge of the plywood pieces B and C into the dowel to lock this joint firmly.

TOWN KITCHEN

This modern kitchen design, which incorporates built-in features like an oven and a hob, still retains the warm feeling of wood. The kitchen includes lots of clever features such as the pull-out wire baskets and pegboard to make the cabinets into neat and useful storage places. Around the hob, where most of the work takes place, a maple chopping block and a tile stand for hot pans have been built into the counter top to make the surface more versatile. The construction of the cabinets is basically the same as in the pine kitchen on page 16, but the doors are much simpler to make. Instead of having to fit accurately within a given opening, the doors 'lay-on', that is each door rests against the front of the cabinet overlapping with the opening, so that the exact size is not so critical. The doors are made from good quality Finnish birch plywood, clear finished with the attractive plywood edges left exposed.
Notice that the plywood edge grain is also used as a design feature on the laminate-covered worktops. Several thicknesses of plywood have been glued together to make an attractive, thick edge which continues all around the worktops.

Planning the kitchen

No matter what the size or shape of your kitchen, most of the features shown here can easily be incorporated into your design. In this kitchen, most of the storage is behind cabinet doors, but you may want to have some open shelf storage as featured in the country kitchen.

The first step in planning a kitchen is to measure the space available, making a note of windows and doors and any irregularities such as pipes, alcoves or columns. The placement of the sink will usually be dictated by the location of the plumbing, but if possible, try to create at least three or four feet of counter space between the stove and the sink as the central work area.

The refrigerator, too, is in frequent use and should be near at hand. Locate other appliances as conveniently as possible depending on how often you use them and on how many appliances there are.

In this kitchen it was important to keep as much uninterrupted work surface as possible, so the refrigerator and built-in oven were placed next to each other at one end of the room.

Draw out the plan of your kitchen on graph paper if possible, indicating the room dimensions and the locations of the various appliances and fixtures.

Making the base cabinets

The construction of these units is very similar to those in the kitchen on page 16. The main difference is that in this kitchen the front edges are covered with dark stained strips of wood. The main structure is made of the same 535mm wide boards of white laminate-covered chipboard. These are available in 2.4 m lengths with the two long edges already edged. You just cut off the lengths you need for the uprights and shelves. Buy some 2.44 m lengths of matching iron-on edging to cover the few places where a cut edge will be exposed.

Screw the components together as shown on page 18. Where the screw heads will be exposed, cover them

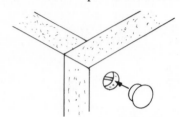

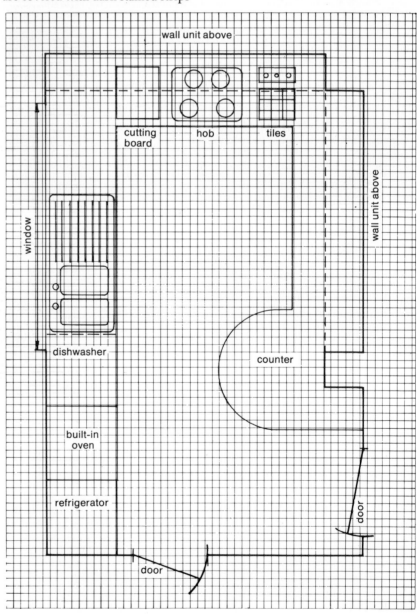

Fitting the wire baskets

The white plastic-covered wire baskets are sold by large department stores in a variety of depths together with pairs of metal slides which are screwed to the sides of the cabinet. Depending on the exact width of the baskets you buy, it may be necessary to screw pine battens to the insides of the cabinets as spacers. These baskets are useful for storing everything from cans to fresh fruit and vegetables. Install three or four big baskets to hold larger items like baking tins and casseroles.

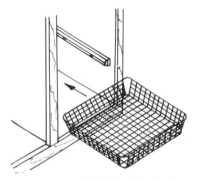

Making the worktops

The plastic laminate is glued down to a base of 19mm thick birch plywood. Plan the length of the worktops carefully, then cut the plywood to the exact sizes. By cutting carefully you will get two 600mm widths out of one standard sheet of plywood so there should not be too much waste. The edge of the plywood, with its thin layers of wood in alternating shades of light and dark, is left exposed. You can leave the edge 19mm thick or you can choose to emphasize it even more by adding a 25mm wide plywood strip glued and screwed from the underside of the front so

with special white plastic screw caps which give a more finished and professional appearance to the cabinets.

After making the basic cabinets, cover the front edges with 19 × 25mm strips of a dark hardwood or pine stained in a dark wood tone to create a contrasting background for the light coloured doors. Use 19 × 50mm wide strips along the top as a fascia.
Use 32mm pins to attach the strips to the framework of the cabinets. Sink the heads below the surface with a nail punch and then fill the holes to match the wood.

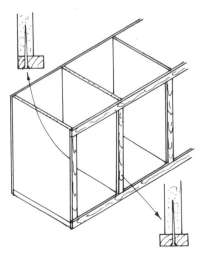

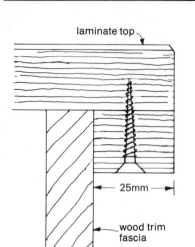

laminate top

25mm

wood trim fascia

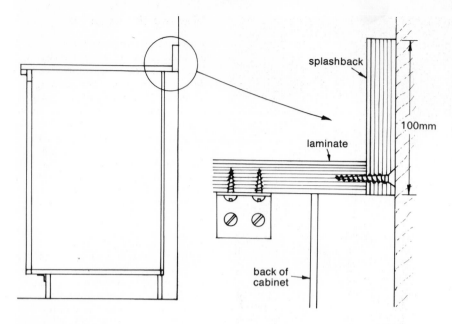

splashback

100mm

laminate

back of cabinet

that the resulting edge is 38mm thick.

It is important to incorporate a board as a splashback to the back of the counter. It not only keeps food and water from falling down the back of

the cabinet it also makes a neater join with the wall, particularly if the wall is not quite straight.

Cover a 100mm wide plywood board with the same laminate as that used

for the counter and then glue and screw it to the back edge of the counter. Use a resin glue and spread it on liberally so that any small cracks will be filled with the glue which is hard and waterproof.

Working with plastic laminates

Plastic laminate has many advantages as a work surface for a kitchen. It is tough and durable, easy to keep clean and quite resistant to heat. It is also inexpensive and available in an enormous range of colours and patterns.

Large sheets of laminate are extremely awkward to handle. If possible, lay the sheet on a solid base such as a sheet of 19mm plywood supported on trestles while you work on it.

Remember to cut the laminate a little larger, about 3mm, than the board you are gluing it to so that it can be trimmed accurately afterwards either with a plane or router.

To cut the sheet, lay it good face upwards and mark the cutting line.

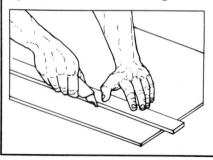

Fit a special hooked blade in the trimming knife and score halfway through the laminate, using a straight edge as a guide. Change blades often to be sure the cutting edge is sharp and score with several strokes of the knife.

To break the laminate cleanly along the scored line, hold the straight edge firmly on the line and lift up the end of the laminate until it snaps off. This takes a little practice to get right so it is a good idea to first make several trial cuts on a scrap of laminate until you get the feel of it.

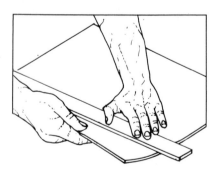

To glue down the laminate, turn the sheet upside down and brush off the surface to make sure it is dust and grease free. Slightly roughen the top of the surface which the laminate is to cover to provide a 'key' for the adhesive. Use coarse sandpaper and

brush off all the dust. Glue the laminate to the base with contact adhesive. Spread a thin, even layer of adhesive on both the underside of the laminate and the top of the base surface.

After ten to twenty minutes, when both surfaces are just dry to the touch, lay several thin wood strips or small dowels along the counter at about 300mm intervals. Once you bring the glued surfaces together you will not be able to move them, so these strips will allow you to keep the surfaces apart while you position the laminate exactly.

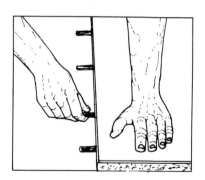

After you have positioned the laminate, making sure the sides and ends are aligned, remove the first strip and press down the laminate firmly. Then remove each successive

Making the oven unit

There is nothing particularly difficult about building in an oven. Each manufacturer supplies exact details for the size of the opening required. You simply build a large box to hold the oven. Place the oven at a convenient working height, which is usually recommended in the manufacturer's instructions. Then within the same large box, build a cabinet above and a large drawer below the oven to hold hard to store items like trays and roasting pans.

Start by planning the height of the unit, and keep in mind that eight feet is the maximum length of board that you can conveniently buy. Usually the depth of the oven from front to back is about 600mm so that the 535mm wide boards used for the cabinets are not enough. Instead, buy a standard sheet of the same laminate-covered chipboard, available at large suppliers, and cut out the pieces as required.

This oven unit was made the full 2.44m in height, so one sheet has simply been cut in half to get the two 0.6 × 2.44m sides.

Cut the four 600mm deep shelves to the required width. Ensure the opening for the oven is the exact size specified. Some ovens require vent holes cut in the shelves below and

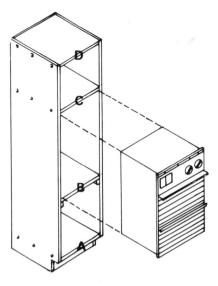

Mark the locations of the two shelves, then screw a 38 × 38mm batten to each side to hold the oven shelf. Start the assembly by screwing shelf B to the battens. Add the second side and then drill and screw the shelf in position. Finally secure the bottom and top pieces A and D and shelf C from the outside, using screws hidden by plastic caps. Then attach the hardboard back by nailing it in place. Notice that the bottom shelf is about 100mm off the floor with a board added underneath set back from the front edge.

In this case it was easy to build in the refrigerator by locating it in the

strip until the entire surface is in contact.

Go over the surface, pressing down firmly over the whole surface to get a strong bond. Then trim the edges with a sharp block plane or with a router fitted with a special cutter designed for cutting laminates, until they are just flush with the surface underneath. Trimming off the laminate takes practice to do well.

In this case you won't need to cover the edge with matching laminate, so the edge can just be trimmed at a 45° angle to keep it from breaking off. Where a front edging is required, apply it first in the same way as the laminate was applied to the top surface before the final trimming.

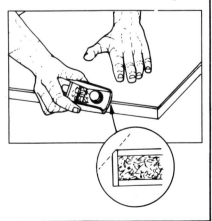

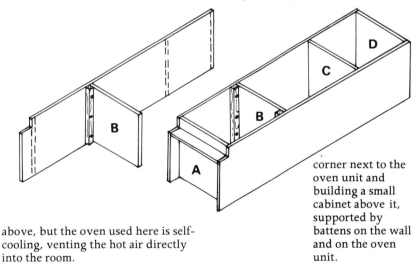

above, but the oven used here is self-cooling, venting the hot air directly into the room.

corner next to the oven unit and building a small cabinet above it, supported by battens on the wall and on the oven unit.

Building in the sink and hob

The sink and hob will require cut-outs so they can be fitted into the worktop. It is best to glue down the laminate surface first and then mark and cut the openings as required.

Follow the instructions provided by the sink and hob manufacturers in laying out the openings. The manufacturers often provide a template indicating the size of the cut-out required. Put the worktop on a pair of trestles, then drill a hole within the area to be cut out to

provide a starting point for the
sabre saw. Make the cut carefully
and then try the sink or hob in place
and if the fit is too tight, trim where
necessary with a plane or coping
saw.

Building in the tiles and chopping block

The small area of tiles next to the
hob is very useful as a hot stand. To
make it easy to install, make the counter out of two 10mm thick pieces of plywood instead of one 19mm thickness.

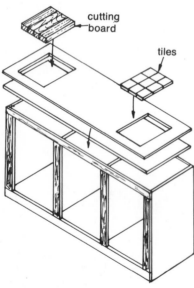

cutting board

tiles

Fit the laminate and cut the holes in
the top piece of plywood and then
glue the two thicknesses together,
adding a few short screws from
underneath to reinforce the glued
joint.

Then install the tiles with tile
adhesive and after it has set, grout in
between the tiles.

Install the chopping board in the
same way. Hold the board in place
using two screws, inserted from
underneath.

Making the wall-hung cabinets

These hanging
cabinets are similar
in construction to
the base units. The
basic carcass is
made from 300mm
wide laminate-
covered panels.

Measure the size and then cut the
top and bottom to that length. Mark
off the cabinet divisions on the top
and bottom. It is convenient to make
all the openings the same width,
about 450mm, and then use any
leftover space to house spices or
cookbooks, as has been done here.

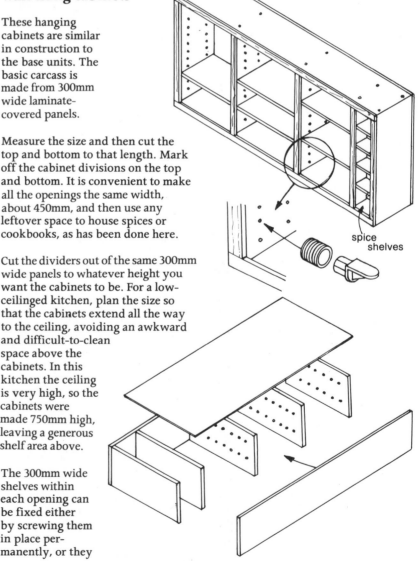

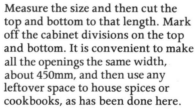

spice
shelves

Cut the dividers out of the same 300mm
wide panels to whatever height you
want the cabinets to be. For a low-
ceilinged kitchen, plan the size so
that the cabinets extend all the way
to the ceiling, avoiding an awkward
and difficult-to-clean
space above the
cabinets. In this
kitchen the ceiling
is very high, so the
cabinets were
made 750mm high,
leaving a generous
shelf area above.

The 300mm wide
shelves within
each opening can
be fixed either
by screwing them
in place per-
manently, or they

can be adjustable, resting on special plastic brackets which fit into spaced holes drilled at, say, 50mm intervals along the sides.

Assemble in the same way as before, first placing the marked bottom piece and one divider on edge. Screw all the dividers in place, then the top. Finally glue and nail a 4mm thick back panel to the back edges, using it to square up the cabinet.

Notice that the extractor unit situated directly above the hob is simply screwed to a wide shelf in the unit above.

The flexible pipe from the extractor goes up through a hole cut in the top and to the outside wall behind the plywood panel fixed above the unit. Follow the manufacturer's instructions to determine the exact position and fixing of the extractor unit.

Hanging the top units

To make it easier to hang the units, first screw a 150mm wide pine board or matching 19mm plywood board to the wall so that the unit will sit directly on the top edge of it.

Make sure to mark a line level on the wall first as a guide for the board.

Before installing the cabinets, screw metal fixing brackets to the top rear inside corners at each divider. Also fix two brackets along the bottom, one at each corner. You will need two helpers to lift the cabinet and hold it in position while you screw through the brackets into the wall.

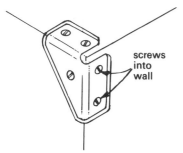

screws into wall

Screw cuphooks and knife racks into the board so that utensils can be hung within easy reach.

Making the doors and drawers

The easiest way to make the drawers is to screw together the four 12mm plywood sides with screws and fibre wall plugs. The 115mm deep drawers

can slide on wooden battens screwed to the sides of the cabinet or on special runners.

Follow the manufacturer's instructions in fixing the runners. The nylon wheels in the runner make the motion so smooth that even a full drawer pulls out with fingertip control.

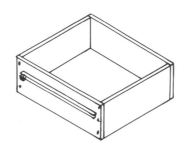

Making the doors is the easiest part of the kitchen construction since they are just pieces of 15mm thick birch plywood with rounded corners. Notice that the cabinet door and the drawer fronts are both cut from the same piece so that the grain is continuous.

Cut each piece of plywood so that it overlaps the cabinet opening by 12mm on all four sides. Try to choose sections of plywood sheet which have the most attractive grain and the fewest flaws. Then round the corners to a 25mm radius before sanding well.

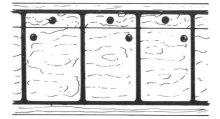

With the drawer in position, measure the exact height of the drawer front, then cut off the top part of the plywood piece which will serve as the drawer fronts.

Apply three coats of clear polyurethane to the sides and paticularly to the edges of the plywood before hanging the doors. The hinges, which fit into a shallow recess drilled with a special bit, allow the doors to open a full 180° Fit the door first before carefully locating the drawer front so that there is an even 2mm gap between it and the door below. Screw the drawer front on the drawer from the inside with four 19mm brass screws and then attach the large wooden knobs

which have been stained a dark wood shade to match the cabinet surrounds.

Use the same technique for all the doors in turn, attaching one at a time to make sure that each one fits correctly.

You can increase the storage area in the cabinets by fixing perforated hardboard to the backs of the doors for hanging lids and other kitchen utensils away neatly.

Nail each piece of pegboard to 25 × 25mm battens around the edge and then screw the battens directly to the insides of the doors. But notice that the shelves behind the doors must be cut back about 75 to 100mm to allow space for the pegboard.

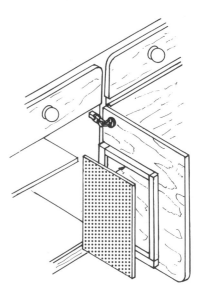

BEDROOM AND BATHROOM PROJECTS

Chest of drawers

Sauna bench

Bedroom closets

Captain's bed

Towel rail and soap dish

This section contains a good mixture of projects for the bedroom and the bathroom, both in traditional and modern designs. The elegant double bed is easy enough to make in a weekend. For a more challenging project, there is the traditional pine bed with a hand carved motif on the headboard, footboard and side rails. This bed uses old-fashioned woodworking joints like mortise and tenon joints in its construction. There are nine other projects for the bedroom and bathroom ranging from an easy-to-make hardwood towel rail to a luxurious chest of drawers in ash veneer.

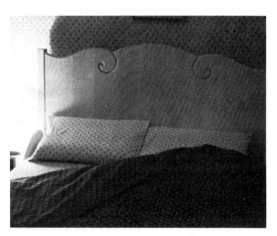

Traditional pine bed

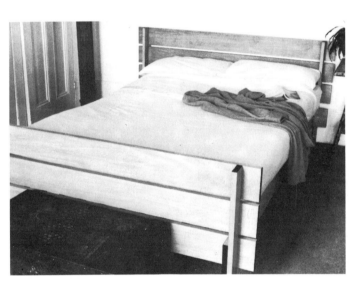

Simple double bed

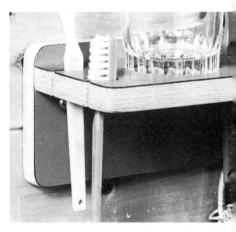

Bathroom cabinet and toothbrush holder

Night table

TRADITIONAL PINE BED

This is an elegant, old-fashioned bed, decorated on the head and footboards with a simple scroll design, made to take a 1375 × 1900mm double mattress. The slatted mattress base is nice and firm to provide good support. The slats are spaced about 50mm apart to allow ventilation for the mattress. If you are using a foam mattress, it is best to check the manufacturer's instructions for the amount of ventilation, and hence spacing, required.

Making the head and footboards

CUTTING LIST

32 × 150mm
    9 pieces 1400mm long
25 × 50mm
    2 pieces 1270mm long

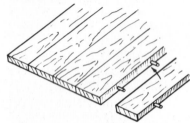

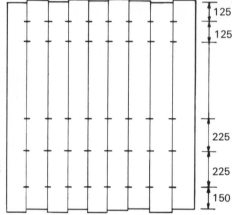

125
125
225
225
150

Dowel joint the pieces of 32 × 150mm into one width (page 232). Join them carefully, making sure that the edges are straight. It is best to clamp them together first without applying glue to see that the joints are a tight fit. Add five 38mm long dowel pegs per joint, positioning them as shown to

avoid cutting through a dowel later when shaping the boards.

Use a dowelling jig (page 233) to drill accurately placed holes, or mark the holes with a gauge and try square and then drill (page 193). Add glue to the holes and edge and clamp up

the boards with bar clamps below and above (page 202).

When the glue has set, remove the clamps and trim both ends to leave them square. It will probably be necessary to plane over the surface with a long plane. Then cut the panel into two parts, one 815mm deep for the headboard leaving at least 450mm for the footboard. Copy the profile for the headboard onto a long piece of paper or cardboard. Trace it onto both pieces and cut out the shape with a sabre saw.

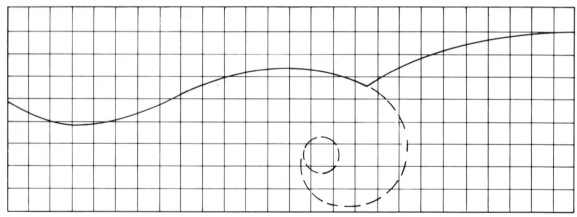

one square = 25mm

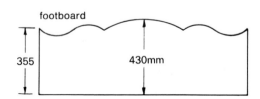
footboard
355
430mm

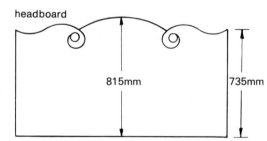
headboard
815mm
735mm

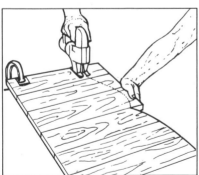

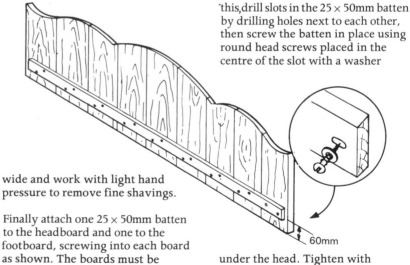

'this, drill slots in the 25 × 50mm batten by drilling holes next to each other, then screw the batten in place using round head screws placed in the centre of the slot with a washer

60mm

Clean up the edges with a Surform, file or spokeshave. Round the shaped edges either with a file, or with a rounding-over bit in a router.

Trace the scroll carefully onto the headboard. Make sure when gouging it out, that the shape follows nicely from the contour of the headboard. Use a very sharp gouge about 12mm

wide and work with light hand pressure to remove fine shavings.

Finally attach one 25 × 50mm batten to the headboard and one to the footboard, screwing into each board as shown. The boards must be allowed to expand and contract across their width and screwing the batten on rigidly could result in splitting at the joints. To prevent

under the head. Tighten with moderate pressure only. Use two screws per board and position the batten exactly 60mm up from the bottom.

Making the legs

CUTTING LIST
75 × 75mm
  2 pieces 965mm long
  2 pieces 585mm long

Use a try square and marking gauge to mark the locations of the mortises. Make sure to put face and edge marks on the legs so that you position the mortises correctly for the left and right legs.

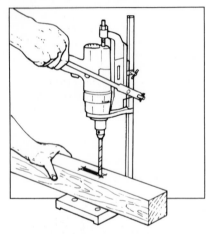

The mortises are 12mm wide so use a 12mm diameter drill bit in a drill stand to drill a series of holes just a little over 50mm deep. Then use a 12mm wide chisel to cut out the mortise, paring down carefully at the end to a straight, square hole.

The tenons will be held in place with two dowel pegs, so mark out two 10mm diameter holes, 50mm apart, exactly

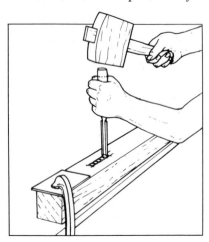

40mm from the mortised edge as shown. Use a gauge to mark all four legs so that the holes will be exactly right. Centre punch the holes, then drill straight through the leg, again using a drill stand to get the holes absolutely vertical.

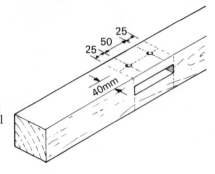

Finally round the edges of the legs to approximately the same radius as the headboard.

Making the rails

CUTTING LIST
32 × 150mm
  2 pieces 2030mm long
  2 pieces 460mm long
25 × 50mm
  2 pieces 1220mm long A

First cut the tenons at each end of the two 2030mm long rails. They should fit snugly into the mortises so make them 12mm thick, 100mm wide and 50mm long, and try them in the mortise slots as you work to get the fit right (page 235). Cut the shoulders first with a tenon saw, exactly 50mm from the end and then chisel away the waste leaving the tenon 12mm thick.

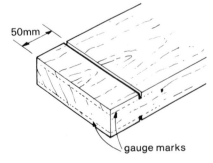

gauge marks

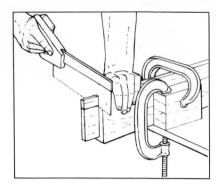

Finally cut away both sides to make the tenon 100mm wide.

To drill the holes for the mortise pegs, insert each tenon into its mortise slot and make sure it is pushed in all the way. Push the 10mm drill bit through the hole already drilled just far enough to make a centre mark on the tenon. Then take out the tenon and drill a 10mm diameter hole, 1.5mm closer to the shoulder than the marked centre. That way the dowel peg, which is sanded to a slight taper, will pull the joint tight in the final assembly.

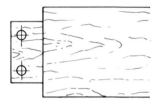

Mark and drill all eight holes, then cut eight lengths of 10mm diameter dowel, 75mm long. Round the ends and sand them, tapering them slightly to make them easier to insert.

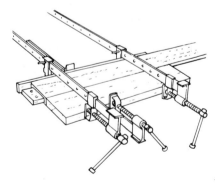

To create the profiled ends of the rails, glue a 460mm piece of 32 × 150mm to one end of each rail making sure the end lines up exactly with the shoulder of the tenon. Then mark and cut out the profile following the diagram and round the edges as before. Carve out the scroll with a mallet and 12mm gouge and then finally glue and screw the 25 × 50mm batten A to the inside, 28mm from the bottom

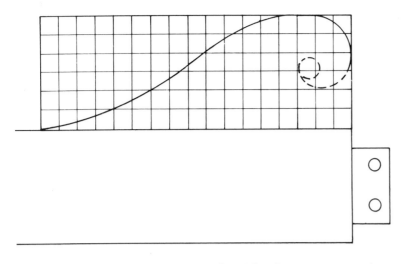

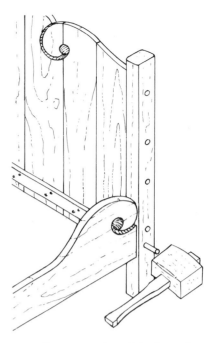

edge. Position it centrally and use four no.10 38mm countersunk screws per batten.

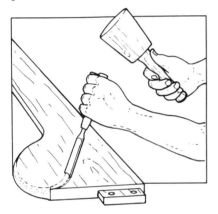

Assembling the bed

CUTTING LIST
32 × 150mm
    2 pieces 1400mm long B
19 × 75mm
    12 pieces 1927mm long

First screw the legs to the head and footboards with the 75mm screws. Position the boards so that they are flush with the inside (mortise) face of the legs. Counterbore by drilling 10mm diameter holes, 25mm deep and then filling the holes with matching pine

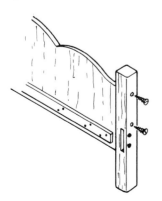

plugs after the screws are in place (page 214). Use two screws per leg in the footboard and three screws per leg in the headboard.

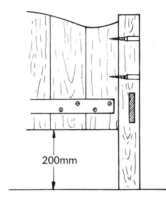

200mm

Next assemble the rails by inserting the tenon into the mortise and tapping in the locking dowel to keep the joint tight. The dowels should be tapped in so that they finish up about 2mm proud of the surface. To remove the pegs and dismantle the bed, simply use another dowel of the

same diameter and tap it in from the back to unlock the joint.

The slat base is made in the same way as the base for the double bed on page 58. First screw down the two 1400mm long cross struts B. If these are slightly too long, cut them to fit and then screw them to the 25 × 50mm battens with two no.10 45mm screws per end.

Finally screw down the twelve slats with the 32mm screws spacing them out evenly and leaving about 50mm between each slat.

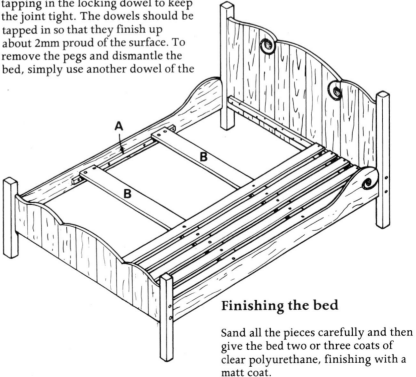

Finishing the bed

Sand all the pieces carefully and then give the bed two or three coats of clear polyurethane, finishing with a matt coat.

NIGHT TABLE

Once you have cut all the pieces for this traditional night table out of veneered chipboard, it shouldn't take more than a day to finish it. The night table measures about 400mm wide, 685mm high and 400mm deep. To make the joinery really easy, all the pieces are glued and nailed together and the drawer is made from a push-together plastic section which is very quick to assemble. Cut the pieces either from a sheet of oak veneered chipboard or, if this is difficult to buy, from veneered chipboard shelving in oak, mahogany or any other finish. These are available in panels of various standard widths.

Making the cabinet

CUTTING LIST
veneered chipboard
  1 piece 405 × 405mm, top A
  2 pieces 400 × 590mm, sides B
  2 pieces 355 × 380mm, shelves C
  1 piece 75 × 355,
  bottom front panel D
  1 piece 60 × 355mm,
  top front panel E
  1 piece 355 × 590mm, back F
  1 piece 75 × 355mm, back rim G
  2 pieces 75 × 200mm, side rims H
  1 piece 22 × 352mm, drawer
  front I

Start by cutting out the chipboard pieces and checking that they are square and accurate. The secret of success in using panels like this is to cut the pieces exactly to size so that each piece fits together perfectly.

When cutting veneered boards, remember first to score the cutting line on the veneer with a sharp trimming knife along a straight edge, so that the veneer does not split when you saw through the board.

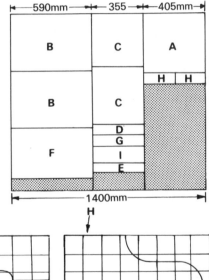

Before beginning assembly, cut out the three shaped pieces, E and H. Then cover all the edges which will be exposed with iron-on veneer edging (page 67).

To assemble the unit, start by gluing and nailing one side B to the back F, covering the edges of the back F. Then continue with the two shelves C. The top shelf is located 125mm down from the top edge, and the bottom shelf is 75mm up from the bottom edge.
Draw guide lines on the sides to locate the shelves when nailing. Make sure to apply glue to the edges, then nail in the pins and finally set them below the surface with a nail punch.

one square = 25mm

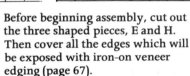

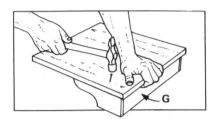

Nail on the other side B and the two front panels, D and E. Then assemble the top A by gluing and nailing it to the back rim G and the two side rims H. Locate the back G about 20mm in from the back edge to allow you space to nail the top to the back F and the sides B.

Construct the drawer from the plastic components, the drawer front I and the 4mm plywood bottom. See page 120 for instructions on using plastic drawer sections. Glue and screw the 12 × 15mm softwood strips to the sides of the cabinet as drawer runners.

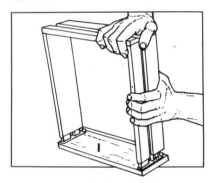

Before finishing the cabinet, fill all the holes with matching wood filler and then sand them smooth.

Finishing the cabinet

Either apply two or three coats of clear polyurethane, or first apply a wood stain to darken the colour of the veneered boards and then finish with polyurethane. This cabinet has been stained a light oak shade and then finished with a coat of matt polyurethane. Finally, add the decorative drawer pull and fit the drawer in place.

SIMPLE DOUBLE BED

Beds with slat supports are firmer and more comfortable than most spring supports and, provided they are spaced right, the slats allow air to circulate around the mattress. The bed is made for a double mattress, 1375 × 1900mm, but the dimensions can be adjusted to fit a mattress of any size. The design would look equally attractive as a single bed. The construction is easy but the pieces must be accurately and squarely cut for the assembly to be easy. All the connections are screwed together except for the bed surround which is composed of simple halving joints. The construction is made easier if you clamp the two pieces together as shown, before drilling the holes and inserting the screws.

Making the base

CUTTING LIST
25 × 25mm softwood
   2 pieces 1320mm long
   2 pieces 915mm long
   4 pieces 150mm long
25 × 150mm hardwood
   2 pieces 1600mm long A
   2 pieces 2095mm long B
25 × 75mm
   2 pieces 1475mm long, for slat supports C (to be trimmed)

Mark and cut the joints on the four pieces A and B as shown. Mark the width of the slot using a piece of

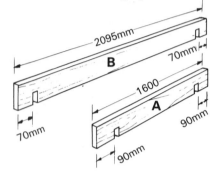

25 × 150mm as a guide. Saw on the waste side of the lines halfway across before removing the waste with a chisel.

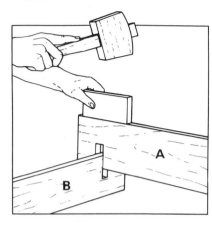

Next assemble the bed frame on the bench or floor. If a corner of 25 × 150mm should break off, glue and clamp it together adding a 90mm screw to strengthen it.

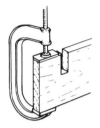

Screw the 915mm long 25 × 25mm battens to the insides of the long rails B, 40mm from the top edge and placed centrally along the length to support the two supports C. Screw the two 1320mm long 25 × 25mm battens to the ends A, 20mm from the top edge. Use four no.8 38mm screws per batten.

Add the short 150mm battens in the corners so that you can screw the plywood corner brackets to them from underneath, using four 19mm long screws per corner.

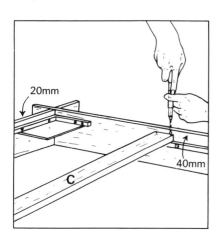

Finally trim the two 25 × 75mm struts C to fit exactly inside the frame, and screw them to the battens with two 38mm no 8 screws per end. Place one about 500mm from the head end of the bed and the other about 685mm from the first.

Making the ends

CUTTING LIST
25 × 150mm hardwood
　5 pieces 1600mm long
25 × 75mm hardwood
　2 pieces 800mm long, for legs
　2 pieces 635mm long, for legs

To make the footboard, screw the two 635mm legs to the end of rails B so that 165mm of leg extends below the rail. Clamp the pieces together first, then drill the holes before attaching with two 38mm long no.12 screws. These round head japanned screws are a feature of the bed design, so be sure to align them vertically.

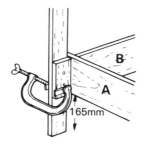

For the footboard, attach two more 25 × 150mm lengths A using a 15mm thick board as a spacer (a piece of 19 × 75mm slat will do).

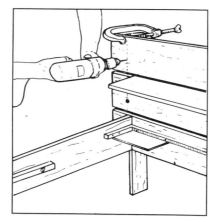

Again clamp the pieces together before attaching them. Make sure the top board lines up exactly with the top of the leg, even if the space is more or less than the 15mm. Also make sure to line the screws up vertically.

Repeat this with the three remaining 25 × 150mm boards to make the

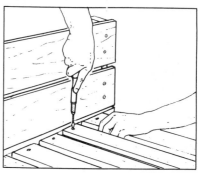

headboard 800mm high. Finally cut twelve 19 × 75mm slats to fit lengthways inside the bed frame. Screw down each slat with four 32mm screws to make the mattress base. Start at one end and leave approximately 50mm spaces between the boards.

Finishing

Sand the bed carefully and then apply one thinned coat of clear polyurethane to the entire bed. Before applying the second coat, carefully paint all the board ends matt black using a small brush. This adds a nice decorative touch to the bed and matches the black screw heads which are left exposed on all connections. Finally, give the whole bed a second coat of polyurethane.

CAPTAIN'S BED

Although this bed is designed to take a standard single mattress about 1020 × 2030mm, you can easily alter the size to fit any mattress, either single or double. The structure underneath is very strong so the width can safely be increased. Don't try to cut out the shapes without a sabre saw; it is very difficult to do accurately by hand. Plan out the work carefully, marking and labelling the pieces. This bed was made from good quality birch plywood stained a light oak shade and sealed with clear polyurethane. It would look equally good left natural or stained a darker colour like mahogany or teak to match darker furniture.

SHOPPING LIST

birch plywood	1½ standard sheets, 19mm thick 1.0 × 1.5m, 12mm thick 760 × 1300mm, 6.5mm thick
chipboard	1.2 × 1.5m, 12mm thick
softwood	about 14m of 38 × 38mm about 25m of 19 × 75mm 6m of 25 × 25mm
hardware	50 no.10 countersunk steel screws, 45mm long 6 no.8 countersunk steel screws, 32mm long 12 no.6 countersunk steel screws, 32mm long 65 no.8 countersunk steel screws, 25mm long 16 no.8 countersunk steel screws, 19mm long 60 finishing nails or panel pins, 25mm long 2 pairs of heavy duty extension drawer slides, 600mm long with 12mm screws 4 brass drawer handles with 12mm brass screws
plus	light oak wood stain clear polyurethane

Making the bed frame

CUTTING LIST
19mm plywood
　1 sheet cut into 2 sides A and
　2 drawer fronts H as shown
　½ sheet cut into 2 pieces
　600 × 1030mm, for ends B
12mm chipboard
　4 pieces 350 × 1030mm,
　for dividers C
38 × 38mm battens
　6 pieces 1030mm long D
　12 pieces 317mm long E
19 × 75mm slats
　10 pieces 2028mm long,
　for slats F
　2 pieces 1025mm long G

First choose the best side of the plywood with the fewest marks and knots and place it face down on the bench. Following the diagrams, mark the sides carefully with a pencil, using the lid of a jar or can to trace the curves.

Cut out the shapes with a sabre saw and then use a block plane to smooth the edges.

To cut the drawer openings, first drill a 12mm diameter hole within the

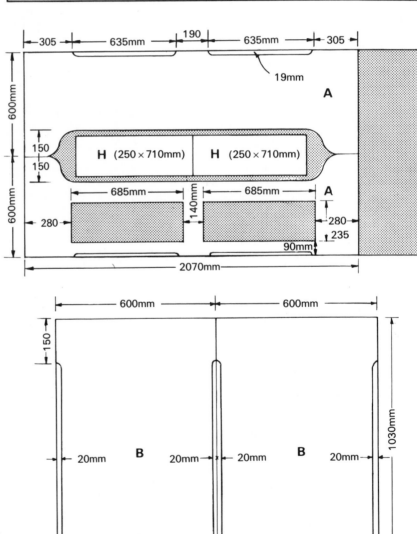

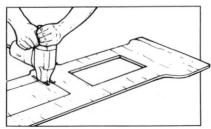

waste area as a starting point for the saw. Cut out the shapes carefully with the saw, being especially careful at the corners so you do not overshoot the marked lines. When the shapes are cut out, plane and sand all the cut edges well and round the top edges of the sides A and ends B to give a more finished look and to make them smooth to the touch.

Next, glue and screw the short battens E to the insides of both sides

A, carefully positioning them as shown. Notice the 19mm space on either end of the sides for the plywood ends B and also the 12mm space on either side of the openings for the 12mm thick dividers C.

Start with the side which has the drawer openings. Use two 45mm screws per batten, screwing through the batten into the plywood. After attaching the six battens, lay the two sides A next to each other to mark

the corresponding batten locations on the other side A, then screw these six battens in place.

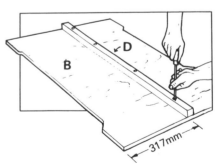

Next glue and screw two of the battens D to the inside of each of the ends B so that the bottom edge of the batten is exactly 317mm from the base. Use three 45mm screws per batten, again screwing through the batten into the plywood.

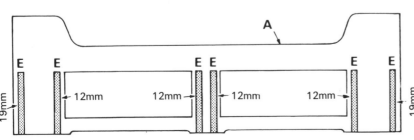

61

Then glue and screw one batten D at the top of each divider C. For a stronger fixing use the 25mm no.8 screws or screw through the chipboard into the battens, four screws per board.

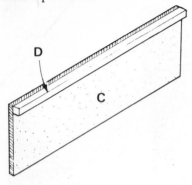

Finishing the bed pieces

Before assembling the bed, sand the pieces well, with an orbital sander if possible. Then stain both faces of the ends B and the sides A.

After you have achieved the depth of colour you want and the stain is dry, apply two coats of clear polyurethane – gloss or matt finish – to the ends and side pieces. There is no need to finish the dividers, but it is a good idea to apply at least one coat of polyurethane to the slats to protect them from moisture.

Assembling the bed

Start assembling the bed by attaching one end B to a side A. First drill two countersunk clearance holes in each connecting batten. Have someone help you by holding the two pieces so that they fit together tightly while you screw through the short battens E into the ends with two 45mm screws.

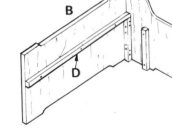

Then attach the other end B and the other side A in the same way. Don't apply glue to these connections since

Assembling the slat support

To assemble the bed slats, space the ten slats F out on the two cross pieces G so that the outside slats are flush with the ends of the cross pieces, making the width 1025mm. The space between the slats will be about 35mm.

Place the cross pieces G carefully as shown, 38mm from the ends of the slats, then glue and nail the slats to the cross pieces using three 25mm pins at each joint. Before the glue sets, check with a try square so that the slat structure will drop squarely into the bed frame. For foam mattresses reduce to nine slats.

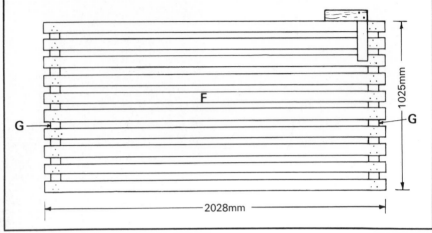

you may at some time want to dismantle the bed.

Attach the dividers C by screwing through the chipboard into the battens E with two 25mm screws per end, countersunk so they won't interfere with the drawers.

After attaching the four dividers, drop the slat assembly in place to check the fit. It may be necessary to push the bed into shape to make it drop in

easily. Remove the slat assembly while you fit the drawer slides but install it again before you fit the drawers.

Making the drawers

CUTTING LIST
19mm plywood
  2 pieces 250 × 710mm,
  for drawer fronts H
  (see cutting diagram)
12mm plywood
  4 pieces 220 × 660mm,
  for sides I
  2 pieces 220 × 620mm,
  for back J
6.5mm plywood
  2 pieces 619 × 647mm,
  for drawer bottoms K
38 × 38mm battens
  8 pieces 190mm long
25 × 25mm battens
  4 pieces 620mm long
  4 pieces 595mm long

Since the type of sliding hardware may vary it is best to determine the width of the drawers from the amount of clearance required for the slides you have bought. Precise instructions are usually supplied with the sliding hardware.

The drawer fronts will remain the same, 710mm wide, but the back J, bottom K and the 25 × 25mm batten lengths may have to be adjusted.

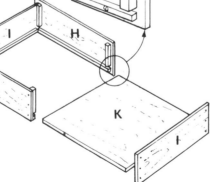

The four corner joints of each drawer are reinforced with 38 × 38mm battens. The 6.5mm plywood drawer bottoms K sit on 25 × 25mm battens glued and screwed to the four drawer sides.

Attach the battens to the backs J and the fronts H. Use 25mm screws through the plywood at the back and 45mm screws through the 38 × 38mm battens at the front, and 32mm no.8 screws through the 25 × 25mm battens into the plywood at the front. The three battens are set flush with the edges of J, but are set in from the edges of the front H to allow the front to cover the opening in the bed. So, position the battens carefully so the sides will be parallel.

Then connect the sides I to the corner battens using 25mm screws, and attach the bottom K to the battens underneath with 19mm screws.

Mark out the locations of the handles and scribe their outlines carefully with a sharp knife. Before attaching them, sand, stain and varnish the

drawer fronts and apply at least one coat of polyurethane to the insides of the drawers.

Then, if you are using the type of inset handle shown, chip away enough wood with a chisel to allow the handle to sit flush with the surface of the drawer front. Attach the handles with the matching 12mm screws.

Attach part of the rolling drawer slides to the sides and corresponding part to the dividers C. Measure very carefully to get the locations correct. Then with the slat assembly in position try the drawers in place. Adjust the runners if necessary.

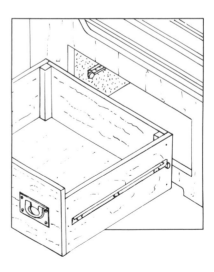

Finally screw down the slat unit with about twelve 32mm no.6 screws, countersunk so that they will not cut into the mattress.

CHEST OF DRAWERS

Chests of drawers come in many styles but the basic construction of them all is very similar. The top, sides and back form a box structure into which the drawers fit. The drawers are supported on runners which are attached to the sides. In traditional work when boards are glued together to form the sides, much more thought and care have to go into the construction to prevent the sides from splitting. However, with modern veneered boards which don't expand and contract, this is not a problem.

This is not an easy project but you can make it a bit simpler by joining the drawers with screws as shown in the Welsh dresser on page 40, instead of the dovetailed method shown here.

A portable router is very handy to cut the housing in the top, to trim the edges of the drawer fronts for the hockey stick moulding, right, and also, with the right attachment, to do the dovetailing on the drawers.

This chest of drawers is made from ash veneered blockboard, but you can use any veneer you like. A blockboard base is more expensive but is much better for this type of work than chipboard. Since you will be spending a lot of time and effort on making it, it is worth buying good materials.

Cutting the veneered blockboard

CUTTING LIST
1 piece 520 × 1105mm, for top A
2 pieces 495 × 930mm, for sides B
2 pieces 125 × 560mm, for drawer fronts C (to be trimmed)
2 pieces 180 × 1065mm, for drawer fronts D (to be trimmed)
1 piece 230 × 1065mm, for drawer front E (to be trimmed)
1 piece 125 × 480mm, for spacer F
1 piece 75 × 1145mm, for plinth G (to be trimmed)
2 pieces 75 × 495mm, for plinth H
1 piece 55 × 1145mm, for cornice I (to be trimmed)
2 pieces 55 × 495mm, for cornice J

Note: cut G, H, I and J at a 60° angle as shown or plane them afterwards.

hockey stick moulding

A sheet of veneered blockboard is expensive so to avoid waste, before you make any cuts in it, double check the dimensions. Follow the cutting list and diagram carefully. Notice that the cuts marked 1 and 2 on the diagram are made first.

If you are using a circular saw, refer to page 209 for hints on making straight and accurate cuts.

Cutting with the grain of the veneered face presents no problems, but, in cutting across the grain, the veneer breaks out causing a rough and unsightly edge which is impossible to fix. To prevent this, first score along the cutting line with a sharp trimming knife and a straight edge. A couple of strokes will be enough to cut through the veneer.

Notice that all the pieces are arranged lengthwise along the sheet of blockboard. This is the same direction as the laminated boards inside the blockboard, in other words the strong direction. Boards cut across the width would have much less strength.

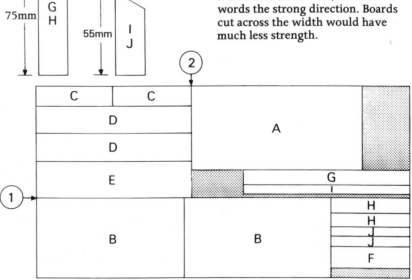

Making the interior frames

CUTTING LIST
25 × 50mm hardwood
   14 pieces 1015mm long
   12 pieces 390mm long

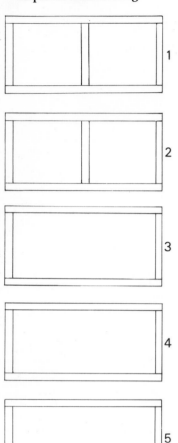

Assemble five frames as shown. Clamp the pieces together with bar clamps, check that the assembly is square then join each corner with two through dowels. Drill two well spaced 6mm diameter holes about 75mm deep. Glue in the 6mm dowel pegs and cut the ends off flush when the glue has set. The dowel ends will be covered with veneer edging later.

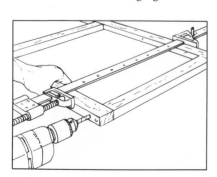

On frames 1 and 2 add a central batten, positioning it exactly in the middle. Join it to the sides by dowelling in exactly the same way as the frames were joined. You should now have five frames as shown, numbered one to five. To avoid confusion, it will help if you mark each frame with its number clearly in pencil.

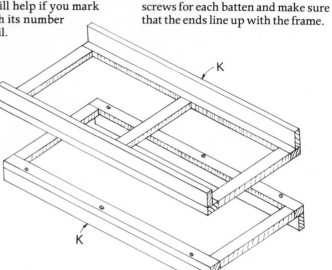

To complete the frames, add the remaining four 1015mm battens (K on drawing) to frame 1 and to frame 5. These are the top and bottom frames. Glue and screw one batten flush with the front and the other flush with the back. Use three 38mm no.8 screws for each batten and make sure that the ends line up with the frame.

Cutting the rabbets and housings

The next step is to cut the rabbets and housings on the top A and sides B. If possible, use a portable router. A straight cutter will cut both rabbets and housings accurately and quickly.

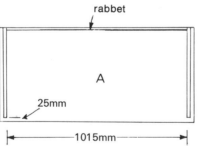

Start by marking the two housings on the underside of the top A. They should be exactly 1015mm apart. Mark the pairs of lines, then cut the stopped housings 6mm deep using a

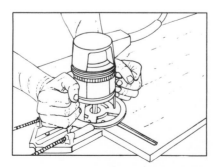

fence on the router. Make them the exact width of the veneered blockboard, so that the sides B will fit tightly into the groove. Cutting them by hand is more difficult. Score the lines with a trimming knife, then continue with a tenon saw and chisel.

Notice that the housing grooves run straight through to the back edge but they are stopped exactly 25mm short of the front edge. Square off the front end of the housing with a chisel.

Cut the rabbets along the back edges of the top A as shown and along the inside back of the sides B. The rabbets run straight through to the ends on the sides B but are stopped at the housing along the top A. Cut all the rabbets 10mm deep and 10mm wide.

Marking the sides

The five frames made earlier must be glued and screwed to the sides B to make up the basic structure of the cabinet. So mark the locations of the frames as shown on the inside faces of both side pieces.

Measure from the bottom upward on each side, then carefully draw the lines with a straight edge or a large square. Lay the sides together to check that the lines match up. Notice that if the thickness of the planed

25×50mm hardwood pieces is not exactly 20mm you will have to make allowance for the difference when you make the drawer fronts.

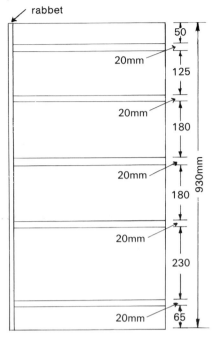
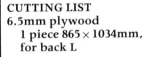

rabbet

50
20mm
125
20mm
180
20mm
930
180
20mm
230
20mm
65

Assembling the cabinet

Stand one side B on the bench with the rabbeted edge upwards. Hold frame 1 against it with the end exactly within the marks. The batten K faces the top end of B but notice that B extends 6mm beyond the top edge of K.

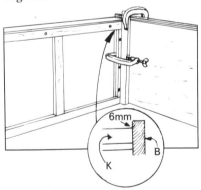

6mm

B

K

Clamp a batten to both the side and the frame while you glue and screw the 25×50mm to the side. Drill three countersunk holes in both frame ends then attach the 57mm no.10 screws.

It is very important to line the frames up exactly within the lines otherwise the drawers will not fit.

After you have attached frame 1, add the other side B, again gluing and screwing with three no.10 screws per side.

Fixing the iron-on edging

This is a good stage to attach the edging along all the facing edges of the top A, sides B and the front edges of the five frames. It is quite easy to do. The edging is backed with a glue which melts at a low temperature. Hold the veneer against the edge, then run a medium hot iron along it, pressing it down with a piece of wood or a cork sanding block as the glue sets on cooling.

Trim the edges with a finely set block plane, then sand them so that it looks like one piece of wood with no edges protruding.

Fixing the top and back

CUTTING LIST
6.5mm plywood
1 piece 865 × 1034mm, for back L

Screw the four shrinkage brackets to the two battens K at the top flush with the top edge. Then add glue to the top of the sides B and drop the top A in place so that the sides fit all the way into their housings. Screw through the four brackets into the underside of the top.

The back panel is a useful device for squaring the cabinet. It may be

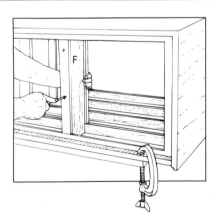

K

B

necessary to push the whole cabinet so that it becomes square and allows the back to fit into its recess.

To fix the back, place the 6.5mm plywood piece L into the rabbets and first pin it in place with a few 19mm pins. Then screw about four 19mm no. 6 screws along each edge to secure it.

Attach frames 2 to 5 in order, the final frames with the battens K facing toward the bottom. To make the cabinet more rigid, it is best to join the top and bottom battens K, to the sides B with a through dowel. Drill a 6mm diameter hole about 50mm

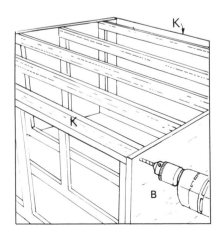

K

F

B

deep through the side B straight into the end of the batten, then glue in the 6mm dowel and cut it off flush. The dowel ends will be hidden later by the plinth and cornice. Finally attach the spacer F centrally between frames 1 and 2. Use two 38mm no.8 screws per side.

Adding the plinth and cornice

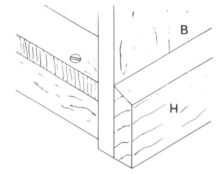

The plinth and cornice are easily fixed by gluing and screwing them to the sides and to the battens along the front.

First attach the side pieces H, flush with the bottom of sides B. Glue and clamp them then reinforce the fixing from the inside with two 32mm no.8 screws per side. The front edges should be exactly flush with the front edges of the cabinet.

Then trim the front piece G to exact shape as shown. To cut the pieces by hand, start the cuts with a coping saw then finish the long straight cut with a hand saw or

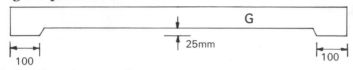

a tenon saw. Remember to score the veneer first to avoid having it break out along the saw cut. Glue and clamp it on before adding three

screws from the inside. Make sure both ends line up with the side pieces H. To finish the plinth, cut off the tips at the corners with a fine saw so that the angle continues round evenly.

Fix the veneer edging to the angled edges and ends of the plinth, paying particular attention to making the joint at the corners very neat. Use a sharp trimming knife to cut off the excess veneer. If possible buy the edging extra wide so that it will cover the angled edges, otherwise use two widths of edging.

Fix the cornice I and J in the same way, tight against the underside of the top. Start with the two side pieces J before trimming and fixing the front piece I and attaching the edging as before. This will be easier to do if you first turn the whole cabinet very carefully upside down, after first laying a blanket on the bench or floor to protect the top.

Making the drawers

Making drawers that fit smoothly and tightly is an art and requires careful work. The dimensions of the pieces in the cutting list, both for the drawer fronts C, D and E and for the plywood backs and bottoms, have been left slightly oversize to allow you to trim each drawer to make it fit its space.

CUTTING LIST
12mm plywood
    4 pieces 125 × 475mm, for sides
    2 pieces 110 × 535mm, for backs
    2 pieces 230 × 475mm, for sides
    1 piece 215 × 1065mm, for back
    4 pieces 180 × 475mm, for sides
    2 pieces 165 × 1065mm, for backs
6.5mm plywood
    2 pieces 510 × 510mm, for bottoms
    3 pieces 510 × 1020mm, for bottoms

Measure each drawer compartment individually, then trim the backs and fronts to exact size. First cut the backs about 1–2mm smaller than the opening for clearance. Try these in place, then trim the veneered blockboard fronts to the same length. The backs are 15mm less in depth than the fronts or sides. This is to allow the drawer back to clear the small 6.5mm thick stop at the front.

The dovetailing can be done either

by hand or with a dovetail attachment on a router which is much quicker and usually neater. Refer to page 236 for complete instructions on cutting dovetails.

Make through dovetails at the backs of the drawers and stopped dovetails at the fronts. Set the front dovetails back 6mm from the front edge.

After cutting the dovetails, check the joints for fit. Dovetails only fit properly once, so leave the final assembly until after you have cut the 6.5mm wide and 6.5mm deep grooves in the sides to hold the drawer bottom. The bottom of the groove should be exactly 10mm from the bottom edge.
Don't cut a groove in the back pieces. These have been cut shallow to allow the bottom to pass underneath for screwed fixings as shown.

Assemble the drawers, starting by

gluing the dovetails of the back and sides. Then measure for the bottoms and cut them the exact size before sliding them into the grooves. Fix each bottom to the back with three 19mm no.6 screws.

Add glue to all the dovetails and grooves before assembly and tap them together with a rubber mallet. It may be necessary to clamp each drawer until the glue sets, checking to be sure it is square.

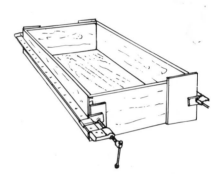

Fitting the moulding

CUTTING LIST
hockey stick moulding
    6 pieces 1065mm long
    (to be trimmed)
    4 pieces 535mm long
    (to be trimmed)
    6 pieces 250mm long
    (to be trimmed)
    4 pieces 150mm long
    (to be trimmed)

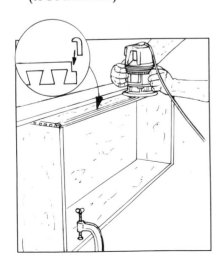

To fit the moulding, cut a recess on all four edges of each drawer front. Make the recess the exact thickness of the beading, using a straight edge and a router fitted with a straight cutter.

Stain the moulding black with ebony stain or another dark colour such as walnut. Give the strips two or three coats to get a dark tone.

Cut the pieces to exact length for each drawer, mitring the corners.

Fix the beading by gluing and pinning it with fine pins, punching the pin heads below the surface and filling the holes with filler dyed to match the beading.

Finishing

This cabinet was simply waxed with a mixture of carnauba and beeswax (page 249), but for a more durable finish, apply a few coats of clear polyurethane with a final coat of wax rubbed in carefully.

Fitting the drawers

CUTTING LIST
6.5mm plywood
    10 pieces 40 × 100mm, for stops

Fix the drawer pulls to the fronts so that they line up in two columns.

Fix the stops, pinning them in place and then try the drawers to make sure they stop at the correct place with the drawer fronts flush. To make the drawers run smoothly, rub candle or other hard wax along the running surfaces.

BEDROOM CLOSETS

There are many ways to build in closets like these but the easiest construction method is using sheet materials such as plywood or plain or veneered chipboard. Instead of having to make a complicated carcass assembly using wood battens, to make these closets you just cut the standard sheets into two 600mm × 2.44m halves to make the uprights and then simply screw on the shelves. That is all there is to it except for the finishing and making the doors.

The only cumbersome part of the project is cutting up the 1.22 × 2.44m sheets. If you don't have the facilities to do this, take the cutting list to your supplier who will usually cut the sheets to size for a small charge.

The doors are made from inexpensive African mahogany but you can just as easily use pine or Douglas fir for the door surrounds and then apply a wood stain before finishing with clear polyurethane. The woven cane applied to the centre panels is available from specialist stores in rolls usually 550mm to 610mm wide. It is quite expensive so it is important to plan carefully for minimum waste. As an attractive and less expensive alternative, use a printed wallpaper or fabric, or even gift wrapping paper, in the central panels as was done with the kitchen doors shown on page 19.

You can make the closet doors extremely simple by using good quality birch plywood and finishing with clear polyurethane as shown in the kitchen doors on page 45.

This closet is built across the middle of a large bedroom to divide the room into a bedroom and a dressing room. If you build the unit directly against the wall it will not require back panels. For this unit 12mm chipboard panels were used to cover the back and also to give the structure more rigidity.

Planning the units

Start by planning the layout of the closets on a piece of graph paper. The first step is to plan the overall size of the unit, drawing the dimensions out on the floor if necessary to see how much space it will take up in the room and then measuring with a tape measure. The front to back distance should be about 600mm to allow enough depth for hanging clothes. You can make the compartments any width you like, but 450 and 600mm are good minimum and maximum dimensions to work to.

Divide the overall length into compartments, allowing for the thickness of each upright. Then draw the front of the unit to decide the height of the compartments. Keep in mind that 2.44m is a convenient height to allow you to use the full length of the standard sheet.

Also plan out the spaces you will need to hang various types of

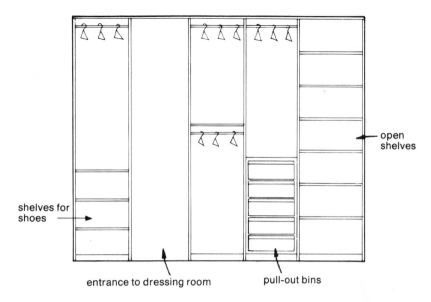

open shelves

shelves for shoes

entrance to dressing room

pull-out bins

clothing. Coats and long dresses require between 1.2m and 1.5m, men's suits about 0.9 to 1.2m, shirts about 0.75m and trousers about 1.2m. The best method is to measure your clothes to decide the exact size you

want the closets to be. Remember to allow an additional 75 to 100mm for clearance above the clothes rail. It is also a good idea to allow about 75mm at the bottom of each cabinet for storing shoes and handbags.

Cutting up the panels

Use either plywood or plain chipboard for the uprights and shelves and paint them after assembly, or use plastic laminate-covered chipboard. Another alternative is to use veneered chipboard, usually available in mahogany, teak and oak, which you can finish with matching iron-on edging. Each 1.22 × 2.44m sheet is cut in half to make into two uprights or several 600mm shelves. You will also need 600mm widths for the top of the unit and as an extra shelf in each compartment at the base.

The pieces are screwed together using 45mm no.10 screws with fibre wall plugs for a tighter fit. The wall plugs are especially necessary if you are using chipboard, as they give the screws something to bite into. Screws have a tendency to pull out of the brittle chipboard but, by using wall plugs, the screws hold by friction giving a stronger fixing.

Making the structure

After cutting the 600mm × 2.44m uprights and shelves, mark the location of the shelves on each upright. Measure from the base with a tape measure along each side and draw a line across with a straight edge. Mark a second line 19mm above the first to locate the shelf.

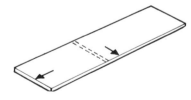

Mark the bottom and front edge so that you will remember which way around to place the panel during assembly. Then drill three 6mm diameter holes straight through the

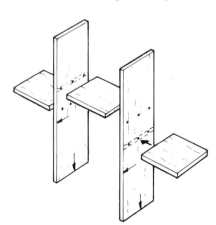

panel, between the lines showing the shelf location.

These holes will take the screws to hold the shelves, so countersink the holes from the other side. On most uprights you will have one set of holes on each side for the shelves.

After drilling all the uprights, cut the top panel to the overall length of the unit. Mark the location of each divider on the underside with lines 19mm apart. Then drill three holes between the lines for screwing the top to the uprights.

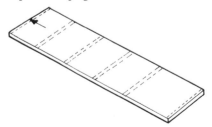

If your ceiling is too low to allow access from above for screwing the top down, you will have to use metal angle brackets or plastic block connectors (page 227) from underneath to connect the top to the uprights.

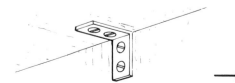

Assembling the structure

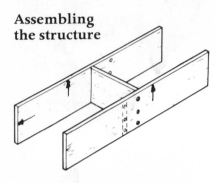

Start by assembling the first compartment on the floor. Get someone to help you to hold the shelf and first two uprights steady, while you drill through the holes into the ends of the shelves with a 6mm drill bit. Drill the first hole, push the plug through and attach the screw before going on to the next hole.

Then place the assembled end unit in position on the floor. If the unit is to lean against a wall the baseboard or skirting will get in the way, so you will either have to remove it or screw a 25 × 50mm batten between the upright and the wall and then cover it with a piece of moulding. Make sure to attach the first upright to the end wall to make the entire structure rigid, and also check with a spirit level that it is exactly vertical.

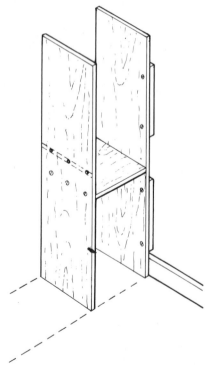

Continue with each shelf and upright in turn, drilling through, inserting the plugs and screwing tight.

Always check with a level and square to be sure that the components are vertical and square. If the last upright is placed against the other wall, you can't get to the other side to drill the last holes, so attach the shelves into this last compartment with metal brackets or plastic block connectors.

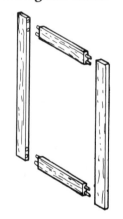

To fit a bottom shelf in each compartment, cut two lengths of plywood or chipboard 40mm wide to place under the bottom shelf. Place one piece 25mm in from the front and the other 25mm in from the back edge.

Making the doors

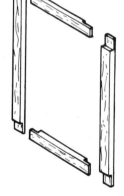

The door frames can be joined together by means of dowel pegs, halving joints or simply held together by screwing on a plywood panel from the back.
Allow an 2mm clearance in each direction when planning the sizes of

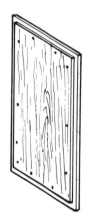

Buy 25mm diameter chromed metal clothes rail cut to the exact inside dimension of each compartment, minus 6mm for clearance. Fit them about 60mm from the top using specially chromed connectors which simply screw to the verticals with matching 12mm screws.

Nail them to the floor, finally nailing the shelf down onto them. Then screw or nail through the side of each upright into the shelf to keep it in place.

After attaching all the base pieces, screw the top down and if your structure is not against a wall, pin a backing piece made of plywood or chipboard onto the back edges.

the doors. Use 19 × 75mm pine or use a dark toned hardwood, like inexpensive African mahogany, for the frames, as in the doors shown here.

After joining up the frames, either cut a rabbet from the back with a portable router or screw on 10 × 10mm strips to take the central panel. You can also cut a decorative moulded edge on the front side with the router, or round the edge with light sanding.

Finish the door frames with two coats of polyurethane, rubbing down between coats. Then cut the

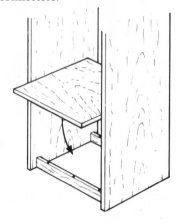

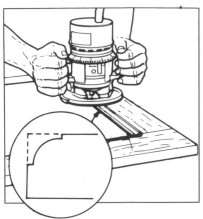

6.5mm plywood infill panels to match the openings in the doors. Cut off lengths of cane and lay them on the panels, stapling around the edges so that when the doors are assembled, the staples will be hidden by the rabbet.

To trim the cane flush with the plywood, turn the panel over and carefully run a sharp trimming knife

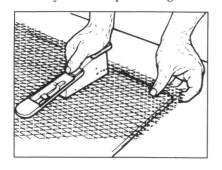

along the edge. Don't bear down too hard or you will pull the strands of cane and distort the pattern.

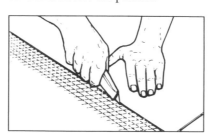

The cane is quite expensive so it is a good idea to stain or paint the side of the panel that faces inward before fitting it in the door frame so that you cane only on the outside of the doors. Then lay the panel in place and secure it with lengths of fine beading pinned to the frame.

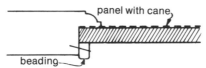

panel with cane

beading

To fit the doors, attach hinges to the edge of each door, fitting them into a recess so that they will sit flush with the wood. Then hang the doors, carefully allowing a clearance on all sides so that they will open and close easily. You may have to trim off a little here and there with a plane to make them fit correctly. Finally, fit magnetic catches and pulls or knobs and you are ready to hang up your clothes.

Making the pull-out bins

It is very convenient to have drawers built into the closets. Make them out of plastic sections as shown on page 247, or, make your own drawers.

These bins were made using 10mm birch plywood for the sides and 6.5mm plywood for the bottom. The plywood is simply cut to size, glued and nailed together and then painted.

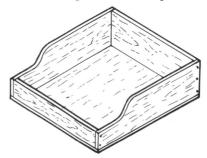

Fitting the bins is very easy. Just glue and nail 12 × 19mm battens, 550mm long to the uprights and locate them so that the bins will be level.

After sliding the bottom bin onto its runners, locate the second pair of strips and so on until they are all in place. Leave room between the bins to allow for the piling up of clothes. Paint or stain the strips to match.

Cut a profile in the side of the bins to pull them out, or attach pulls or drill 35mm diameter fingerholes.

SAUNA BENCH

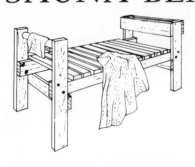
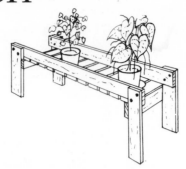

This bench will serve not only as a seat, but also it has a towel rail at one end and a shelf to hold books or toilet articles at the other end. The simple bolt-together construction can be used equally successfully to make an attractive coffee table or a planter for indoor or outdoor use. When buying the wood, try to select straight, clear boards.

Making the framework

CUTTING LIST
25 × 100mm
   2 pieces 1375mm long,
   for rails A
   4 pieces 685mm long,
   for legs B
   2 pieces 380mm long,
   for braces C

First make two side frames. On each leg B mark the location of the top of the rails 430mm from the bottom. Then arrange two legs B and one rail A on the bench so that the ends of the rail are flush with the legs and the top of the rail lines up with the marks. Either clamp the rail to the leg at each end, or pin them temporarily together from the back.

At each joint, drill two holes straight through both pieces with a 10mm diameter drill.

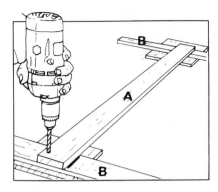

Insert the coach bolts from the leg side and tighten the nuts with a wrench.

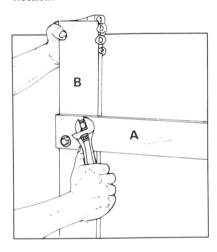

Glue and pin the two braces C to the legs. Get someone to hold the two frames vertically while you attach the braces. To make the nails hold better, hammer them in at a slight angle, as shown.

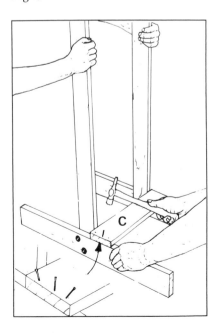

SHOPPING LIST	
softwood	about 8.5m of 25 × 100mm pine or Douglas fir 5m of 32 × 75mm
dowel	400mm of 38mm diameter
hardware	8 coach bolts 10mm diameter, 50mm long with nuts and washers about 80 finishing nails or panel pins, 38mm long
plus	wood filler clear polyurethane

Attaching the slats

CUTTING LIST
32 × 75mm
    12 pieces 380mm long,
    for slats D

Cut the slats to length, then round the top edges with a file, block plane or a router with a rounding-over bit.

Glue and pin each slat to the rails using two pins per end. Drive the pins in at an angle and leave an equal overhang at both ends. It makes it easier to line up the end of the slats if you temporarily pin a batten along the rail, as shown.

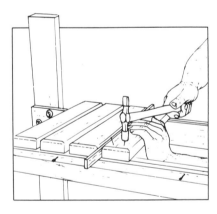

Start the first slat 75mm in from the leg. Use a thin batten about 12mm wide as a spacer. Set all the pins well below the surface and fill the holes.

Making the towel rail and shelf

CUTTING LIST
25 × 100mm
    1 piece 405mm long,
    for shelf E (to be trimmed)
    2 pieces 380mm long,
    for sides F

First glue and pin one side piece, F to the legs as shown. Then measure the distance between the legs at the top and cut the shelf E and the 38mm diameter dowel to that exact length.

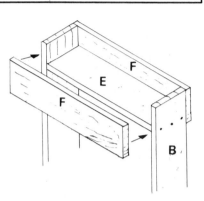

Alternatively, hold them in position to mark the cutting length. Then glue and pin the shelf E to the legs and to the side piece F.

To finish the shelf, glue and pin the last side F to the shelf and leg.

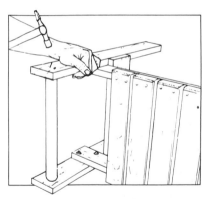

The dowel is pinned between the legs at the other end, about 50mm from the top, using two pins per end. Set all the pin heads and fill the holes.

Finishing the bench

Sand the pieces first, making sure that the ends of the slats are smooth. The finish can be either clear polyurethane as here, or a coloured polyurethane such as green or red to add a cheerful touch to the bathroom. Apply several coats of polyurethane to the bolt heads and nuts to prevent them from rusting in the damp atmosphere.

75

BATHROOM CABINET AND TOOTHBRUSH HOLDER

Natural pine looks so much better for bathroom cabinets than the white plastic laminate which is normally used. This cabinet has no complicated joints, it is simply screwed together using fibre wall plugs to get over the problem of screwing directly into the end grain. The usual rule is never to drive screws into the ends of boards, but by drilling a slightly larger hole and inserting a fibre wall plug before driving in the screw, the joint will be very strong. As an alternative, nail the pieces together as for the bench on page 74

Making the cabinet frame

CUTTING LIST
25 × 150mm
    2 pieces 380mm long, for ends A
25 × 125mm
    2 pieces 710mm long,
    for top and bottom B
25 × 100mm
    1 piece 380mm long,
    for upright C (to be trimmed)
    2 pieces 340mm long,
    for shelves D
    1 piece 380mm long,
    for shelf E (to be trimmed)

Join the pieces by screwing through the uprights into the fibre wall plugs inserted in the end of the shelves.

First mark the locations of the shelves on the inside of the ends A with pairs of light pencil lines.

With a ruler or a marking gauge mark the hole centres for the screws between these two lines. Drill each hole with a 5mm diameter drill, straight through the uprights.

Drill the corresponding holes in the ends of the shelves, using the same drill bit. To mark the centres for these holes, insert the 38mm screws in the uprights, hold the shelf in its location and tap the screws to make a mark at the end of the board.

Before joining the pieces, sand them well and round the front corners of the ends with a file.

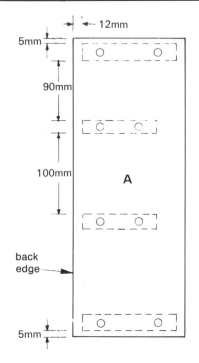

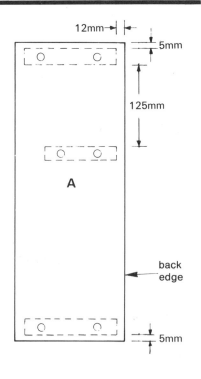

Drill the hole in the end of each shelf about 20mm deep, insert the wall plug and then screw the four pieces together with 38mm screws. Don't forget to put the screw cup washers on the screws before attaching each one.

Make the surround for the cabinet first, attaching the top and bottom pieces B to the ends A. Notice that they are set in 12mm from the back edge.

Then trim the central upright C exactly to length after trying it in place. Mark the shelf locations on it by transferring the marks from the end pieces. Notice that it supports two shelves D from the left and one E to the right so it will have three pairs of holes.

Mark and drill the holes in C as before, then attach shelves D to upright C. Lay the cabinet surround flat and place the upright and shelves into it to mark and trim shelf E to exact length.

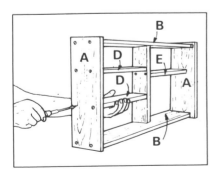

Finally screw shelf E to the upright C and then insert and screw all the pieces to the surround.

Attaching the back and doors

First glue down the sliding door channels with contact adhesive, gluing the deeper channel to the top (page 126).

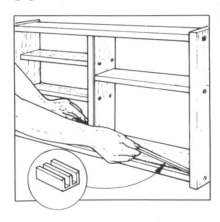

Before attaching the back, glue plastic laminate to the 6.5mm plywood using contact adhesive (page 225). Nail this panel to the back of the top and bottom pieces B.

Finally cut two pieces of 12 × 38mm, 710mm long, and screw them with three 25mm screws and cup washers to the top and bottom pieces to hide the plastic channels.

Now order the two 380mm wide mirrors with rounded edges to the exact size. It's best to cut a piece of scrap 6.5mm plywood and try it in place to get the size right.

For handles, glue on two thin pieces of matching pine with contact or epoxy adhesive. Finish with two coats of polyurethane.

Toothbrush holder

Use a piece of matching plastic laminate and plywood to make this simple and attractive toothbrush and glass holder.

Glue the laminate to a piece of 19mm thick plywood 125 × 175mm. Cut into two pieces, 75 × 125mm for the shelf A and 100 × 125 for the back B.

Round the corners as shown, trim the edges with a fine file and then sand the edges well before cutting the holes and slots as shown.

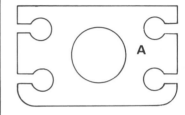

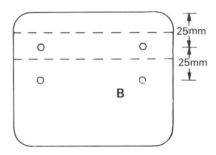

Drill four 20mm diameter holes in piece A and cut slots as shown for the toothbrushes. Cut a central hole with a coping saw to hold the glass. Drill the four 5mm diameter holes in the back B, two to attach the shelf and two for screwing to the wall.

TOWEL RAIL AND SOAP DISH

These two small, attractive projects for the bathroom require very different degrees of skill. The 1m long towel rail is very simple to make while the veneer soap dish is quite difficult. The construction of the towel rail is straightforward; the only difficult step is to drill the holes accurately. Making the soap dish is time consuming, but assembling and then carving through the layers of veneer produces beautiful results and you may want to use this technique on other projects. Plywood end grain is also a design feature of the coffee tables on page 166 and kitchen counters on page 45.

Gluing the veneers for the soap dish

Cut the veneer strips into about 30 pieces of light and 30 pieces of dark veneer roughly 200mm square.

Glue the layers together alternating

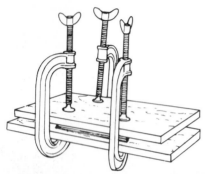

dark and light wood. Spread a thin layer of glue between each layer, then clamp between two heavy pieces of plywood and allow plenty of time for the glue to set.

Carving the shell

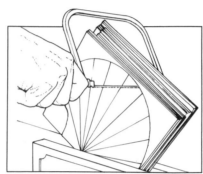

SHOPPING LIST	
veneer	about 7.5m of dark veneer strips such as teak or mahogany at least 200mm wide about 7.5m of light veneer strips such as sycamore or maple at least 200mm wide
plus	white woodworking glue clear polyurethane

Draw the shell shape on both sides of the block and then cut out the shape with a coping saw.

To hold the piece flat on the bench while you carve, you can either glue it down temporarily to a

piece of plywood or use small clamps at two corners.

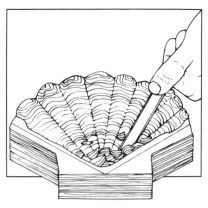

Use a very sharp gouge to carve out the scallop shapes of the shell, working with firm and even strokes. If you use a real scallop shell as a model, it will make the carving easier as you can refer to the shell as you work.

After finishing the inside of the shell, hold it gently in a vice and shape the back, first with a Surform and then with a gouge to carve out the details of the scallop shapes. The flutes on the back of the shell are not nearly as deep as those on the inside.

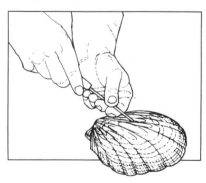

When you are satisfied with the overall shape, finish the shell by sanding it very smooth. Then seal it with many coats of polyurethane to make it completely waterproof. Rub it down with fine sandpaper or steel wool between successive coats.

Making the towel rail

Mark and drill a 25mm diameter hole through each block of hardwood, then round the corners of the blocks, as shown, with a Surform or file.

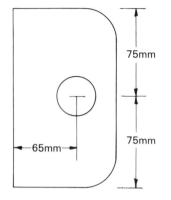

Mark the location of the escutcheon plates on the back edge of each block and cut out a small groove or hole under the keyhole to accommodate the screw head before screwing the plate to the back edge.

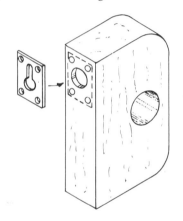

Before assembly drill four 10mm diameter holes in the large dowel and sand the dowels and blocks.

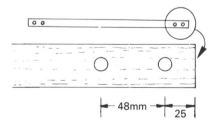

To assemble the towel rail, slide the blocks onto the 25mm dowel and lock them in position with the four short lengths of 10mm diameter dowel. Then apply several coats of clear polyurethane. If you like, you can stain the wood a darker wood tone or a bright colour to match your bathroom fittings, but test scraps first to be sure that the dowel and the hardwood finish the same shade.

Hanging the towel rail

Hold the rail in position against the wall and check that it is level before marking the two screw locations. Then drill the holes for the plugs and insert the screws, leaving about 3mm extending. Finally hang the rail onto the screws.

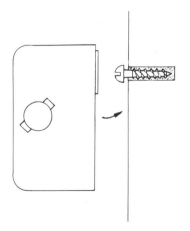

CHILDREN'S PROJECTS

There is something especially satisfying in making things for children whether it is furniture or toys. Not only can you make individual designs, but the children can take part. This section includes the essential furniture for a child's room, a traditional cradle, bed and playpen, high chair and bunk beds with built-in ladder. The designs are simple, good looking and sturdy. A selection of delightful toys including a rocking elephant, completes the chapter.

Rocking elephant

Child's bed

Bunk beds

Truck

High chair

Baking kit

Cradle

Doll's house

Child's bed

BUNK BEDS

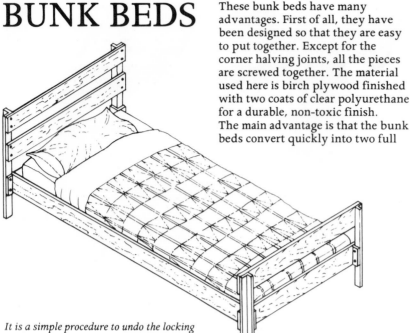

These bunk beds have many advantages. First of all, they have been designed so that they are easy to put together. Except for the corner halving joints, all the pieces are screwed together. The material used here is birch plywood finished with two coats of clear polyurethane for a durable, non-toxic finish.

The main advantage is that the bunk beds convert quickly into two full sized single beds when the bunks have outlived their usefulness. You just undo the four screws which hold the two bunks rigidly and safely together, switch the ends and you have two identical single beds, each with a tall headboard and a low footboard.

The two spacious drawers underneath are optional as the beds will look fine without them. The two drawers slide on wooden battens which must be fixed accurately. As a simple alternative, screw four castors under each drawer.

You will need a circular saw to cut the plywood sheet into boards. Clamp a straight board to the plywood as a ripping guide for the saw as shown on page 209.

Keep in mind that these instructions are for a bunk bed to suit standard 750×1900mm mattresses. If you are using mattresses of a different size, make sure to alter the cutting list accordingly.

It is a simple procedure to undo the locking screws and convert the bunk bed into two good looking, full sized single beds.

Cutting up the plywood sheets

CUTTING LIST
(see diagrams opposite)
19mm plywood
   6 pieces 140×2145mm, rails A
   10 pieces 140×1000mm, cross rails B
   4 pieces 90×780mm, legs C
   4 pieces 90×580mm, legs D
   4 pieces 70×780mm, legs E
   4 pieces 70×580mm, legs F
   3 pieces 105×785mm, drawer supports G
   2 pieces 150×775mm, drawer fronts H
   8 pieces 150×685mm, drawer sides I
6.5mm plywood
   2 pieces 695×655mm, drawer bottoms J

Check the cutting diagrams carefully before starting work. Because there is little waste, there is no margin for error. Notice that the order in which the cuts are to be made is indicated by the circled numbers. It is important to proceed in this order.

The easiest way to cut up a large sheet of plywood is to lay it over two trestles with supporting battens underneath (page 207). Make each cut carefully with a circular saw, using a homemade straight edge to guide the saw in a straight line, or use a table saw.

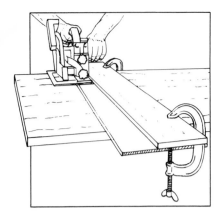

As you cut each piece, letter it in pencil and place all the rails in one group and all the leg pieces in another, so that it will be easy to identify them when it is time to assemble the beds.

If the saw leaves rough edges, run a block plane over them lightly to smooth them off. This is also a good time to sand the pieces since they are much easier to finish when lying flat. Sand along the grain at all times paying particular attention to the edges, and remember to lightly re-mark each piece if you sand off the pencilled letter.

To make finishing easier later on, try not to leave scratches or finger marks on the pieces as you work. Professional furniture makers make a habit of always working with clean hands and keep a cloth nearby to wipe off glue drips and smudges. It is also a good idea to lay an old blanket over the bench while sanding and assembling to avoid marring the work.

Making the legs

The legs are L-shaped to make them stronger. There are four 780mm long legs for the bottom bunk and four 580mm long legs for the top bunk.

Glue and clamp the two parts of each leg together. Glue C to E and D to F making four long and four short L-shaped legs. Unless you have a lot of clamps, it will be necessary to glue one or two legs at a time with white woodworking glue, letting the glue set for 20 to 30 minutes.

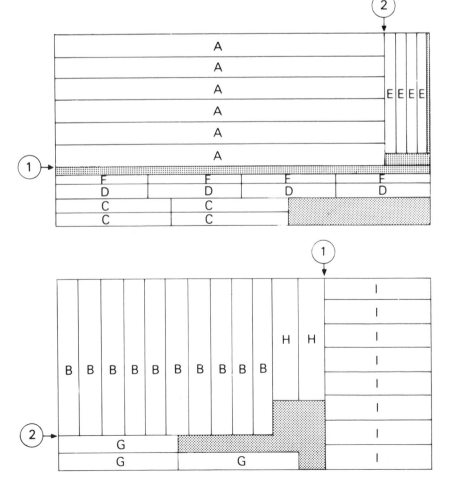

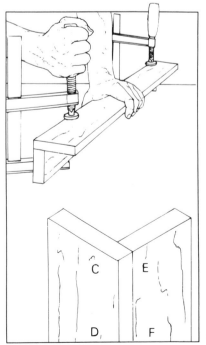

After all the legs have been glued, arrange the eight legs, four left-hand and four right-hand, on the bench. Mark the ends to indicate the bottom end, then measure up as shown on each piece. Draw the marks across the board with a try square and then crosshatch the areas to indicate the rail location.

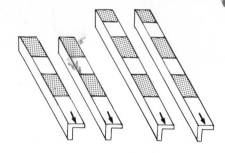

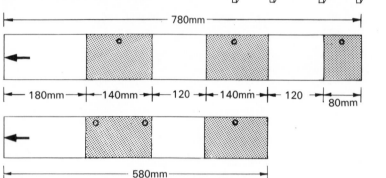

To reinforce the glued joint of the legs, drill three countersunk holes in each leg and insert the 45mm no.10 screws. Notice that the holes are located within the hatched areas, so that the crossrails B will eventually hide the screw heads.

Check to make sure that all the leg components are firmly joined together. One or two may need an additional screw to hold them tight.

Preparing the rails

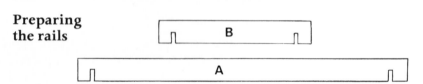

There are six long rails A and ten cross rails B. All six rails A must have halving joints cut at each end and in addition, six of the cross rails B must have halving joints as shown.

It is important to measure and cut these joints carefully so that they fit together snugly. Measure exactly 90mm in from each end. Then use a scrap piece of the same plywood to mark the width of the groove. Finally, measure and mark across exactly half the width of the rail to give the depth of the groove.

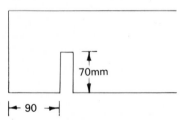

To cut the slots, hold the rail in a vice, if possible, then make a saw cut on the waste side of each line. To finish off, lay the rail on the bench and chisel out the waste.

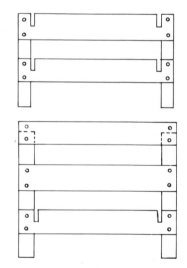

A sabre saw is very useful for cutting halving joints like these. It is easy to trim off a little extra if the joint is too tight, and the rough edges make the joint fit nicely.

Then cut four 25mm battens 1900mm long and glue and screw them to the insides of four of the long rails A, 65mm down from the top edge, placing the best face outwards. Use five 32mm no.8 screws per batten. The other two nails A will serve as guard rails at the top.

Assembling the ends

The cross rails B are simply screwed to the legs to make four ends, two high and two low. The screws should be located carefully so that they all line up above one another

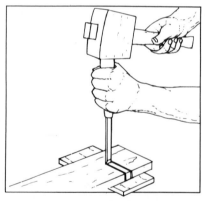

when the bed is assembled. Measure in 65mm from the ends and drill the 5.5mm diameter clearance holes for the no.10 brass screws. Drill two

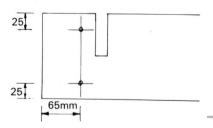

holes at each end of all the rails except the two long rails A without battens. These guard rails will not be screwed in place to allow them to be removed for making the upper bunk.

Assemble the tall ends first. Lay two long legs on the bench or floor, one left-hand and one right-hand as shown. Then place the first rail, slots uppermost, between the guide lines drawn earlier, with the slot flush against the leg.

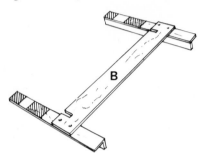

Mark the screw holes, drill the pilot holes in the legs, then attach the rail with the no.10 brass screws with screw cup washers under the heads.

Attach the next two rails within the guide marks in the same way. Notice that these two rails have no slots. Also note that the top rail extends 60mm above the top of the leg. This rail will tie the top and bottom bunks rigidly together with one screw going into the bottom leg and one into the top leg at each corner.

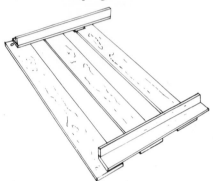

Make the short ends in the same way, this time with two rails per end, both rails having slots facing upwards.

Finishing the pieces

This is a good time to polyurethane the pieces since you can lay them flat. First erase any marks or letters and give the pieces a quick sanding with fine paper, rounding the top edges of the rails slightly. Apply two or preferably three coats of clear polyurethane rubbing down between coats.

Assembling the beds

First assemble the bottom bunk using the two high ends and two

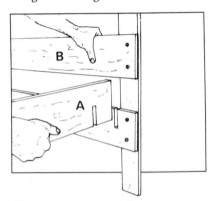

long rails with battens A. If possible, get someone to help hold the ends

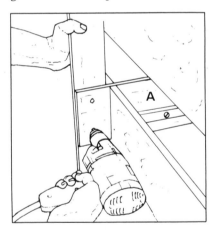

while you slot the long rails in place, with the battens facing inwards. Slot both rails in place, then screw these rails to the back of the leg by first drilling countersunk holes, then driving in two no.10 brass screws and washers per end.

The two beds are assembled separately then stacked and screwed together. This requires a lot of room so it is a good idea to clear a space in preparation for this step.

Before assembling the top bed with the two shorter ends, it's a good idea to make and fit the drawers to the bottom bed while you still have the space.

Making and fitting the drawers

CUTTING LIST
25 × 25mm hardwood strips
8 pieces 685mm long

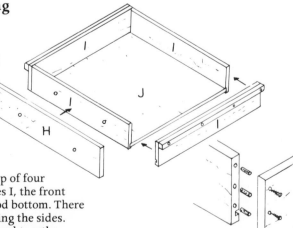

Each drawer is made up of four identical plywood sides I, the front H and a 6.5mm plywood bottom. There are many ways of joining the sides. These are simply screwed together into fibre wall plugs which makes the assembly very easy. Refer to the instructions on page 217 for cutting the 6.5 × 6.5mm groove for the drawer bottom and for assembling the sides. Use three 45mm no.10 screws per corner.

Clamp the front in place temporarily with 1in overlapping at each end while you drill two small holes straight through both pieces as pilot holes for the 35mm diameter finger holes.

Remove the front and drill the 35mm holes, using the pilot holes as guides.

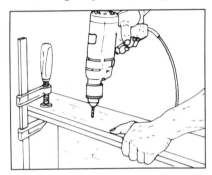

Drill from the face side of the front H and from the inside of the drawer so that any splintering or breakout will be hidden when you screw the front in place.

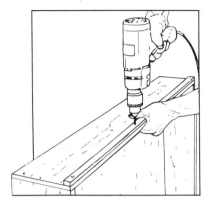

Before securing the front to the drawer with five 32mm no.10 brass screws with cup washers, stand the drawer up on its side and screw on each hardwood runner to the two sides flush with the top edge, using four no.8 countersunk steel screws, 38mm long.

The drawer supports

The drawers are supported by the three plywood boards G which are secured to the long rails A with metal brackets. First screw the brackets to the ends of the boards G using the 12mm long round head screws. Then screw the hardwood runners flush with the bottom edge and front

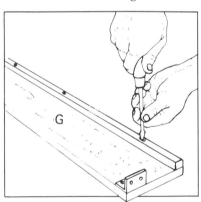

end of the boards G using 38mm screws. Two of the supports G have runners on one side but the central support has one on each side.

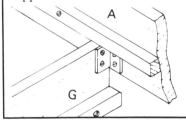

Attach the supports G to the inside of the rails A. Start by locating the central one exactly in the middle. Make a pencilled mark and then hold the support up to the mark with the top edge against the rail batten and mark the hole locations through

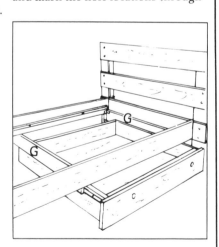

the brackets. Drill the screw holes and attach the support with two 12mm screws per bracket. To locate the left and right supports, hold the drawers in place and mark their locations. The supports extend about 50mm below the rails.

Slide the drawers in and make any slight adjustments to the runners if necessary to make them run smoothly.

Attaching the bed slats

CUTTING LIST
19 × 75mm
   32 pieces 780mm long

Assemble the top bunk by slotting the long rails A in place with the battens facing inwards. Screw the rails A to the back of the legs exactly

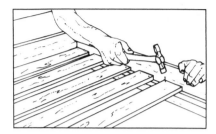

as for the bottom bunk. Leave the two removable guard rails A off until the bed is assembled.

Secure the slats to both beds, sixteen slats per bed, by gluing and pinning them to the battens with the 32mm long pins, two per end.

Fix the first slat at one end, then space them about 50mm apart, securing each one in turn.

Final assembly

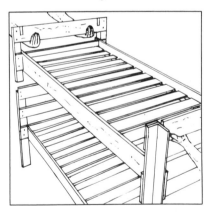

Lift the top bunk onto the bottom one, lining up the legs carefully. Secure the top bunk by screwing through the rail which overlaps the joints in the legs. Then slot the guard rails A into position. The joints for these rails should be quite loose to make them easy to remove.

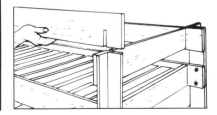

BABY'S BED AND PLAYPEN

The bed: making the end frames

CUTTING LIST
25 × 75mm
   4 pieces 1050mm long A
   4 pieces 550mm long B

The bed is designed for a 610 × 1220mm mattress. Cut the pieces and mark the long pieces A for dowel jointing to pieces B (page 232). Drill two holes per joint for 10mm diameter dowel pegs 75mm long, and then assemble the pieces.

Tapping the frame together with a

mallet should be enough to tighten the joint but, if necessary, clamp with bar clamps across the width until the glue sets.

Mark the two upper corners and bottom of the legs with a radius of about 30mm, cut the corners with a coping saw and smooth the cut with a file or as shown, with a Surform, taking care to make them even.

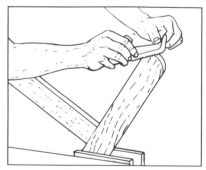

It is a good idea to round all the edges with sandpaper so that they feel nice and smooth to the baby's touch. Make both frames and put them aside for assembly later.

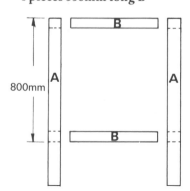

Making the side frames

CUTTING LIST
32 × 50mm
  6 pieces 1225mm long C
  2 pieces 210mm long D
  2 pieces 360mm long E
  2 pieces 660mm long F
19mm diameter dowel
  11 pieces 240mm long
  11 pieces 395mm long
  11 pieces 690mm long

There are three frames, each with eleven dowels. The two front frames are hinged together to allow easy access to the bed. The procedure for each frame is the same, the only difference between them being the height.

On the edge of one of the six pieces C, first mark the location of the 32 × 50mm uprights at each end. Divide the remaining distance into twelve equal spaces about 95mm wide. Then clamp the six pieces C together with the ends lined up and transfer the marks across to the other five pieces using a try square. Unclamp the pieces and use a marking gauge to mark the hole centres midway across the eleven centre lines before centre punching the holes.

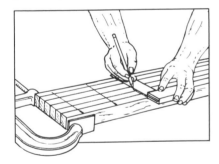

Drill the eleven 19mm diameter holes on each piece C, preferably in a drill stand. Use a depth stop to make the holes just over 15mm deep (page 195).

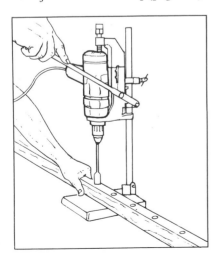

SHOPPING LIST

softwood (Douglas fir or pine)	7.5m of 25 × 75mm 15m of 32 × 50mm 5.5m of 25 × 25mm
Douglas fir plywood	2 pieces 590 × 710mm, 6.5mm thick
perforated hardboard	2 pieces 610 × 1220mm, 3mm thick
dowel	about 17m of 19mm diameter 3.6m of 110mm diameter for pegs 150mm of 6mm diameter for pegs
hardware	8 no.8 countersunk steel screws, 50mm long 10 no.8 countersunk brass screws, 38mm long 24 no.8 countersunk brass screws, 19mm long 34 no.8 brass screw cup washers about 50 finishing nails or panel pins, 19mm long 4 metal brackets with 12mm screws, to support base 3 brass hinges, 50mm long with 12mm long brass screws
plus	2 plastic-covered wire baskets with matching runners and screws clear polyurethane

Add a dab of glue to each hole and tap the 240mm dowels into one piece C. Then tap the other piece C on top. It may be difficult to get the top piece on. To make it easier, slant the top piece so that the dowels fit progressively, each into its hole.

Get the two pieces C straight and clamp them parallel, with the uprights D in position at each end. Before the glue sets, attach the uprights D by dowelling through the pieces C using two 75mm long, 10mm diameter dowels per joint. Make the next frame in the same way using two pieces C, two uprights E and the 395mm long dowels. The large back frame uses up the remaining pieces C and F, and the 690mm long dowels. Round the corners and edges.

Finally join the two small front frames together with the three brass hinges. Remember to chisel out a recess for each hinge so that the two frames fit flush together.

Assembling the bed

CUTTING LIST
32 × 50mm
  4 pieces 675mm long,
  basket supports G

Screw the four sides together to form the frame leaving 620mm inside. Clamp the side and end frames together so that they are all aligned for drilling and screwing. Position the ends so that they extend 50mm above the top of the side frames. Use three 38mm brass screws with cup washers per end on the large side frame, then two screws per end on the lower of the two front panels.

Notice that the upper hinged panel is not screwed to the ends. See the instructions for making a baby-proof lock with dowels. Next attach the plywood end panels with the 19mm brass screws and cup washers. Centre the panel over the outside of the end, allowing 25mm overlap on each side, then drill holes and attach the screws, twelve per panel.

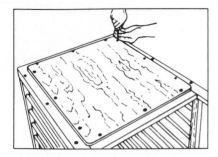

Finally fit the slides for the pull-out baskets. There are many sizes of basket available, so follow the manufacturer's instructions for the placement of the 675mm long battens G. Use one 50mm screw per end. Then screw the runners to the insides of the battens and slide the baskets in place.

Making and installing the base

CUTTING LIST
25 × 25mm
  2 pieces 1220mm long
  4 pieces 570mm long

Making a baby-proof lock

This locking mechanism for the baby's bed is much easier to make than it is to explain. The diagrams show the details. With the front flap clamped in the closed position, drill a 13mm diameter hole X through the end piece A, into the edge of the end frame C just far enough to make a centre hole.

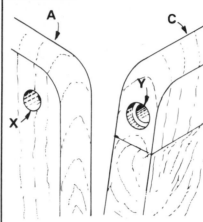

Then unclamp and drill a 19mm diameter hole Y, just over 6mm deep into that centre, continuing with a 13mm diameter drill bit in the centre, another 6mm into the wood. On the inside of hole X, make a notch about 6 × 6mm and 10mm deep.

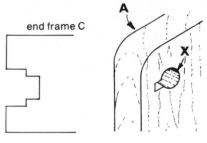

end frame C

To make the key, drill two 6mm diameter holes exactly 28mm apart in a piece of 12mm diameter dowel 50mm long.

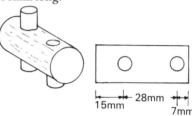

Glue a 25mm length of 6mm diameter dowel into one hole 15mm from the end with the ends extending equally as shown. Push the 12mm diameter dowel through hole X, then glue a second 6mm diameter dowel 20mm long in the other hole with one end flush.
To open the lock, turn the dowel until it can be pulled out so the 6mm dowel sits in the notch cut in hole X.

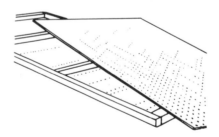

You can use a sheet of plywood for the bed base, but perforated hardboard with spacers between

allows the mattress more ventilation. Alternatively, use two pieces of 4mm plywood and drill holes through both.

Simply glue and nail the 25 × 25mm pieces first to one panel and then to the other using the 19mm pins. To support the mattress base in the bed, screw the four metal brackets to the insides of pieces A, one per corner, at a height which is convenient for the baby's age; lower down for older babies so that they have room to stand up safely in the bed.

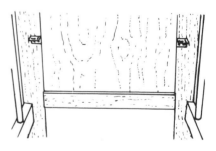

Then drop the base in place and attach it to the brackets from underneath. To adjust the height of the mattress as the baby grows, just alter the placement of the brackets.

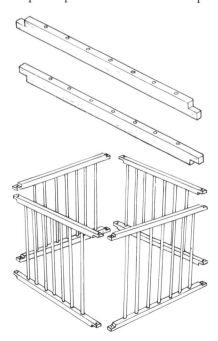
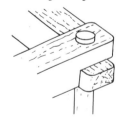

Making the playpen

CUTTING LIST
32 × 50mm
  8 pieces 965mm long
19mm dowel
  28 pieces 610mm long
  4 pieces 675mm long,
  for corners

The playpen is designed to take a
vinyl mat about 865 × 865mm. Mark
the centres of nine 19mm diameter
holes, 115mm apart, in each of the
softwood pieces, starting 25mm from
each end. Before drilling the holes,
cut the corner halving joints as
shown, 40mm from each end.

When drilling the holes, remember
to drill on the top edges of four of the
pieces and bottom edges of the
other four. Drill the seven middle

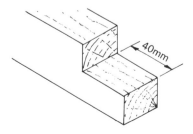

SHOPPING LIST	
wood	8.5m of softwood, 32 × 50mm
	21.5m of 19mm diameter dowel
	clear polyurethane

holes first, using a drill stand with a
depth stop to make them 15mm deep.

After assembling them, hold the four
frames together while you drill the
corner holes. Assemble the playpen
by pushing the 675mm long dowels
through the corner holes. Make a
hardboard base for the playpen or
simply tie a vinyl mat at the four
corners to keep it in place.

Finishing the bed
and playpen

The easiest way to finish the bed and
the playpen is to apply two or three
coats of polyurethane, but it would
look equally nice painted a bright
colour. Remember that babies will
chew on the paint, so be absolutely
sure to finish with a non-toxic
substance. Check with the
manufacturer if you are not sure
about the paint and if you are still
uncertain, finish with polyurethane
which is safe.

BAKING KIT

This very grown-up toy is extremely easy to make and is popular with boys and girls alike.

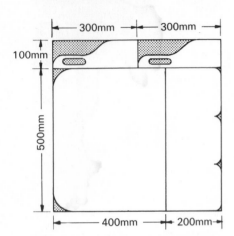

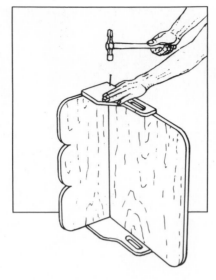

Cut out the four pieces of plywood and cut handle slots in the ends to make it easy to carry around. Then, after gluing and nailing the back in place, glue and nail the two side pieces on and the toy is made after about an hour's work. Now add as many small baking utensils as you have room for by hanging them from cup hooks simply screwed into the back panel.

SHOPPING LIST	
plywood	610 × 610mm, 12mm thick, cut into 4 pieces as shown
hardware	about 20 finishing nails or panel pins, 32mm long several small cup hooks two large cup hooks for the rolling pin
plus	a selection of small baking utensils such as measuring spoons, small wire whisk, pastry cutters, pastry wheel and rolling pin

DOLL'S CRADLE

This cradle is made to a doll's proportions but, by altering the dimensions and fixings, you can make a full size rocking cradle for a baby.

Making the support

CUTTING LIST
25 × 50mm
    2 pieces 355mm long A
    2 pieces 430mm long B

Start by rounding one end of both B pieces then drill a 19mm diameter hole as shown.

Attach A to B by through dowelling from underneath using two 90mm long dowel pegs per joint (page 232).

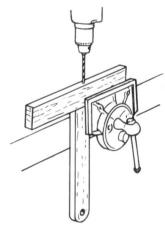

Make two identical ends then, to complete the support, glue and screw the 545mm long 25 × 75mm piece between the two ends. Screw the 50mm screws into fibre wall plugs inserted into holes drilled in the ends of the 25 × 75mm piece.

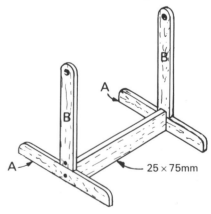

Making the cradle

CUTTING LIST
19 × 38mm
   4 pieces 515mm long C
12 × 25mm
   18 pieces 190mm long D
12mm plywood
   2 pieces 250 × 250 for ends E
   1 piece 150 × 515mm, for base F

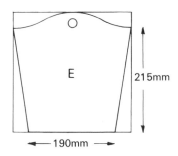

Cut out the ends E to the shape shown, using a sabre or coping saw. Sand the edges smooth and drill a 19mm hole as shown. Nail the ends E to the base F, placing F between the ends flush with the bottom edge. Use four 32mm pins per end. Make the sides by gluing and nailing the slats D to the pieces C, nine slats per side. Use two 25mm nails per end and space pieces C as shown.

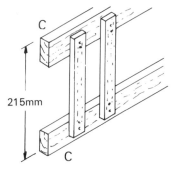

Then glue and screw the sides C to the ends E using two 38mm screws and two fibre plugs per end. Add a few 32mm pins through the bottom of the sides C into the base F.

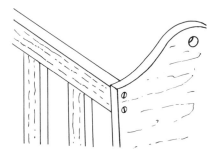

Finally assemble the cradle by pushing the 19mm dowel pegs through the holes from the support into the cradle.

SHOPPING LIST	
softwood	545mm of 25 × 75mm / 1.8m of 25 × 50mm / 2.1m of 19 × 38mm / 4m of 12 × 25mm
plywood	460 × 610mm, 12mm thick
dowel	two 57mm lengths of 19mm diameter / 610mm of 10mm diameter for pegs
hardware	4 no.8 countersunk steel screws, 50mm long
	16 no.8 countersunk steel screws, 38mm long
	20 no.8 fibre wall plugs, 25mm long
	about 25 finishing nails or panel pins, 32mm long
	about 80 finishing nails or panel pins, 25mm long
plus	bright coloured paint / transfers / clear polyurethane

Finishing

Set the nails below the surface of the wood with a nail punch and fill the holes with matching filler. Sand the pieces smooth and finish by painting the cradle a bright colour. Remember to use non-toxic paint.
Alternatively, leave the pine natural and finish with clear polyurethane. In either case, transfers or stencils can be used to decorate the ends.

TRUCK

The best wood to use for the truck is beech which is often used for toys since it is hardwearing and has a nice, warm colour.

Hardwood is usually not available already planed up, so you must find either a supplier or workshop who will plane the boards to 12mm thickness. You will need about 4.5m of 215mm wide boards.

Alternatively, use 12mm birch plywood which is also very hardwearing, and more readily available.

SHOPPING LIST

hardwood	about 4.5m of 12 × 215mm beech or similar wood (alternatively 1m × 1m of 12mm birch plywood)
dowel	125mm of 19mm diameter about 1.2m of 10mm diameter 150mm of 6mm diameter
hardware	about 40 no.6 countersunk brass screws, 32mm long 40 no.6 brass screw cup washers 8 large washers to fit over 10mm diameter dowels behind wheels
plus	8 toy rubber wheels about 100mm diameter (available from specialist shops) clear polyurethane

Making the cab

CUTTING LIST
hardwood
- 2 pieces 210 × 230mm A
- 1 piece 140 × 170mm B
- 1 piece 170 × 180mm C
- 1 piece 205 × 210mm D
- 1 piece 145 × 405mm E
- 2 pieces 65 × 405mm F

Cut out and letter the pieces. Drill the 4mm diameter screw clearance holes. Then glue and screw the sides together using cup washers.

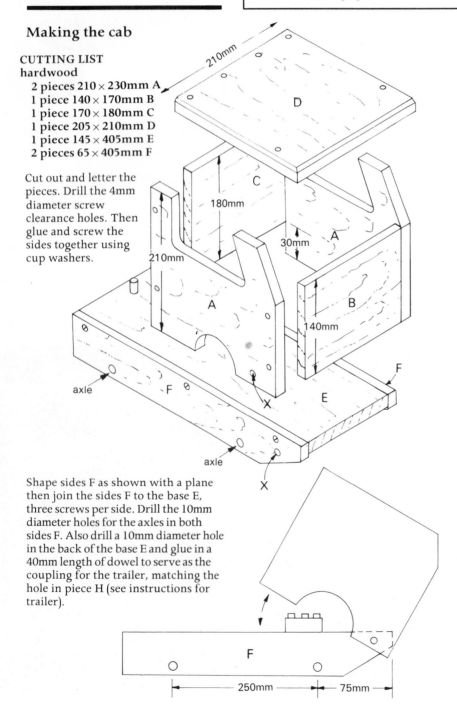

Shape sides F as shown with a plane then join the sides F to the base E, three screws per side. Drill the 10mm diameter holes for the axles in both sides F. Also drill a 10mm diameter hole in the back of the base E and glue in a 40mm length of dowel to serve as the coupling for the trailer, matching the hole in piece H (see instructions for trailer).

Before assembling the top part cut out the opening for the windows in each side A. Don't cut the semi-circular shape to fit over the wheels until later. Notice when you screw the pieces together that they fit flush at the corners and that the back of the cab C is 30mm shorter than the sides A to allow the sides to extend over the base sides F.

After assembly, hold the cab in place on the base while you drill one 6mm diameter hole X in each side at the front. Drill straight through sides A and F to form a pivot, allowing the cab to tilt forward and expose the engine which is simply made from various scrap pieces of wood which are glued together.

Cut off two 230 mm lengths of 10mm diameter dowel as axles and attach the four rubber toy wheels as shown in the drawing.

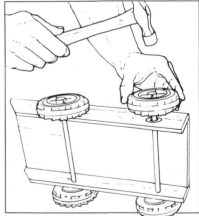

Cut two 25mm lengths of 6mm dowel, then temporarily insert them as pivots into holes X and draw the semi-circular shapes on sides A over the wheels. Remove the pivots, cut the semi-circles, then attach the cab with the pivots again.

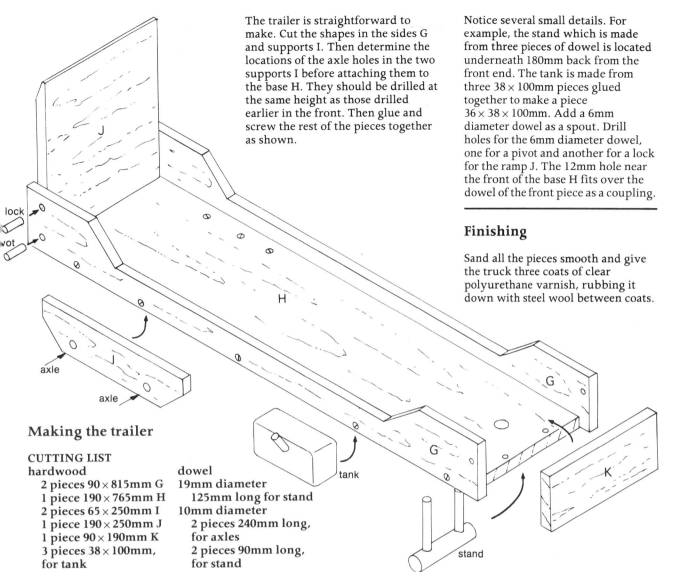

The trailer is straightforward to make. Cut the shapes in the sides G and supports I. Then determine the locations of the axle holes in the two supports I before attaching them to the base H. They should be drilled at the same height as those drilled earlier in the front. Then glue and screw the rest of the pieces together as shown.

Notice several small details. For example, the stand which is made from three pieces of dowel is located underneath 180mm back from the front end. The tank is made from three 38 × 100mm pieces glued together to make a piece 36 × 38 × 100mm. Add a 6mm diameter dowel as a spout. Drill holes for the 6mm diameter dowel, one for a pivot and another for a lock for the ramp J. The 12mm hole near the front of the base H fits over the dowel of the front piece as a coupling.

Finishing

Sand all the pieces smooth and give the truck three coats of clear polyurethane varnish, rubbing it down with steel wool between coats.

Making the trailer

CUTTING LIST
hardwood
  2 pieces 90 × 815mm G
  1 piece 190 × 765mm H
  2 pieces 65 × 250mm I
  1 piece 190 × 250mm J
  1 piece 90 × 190mm K
  3 pieces 38 × 100mm,
  for tank

dowel
19mm diameter
  125mm long for stand
10mm diameter
  2 pieces 240mm long,
  for axles
  2 pieces 90mm long,
  for stand

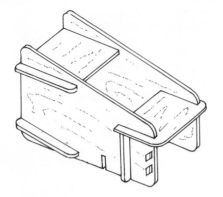

CONVERTIBLE HIGH CHAIR

This is really an ingenious design which is very simple to make out of half a sheet of 12mm thick plywood. The pieces simply slot together and no complicated joints are involved. The tray is secured with a clever lift-off detail which doesn't require any hardware. When the child isn't using the high chair, remove the footrest F and turn the chair on its side to serve as a writing desk with built-in seat, shown left. And when it has outlived its usefulness as a high chair, it can easily be turned into a racing car with the addition of wheels and painted numbers.

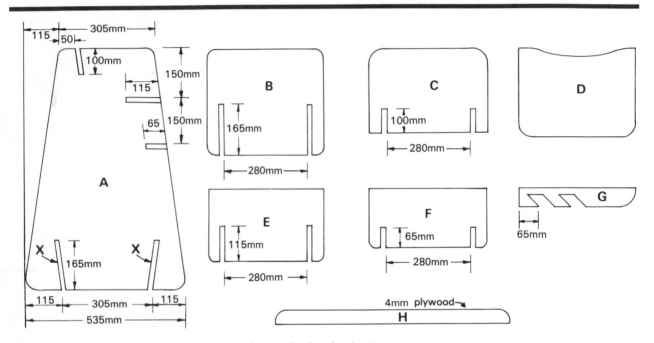

Making the high chair

CUTTING LIST
12mm plywood
 1 piece 750 × 975mm,
 cut in half as shown A
 2 pieces 330 × 380mm B
 2 pieces 280 × 380mm C and D
 1 piece 230 × 380mm E
 1 piece 180 × 380mm
 2 pieces 50 × 380mm G

First cut out all the pieces. Accuracy isn't as crucial in cutting out since

SHOPPING LIST	
plywood	12mm standard sheet 12mm thick 40 × 750mm, 4mm thick
hardware	10 finishing nails or panel pins, 32mm long 20 finishing nails or panel pins, 19mm long
plus	wood filler sealer and paint

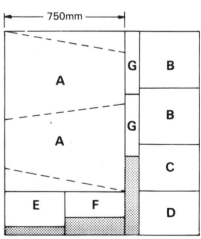

all the pieces overlap, but when you are cutting the halving slots be careful not to make them too large. An over tight fit can be corrected, but there is nothing you can do about a loose fit and the stability of the chair depends on the joints fitting together tightly. Don't forget that the paint will make the joints a little tighter.

Mark the lines for each slot exactly 12mm apart, then cut on the *waste* side of the lines, using a sabre saw or a panel saw. Chop off the waste at the end with a 12mm chisel. Round the ends of all the pieces as shown, including the 4mm thick strip H. Notice that slots X on both pieces A are parallel to the sloped sides.

The pieces should not fit together too tightly as the coats of paint will make the joints tighten.

Now cut angled slots in the tray supports G. Use a fine blade such as a coping saw or a fret saw and save the small waste pieces Y. Fit the waste pieces back into the pieces from which you have cut them and then lay one of these tray supports on piece A so that the top edges line up. Glue and nail the small waste pieces to the side A using 19mm pins. Make sure the tray support G doesn't move as you nail.

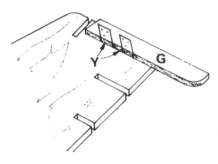

Slot the whole chair together and then clamp the tray D to its supports as you carefully glue and nail it down with 32mm pins. The curved back edge of the tray should be just above the front edge of the seat E.

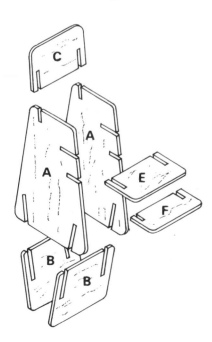

After nailing in about four pins, remove the tray and finish with a few more pins. Set the nail heads then glue and nail piece H around the edge of the tray, bending it tightly and nailing with 19mm pins.

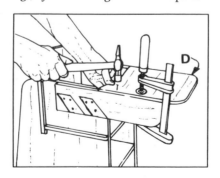

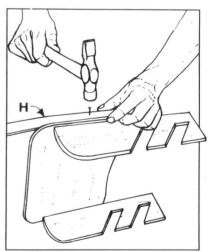

Finishing the high chair

Take the pieces apart and sand them carefully paying special attention to the edges of the plywood. Fill the rough edges and any gaps between the tray and the lip with wood filler and after this has dried, sand it off again with fine sandpaper so that the edges feel smooth. Apply a coat of sealer to all the pieces and then finish the chair in a bright glossy colour or in two tones for a more exciting effect as was done with this chair. As when finishing any project for children, check that the paint is non-toxic.

DOLL'S HOUSE

There are three steps in making this doll's house which measures about 305 × 635 × 560mm high. First cut out the pieces, then glue and nail them together and finally decorate and paint before the dolls move in.

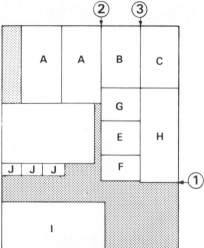

CUTTING LIST

10mm plywood
2 pieces 280 × 535mm, for gable ends A
2 pieces 280 × 436mm, for internal   walls B and C
1 piece 430 × 650mm, for front D
1 piece 230 × 280mm, for floor E
1 piece 150 × 280mm, for floor F
1 piece 230 × 280mm, for floor G
1 piece 280 × 630mm, for top H
1 piece 330 × 700mm, for ground floor I
3 pieces 75 × 150mm, for stairway J
4mm plywood
1 piece 445 × 650mm, for back
2 pieces 165 × 650mm, for roof K

Cutting the pieces

It is best to cut the pieces with a circular saw to get a straight even cut (page 208). However, the cutting can be done with a sabre saw, or a hand saw, if you plane the edges after they are cut to make sure they are straight and even. Place the face side down when cutting with a sabre saw.

Cut out the shapes of the gable ends A, the walls B and C and the front D. Use either a sabre or coping saw to cut out the door and the windows. The windows are 65 × 120mm and are 12mm apart.

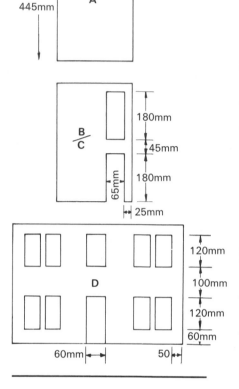

Assembly

Mark the rooms and walls on the top H. The central hall is 150mm wide, the rooms on each side of it 230mm wide and the two walls 10mm thick.

Glue and nail the gables A and the walls B and C to the top H, following the guide marks, using 25mm pins.

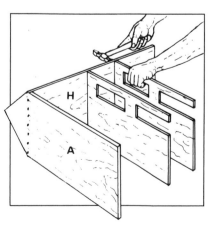

SHOPPING LIST	
wood	50 × 100mm softwood, 305mm long / 6 × 12mm batten, 1m long 1.2 × 1.5m plywood, 10mm thick / 650 × 790mm plywood, 4mm thick 300mm dowel, 12mm diameter
hardware	4 no.8 countersunk steel screws, 25mm long about 30 finishing nails or panel pins, 25mm long about 20 finishing nails or panel pins, 12mm long pair of brass hinges, 38mm long with 10mm screws
plus	various wood scraps, such as triangular moulding for stairway doll's house wallpaper or gift wrapping paper

Glue and nail floors E and G in place so that all the rooms are 213mm high. Use the doorway cut-outs as a guide.

Attach the ground floor I, first marking the wall locations on it. Notice that it extends 1in beyond the gables in each direction.

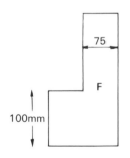

Cut floor F to serve as a landing. To attach it and the stairways, first glue and nail battens to the walls B and C.

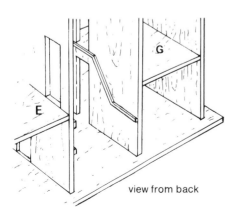

view from back

Then glue the half landing J in place on the battens.

Make the stairway by gluing triangular blocks onto the two pieces J, then glue these onto the battens.

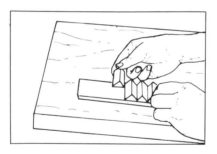

The chimneys are made of two 150mm lengths of 50 × 100mm softwood with 12mm dowels drilled and glued into the top for chimney pots. The chimneys are fixed against the gable ends A with glue, adding a couple of

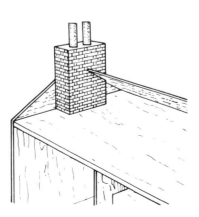

screws for reinforcement. The 4mm plywood roof pieces K are held in place and marked, then cut out around the chimneys. Pin the roof pieces to the gables A with 12mm pins and hold the ridge together with adhesive tape until the glue sets.

Finally nail on the back and attach the front with hinges.

Decorating

Here's where you can really have fun with this project. Buy paper in various patterns such as slate roofing, brickwork, parquet flooring and wallpaper from specialist shops selling things for dolls' houses, or use gift wrapping paper with small patterns. Glue it in place with any adhesive suitable for paper.

Glue 12mm wide wooden strips under the windows and either paint them or leave them plain as here. Also add small strips across the windows for mullions. Make a front door and paint it, then add the details for a letter box and a door knob and an arched lintel.

Cover the roof edge with 25mm wide wooden strip which can be painted to match the door or left plain.

And when this is all finished, start thinking about the furniture . . .

CRADLE

This is a copy of an early American cradle design, and it is just as handsome and functional today as it was then. Early American furniture was most often designed to be sensible and straightforward with clean proportions and functional details like the cut-out handles on this cradle which make it easy to carry, or even to hang up.

It is undoubtedly easier today to obtain suitable boards for this project than it was in the eighteenth century when making a cradle like this meant felling and hewing a tree which would then have to be hand sawn into boards. Cherry, oak and walnut were often chosen for fine pieces of furniture and it would be well worth the extra cost and time to use one of these woods to make a real family heirloom. This cradle is made from less expensive pine, but you can just as easily use 19mm thick plywood, painted and decorated with stencils of early American motifs. The instructions are for a 305 × 915mm mattress and you must alter the dimensions to suit any other size.

Making the ends

CUTTING LIST
25 × 125mm   3 pieces 915mm long

After cutting the three pieces to length, glue them together to make the two ends (page 231). There is no need to dowel joint the boards. If they are nice and straight, the glued butt joints should hold very well. Arrange the boards so that their end grain alternates so as to minimize warping. Use three bar clamps when gluing up, alternating them over and under the boards.

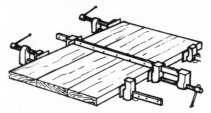

While the glue is setting, follow the diagram to make a template for shaping the ends. The template is best made by first drawing a grid of 1in square lines on a piece of cardboard and then following the diagram to draw the shapes out freehand. Take your time and smooth out the curves on the drawing afterwards until they are pleasing to the eye. Each square on the diagram is 1in on the cardboard.

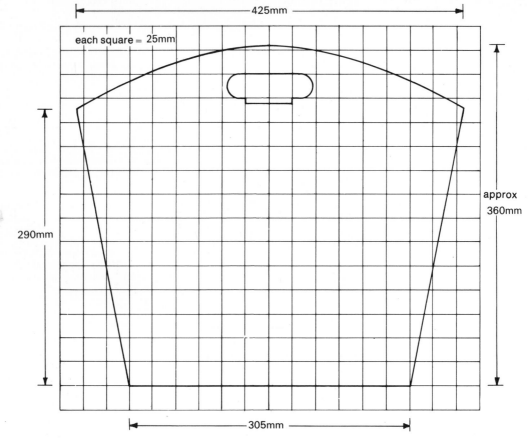

each square = 25mm

425mm

290mm

approx 360mm

305mm

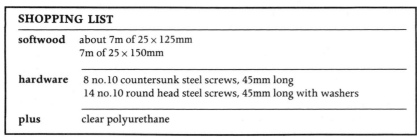

SHOPPING LIST		
softwood	about 7m of 25 × 125mm	
	7m of 25 × 150mm	
hardware	8 no.10 countersunk steel screws, 45mm long	
	14 no.10 round head steel screws, 45mm long with washers	
plus	clear polyurethane	

Plane off the gluetop boards, then trace two outlines of the end panel, using the template. Cut the panel in half then use a sabre or a coping saw to cut out the shapes. If the sabre saw is powerful enough, clamp the pieces together and cut through both at once. This will mean less hand work later on when you come to plane the pieces to the same size.

Cut on the waste side of the line, then clamp the two roughly shaped

pieces in a vice while you plane the edges down to the marked outline. Work from both ends towards the middle to avoid splitting the wood. Smooth the curved top edges with a file or a Surform.

Clamp the two end pieces to the bench, keeping them lined up. Then trace the outline for the handle from the diagram and transfer it to the wood. Drill two 25mm diameter holes within the waste area and cut out the handle shapes with a sabre saw. Smooth the rough edges with a file and then with sandpaper, rounding the edges and making the handles feel smooth and comfortable to hold.

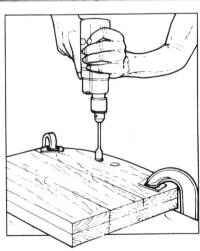

Making the sides and base

CUTTING LIST
25 × 150mm
    4 pieces 1220mm long, for sides
25 × 125mm
    3 pieces 1220mm long, for base

First glue each pair of 25 × 150mm boards together to make two side panels, each measuring approximately 290 × 1220mm. Use three bar clamps for the gluing operation, one in the centre and the other two about 150mm

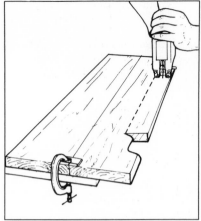

before, using a sabre saw and cutting out both sides at once if possible. Use a rounded file to smooth out carefully the curves in the shapes. Work slowly, checking that the curve is regular.

Cut the slope at each end either with a sabre or a panel saw. Finish off with a plane so that they are straight and smooth, and slope at the same angle as the end pieces so that they will be flush when joined together. To make the base, simply glue and clamp the three 1220mm long 25 × 125mm boards together and trim the ends square to a length of 970mm.

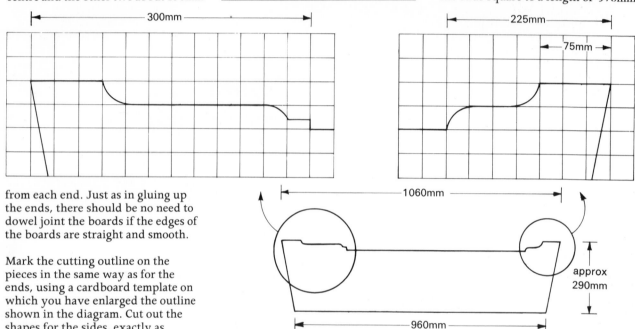

from each end. Just as in gluing up the ends, there should be no need to dowel joint the boards if the edges of the boards are straight and smooth.

Mark the cutting outline on the pieces in the same way as for the ends, using a cardboard template on which you have enlarged the outline shown in the diagram. Cut out the shapes for the sides, exactly as

Cutting out the rockers

CUTTING LIST
25 × 150mm   2 pieces 710mm long

Make a cardboard template and trace out the shape of the rockers and cut them both out with a sabre saw. It is important that the curves on which the cradle rocks are identical so, if possible, clamp the pieces together in a vice and cut out both at once. After cutting the pieces

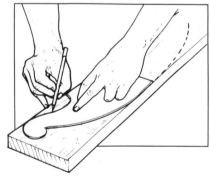

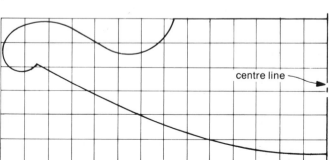

centre line

roughly to shape, clamp them together and shape them with a file or Surform. Smooth the wood evenly to the marked line.

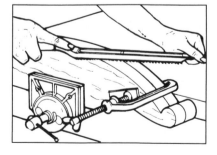

The rocker edges are quite fragile so cut them out and smooth them with care. If an end should break off, glue it back in place, reinforcing it from below either with two 10mm dowel pegs, cut off flush with a saw, or with two no.8 screws, 38mm long. Countersink the screws or hide them with wooden plugs, cut off flush.

Assembling the cradle

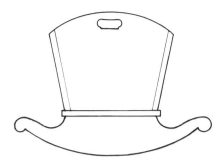

First drill the clearance holes for the screws at the ends of each side. If you conceal the screws with plugs cut from matching wood (page 214) the cradle will have a more finished appearance, so counterbore the screws by first drilling a 10mm diameter hole about 6mm deep. Then drill the 4.5mm diameter clearance hole straight through the sides.

Clamp the sides to the ends using the

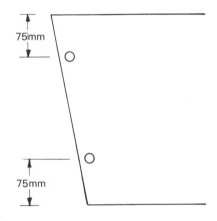

angled scraps under the clamps to make the clamping easier.

Make sure that the end pieces line up flush at the joint before marking through the holes with a marking awl.

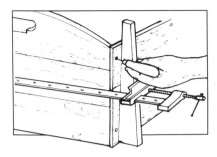

Drill the four holes in each end with a 2.5mm diameter drill bit about 25mm deep, and then screw the pieces together with the 45mm countersunk

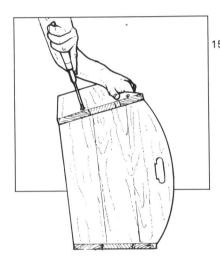

screws before plugging the holes. Plane the lower edges of both sides so that they are flush with the ends.

Screw the base of the cradle to the assembled pieces using two round head screws per side. Since the screw joint tends to restrain the bottom from expanding and contracting, drill the clearance holes oversized using a 8mm diameter drill bit. Put washers under the screw heads to help the screws to move sideways as the wood expands and contracts with the changes in the moisture in the air. The joint which was screwed earlier between the ends and the sides will not be affected by expansion and contraction since both pieces tend to move in the same way.

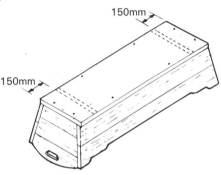

Finally attach each rocker to the cradle, screwing from the inside with three round head screws in oversized holes. The screw heads will be hidden by the mattress, so there is no need to hide them unless you want a perfectly neat finish. If so, use countersunk screws instead and sink them below the surface of the wood, covering them with matching wood plugs. Locate the rockers 150mm from each end of the base.

Finishing the cradle

Sand all the pieces well, paying particular attention to all the curved surfaces which were cut with the sabre saw. All the edges should be rounded so that there is nothing sharp protruding to hurt the baby.

Apply two coats of clear polyurethane, sanding with fine sandpaper between each coat. To give the cradle an extra smooth finish, apply a coat of wax and buff well. Polyurethane is a non-toxic finish so it is safe for the cradle. If you decide to use plywood and to paint it, be sure to use non-toxic paint.

ROCKING ELEPHANT

The most important step in making this delightful rocking elephant which stands 685mm high, is to get the shapes of the head, ears, legs, trunk and tusks just right. So spend a little time drawing the pieces out on paper so that they can then be transferred to the plywood for cutting. Follow the diagram in laying out the pieces, then trace the shapes and cut them out with a sabre saw.

You will need a fairly sturdy saw to cut through the 25mm thickness of plywood so be sure to check the manufacturer's instructions on the capacity of your saw. Buy coarse blades for this rough work which, although they don't cut as cleanly,

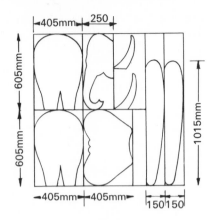

go through the wood more easily. It will not take you long to clean up the cut edges of the plywood.

To mark the arc for the runners use a piece of string. Lay the plywood runners on the floor and have someone hold the circle centre 2.1m away while you wrap the other end of the string around a pencil to mark the arc. Notice that the centre line is not in the middle of the runner because the elephant's centre of gravity is toward the front.

After cutting out all the plywood pieces, hold them in the vice and smooth them and round the corners with a rasp or a Surform.

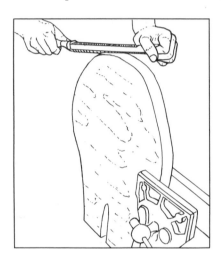

Before attaching the body pieces to the runners, mark and cut out matching notches in the legs and runners so that they fit together snugly. Make the notches about 40mm deep on each piece and position them as shown so that the length of the slats for the body will be 585mm.

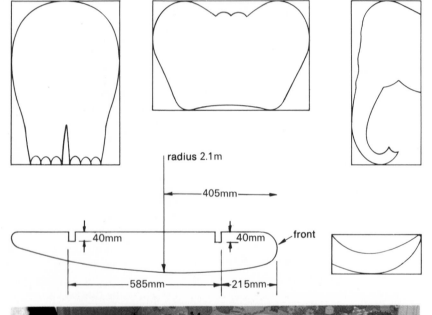

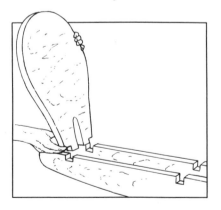

Next screw the legs to the runners using one 65mm screw per leg. Hide the screw head with a wooden plug if possible.

Now cut twenty five slats each 585mm long to make the body of the elephant.

Before screwing the slats on with the brass screws and decorative cup

SHOPPING LIST

wood	1.2 × 1.2m of 25mm thick plywood (or glue two thinner pieces together) 15m of 19 × 38mm softwood battens
hardware	7 no.10 countersunk steel screws, 65mm long 10 no.10 countersunk steel screws, 45mm long 50 no.6 countersunk brass screws, 32mm long 50 no.6 brass screw cup washers
plus	clear polyurethane

washers, either sand or plane the top edge of each piece to smooth off any rough edges on the elephant's back and bevel each top edge slightly with a plane.

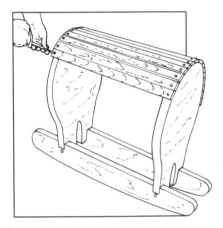

Next screw the ears to the head with three 65mm screws. Mark parallel lines so that the head will be attached vertically exactly in the centre of the ears.

To attach the ears to the body, first turn the elephant upside down and place blocks to support and steady the rounded shape. Then glue and clamp the ears to the front of the

body. When the glue has set, remove the clamps, drill holes and insert six 45mm screws from the inside.

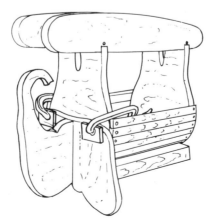

Turn the elephant right side up and before allowing the children to try it out, add the finishing touches. Glue and screw the tusks in place hiding the four 45mm screws with plugs, and add the eyes either by painting them on or by inserting a plug cut from a dark wood. Finally thread a piece of thick rope through a drilled hole and knot it from the inside to form the tail.

Finishing

The best protection is a few coats of clear polyurethane, rubbed down between coats with fine sandpaper or steel wool so that the body is smooth to sit on.

WORKROOM AND STORAGE PROJECTS

Storage cabinet

Simple shelving system

Honeycomb wall unit

Large work table

Roll top desk

Storage and work space are always at a premium. This section includes all manner of useful projects to solve this problem; an easy-to-assemble honeycomb wall unit for the kitchen or living room, two designs for shelving systems, one supported on the wall by track and the other free standing, a large work table with drawer legs, a sturdy workbench and tool cabinet and a real pièce de resistance – a roll top desk in solid hardwood.

Roll top desk

Workbench

Tool cabinet

Boxes and cubes

Storage cabinet

Versatile trestles

107

VERSATILE TRESTLES

Trestles are immensely versatile. They can be used with a couple of planks as a platform for painting or wallpapering, and they serve just as well as a base for a dining or work table. These trestles are 735mm high and 600mm wide. They fold up flat for easy carrying and the cut-out handles make it easy to hang them on the wall within easy reach when they are not in use.

Preparation

CUTTING LIST
chipboard
    4 pieces 600 × 750mm A
    4 pieces 170 × 290mm B
continuous hinge
    2 pieces 600mm long
    6 pieces 285mm long

Cut out the pieces following the cutting diagram, then cut out the

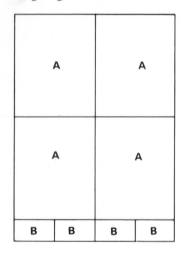

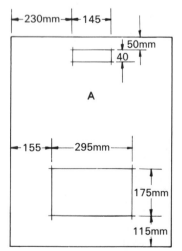

SHOPPING LIST *to make two trestles*

chipboard	1.2 × 1.8m, 19mm thick
hardware	3m chrome-plated continuous hinge with 12mm screws
plus	sealer, undercoat, black glossy paint flush hardboard door, about 750 × 1900mm

slots in the four pieces A. Start by carefully marking the openings, working with a large try square if possible, to make sure they are square.

Before cutting out the slots with a sabre saw, drill a hole in one corner inside the waste area of each rectangle to make it easier to get the saw blade in. If you are using a compass or keyhole saw, drill holes first in all the corners to start each straight cut.

Cut two openings in each of the four pieces, one for the handle and one for the folding flap, then use a file and sandpaper to clean off and smooth the inside edges of the openings. At the same time, sand all around the outside edges to remove the saw marks and to round the edges slightly.

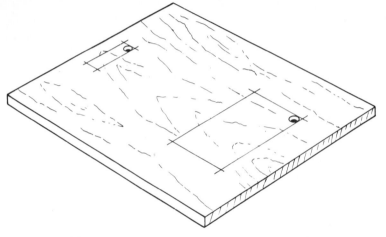

Assembling the trestles

The assembly is very easy. Lay the pieces A down on the bench in pairs with the handle ends tight together. Then carefully lay the long lengths of continuous hinge centrally over the join and mark through four holes with a pencil, two on either side, one hole at each end of the hinge. The easiest way to make a small clearance hole for the 12mm screws is to use a bradawl or even a nail.

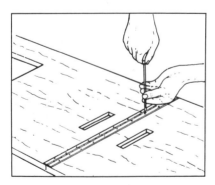

Insert these four screws to hold the hinge in position and continue fixing the rest of the screws.

Attach the B pieces using the short lengths of hinge. Lay one piece in each opening tight against the outside (bottom) edges and attach the hinges as before. Make sure that the two edges are aligned so that the flap won't be askew when opened.

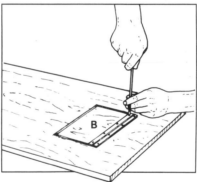

Finally stand the trestle on its side and connect the two flaps from underneath with another piece of hinge.

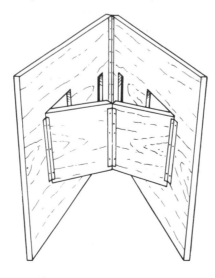

Now fold the trestle up to make sure the flaps lie flat in the openings. It may be necessary to take them off and trim a bit off here and there.

Notice that the bottom edges don't sit flat on the floor. Plane off the ends to the correct angle for a firm footing.

Making the table top

The top is easily made from a flush hardboard door available in various widths; 750 or 900mm are the most versatile widths. Paint the top, first sanding it smooth and applying a coat of sealer.

You can make other trestles using plywood or even acrylic sheet for an elegant desk or dining table base.

You can also use glass or acrylic sheet as the table top which looks extremely attractive. Place lengths of rubber strip over the hinges to protect the top.

Finishing

The table looks best with a shiny finish. Apply a sealer, undercoat and at least one coat of glossy paint, rubbing down lightly. These trestles and top were painted black to contrast with the red chairs.

HONEYCOMB WALL UNIT

Ready-to-use panels of 15mm thick plastic laminate-covered chipboard are very convenient for the quick assembly of cabinets, shelves and wall units. The 2.44m long panels are available in various widths from 150 to 610mm wide in a selection of colours with matching iron-on edging. This storage wall unit consists of shelves, five uprights, a top and a bottom surface and requires two standard sheets of hardboard for the backing. The pieces are connected with screw-together block joints (page 226). The shelves are adjustable, using small plastic shelf supports which fit into holes drilled at 50mm intervals along the uprights.

To make the base

CUTTING LIST
150mm wide panels
    2 pieces 2.44m long,
    for front and back
    5 pieces 230mm long,
    for cross pieces

Before assembly, cover the four ends of the front and back with matching iron-on brown edging. Then attach the cross pieces to the front and back using one plastic block per joint (page 226).

To make the wall unit

CUTTING LIST
brown panels
    5 pieces 2410mm long,
    for uprights
    2 pieces 2440mm long,
    for top and bottom
orange panels
    20 pieces 589mm long,
    for adjustable shelves
    4 pieces 591mm long,
    for fixed shelves

For adjustable shelving refer to the instructions on page 115 for making a drilling jig for the plastic shelf

support studs. The diameter of the drill bit and the depth of the holes will depend on the type of shelf studs you buy. It's best to experiment on a scrap piece first to get the drilling right. Using the drilling jig clamped to the board, drill two lines of holes in each upright starting about 300mm from either end of the board. Space the holes 50mm apart. Then tap the stud sockets into the holes.

It is best to assemble the unit on the floor and then lift it onto the base. Before assembly, apply edging to the ends of the top and bottom pieces.

Alternative shelf supports

It is very tedious to drill hundreds of holes so, as an alternative, you can attach the shelves by gluing and nailing 19 × 19mm battens to the uprights. Paint the battens brown to match the uprights before attaching them. Mark out the shelf locations by measuring from the bottom of each upright and then squaring across with a try square. The shelves can then either rest on the battens or be glued and nailed rigidly to them.

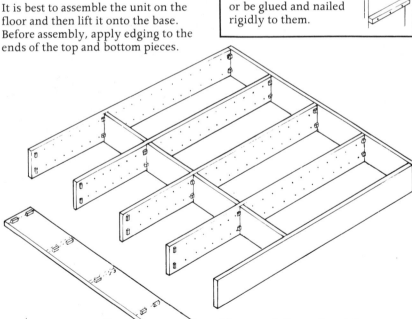

Then carefully mark out the locations of the uprights on them. The spaces between uprights should be exactly 591mm allowing about 2mm clearance for the adjustable shelves.

Attach the block joints and join the uprights to the top and bottom pieces. Use two plastic block joints at each connection.

To keep the uprights rigid, also attach the four 591mm long shelves with block joints, positioned about 900mm from the bottom.

With the pieces still flat on the floor, nail the hardboard backing in place. Nail two corners, then use the hardboard as a guide to square up the assembly before nailing the other corners. Nail at approximately 400mm intervals. Attach the base with six block joints from underneath. Get help to lift the unit upright and install the adjustable shelves. To make sure that the unit doesn't topple over, attach it to the wall either with a few screws through the back, or preferably with a couple of brackets attached to the top.

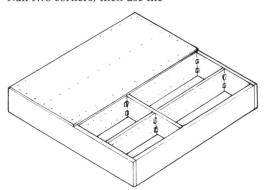

SHOPPING LIST *to make a unit 2.44m × 2.44m × 305mm*	
laminate-covered chipboard	13 panels 2.44m long, 305mm wide (7 brown and 6 orange) 3 panels 2.44m long, 150mm wide for base components (brown).
hardboard	2 standard sheets, 4mm thick
hardware	about 75 finishing nails or panel pins, 19mm long 46 plastic block joints with 19mm screws about 320 plastic shelf sockets about 80 plastic shelf support studs
plus	2.44m length of brown iron-on edging, 15mm wide

SIMPLE SHELVING SYSTEM

Two standard sheets of plywood are enough to make four uprights and eleven shelves for a 3.6m wide shelving system. To make a smaller 2.44m wide system, use only one 1.22 × 2.44m sheet to make three uprights, five shelves and one drilling jig. You can use chipboard equally well to make

a less expensive system. The shelves simply plug into the uprights at any height you require with 6mm dowel peg supports. However, drilling

the holes in the uprights and shelf ends must be accurate so that the shelves fit tight against the uprights to stabilize the system.

CUTTING LIST
19mm plywood
cut the sheets into
twenty four 1220mm lengths:
11 pieces 235mm wide,
for shelves A
8 pieces 130mm wide,
for uprights B
4 pieces 236mm wide,
for uprights C
1 piece 130mm wide,
for drilling jig D

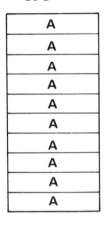

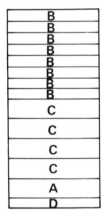

should be exactly 90mm apart as shown. Measure in 20mm from one edge for the first line. Place the uprights B in pairs on the bench on top of a piece of waste plywood, then put the drilling jig carefully on top and clamp the pieces tight to the bench aligning one side and one bottom edge exactly. Drill straight through with a 6mm diameter drill bit. Make sure not to drill through the waste piece into the bench.

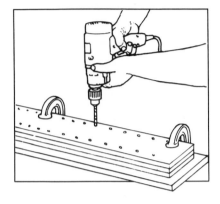

Mark the bottom edge on each pair. After drilling the four pairs of uprights, mark each one along the centre with two lines 20mm apart, as a guide for attaching the middle piece C.

Spread glue along the long edges of uprights C, then nail the two B pieces to piece C with 38mm pins to hold them in place temporarily. Before putting in screws to fix the pieces rigidly, check that the middle piece C is centred.

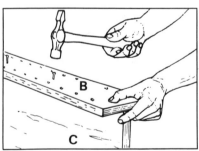

Then carefully drill six countersunk screw holes spaced about 150mm apart through the outside B into the centre upright C. Fit six 45mm no.10 screws per side and fill the holes to hide the screw heads.

Drilling the shelves

Make a small jig by drilling a hole in a 150mm long piece of 19 x 19mm softwood with a 6mm diameter drill bit, exactly 35mm in from the end as shown. Use a drill stand if possible to

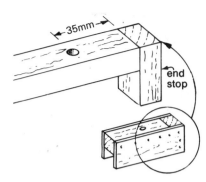

make the hole absolutely straight. Then glue and nail on a 50mm long end stop out of the 19 x 19mm softwood. Also glue and nail two 50 x 150mm pieces of 6mm plywood to the sides as shown with the 19mm pins.

Hold this over the end of the shelves and drill holes 25mm deep, four holes per shelf. It is vital that the drilling be done accurately, so the shelves will be correctly aligned. Spend enough time making the jig to ensure that the spacing is precise and use a depth stop when drilling the holes. To assemble, simply push the 50mm pegs through the holes in the uprights B and into the shelves at the far corners.

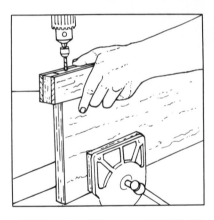

Finishing the shelves

Finish the shelves and uprights as here by painting the plywood to suit your taste and decor. After sanding the edges and faces carefully, apply a sealer, undercoat and one or two coats of glossy paint to get a really smooth finish.

Alternatively, if you use a good grade of birch plywood, you can leave it natural and just seal it with two or three coats of clear polyurethane, like the wall unit shown on page 124. Leave the plywood edges exposed or nail on half round or other moulding, setting the nails and filling the holes before painting the moulding.

Making the uprights

First make a drilling jig (page 115) for 6mm holes spaced 50mm apart to drill the uprights B. The two rows of holes

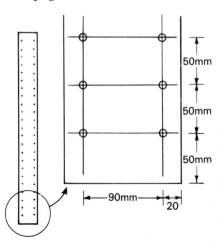

UPRIGHT BOOKCASE

This bookcase with adjustable shelves is 845mm wide and 2.1m high, but you can adapt the instructions to make a bookcase of any size. Make it in teak veneered blockboard or more economically out of painted or stained chipboard. Six of the shelves are adjustable and rest on brackets which slot into sockets set into the uprights at 50mm intervals. Brass sockets and studs look best with teak, but white plastic ones would look handsome on painted chipboard.

Preparing the pieces

CUTTING LIST
19mm blockboard
   2 pieces 235 × 2100mm,
   for uprights A
   9 pieces 230 × 805mm,
   for shelves B
   3 pieces 50 × 805mm,
   for support C

Cut the sheet of blockboard into six strips as shown, scoring the veneer with a knife before sawing. The uprights are 6.5mm wider than the shelves to allow for setting in the back. Don't trim the 6.5mm plywood sheet for the back until the bookcase is assembled

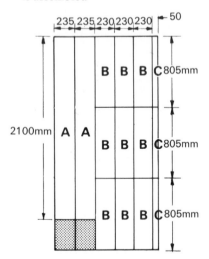

Making the uprights

First cut a rabbet to hold the back panel along the back edge of each upright. Use a rabbet plane (page 200) or router (page 216). Carry the rabbet through to the board ends.

Now make a drilling jig about 900mm long out of a piece of waste plywood 230mm wide as shown. Clamp it to each upright in turn, using it to drill 6mm diameter holes centred every 50mm along the length of the uprights. Make sure the end of the drilling jig matches up exactly with the bottom of the upright so that the first pair of holes will line up on both uprights and the shelves will be horizontal. Move the jig further up the upright by pushing a pair of 6mm dowel pegs through the jig into the last pair of

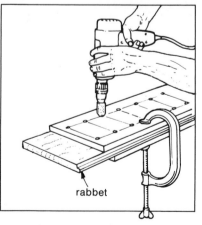

drilled holes. Remember to use a depth stop as shown to make the holes the exact depth required to fit the shelf sockets.

Making the shelves

The bookcase shown here has nine shelves B. Six of these are adjustable and the remaining three are screwed to the 50mm supports C. Screw the supports to the underside of the three shelves 25mm from the front edge using four 50mm screws per shelf. Sink the screws 12mm into the strip by first drilling a 10mm diameter hole exactly 12mm deep. You can of course make more or fewer shelves for the bookcase.

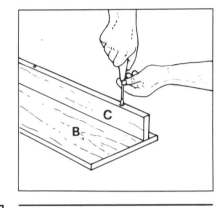

Making a drilling jig

Drilling holes at regular intervals is made easier by using a jig made from a piece of plywood 12 or 19mm thick. Cut one end so that it is exactly square and mark it with an arrow so that you will remember to start at this end.

holes every 50mm
230
approx 900mm
125 50

Also mark one edge as the front edge. Measure out 50mm intervals with a tape measure or ruler, then square lines across the board at each mark with a try square. Finally draw two lines from the arrowed front edge, one 50mm in from the edge and the other 125mm from the first. Use a centre punch to mark carefully all the holes. Drill the holes with a 6mm drill bit. If possible use a drill stand to get the holes exactly vertical (page 214). If one is not available, stand a try square next to the drill as a vertical guide.

Applying the edging

To match the veneer, apply 19mm wide iron-on teak veneer strips to the front edges of all the shelves B, uprights A and supports C. The back of each strip is covered with Scotch glue which is the same type of glue used in traditional veneer work. It

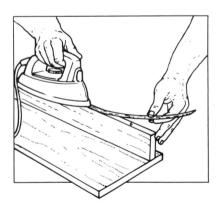

Finishing the bookcase

Finish the bookcase by sanding with fine sandpaper. Wipe with a clean, dry, lint-free cloth and then rub in two even coats of teak oil, allowing the surface to dry between coats. Alternatively you can apply two coats of clear polyurethane.

has the advantage of melting at a low enough temperature to allow you to remove or relocate the veneer by applying a medium hot iron until the glue melts. The glue sets almost as soon as the heat is removed. Trim off any excess edging with a sharp block plane and then carefully sand the edges smooth so that there is no join and it looks as if the boards are solid teak.

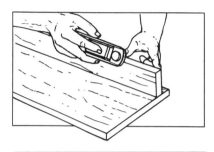

Assembling the bookcase

Mark the insides of the uprights A with a light square line 900mm from the bottom as a guide for the middle shelf. Lay one upright on the bench or on the floor and hold the middle shelf in place while drilling through from the outside with a 4.5mm diameter drill bit. Hold the shelf in position flush with the front edge of A while you drill straight through about 25mm into the ends of the shelf. Push a wall plug through the upright into the hole in the shelf, then screw a 45mm brass screw with the cup washer into the wall plug. Drill a second hole through the upright into the shelf and screw it tight, and finally drill a third hole into the end of the 50mm support C. Repeat for the other end of the shelf and for the top and bottom shelves, holding them straight while drilling. Use a bar clamp to hold the shelf tight.

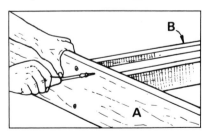

Remember to allow for the back by setting the shelves 6.5mm in from the back edge of the uprights.

Finally lay the bookcase flat with the back upwards and measure the exact size required for the back panel and trim the 6.5mm sheet. Pin it onto the uprights and the backs of the three fixed shelves with 19mm pins.

STORAGE CABINETS

Spice rack

It shouldn't take more than an hour or two to make this simple pine spice rack which measures 340 × 760mm. To make it really easy, the shelves are just glued and nailed to the uprights. The cabinet is strengthened by nailing on a hardboard back. Make the spice rack as small or as large as you like. You can even make it to fit into an alcove as shown on page 16.

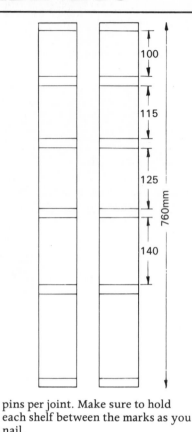

To make the spice rack

CUTTING LIST
softwood
   6 pieces 300mm long
   2 pieces 760mm long

First mark the shelf locations on the two 760mm uprights with a try square. Mark both uprights at the same time to make them match up exactly.

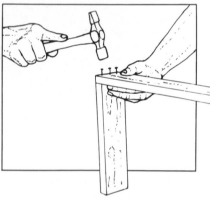

Glue and nail the top shelf and then the bottom shelf to one of the uprights. Continue by attaching the other four shelves using three 38mm

pins per joint. Make sure to hold each shelf between the marks as you nail.

Continue by turning the frame over and gluing and nailing the other upright to the shelves.

Finally lay it face down on the bench to nail on the back. Use the 12mm pins to attach the back, two per shelf and three for each upright.

To make the spice rack look more finished, set all the nails with a nail punch and fill the holes with filler. Sand smooth and finish with two coats of clear polyurethane or paint the shelf unit in a colour to match your kitchen. If you don't want to paint the hardboard back, finish painting the shelves first.

SHOPPING LIST

softwood	about 3.6m of 19 × 75mm
hardboard	330 × 760mm, 4mm thick
hardware	36 finishing nails or panel pins, 38mm long 18 finishing nails or panel pins, 12mm long
plus	wood filler clear polyurethane

Drawer cabinet with circular handles

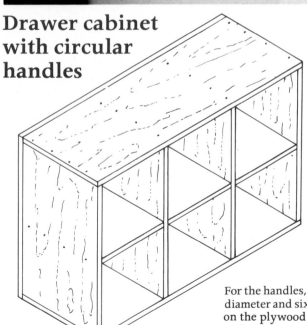

This cabinet which measures 275 × 405mm is made entirely of 6.5mm birch plywood, glued and nailed

together. The dividers are slotted together to make internal spaces 127 × 127 × 150mm deep. The drawers are made either 126 × 126mm, 63 × 126mm or 63 × 63mm to fit either one, two or four drawers in each space. Drawers of three different sizes make the cabinet a perfect storage place for all kinds of sundries.

For the handles, mark six 90mm diameter and six 50mm diameter disks on the plywood using a compass, and cut them out with a coping saw. Then sand them round and smooth. Glue the disks together in pairs before fixing them on. Depending on the number of drawers in each space,

leave the disks as they are, cut them in half or in quarters to make the required number of handles for the cabinet. Fix the handles by screwing them to the drawer fronts from the inside. Paint the cabinet a bright

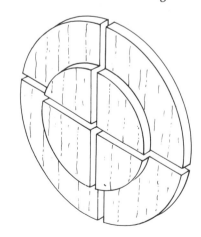

colour and accent the handles by painting them in a contrasting colour and fix labels to the drawers if you like.

Teak cabinets

Small cabinets with drawers are always useful. These handsome teak cabinets with drawers of varying sizes can be used to hold a variety of small items.

The cabinet must be made carefully so that the drawers fit smoothly. It is best to make the cabinet first and then make the drawers. It is usually necessary to fit the drawers and to plane off a little to make them slide smoothly.

Both the cabinets shown here are made in the same way, but of course the larger version requires that much more time and patience. The instructions given are for making the small cabinet which is 350mm long, 190mm high and 160mm deep.

Then cut rabbets 6.5 × 10mm wide along the back edge of pieces A and B for the 6.5mm thick back panel. Finally run a 6.5 × 6.5mm groove along the centre line of both pieces A as shown. Remember to score the veneer with a knife before cutting the grooves.

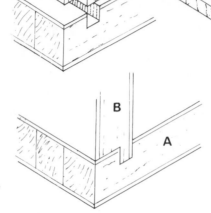

To make the cabinet

CUTTING LIST
teak blockboard
    2 pieces
    160 × 350mm, for top and
    bottom A
    2 pieces
    160 × 165mm, for sides B
6.5mm plywood
    1 piece
    153 × 165mm, for divider C
    1 piece
    170 × 330mm, for back D
6 × 12mm softwood
    4 pieces 145mm long

After cutting out the 19mm blockboard, cut 6.5 × 6.5mm tongues in the ends of sides B and matching grooves in pieces A for the corner joints. The easiest way is to use a 6.5mm straight cutter in a router with a guide (page 216) but you can also use a plough plane or combination plane (page 200) as an alternative.

Before assembling the sides, screw the 6 × 12mm softwood along the sides as battens for the top two small drawers, using two 12mm countersunk screws per batten.

Don't add glue to the battens so they will be easier to move if necessary. The drawers are 42mm deep so the spaces between battens should be just deeper than this.

Assemble the sides by gluing them together and reinforcing the joints with two or three pins set below the

surface. Then cover the pinheads by applying iron-on teak edging over the ends of pieces A (page 115).

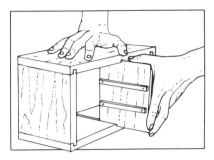

Glue the central divider C in place then finally apply iron-on edging to the front. Overlap the corners, cut through both pieces at a 45° angle using a sharp knife, and then remove the waste by warming the join with an iron so that the glue melts.

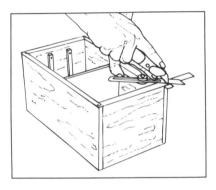

Making the drawers

CUTTING LIST
6.5mm plywood
   2 pieces 150 × 150mm, for sides E
   2 pieces 140 × 150mm, for front and back F
   6 pieces 38 × 150mm, for sides G
   6 pieces 38 × 140mm, for front and back H
4mm plywood
   4 pieces 150 × 150mm, for bottoms
solid teak
   3 pieces 54 × 160mm, for fronts
   1 piece 160 × 165mm, for front
   3 pieces 32 × 50mm, for handles
   1 piece 32 × 150mm, for handle

Glue and nail together the drawer sides, backs and bases, making one large and three small drawers. Then slide these into the cabinet and number them and their locations so that you will remember where they go. Trim off with a plane where necessary to make them fit smoothly.

Before fitting the fronts, drill 20mm diameter holes in the handles, then glue and screw them from the back

SHOPPING LIST	
teak	215 × 330mm, 10mm thick for drawer fronts and handles
teak veneered blockboard	160 × 1075mm, 19mm thick
plywood	330 × 900mm, 6.5mm thick 330 × 330mm, 4mm thick
hardware	8 no.4 countersunk brass screws, 25mm long 16 no.4 countersunk brass screws, 12mm long 12 finishing nails or panel pins, 25mm long about 50 finishing nails or panel pins, 19mm long
plus	6 × 12mm softwood, 600mm long 2.44m length of teak veneer iron-on edging, 19mm wide contact adhesive

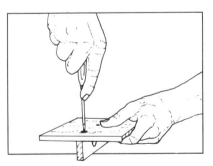

to the loose fronts with the 25mm brass screws, countersinking the holes.

To fit the fronts, leave the drawers in the cabinet and spread contact adhesive on both surfaces. After the glue is touch dry, carefully glue on each front in turn, leaving a 1mm gap between the small drawers. The front should overlap the 19mm surround by about 6mm on all sides. Then gently take the drawers out and reinforce the front by

adding 12mm screws from inside the drawer. Finally, pin the cabinet back in place with 19mm pins.

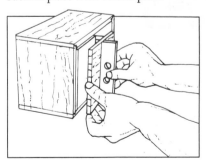

Finishing

The best finish for teak is linseed oil or teak oil. Sand the cabinet well, but be careful not to rub through the veneer. Then rub in two or three coats of oil, allowing the surface to dry between coats.

LARGE WORK TABLE

A table with a work surface this size, 990 × 2210mm, is ideal as a kitchen work table, as a sewing or hobby table or as a drawing table. The plywood legs, which are made large enough to contain either drawers or shelves, provide valuable storage space. They are simply glued and nailed together. And to keep the project quick to make, the drawers are made of push-together plastic sections with fronts made from plywood covered with bright plastic laminate.

SHOPPING LIST		
softwood	6.7m of 38 × 38mm	
	6.7m of 12 × 19mm for drawer supports	
plywood	1 standard sheet, 12mm thick	
	1 standard sheet, 4mm thick	
chipboard	1 standard sheet, 19mm thick	
plastic laminate	1 standard sheet, white alabaster slate finish	
	small bright red pieces for drawer fronts	
hardware	28 no.10 steel screws, 38mm long	
	40 no.6 round head steel screws, 12mm long for drawer fronts	
	70 finishing nails or panel pins, 38mm long	
	140 finishing nails or panel pins, 19mm long	
plus	9m of plastic drawer section, 100mm wide, with 20 corner connectors and 20 front plates	
	contact adhesive for laminate	

Making the top

CUTTING LIST
38 × 38mm
   2 pieces 2160mm long
   2 pieces 865mm long
chipboard
   2 pieces 85 × 2440mm A
   (to be trimmed)
   2 pieces 85 × 990mm B
   1 piece 990 × 2210mm, for top
laminate
   2 pieces 110 × 2440mm C
   (trim after gluing)
   2 pieces 110 × 1000mm D
   (trim after gluing)
   remainder, about 1000 × 2220mm
   for top (trim after gluing)

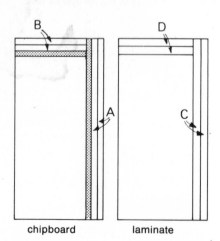

chipboard   laminate

The chipboard edge boards A and B are joined to the top with 38 × 38mm softwood battens glued and screwed to both the top and the edge for an extra strong fixing. Cut them out as shown and trim pieces A to length after screwing pieces B in place.

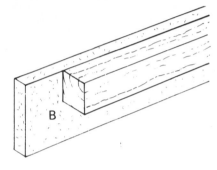

Fix the battens to the pieces B first, leaving a 65mm space at each end. Glue them flush with the top edge of the chipboard then add three 38mm screws from the chipboard side. Make sure to countersink these holes carefully so that the screw heads will not interfere with the laminate when it is glued on later.

Clamp and glue these two ends to the top with all the edges flush. At the same time measure the distance between the pieces B and cut the edge boards A to this exact length.

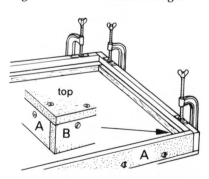

Glue and screw one 2160mm batten to each piece A with 38mm screws as before, then clamp and glue these in place as shown. Make sure to line up the

chipboard edges carefully before clamping.

After the glue has set, remove the clamps and turn the top over. Add 38mm screws through the top and into the battens along all four edges.

It is important that all the edges line up exactly so that the laminate will fit neatly and smoothly. Plane with a block plane and fill gaps with wood filler if necessary.

Gluing the laminate

Turn to page 46 for general instructions on cutting and gluing plastic laminates. Start with the end strips D. Glue them to the ends B and trim them flush on all four edges with a sharp block plane. Continue by cutting strips C with a panel saw 6mm overlength. Glue down the top and then trim all around.

Making the legs

The legs consist of four boxes made of 12mm and 4mm plywood. The sides are simply glued and pinned together which makes them easy to assemble. Two of the boxes have open shelves which can be closed off, if desired, by attaching hinged doors (page 244). The other two each contain one large and four small drawers with fronts covered in bright red plastic laminate.

It is important to cut the pieces accurately. If possible use a table saw or a circular saw with a straight edge (page 208) to do all the cutting.

Number the pieces to keep them in order during assembly.

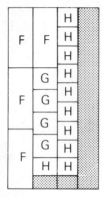

CUTTING LIST
softwood
  20 pieces 12 × 19mm, 280mm
  long for drawer runners
12mm plywood
  8 pieces 290 × 805mm,
  for cabinet sides A
  8 pieces 90 × 290mm,
  for cabinet fronts B
  8 pieces 105 × 315mm,
  for drawer fronts C
  2 pieces 190 × 315mm,
  for drawer fronts D
  4 pieces 290 × 290mm,
  for shelves E
4mm plywood
  4 pieces 315 × 805mm,
  for cabinet backs F
  4 pieces 293 × 315mm,
  for cabinet tops G
  10 pieces for drawer
  bottoms H (size to be
  determined at assembly)

Start by making four identical boxes. First glue and nail the back F to the two sides A, using about five 19mm pins per side. Make sure the distance between the sides A is exactly 290mm so that the fronts B and the shelves E will fit correctly. It is a good idea to hold a shelf E between the sides as a spacer.

Attach the two fronts B with two 38mm pins per side, keeping the edges carefully lined up while nailing. Fix the nails slightly askew so that they hold better.

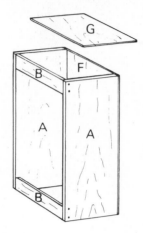

Finally glue and pin the top G in place with 19mm pins.

Open cabinet legs

Two of the legs have drawers and the other two have open shelving. Start with the open cabinets. The bottom shelf E sits directly on the front B. Mark a line, glue the edges, then hold the shelf in place while you nail it from the outside using three 38mm pins per side. Next decide on the location of the middle shelf, mark it with a try square then glue and nail it in place.

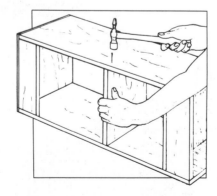

Drawer legs

Make the drawers from ready-made plastic drawer sections available in long lengths to be cut to size and simply pushed together using special corner joints available with the sides (page 247). It is important to follow the manufacturer's instructions carefully to determine both the

length of sides and back, and also to work out the exact locations of the 12 × 19mm drawer runners which run in a groove in the plastic sides. Cut the plastic with a fine saw.

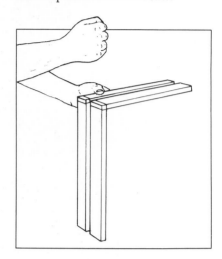

Don't attach the plywood drawer fronts C until you have glued on the red plastic laminate and cut out the handle shape with either a coping saw, sabre saw or router. Notice that the 190mm fronts D have the same drawer backs as the 105mm fronts C, and all the handle cut-outs are identical.

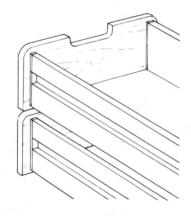

After assembling the ten drawers with bottoms H, determine the exact locations of the 12 × 19mm drawer

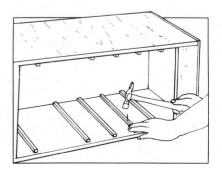

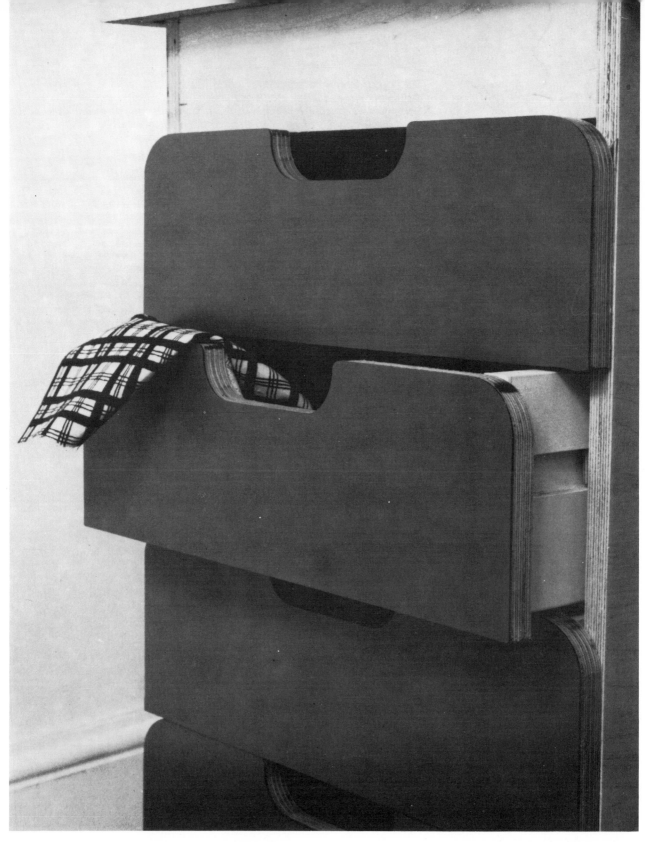

runners by leaving a 3mm gap between drawer fronts. Lay the cabinet on its side and nail the runners in place with 19mm pins. Then turn it upright to install the drawers. It may be necessary to adjust one or two of the drawers or runners to get the fit just right before finally adding a few more pins to make the runners secure.

Finishing

The cabinets can either be painted or varnished with two coats of clear polyurethane.

Before finishing the cabinets, make sure to trim off any protruding edges of laminate with a block plane, or with a router fitted with a special laminate-cutting bit. Set the nails with a nail punch and fill the holes with filler before sanding the cabinets carefully.

To assemble the table, lift the top onto the four legs so that the 38 × 38mm battens sit on the legs. There is no need to screw the table top down, its weight holds it firmly in place.

BOXES AND CUBES

The only difficulty about making boxes is cutting the wood accurately. The sides must be square and the correct length for the pieces to fit together well. The best material to use is plywood. It is stronger and easier to join than chipboard and it is simpler to finish. However, it is also more expensive. This wall unit is made of 12mm thick birch plywood with painted, half round edging nailed on. This type of edging requires mitre joints. For a butt jointed edging, use 6 × 12mm rectangular strips. The sides are simply glued and nailed together and the nails set and filled to hide the holes.

Wall storage system

Using only glue and nail construction, this is one of the easiest projects in the book. Yet with the teak veneer doors and the brown, half round edging, it is an elegant wall unit. Support the units, which are all 685mm wide, with any adjustable shelving system, choosing a colour which complements the edging and wood.

Making three large boxes

The three large boxes along the bottom of the wall unit are the same basic box. One is made into a cocktail cabinet by adding a shelf and a door, one serves as a record cabinet, the third as a storage box.

CUTTING LIST
12mm plywood
6 pieces 355 × 355mm, sides A
6 pieces 355 × 660mm, tops and bottoms B
1 piece 205 × 330mm, divider C for cocktail cabinet
1 piece 205 × 320mm, shelf D for cocktail cabinet
4mm plywood
3 pieces 355 × 684mm, backs E

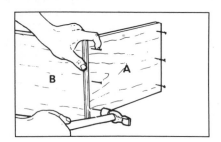

For each box, first nail the sides A to the tops and bottoms B with 32mm pins. Start the pins in one of the sides A, then glue and nail it to the top B. Make sure the edge fits flush along its length by feeling with your thumb as you nail.

Attach the bottom B, then turn the box over and nail on the second side.

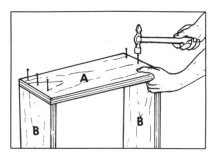

Four ways of making boxes

1 Glue and nail. Start nails or pins in side pieces. Drive nails at a slight angle to increase strength. For 12mm plywood use 32mm long finishing nails or panel pins.

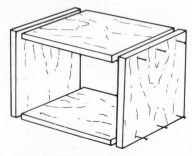

2 Glue and screw. Temporarily nail the pieces together with three nails, leaving the heads protruding. Then

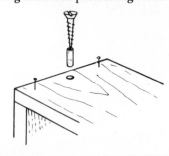

pull out each nail in turn and drill straight through the nail holes at least 25mm into the end grain with a 4.5mm diameter drill. Push a no.8 fibre wall plug in and add a no.8 screw. Start the screw in the plug then tap it with a hammer to push it to the bottom of the hole before screwing it tight. The screws can be countersunk and filled for painted work, or decorated with brass or chrome cup washers.

For chipboard, use special chipboard screws with coarse threads, countersunk in a 10mm diameter hole and capped with a plastic screw cover on laminate-covered chipboard (page 226).

3 Corner block joint. This is probably the easiest way to join panels, but the blocks, which are exposed on the inside, tend to look clumsy. (page 226).

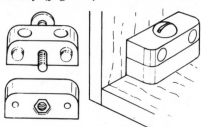

4 Grooved corner joints. Use a table saw or router to make matching grooves. This connection is often used for drawers (page 247). Glue the joint and reinforce with skew nails.

Adding the back
The simplest way is to nail or screw the 4mm plywood or hardboard back directly onto the back edges of the box. But to avoid leaving the edges of the back panel exposed at the sides, rabbet the back edges. Rabbets must be 'stopped' before the end of the board to avoid showing through.

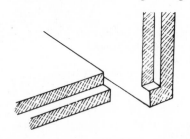

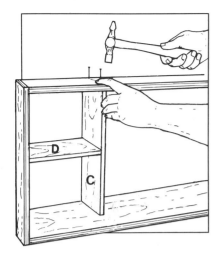

Before fitting the back, nail the divider and shelves in place in the cocktail cabinet. Mark the location in the box with a try square. Glue and nail the divider C to the shelf D before nailing them into the box.

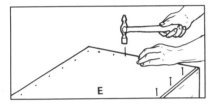

Then glue and nail the backs E in place using 12mm pins. Use the back panel to square up the box. Nail one edge, then check all the corners for flush fit before nailing the other sides.

SHOPPING LIST
to make the unit shown which includes 6 boxes and 7 shelves

birch plywood	2½ standard sheets, 12mm thick 1 piece 355 × 1220mm, 6.5mm thick ½ standard sheet, 4mm thick
teak veneered plywood	1 piece 355 × 710mm, 12 or 19mm thick (to be trimmed) 1 piece 610 × 710mm, 6.5mm thick (or stain birch plywood with teak stain)
hardware	150 finishing nails or panel pins, 32mm long 150 finishing nails or panel pins, 12mm long for backs 150 finishing nails or panel pins, 19mm long for moulding pair 38mm brass hinges with matching 12mm screws for fold-down door small catch for fold-down door sliding stay in chrome or brass with 12mm long screws for fold-down door 8 pieces adjustable shelving track, each 1.5m long with screws for wall 20 brackets, 225mm long 6 brackets, 300mm long
plus	30m half round moulding, 12mm wide 1.5m each matching top and bottom plastic door slide for doors 6.5mm thick 2.4m plastic channel for record cabinet dividers, 6.5mm thick 5.5m teak iron-on veneer edging, 12 or 19mm wide, to match veneered plywood, or use teak stain contact adhesive clear polyurethane dark brown paint

→

Making two small boxes

CUTTING LIST
12mm plywood
　4 pieces 240 × 240mm, for sides
　4 pieces 240 × 660mm,
　for tops and bottoms
4mm plywood
　2 pieces 240 × 684mm, for backs

Make these boxes in exactly the same way as the large boxes, nailing the sides to the top and bottom before attaching the backs.

One open box with dividers

CUTTING LIST
12mm plywood
　2 pieces 205 × 455mm, sides A
　3 pieces 205 × 660mm,
　top, bottom and shelf B
　1 piece 205 × 380mm, shelf C
　1 piece 205 × 230mm, divider D
　1 piece 125 × 205mm, divider E
4mm plywood
　1 piece 455 × 684mm, back F

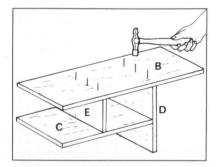

This box measures 455 × 684mm. Follow the same procedure as before. Make the internal dividers and fix them as a unit into the box. Start by nailing divider E to shelf C, then attach these two to divider D and then finally to shelf B.

To make seven shelves

These shelves, which are 240mm deep, are small boxes without the top panel and are made using 12mm instead of 4mm plywood for the back panel.

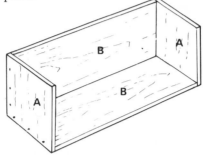

CUTTING LIST (for each shelf)
12mm plywood
　2 pieces 240 × 252mm, sides A
　2 pieces 240 × 660mm,
　shelf and back B

Finishing the unit

Set all the nails, fill the holes with wood filler and sand the boxes well. Pay particular attention to the filled holes, making sure any marks from the filler are sanded off. Then apply two coats of clear polyurethane to the boxes and dividers.

Attaching the edging

The half round edging must be mitred at the corners. Use a small mitre box (page 205) and tenon saw to cut the moulding to fit the front edges of the boxes and shelves. Number each piece on the back as you cut them to avoid confusing the

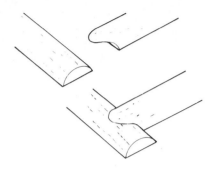

lengths. Paint each strip with dark brown paint over the appropriate undercoat. Nail the pieces in place with 19mm pins. To make T-joints for applying edging to the shelves, cut the ends in an arch with a coping saw so that they fit over the moulding.

Although a mitred corner looks more elegant it is much more work and also more difficult to do accurately. To make the job easier, use rectangular edging such as 6 × 12mm strips which can be simply butt jointed at the corners.

Record cabinet dividers

To attach the dividers to the record cabinet, first cut the plastic channel into eight 300mm lengths. Then mark the location of each length inside the box and spread a line of contact adhesive along the lines and along the backs of the plastic channels. After fixing the channels, cut the 6.5mm plywood to size, round the corners with a coping saw and file or sand them smooth before giving them two coats of polyurethane and sliding them into place in the channels.

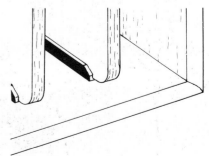

Sliding doors

Glue the plastic slides in place with contact adhesive. Attach the slides before trimming the 6.5mm teak veneered plywood doors to size. Cut the doors 355mm wide to overlap slightly and trim the height so they can just be pushed in place in the track. Drill holes or attach knobs for pulls before fixing the doors in place.

Fold-down door

The hardware for this fold-down door is somewhat more difficult to install and can only be done by trial and error to get the door to open and close smoothly. Attach the brass hinges and the catch to the door before screwing the hinges to the cabinet and attaching the sliding stay with matching screws.
To finish the edge of the veneered plywood, either cover it with iron-on teak edging (page 67) or stain it to match.

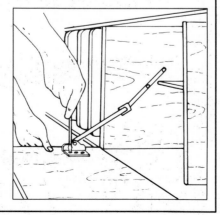

Other ways to use boxes

Storage boxes are very useful in the kitchen for the endless array of equipment needed. Hang boxes as shown here in a row on the wall, with L-brackets mounted inside, or stack them under worktops. These boxes, made of 19mm chipboard, are glued and nailed together and then painted with two coats of glossy paint over a sealer. The backing is white painted hardboard simply nailed on. To get the chipboard edges smooth before finishing, rub in filler and sand smooth. Notice that the top edges have been slightly bevelled.

Cubes are amazingly versatile. Make them out of chipboard or plywood or even 6.5mm hardboard. Stack them in any number of combinations or use them individually.

These cubes are made of white, laminate-covered chipboard which is available in many other colours in 2.44m boards in widths from 150 × 535mm, with iron-on edging to match. Use 380mm wide boards to make these boxes. Plan out the cutting list for the five sides and dividers and then cut the boards and iron on the matching edging before joining the pieces. Use 38mm chipboard screws countersunk and covered with white plastic caps to match the laminate. Three cubes have a central divider, one of which holds a simple drawer made from a push-together plastic drawer system (page 247). Arrange four cubes together as a coffee table. The cubes can sit directly on the floor or on a base made from four 50mm high laminate-covered boards nailed together at the corners.

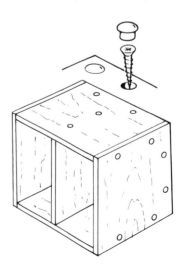

ROLL TOP DESK

No book of furniture making would be complete without including one really demanding project. This beautiful roll top desk is very exacting to make because the cabinet must be absolutely square and the lengths exact so that the roll top works smoothly. But with the right tools and plenty of patience, it is a very rewarding project to make. Even if you don't plan to make a roll top desk right away, the technique of making a roll top, or tambour, is useful. It consists of narrow strips which are glued onto a backing of heavy cloth or leathercloth so that it is flexible enough to run in a groove around corners.

A tambour can be used horizontally

as it is for this desk or vertically for cabinets and chests. It is an extremely elegant and professional method of furniture making which not only looks attractive, but also saves space since the sliding door is contained within the cabinet.

To make this desk you will need facilities for planing down the

hardwood which is usually bought rough sawn. A local joinery or woodworking shop will probably do this for a small charge, but make sure to specify the exact thickness that you want the finished boards. The main cabinet is made from 20mm thick boards, but the other parts such as the interior dividers,

SHOPPING LIST	
sawn hardwood	about 7.5m of 25 × 225mm / about 9m of 25 × 150mm 10.5m of 32 × 75mm
plywood	1 × 1.22m, 6.5mm thick (preferably veneered to match the hardwood) 300 × 900mm, 6.5mm thick for template
hardware	8 no.6 countersunk brass screws, 32mm long 35 no.6 countersunk brass screws, 19mm long 18 no.4 countersunk brass screws, 12mm long a few finishing nails or panel pins, 12mm long brass cabinet lock with matching screws
plus	900 × 1020mm thin leathercloth (to be trimmed)

drawers and tambour require 8mm thick pieces. The legs and rails are all 28mm thick.

The essential tools for making the desk are a table saw or radial arm saw for cutting the pieces to size and in particular for ripping the boards into the fine tambour slats, and a router for cutting the grooves and rabbets. See pages 210 and 216 for instructions on using these tools. Choose a rich, dark coloured hardwood which is relatively stable and straight grained such as South American mahogany, walnut or cherry.

This desk is made of muninga, a lovely African hardwood which is brownish red with orange patches in some boards. It has a sweet almost perfumed smell when it is being worked.

The design of the desk has been kept modern and elegant in contrast to the usual roll top desk which is more old-fashioned and heavy looking. The desk has a good sized writing surface and ample space for storing stationery and writing implements in the drawers and open storage compartments. The leg structure too is kept light and elegant. Slanting the leg and rail not only makes it look interesting, but also gives the desk greater stability and allows more leg room by eliminating the need for a rail across the front.

You can of course make the desk larger to suit your requirements. It is difficult to alter the front to back dimension of the desk, but it is relatively easy to change the width by adding or subtracting a constant dimension to all the components which span across the width.

Preparing the wood

All the sawn boards must first be planed to the exact thickness required. If you are having them planed by your wood supplier or by a local woodworking shop, you should first cut the sawn boards to rough length and organize them in groups according to the required finished thickness. The shopping list allows for about twenty per cent waste in the length which is adequate for cutting off split ends and trimming the boards.

The base C and the top B are made from glued up 25 × 150mm boards which must first be planed square and straight before they are dowel jointed and glued together to make a surface (page 231).

List of parts for cabinet

name	location	no. of pieces	material	thickness mm	width mm	length mm	remarks
A	sides	2	hardwood	18	215	750	
B	top	1	hardwood	18	290	990	glue up two 150 boards
C	writing surface (base)	1	hardwood	18	655	965	glue up three 225 boards
D	inside top	1	hardwood	18	215	965	
E	front and back rails	2	hardwood	18	45	988	
F	tambour stop	1	hardwood	18	18	960	
G	bottom	1	plywood	6.5	725	962	
H	back	1	plywood	6.5	165	1962	
I	inside back	1	hardwood	8	150	1950	
J	tambour slats	60	hardwood	8	12	1020	cut from three 25 × 150 boards
K	storage dividers	6	hardwood	8	120	210	
L	storage shelf	1	hardwood	8	210	310	cut from 225 board
M	drawer sides	8	hardwood	8	55	205	
N	drawer sides	4	hardwood	8	113	205	
O	drawer bottoms	3	hardwood	8	195	195	cut from 225 board
P	drawer and tambour handles	4	hardwood	8	25	60	
Q	drawer handle	1	hardwood	8	25	120	
R	front legs	2	hardwood	28	65	760	to be trimmed to length
S	back legs	2	hardwood	28	65	760	to be trimmed to length
T	diagonal rail	2	hardwood	28	65	760	to be trimmed to length
U	cross rails	3	hardwood	28	65	1025	

To economize on wood, rip 25 × 150mm boards in half to make up two 8mm thicknesses out of each board for making the drawer components and for the tambour. The appearance of the tambour is greatly improved if you arrange the 8mm slats so that you re-create the grain pattern of the board. Carefully number the pieces as they come off the saw so that you can arrange them in the same order.

Preparing the sides A

For the tambour to slide smoothly, the sides must be absolutely square and parallel. You must take care in cutting the grooves and dovetails, and be very exacting in the assembly procedure to check and double check that everything is straight and square before the final gluing. ➡

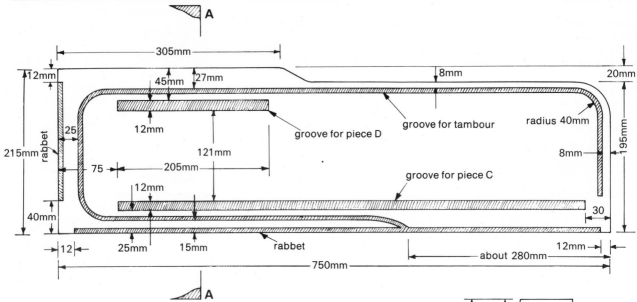

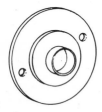

Start with the two sides A. First perform the delicate job of cutting the grooves for the cross pieces C and D and then the curved groove which holds the edge of the tambour. This can be done by hand, but it is a lot easier and can be done more evenly and accurately with a router. Cut the tambour groove with a template and use a straight edge guide to cut the straight grooves. You will need a router fitted with a template guide and 5mm and 12mm straight cutters.

Make an accurate full scale drawing of the side view of the cabinet on a piece of 6.5mm plywood. Then make a template out of the plywood for cutting the tambour groove.

File the edges of the template and sand them smooth. It must be marginally smaller than the groove,

to allow for the template guide on the router.

Mount each side A within 25 × 50mm pieces nailed to the bench, then locate the template carefully with pins or temporarily spot glue it to the board with a piece of paper in between.

The 5mm wide groove should be exactly 5mm deep so that the tambour will run on the bottom of the groove not on the shoulders.

Run the router along smoothly in one movement. Notice that the end of the groove continues out to the edge along the bottom to allow the tambour to be run in from underneath when the cabinet is assembled. The groove usually has to be widened slightly at the curves. You can do this best by hand with a chisel, smoothing the groove out afterwards with sandpaper.

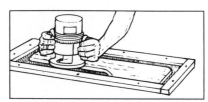

Use a straight edge to rout the 12mm wide and 8mm deep grooves to take the shouldered tongues of C and D. Next cut the stopped rabbets along the bottom and back edges. Cut the profile of each side A and finish the cut edges with a small plane. Leave the rounding of the edges until the cabinet is assembled.

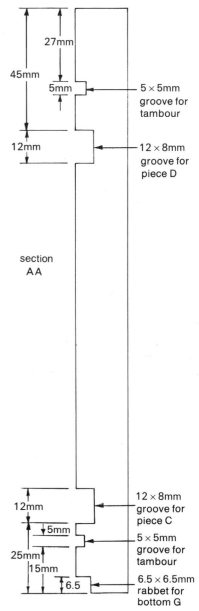

Preparing the base C and inside top D

These two pieces will be joined to the sides. Each will have a shouldered tongue cut along the ends to fit into the grooves cut in the sides A.

First glue together the three pre-pared 25 × 225mm boards C to make up the base, adding dowel joints for reinforcement (page 232). Then cut the base to size and check to make sure that it is absolutely square. This is critical, for the sides A must be parallel after assembly. Mark the top face on both C and D.

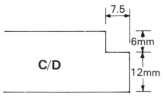

Cut the shouldered tongues, cutting the rabbets along the top so that the tongue is located along the bottom edge. This can be done by hand with a rabbet plane, but again it is more easily done with a router. Follow the same procedure in cutting the identical profile on the ends of piece D.

Then trim off the last 12mm of tongue at the front edge so that it will match the grooves which are stopped 12mm short of the front.

The next stop is to cut the 5mm wide grooves in these two pieces to take the storage dividers K. Lay out the dimensions carefully on the base (see below), cutting the grooves on the top face of C but on the underside of D.

Then run the router fitted with a 5mm straight cutter against a home-made T-square guide to cut the grooves just a little over 3mm deep. Notice the stop nailed to the T-square to make grooves 200mm long.

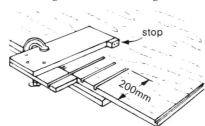

It is important that the grooves in the top D match up exactly to those in the base C, so after cutting the grooves in the base, transfer the marks from one to the other by laying them edge to edge. Then after cutting the same stopped grooves in the top D, square off the ends of the grooves with a narrow chisel.

Preparing the top B and rails E

The top and rails are dovetailed to the sides (page 236). This is not only decorative, but also keeps the sides together accurately.

Start with the top B. Lay out the dovetails and make the saw cuts along the lines to the gauge mark. Slant the board in the vice so that the saw cut is vertical.

Before cutting out the waste, transfer the saw marks to the sides A with a light scraping of the saw teeth.

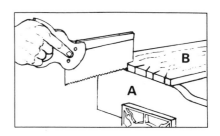

Remove the waste on B along the gauged line, first with a coping saw and then with a chisel. Finally cut the pins on A making sure to saw on the waste side of the scribed lines. Try the joint for fit, tapping it only partway home. Dovetails should only be fitted together at final assembly.

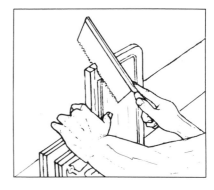

The single dovetails for the front and back rails E are cut in the same way, starting by cutting the tails in the rails E and finally cutting the pins.

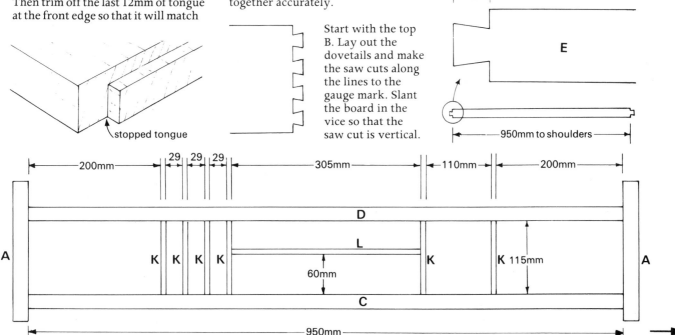

Again try the joints partway to make sure that the fit is right and adjust by trimming if necessary. If the joint is too loose, you will have to add a filler strip later during assembly.

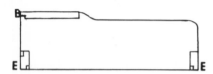

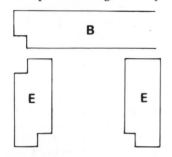

Before assembling the pieces, cut 6.5 × 6.5mm rabbets on the three dovetailed pieces B and E to hold the back and bottom plywood panels. Notice that the back rail has two rabbets.

Assembling the cabinet

Glue the two tongued boards C and D into their grooves. The tongues should be tight enough so that they have to be clamped gently together. Make sure the two boards C and D are arranged the right way, with the grooves for the dividers K matching up.

Then glue the three dovetailed B and E boards, starting with the top B and then the two rails E. Glue and clamp down the top, then glue the rails in place clamping front to back. Also glue the front rail E to the front edge of the base C.

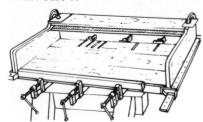

Fitting the dividers and drawers

Prepare and fit the dividers and drawers. Start by cutting the 5mm tongues at the top and bottom of the dividers K to fit into the grooves. Cut them with a saw or router, cutting off the last 10mm of the tongues. Then slide them in from the back to make sure that they fit. Cut 5mm wide grooves in the central dividers to take the shelf L which has the same 3 × 5mm tongue. Before you finally glue them in position, make the three drawers, dovetailing or finger jointing the sides together. The sides have 3 × 12mm grooves to take the battens. Glue the 8mm bottoms in place in grooves cut along the inside of all four sides. Then shape and attach each handle from the inside with two 19mm long no.6 brass screws.

120mm

115mm shoulder length

K

5mm

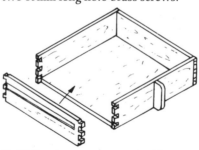

To fit the drawers, screw 3 × 12mm hardwood battens to the dividers locating them to match the grooved sides of the drawers precisely. Use two 12mm no.4 screws per batten. You may have to adjust them slightly to get the right fit, so pin them temporarily in place until you find the right location.

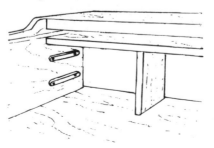

Then shape two of the dividers K before sanding them and finally gluing them in position. With all the dividers and drawers in final position, screw on the inside back I to C and D with about eight 19mm no.6 brass screws.

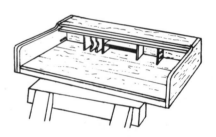

Making the tambour

First lay out all the 8 × 12mm strips preferably in the order in which they were cut from the board so that the grain of the board is re-created. Examine the 60 slats and choose 54, rejecting any which are not straight or perfect. Line up the ends against a straight edge, then clamp them together gently, clamping two

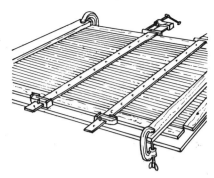

boards across the top to hold them down. Then put four or five strips of wide masking tape across the slats to hold them together.

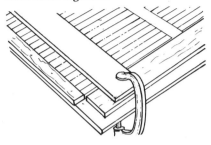

With the strips still clamped down to the bench, trim the ends straight across with a straight cutter mounted in the router so that the strips are exactly 960mm long. Use a straight edge as a guide for the router and make sure it is mounted absolutely squarely.

Then move the straight edge sideways 5mm to cut the tongues. This is a delicate operation so take your time. After completing one edge, repeat for the other edge, again making sure it is cut square and parallel.

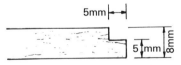

After the tongues are cut, remove the clamps and turn the taped slats over and with battens holding them in place along the four sides, plane off any irregularities with a smoothing plane. After the surface is smooth, clean off all the dust and shavings in preparation for gluing down the cloth.

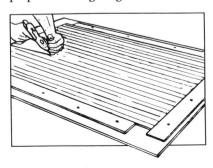

Leave the strips in place between the four battens. Then cut the leathercloth 945mm across the width so that it doesn't interfere with the tongues but leave it about 25mm longer at top and bottom.

Spread white woodworking glue over the rough side of the leathercloth and lay it over the planed tambour surface. Lay a weighted piece of plywood on top and let the glue set. Then trim the leathercloth making the back edge flush and leaving 10mm extending along the front edge.

Remove the tape and rub wax on the tongues and in the grooves. Then with the cabinet upside down on the bench, slide the tambour into the grooves. Check for spots where they rub or stick, where the grooves may need widening out a little more.

Prepare the tambour stop F, cutting a 5mm tongue at either end to ride in the grooves and a 6.5 × 10mm rabbet along the length to take the leathercloth and cover strip as shown. Shape the two handles P as shown. Cut a groove for each on either side of F and then glue the handle so that it extends 6mm beyond the stop.

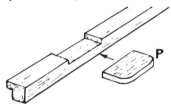

After you have worked on the tambour until it rides smoothly, ease the stop F into the grooves by bending it slightly until it goes in.

Then glue the extending leathercloth to the back of the rabbet covering it with a small strip screwed in place with six 12mm no.4 screws.

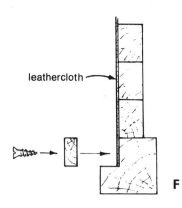

Fix the lock to the cabinet, marking and chiselling out space for the body and drilling out for the keyhole. Set the corresponding plate into the underside of the tambour stop F, then test the lock mechanism.

Now round all the edges and sand with progressively finer paper until all surfaces are smooth.

Making the leg structure

A structure involving pieces which join at an angle should be set out on a full scale drawing, so that all the angles can be copied accurately.

510mm

40mm

bridle joint

S

T

660mm

R

bridle joint

710mm

First draw out the end frame full size on a piece of cardboard or plywood following the diagram. Then cut the four legs and two rails T to exact shape.

Use a sliding bevel set precisely against the full scale drawing to mark the angles to be cut. Mark and cut the mortises for the exposed tenons. Do these very carefully to prevent the wood from breaking out along the back.

Start by marking the joints on the legs, again setting the sliding bevel against the drawing, and then cut them out as shown, first with a saw to the gauged lines and finally chiselling out the waste on either

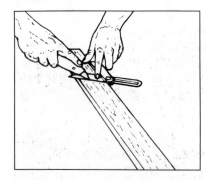

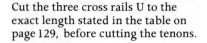

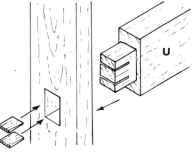

U

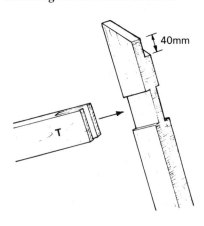

40mm

T

Cut the three cross rails U to the exact length stated in the table on page 129, before cutting the tenons.

After you try the tenons for fit, tapping in part of the way, mark and cut the bridle joints for the diagonal end rails T.

side. Also cut a 10 × 40mm notch at the top of the four legs as shown.

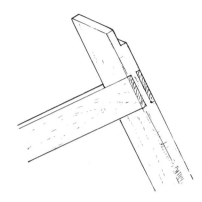

The ends of the diagonal rails are marked in the same way; first with the sliding bevel, then with the marking gauge left at the same setting as was used for the legs.

Cut out the slot and then try the joints partway to make sure that they fit tightly.

Then shape all the pieces, clamping them in matched pairs in the vice. Use a Surform, a spokeshave or a rasp, but make sure to stop the curve

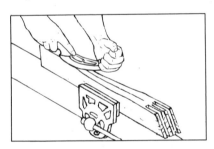

before the joints so that the joints will fit together. You can round the legs at the joint after assembly.

After sanding the pieces, assemble the end frames. Glue both together at the same time with paper between them.

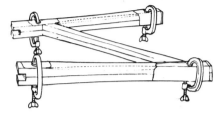

Then assemble the structure by adding the cross rails. Before gluing the tenons into the mortises make two sawcuts in each tenon. Add glue to the joints, then tap them in place with a soft-faced hammer or a mallet.

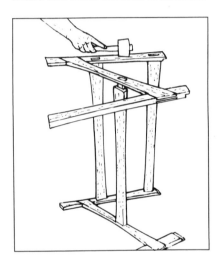

Make up twelve small wedges about 12mm long from a dark wood such as walnut or teak. Make them about 3mm thick at the top. Tap in the wedges and then plane the tenon end flush. Sand well, rounding all the edges. Clamp the base assembly across with bar clamps, checking that it is square. Use a try square or two pointed strips to check that the diagonals are equal.

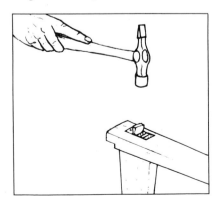

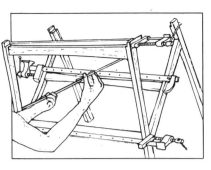

Final assembly

First lay the cabinet upside down on blankets placed on the bench. Then place the leg structure on it with the back leg 12mm from the back of the cabinet. Drill holes from the inside, then screw the legs to the sides A using two 32mm no.6 screws per leg.

Finally attach the bottom G and the back H with 19mm long no.6 screws, notching corners and trimming to fit if necessary.

Finishing

The final finish of a hardwood project like this depends entirely on the preparation of the wood. If the wood is beautifully sanded at each stage as directed in the instructions, it will take a finish much better.

This desk was finished with three coats of wax polish made up from a mixture of carnauba, beeswax and turpentine. Alternatively you can apply an oil finish such as teak oil which is hard and durable. Whichever finish you use, it should be well rubbed in and carefully buffed for a really deep shine. Taking time to produce a good looking finish is important when you have devoted so much effort to a project.

WORK BENCH

You can make most of the projects in this book on temporary work surfaces such as an old table or a door laid across two trestles, or even on the floor. But this 610 × 1525mm work bench, 920mm high, makes your work so much easier and more professional. It is the right height for comfortable working and it has a well and a tool rack along the back and a large shelf underneath to store tools and equipment while working. Most important of all, it is sturdy without having a lot of complicated joints. The most useful feature besides the rugged vice is the replaceable top designed for the work surface. The first two layers of 19mm plywood are screwed down firmly, but the final 6.5mm layer is just pinned on so that it can be replaced with the minimum of trouble when it gets worn and dirty.

Making the frame

CUTTING LIST
75 × 75mm
   4 pieces
   875mm long, for legs A
32 × 100mm
   4 pieces
   540mm long, for end rails B
   3 pieces
   1180mm long, for rails C

The basic frame is quite simple. It consists of two end frames joined together with four long rails.

Start by making the two end frames. Each is composed of two legs A and two end rails B. Mark the slots or halving joints on the legs, using a scrap piece of 32 × 100mm to measure the width correctly. Cut the slots 20mm deep with a saw and chisel. Then simply glue and screw the end rails into the slots with the 65mm screws and chrome cup washers. It is

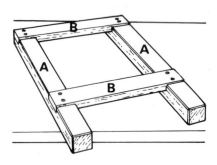

SHOPPING LIST	
plywood	1 standard sheet, 19mm thick
	460 × 1500mm, 6.5mm thick
	about 300 × 460mm, 12mm thick
softwood	3.6m of 75 × 75mm
	6m of 32 × 100mm
	1.5m of 38 × 150mm
	3.6m of 12 × 50mm
hardware	2 no.12 countersunk steel screws, 65mm long for rail D
	3 no.12 countersunk steel screws, 25mm long for bench stop
	48 no.10 countersunk steel screws, 65mm long
	22 no.10 chrome cup washers
	15 no.8 countersunk brass screws, 38mm long
	18 no.8 brass cup washers
	10 finishing nails or panel pins, 32mm long
	30 finishing nails or panel pins, 19mm long
plus	woodworker's vice with coach bolt fixings
	1 Record bench stop
	clear polyurethane

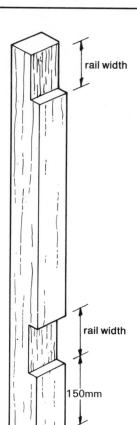

important that the ends are square so do this work carefully.

Notice that the legs and rails have bevelled edges and ends as a decorative touch. This can be done with a block plane or router.

Next place the two ends on their sides as shown, either on a bench or on the floor. Drill two clearance holes for the no.10 screws 32mm from

each end of the three rails C. Then hold the rails C in position to drill the pilot holes through the rails into the legs.

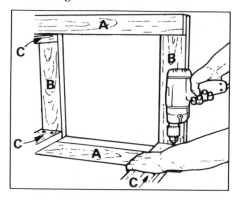

Screw the three rails C to the legs A with the 65mm screws, locating them at the same height as the end rails B. Two are fixed at the back, top and bottom, and only one at the front bottom. Notice that all three of the long rails C are attached to the insides of the legs A.

Preparing the top, shelf and back

CUTTING LIST

38 × 150mm
   1 piece
   1370mm long, for front rail D

12 × 50mm
   2 pieces
   1575mm long, for tool rack E
   3 pieces
   100mm long, for tool rack spacers F

19mm plywood
   1 piece 610 × 1525mm, for top G
   1 piece 460 × 1525mm, for top H
   1 piece 375 × 1220mm, for shelf I
   1 piece 525 × 1220mm, for back J

Cut out the pieces and then attach first the back J and then the shelf I.

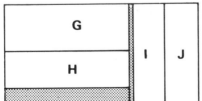

Screw each in place using three 38mm brass screws with cup washers at either end.

To make the top, glue and pin pieces G and H together with 32mm pins. Keep the front edges flush, leaving a 150mm well at the back. The top will be screwed down permanently later, so the 32mm pins are just to hold the two pieces together until the glue sets.

The top will later be covered with a 6.5mm layer of plywood.

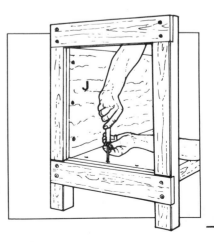

Mounting the vice and bench stop

After the top has been firmly glued together, attach the vice and bench stop to the underside. If you are right-handed, the bench stop should be located near the front left corner of the bench, and near the front right corner if you are left-handed. The vice is usually located on the left, although there is no definite rule about the location.

Temporarily place the top on the underframe and mark the locations for the vice and bench stop. Be careful to locate the bench stop away from the end rail, about 75mm from the end should be about right. Trace the outline of the wood block which is part of the bench stop onto the top, then drill several holes within the marks and finally chisel out the rest of the wood to form a clean rectangular hole into which the bench stop fits.

Place the 6.5mm plywood piece on top with the edges lined up exactly then trace the hole for the bench stop on it from underneath and cut out this hole in the same way. Put aside the 6.5mm top until later.

Turn the 38mm thick top over and attach the bench stop to the underside with the three no.12 screws.

Before fixing the vice, cut a 25mm deep notch in the bench top, the exact width of the front plate of the vice. This way the vice will be recessed with the front plywood 'softening' in line with the front edge of the bench. Then lay one or two small pieces of 12mm plywood under the vice to pack it up so that the top of the vice is flush with the top of the bench.

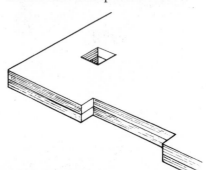

Then mark and drill the holes for the coach bolts which secure the vice to the bench.

Counterbore the holes in the top surface so that the bolt heads will be flush with the top, then bolt down the vice. Also measure and cut to size two pieces of 12mm plywood softening for the vice faces to prevent the metal jaws from marking the work. Fix the plywood pieces to the vice jaws with machine screws in the holes provided.

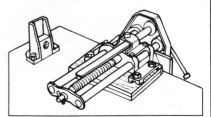

Before turning the top over, cut out the notch in the front rail D for the

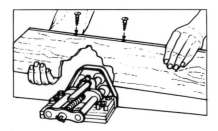

vice. Work carefully, marking and cutting a little at a time until you get the fit just right. After cutting out the notch, it may be necessary to add a couple of 65mm no.10 steel screws into the rail from underneath on each side of the notch to reinforce the rail at the weak points.

Turn the top right side up and lay it on the frame so that there is an equal overhang on each side and the

back edge is flush with the legs. This will leave a generous overhang at the front to allow you to clamp work down to the top.

Secure the top by screwing two 65mm no.10 screws into each end rail B and three 38mm no.8 brass screws with cup washers through the well into the back rail C. The 65mm screws should be countersunk flush with the surface.

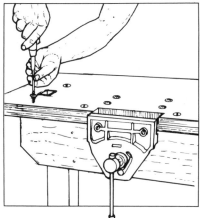

Add the front rail D. Counterbore the screw holes with a 10mm diameter drill bit and after fixing D into each leg with two 65mm screws, plug the holes with plugs cut from a waste piece of the same wood (page 214). Then screw down the front of the top to the rail D with four 65mm countersunk screws.

Finally pin down the removable 6.5mm plywood top surface thereby hiding the screws and bolts of the permanent top surface. Space the 19mm pins evenly over the surface, then punch them well below the surface and fill the holes with wood filler.

Fixing the tool rack

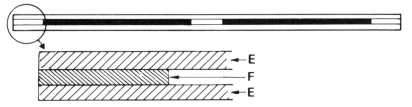

The final step before applying the finish to the bench is to attach the tool rack to the back. First glue and pin the 12 × 50mm pieces together with the 100mm long spacers placed in between the two strips at either end and in the middle. Clamp the pieces until the glue sets, then screw them to the 19mm plywood edge at the back of the bench with six 65mm steel screws and cup washers. Trim off

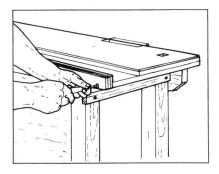

both ends flush with the bench. To hold chisels, you may want to arrange dowel spacers at more frequent intervals.

Finishing the bench

Some woodworkers prefer their benches to be unfinished but, to make it easier to remove glue and paint from the surface, it is best to apply at least two coats of polyurethane particularly to the top surface. The plywood shelf and back can also be painted a dark colour as a contrast to the light wood tones of the rest of the bench.

When working on the bench, keep the top clear of nails and screws and scrape off dried glue so that it will not damage the pieces you are working on.

TOOL CABINET

Hand tools such as planes, hammers, saws and chisels should be kept organized in a wall-hung tool cabinet so that they are within reach and not cluttering up the surface of your workbench. Some woodworkers make their tool cabinet of solid hardwood with hand-cut dovetail joints, but this cabinet is for the beginner who wants to make a quick storage place for tools. It is made of plywood simply glued and nailed together. The door knobs are two small wooden balls painted red and screwed on from the back of the door. You can of course vary the storage facilities and size of the cabinet to suit your own needs; this one measures 610 × 815mm.

SHOPPING LIST

birch	1.22 × 1.22m, 12mm thick
plywood	1.22 × 1.22m, 6.5mm thick
dowel	about 1.2m of 10mm diameter
hardware	16 no.6 countersunk steel screws, 19mm long
	2 no.8 round head brass screws, 19mm long for knobs
	about 100 finishing nails or panel pins, 25mm long
	about 50 finishing nails or panel pins, 12mm long
	2 lengths of brass plated continuous hinge,
	each 815mm long with 12mm brass screws
	2 chrome cabinet catches with 12mm screws
	2 mirror brackets with 12mm screws to hang cabinet
plus	2 small wooden balls for handles
	small quantity of bright red paint
	clear polyurethane
	bright red plastic laminate for drawer fronts, 65 × 610mm

CUTTING LIST

12mm plywood
  5 pieces 90 × 585mm A
  2 pieces 90 × 815mm B
  1 piece 150 × 585mm C
  5 pieces
  50 × 278mm D
  4 pieces 50 × 815mm E
  1 piece 150 × 278mm F
  2 pieces
  75 × 278mm G
  2 pieces
  21 × 278mm H
6.5mm plywood
  1 piece 610 × 815mm I
  2 pieces
  302 × 815mm J
  4 pieces
  66 × 90mm K
  4 pieces 90 × 140mm L
for the drawers
  6 pieces
  57 × 90mm, for sides M
  6 pieces
  57 × 170mm, for fronts
  and backs N
  3 pieces
  90 × 185mm, for bottom O

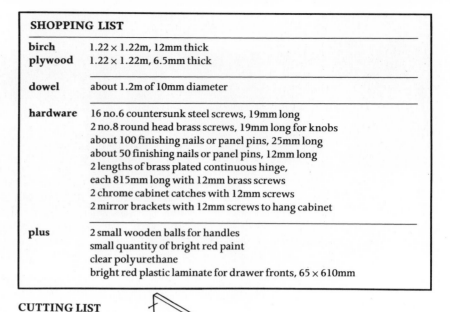

Making the cabinet

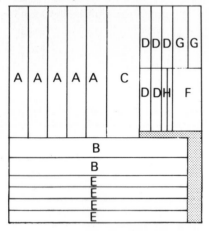

First cut all the pieces accurately and squarely, using a table saw or a circular saw with a straight edge (page 208). If the pieces are exact, the cabinet will go together very easily. Before assembling the cabinet, sand all the plywood edges.

Assembly

To make the box, glue and nail together the four sides A and B. Use three 25mm pins per corner. It is best to hold the pieces in a vice while nailing. Then glue and nail the back I in place with 12mm pins to make the box square. Glue and nail the 6.5mm thick spacers K in place with equal spaces between them. Continue by attaching pieces L to the sides to support the three shelves A, which are pinned to the supports.

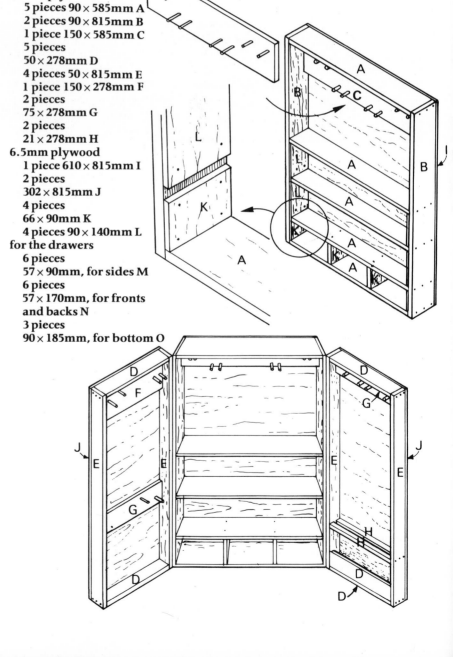

Before attaching the plate C which holds the dowel pegs, lay the box flat on the bench and place your tools in it so that you can mark their locations and decide where to fix dowel pegs. Mark and drill 10mm diameter holes for the 50mm long dowel pegs. After the pegs are glued in place, attach the plate to the box by gluing and screwing from the back, with four no.6 screws.

Make the two door boxes in the same way. Glue and nail the sides D and E together, then add the backs J and attach the shelves and plates. Notice the chisel and screwdriver rack. The two pieces H are separated by a 12mm space to hold the blades of the tools, and the guard D covers the blades and sharp points of the tools.

Attach the doors with two lengths of continuous hinge. Then add the catches and mirror brackets on the top and screw on the red painted wooden knobs from the inside of the doors. Seal the whole cabinet with at least two coats of clear polyurethane.

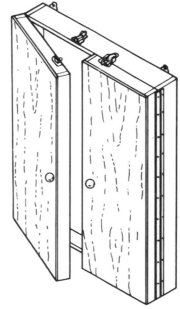

Making the drawers

Assemble the small drawers by gluing and nailing together the sides

M and the front and back N. Then nail on the bottom O. Make three identical drawers in the same way. Cut out a finger hole as shown. To decorate the drawers, either paint them red or glue bright coloured plastic laminate to the fronts.

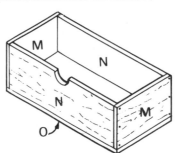

Hang the box on the wall of your workroom from the two mirror brackets which should be more than adequate to take the weight. If the cabinet will be filled with especially heavy tools like planes, screw a 25 × 25mm softwood batten to the wall under the cabinet for additional support.

141

LIVING ROOM PROJECTS

Projects for the living room include several designs for coffee tables, one with an oak parquet top, another with a mirror top, a third made of end grain plywood strips glued together for a dramatic effect and a fourth which can convert to a full height dining table to seat four to six. There are two useful sofas, one with underneath storage and another which pulls out to convert into a double bed. Veneer lampshades, a traditional corner cupboard and a floor and table lamp complete the furniture in this section.

Table lamp

Plywood end grain coffee table

Convertible sofa

Dual height table

Oak corner cupboard

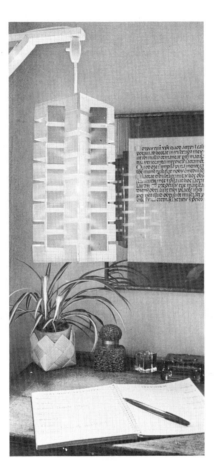

Veneer lampshade

Parquet coffee table

Sofa with storage

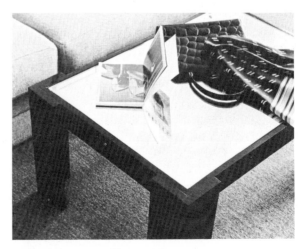

Mirror top coffee table

TWO COFFEE TABLES

These two coffee table designs can be adapted to go well with any decor. They are similar and both are quite easy to make. The first table has a frame which involves halving joints. The top is 915mm square, consisting of oak parquet flooring simply glued to a chipboard base.

The second table frame is just glued and nailed together, making construction even simpler. It too can be made with a parquet inset top but, as here, a completely different look can be achieved by using a mirror top and painting the table glossy black.

Parquet table

Parquet flooring is sold by the square metre, ready to be glued down. It is available in various hardwoods such as teak, oak or mahogany. Whichever you choose, try to match it to the table frame either by using the same wood or by staining pine to match. The frame consists of 25 × 75mm and 25 × 50mm sections with simple halving joints at each corner.

SHOPPING LIST

wood	about 7m of 25 × 75mm
	2.1m of 25 × 50mm
	3.6m of 12 × 25mm
	915 × 915mm chipboard, 12mm thick
	1m of parquet flooring
hardware	20 no.8 countersunk steel screws, 38mm long
	16 finishing nails or panel pins, 25mm long
plus	contact adhesive
	wood filler
	clear polyurethane

Making the frame

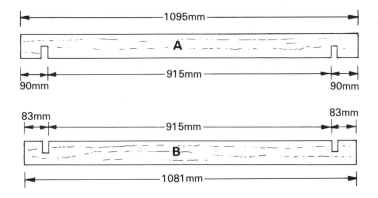

1095mm

A

915mm — 90mm — 90mm

83mm — 915mm — 83mm

B

1081mm

CUTTING LIST

25 × 75mm
- 2 pieces 1095mm long, for rails A
- 2 pieces 1081mm long, for rails B
- 4 pieces 460mm long, for legs

25 × 50mm
- 4 pieces 460mm long, for legs

12 × 25mm
- 4 pieces 860mm long, for battens

As always, make sure to cut the pieces accurately and squarely. Then mark and cut the halving joints on the four rails A and B. The important dimension on both is the 915mm between the joints, leaving just the right space for the chipboard and parquet top. Mark the joints with a try square and marking gauge and be sure to make the saw cuts inside the lines so the joints will be snug. Test each joint with a 25 × 75mm scrap and trim it with a chisel if it's tight.

Before assembling the joints, glue and nail the 12 × 25mm battens to the insides of the rails 25mm from the top edge. Notice on the diagram that the rails are in pairs with the slots facing downwards on one pair A, and upwards on the second pair B.

Next, glue and screw the L-shaped legs together. Each leg is made up of one 25 × 75mm piece and one 25 × 50mm

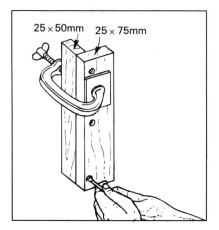

25 × 50mm   25 × 75mm

piece. It is best to counterbore the hole, sinking the screw about 6mm deep and then plugging it. Alternatively, use a matching wood filler to conceal the screw or use a decorative brass screw with a washer.

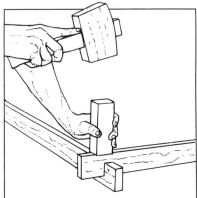

Assemble the frame by slotting the halving joints together. At each corner, clamp rail A to the 25 × 75mm part of the leg while you glue and screw it in place. Hide the screws under plugs or wood filler.

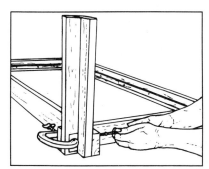

Making the top

Before dropping the chipboard in place on the battens, glue the parquet flooring to it using the same procedure as that used for gluing plastic laminates (page 46). Spread a thin layer of contact adhesive on both surfaces, let them dry and then carefully position the parquet, putting it down in four 457mm sections.

Finally, drop the top onto the battens, trimming the edges with a plane if the fit proves to be too tight.

Then sand the frame and finish the entire table with at least three coats of clear polyurethane. The top looks best with a deep finish so give it even more coats to make it really lustrous.

Glue and nail the 12 × 25mm battens with 25mm pins along the insides of the four rails, 20mm down from the top edge. These will support both the chipboard and the mirror which lies on top. Centre the battens on each of the four rails.

Allow the glue to set on all the pieces, then glue and nail one leg to each end of the long rails, using about three 38mm pins per joint. Make sure the rail and leg are square by checking with a try square.

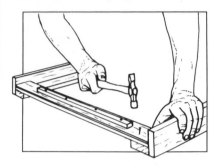

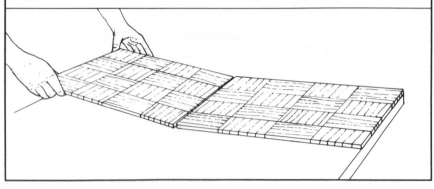

Join these two frames together with the short rails, again gluing and nailing the joints.

Mirror top coffee table

This 500 × 760mm coffee table is easier to make than the parquet flooring design because it doesn't involve cutting halving joints at the corners, and the connections are just glued and nailed. The table top is made by simply laying a mirror onto the chipboard.

Start by gluing and nailing the L-shaped legs together as for the parquet table. Use about four 38mm pins per leg. Then set the nails and fill the holes with a matching filler.

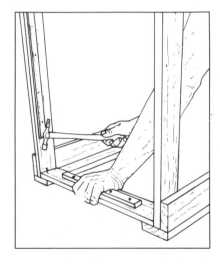

Making the frame

CUTTING LIST
25 × 75mm
   2 pieces 470mm long, for rails
   2 pieces 760mm long, for rails
   8 pieces 460mm long, for legs
12 × 25mm
   2 pieces 500mm long
   2 pieces 300mm long

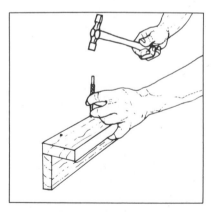

SHOPPING LIST	
softwood	about 6.7m of 25 × 75mm 1.8m of 12 × 25mm
chipboard	500 × 760mm, 12mm thick (cut to exact size after the frame is complete)
hardware	about 40 finishing nails or panel pins, 38mm long 20 finishing nails or panel pins, 25mm long for battens
plus	mirror, 4 or 6mm thick, with rounded edges (cut to exact size after frame is complete) wood filler / wood primer undercoat for black paint black glossy paint

Making the top

Measure the exact inside dimensions between the rails and subtract about 1mm for clearance. Then cut the chipboard precisely to that size. Make sure to cut it square so that it will force the frame square as you drop it in place on the battens. You may want to bevel the chipboard edges slighlty towards the bottom to make it easier to drop it in place. Plane off the edges if necessary to make it fit right. Then subtract about 1mm from the chipboard dimensions and have a glass supplier make up a piece of mirror with rounded edges to this exact size.

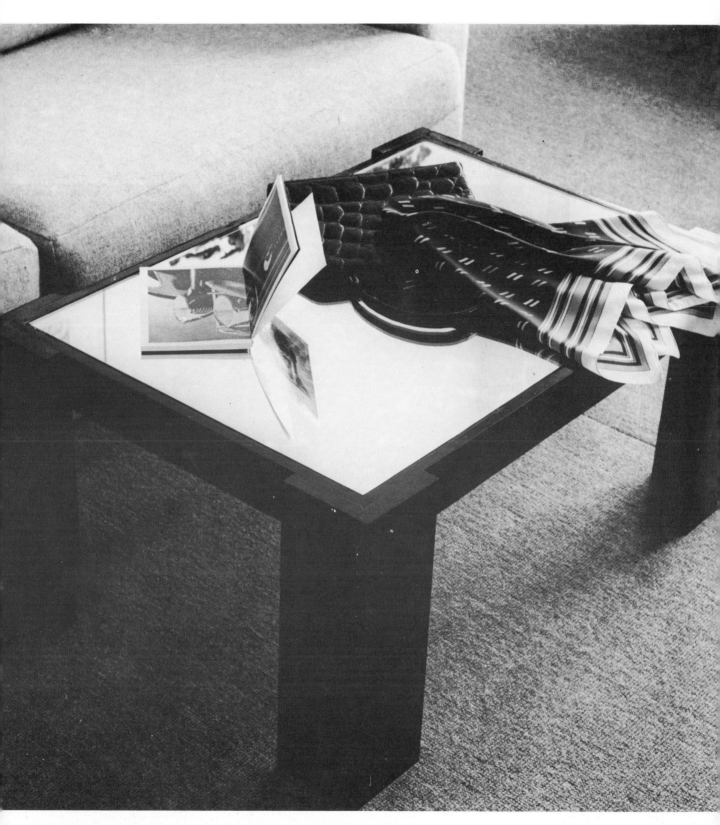

Finishing the table

Carefully set and fill all the nails so that they will not show under the paint, then sand the frame until it is smooth. Round the edges slightly with the sandpaper, particularly along the top edges of the rails. Apply first a primer then an undercoat. Then apply the first coat of glossy black paint. Sand the surface with very fine paper (240 grit) between each coat so that the final surface will be perfectly smooth. Be sure to brush off the sanding dust before applying the next coat.

When the final coat of paint is dry, simply place the chipboard and then the mirror onto the battens and the table is ready for use. If you would rather use glass instead of a mirror and chipboard, it will be necessary to provide a more elegant support for the top such as a few small metal brackets rather than the nailed battens used with the mirror.

SOFA WITH STORAGE

This design is really three pieces of furniture in one. It is a comfortable three-seater sofa, and it is long enough to serve very well as a spare single bed. There is also a useful storage chest underneath with plenty of room for anything from blankets to toys.

It is truly easy to make. Once the pieces are cut out, the assembly shouldn't take more than an afternoon. The construction is straightforward as the sides simply screw into the back and the front, with fibre wall plugs being used in the plywood to give a better grip.

This sofa was made completely out of birch plywood which is an attractive wood that only needs polyurethane varnish to give it a beautiful clear finish. Notice that the ends are made of a triple thickness of plywood. The three layers glued together make an attractive decorative feature out of the thin layers of veneer which make up the plywood.

To make the sofa even more

economical you can just as easily use 19mm chipboard. Paint the finished sofa a bright, glossy colour with perhaps an edging painted a contrasting colour nailed on. Refer to the instructions for details on producing a really perfect finish on chipboard or inexpensive grade plywood.

Another possibility is to turn the project into an upholstered sofa simply by covering the chipboard with a suitable upholstery fabric. To make it softer, first glue 1in foam sheet to the chipboard before wrapping the fabric around it. Secure the fabric with fabric adhesive and upholstery tacks. For instructions to make cushions, see the convertible sofa on page 160.

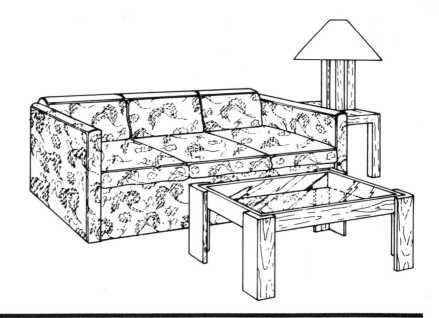

see the convertible sofa on page 160.

SHOPPING LIST

birch plywood	2 standard sheets, 19mm thick
	2 pieces, 725 × 911mm, 10mm thick for seat
	725 × 1825mm, 6.5mm thick for bottom
softwood	about 8.5m of 25 × 25mm
hardware	10 no.12 countersunk steel screws, 75mm long
	10 no.8 countersunk steel screws, 32mm long
	10 no.12 fibre wall plugs, 38mm long
	about 30 finishing nails or panel pins, 32mm long
plus	clear polyurethane or paint

Making the sofa ends

CUTTING LIST
19mm plywood
 6 pieces
 605 × 805mm, for ends A

After cutting up the pieces, make the two ends by gluing three pieces A together for each end. The easiest way to do this is to select carefully the best face and lay it down on the bench or floor with a blanket underneath to protect it from being marked. Then spread a thin, even

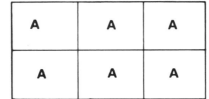

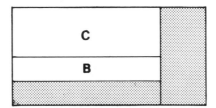

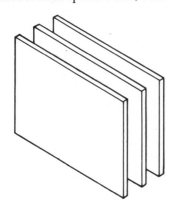

layer of glue over the plywood and lay the next piece on top. The pieces may not be identical so keep two sides, for example the bottom and left-hand edges, lined up and trim the others later.

To help locate the plywood pieces, nail in three or four pins. Then apply glue to the second plywood piece, add the last piece and pin it in place keeping the same edges flush throughout. These few locating pins

placed near the bottom of the sofa end will be hidden later under the seat.

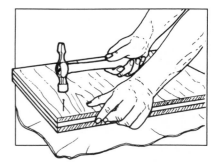

Repeat this procedure to make the other end. Then lay the two ends on top of each other, place heavy weights on top and leave them until the glue sets. Make sure not to put any glue between the two ends; wipe over the two surfaces to ensure that none has accidentally been spilled. Also wipe away any excess glue that oozes out between the layers of plywood. If you have a few clamps, it is also a good idea to clamp the edges to make sure that the glue bonds firmly and evenly.

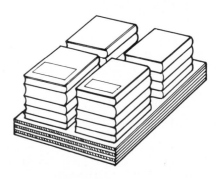

After the glue has set, plane off all the edges to make them smooth and even. A small block plane works very well on plywood end grain. Also, round the corners with a file.

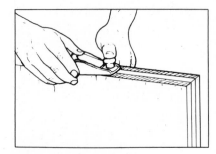

Next mark and drill the five holes on each end for the screws. Use wood plugs to hide the screws. First drill 10mm diameter holes about 20mm deep to take the wood plugs, then drill straight through with a 6mm diameter drill bit. Keep in mind that one end is for the left and the other for the right-hand side of the sofa.

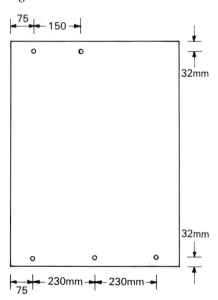

It is important to drill these holes fairly straight so that the screws will go straight into the ends of the front and back pieces.

Assembling the sofa

To assemble the four sides you will need quite a bit of floor space and someone to help you hold the pieces while you work. To make the assembly easier. pin or clamp two pieces of 25 × 25mm to the inside faces of each end, as shown. Leave the pin heads exposed for easy removal later, or if you don't want to leave marks in the plywood clamp the

Preparing the front and back

CUTTING LIST
19mm plywood
1 piece 330 × 1830mm, for front B
1 piece 605 × 1830mm, for back C
25 × 25mm softwood
4 pieces 1800mm long

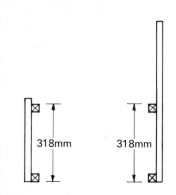

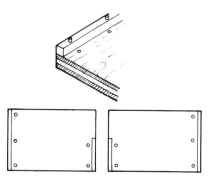

25 × 25mm pieces to the ends. Then pin the front A and the back B to these battens from the inside to hold them temporarily in place.

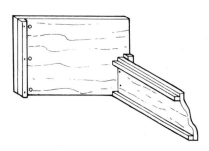

With all four pieces held together in this way, drill straight through the holes into the ends of the front and

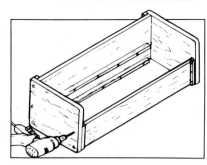

The lift-up seat and the bottom will simply rest on battens which are attached to the insides of the front B and the back C. Mark the locations of the battens, measuring from the bottom edge, then glue and pin them in place. Reinforce the top battens, which will hold the seat, with five 32mm long no.8 screws per batten.

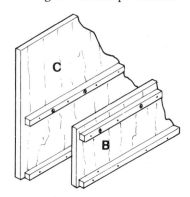

back with the same 6mm diameter drill bit. The drill bit should penetrate about 40mm into the ends.

Now push the fibre wall plugs into the holes. Make sure to push them to the ends of the hole. Then insert the 75mm screws and give them a light tap with a hammer before screwing tight.

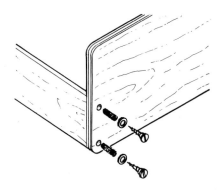

Fit a wood plug into the 10mm hole to hide the screw. These can be made from two pieces of dowel as a

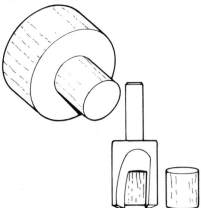

decorative feature or simply cut with a plug cutter to be glued flush with the surface.

Another interesting possibility is to attach the sides to the front and back using threaded dowels made with a special tool called a screwbox and tap, described on page 205. The screwbox makes threads on dowels 12 or 19mm diameter and the tap makes matching threaded holes in wood to take the dowel. You could, for example, glue the end of the threaded dowel into a block of wood cut into a hexagonal shape to look like a bolt head.

Before placing the seat and bottom on the battens, drill four finger holes about 25mm diameter in the bottom piece, one near each corner. Also drill two holes near the front edge of each of the seats as finger holes to make it easier to lift up to get into the storage compartment.

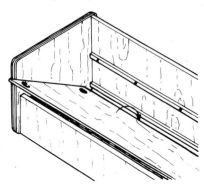

Now lay the bottom piece onto the lower battens. Then lay the two seat pieces on the top battens. The seat can just rest on the battens but, if you wish, you can attach butt hinges along the back edges to make it easier to open and close the storage compartment.

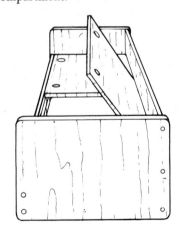

Finishing the sofa

For a clear finish on birch plywood, apply two or three coats of polyurethane to the well-sanded plywood. When sanding, pay particular attention to the thick edges of the two ends. It is especially nice when exposed end grain like this is very smooth to the touch, so, sand the ends first with rough, then medium and finally with very fine sandpaper.

To make a sofa with a darker finish, the birch plywood can be stained in a wood tone such as mahogany or oak before the polyurethane is applied. If you used chipboard or an inexpensive grade of plywood, apply a fine layer of filler overall to fill the grain and allow it to dry. Then sand smooth and apply two coats of paint over a sealer. This will result in a really smooth and professional finish to even the roughest boards.

Making the cushions

You can easily make soft cushions such as these filled with kapok or less expensive foam chips. Make each seat cushion 610 × 725 × 125mm thick and the back cushions 610 × 250 × 125mm.

The cushions can be made with inexpensive firm cotton fabric, machine stitched around three sides with one end left open for stuffing. Before filling the pillows, turn them to the right side and then fill with foam chips or kapok making the cushion firm but not overfull. Close the opening by oversewing by hand.

Use furnishing fabric to suit your decor when making the cushion covers. These have a zipper along the back seam so that they can be removed for washing or dry cleaning.

DUAL HEIGHT TABLE

In small city apartments there often isn't enough space for both a dining table and a coffee table. This table is designed to serve both functions. It takes only an instant to convert this handsome design from a coffee table with a general shelf space underneath into a dining table of full height which can seat four people

comfortably. All you have to do is remove the top, stand the under frame upright and replace the top, locating the under frame against battens screwed to the underside of the table top.

The table is basically very simple in design and construction, but for its dual role to work successfully it must be accurately made. Drilling precise holes in the large dowels is quite difficult without a drill stand so, if possible, buy or borrow one for this job. Alternatively use 50 × 50mm softwood for the legs instead of dowels. These are easier to drill accurately since they will lie flat on the bench.

Making the frame

Before making the frame, prepare the 19mm top and the 12mm plywood shelf by sanding them and staining both sides blue or any other bright colour.

CUTTING LIST
45mm dowel
   4 pieces 460mm long, legs A
25mm dowel
   4 pieces 638mm long, struts B
   2 pieces 890mm long, surround C
38 × 38mm
   2 pieces 460mm long, holding jig

The first step is the most difficult. The two holes in the large dowels A

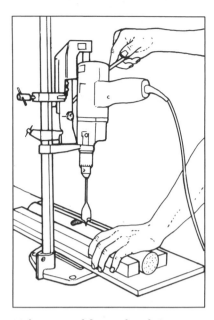

SHOPPING LIST

birch plywood	815 × 1145mm, 19mm thick for top 610 × 915mm, 12mm thick for shelf (this piece *must* be square and accurate) about 150 × 460mm 12 or 19mm thick for holding jig
dowel	10m of 25mm diameter 2.1m of 45mm diameter for legs (or use 50 × 50mm softwood)
softwood	5m of 38 × 38mm
hardware	18 no.10 countersunk steel screws, 45mm long 6 no.8 countersunk brass screws, 50mm long 8 no.8 countersunk brass screws, 38mm long 14 no.8 brass screw cup washers 20 finishing nails or panel pins, 38mm long
plus	blue stain clear polyurethane

must be drilled accurately so that they are parallel and so the frame will be square when it is put together.

To make it easier, make up a holder out of a piece of plywood, about 150 × 460mm and two pieces of 38 × 38mm batten about 460mm long. Glue and nail the first batten to the plywood then use one of the legs A as a spacer to nail the second batten.

For each leg A, mark the centre of the dowel, then mark the hole

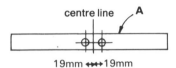

centres 19mm on either side of the centre line so that they are 38mm apart. Centre punch both holes and with the dowel in the holder, drill the two 1in diameter holes. Set the depth stop so that the holes are exactly 22mm deep. Drill two holes in each of the four legs A in the same way.

Make two end frames by gluing a pair of struts B, to a pair of legs A. If they are loose, wrap paper around the ends to ensure that it is a tight fit. Make sure that the two legs are parallel by measuring the distance

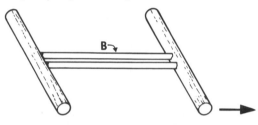

between them at both ends, and also make sure the struts are as far as they will go into their holes.

Now mark and drill another 25mm diameter hole, 22mm deep into each leg.

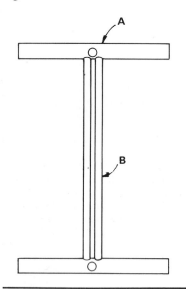

These should be located exactly in the centre as shown. Again, use the drill stand to ensure that the drilling is accurate and square.

Put one end frame on the floor and glue the two 1in dowels C into the drilled holes. Then, before sliding the stained 12mm plywood shelf in place, make a cut-out in each corner with a coping saw.

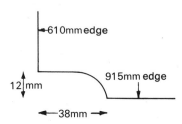

Drop the shelf in place between the two struts and glue the top end frame to the two dowels C. Before the glue sets, screw the plywood shelf in place with three 50mm long no.8 brass screws and screw cup washers

through the struts B at each end, and four 38mm long no.8 brass screws and screw cup washers through the two dowels C.

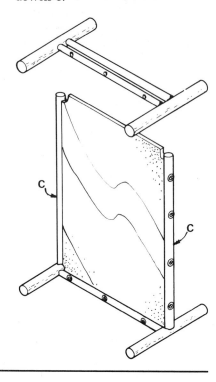

Making the top

CUTTING LIST
25mm dowel
  2 pieces 1220mm long D
  2 pieces 915mm long E
38 × 38mm battens
  2 pieces 685mm long F
  2 pieces 1000mm long G
  4 pieces 100mm long H

Lay the 19mm top face down on a blanket so that the surface will not be scratched while you are working with it. Glue and screw one short batten F 70mm in from one end with an equal space on either side, using three 45mm screws. Then stand the frame on the plywood with two of the legs A butting against the batten. To locate the other three battens, mark around the other pair of legs, then glue and screw the other battens in place so that the battens hold the four legs in a rectangle as shown.

Turn the frame over so that the legs now lie on the plywood against the battens. Measure in from

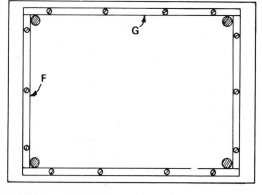

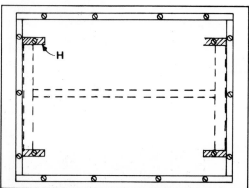

both edges to make sure the dowels are located centrally in the frame. Then mark the locations for the four blocks H, which when screwed down will serve to locate the legs when the table is used at dining height.

Now stand the table up with the top in place and attach the 25mm dowel edging D and E to the top, mitring the corners carefully. Glue and nail the edging to the plywood edge with the 38mm pins, punching the pins below the surface.

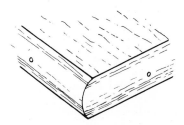

Finishing the table

Fill the holes left by the pins around the edging, using light wood filler. Be sure to let the filler dry completely and then sand the edges smooth. Apply two coats of clear polyurethane over the whole of the table – the blue-stained surfaces as well as the unfinished dowels.

Applying clear polyurethane on top of a stained surface gives a particularly lustrous final finish. Make the final coat of polyurethane matt if you don't want the surface to be too shiny.

OAK CORNER CUPBOARD

The corner cupboard is a wonderful piece of furniture which provides storage and display space without taking up too much room. As here, the door can have a glass panel to show off china or silver or it can be of solid wood, to enclose a cocktail cabinet for example.

This cupboard is made from oak veneered chipboard with matching iron-on edging. It may be necessary to go to a large supplier to find oak chipboard, but if you have trouble buying it, you can use oak veneered shelving panels which are widely available in several widths. Remember to buy sheets with oak veneer on both faces. Sheets are often sold with the 'good' face in oak and a balancer of mahogany on the other side.

Alternatively you can use a good grade of plywood to make the cupboard and stain it oak or another suitable shade.

Making the cupboard

CUTTING LIST
oak veneered chipboard
   1 piece 610 × 610mm,
   for top A and base B
   1 piece 610 × 610mm,
   for shelves C
   1 piece 510 × 800mm,
   for back D
   1 piece 491 × 800mm,
   for back E
   2 pieces 95 × 800mm,
   for side panels F
   2 pieces 65 × 815mm,
   for door sides G (to be trimmed)
   2 pieces 65 × 610mm,
   for door stiles H (to be trimmed)

Follow the cutting list in marking out the pieces. Remember when you are cutting the pieces first to score the veneer along the cutting line to prevent it from breaking out when sawing. Fit a new blade in a trimming knife and score the veneer in two or three light strokes along a metal straight edge. Then saw along the side of the scored line. If you use a hand saw or a sabre saw, it is best to saw about 1mm away from the line and then finish off by planing.

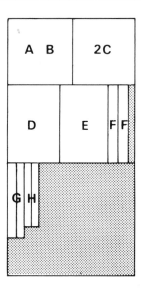

The best procedure to follow is to iron the veneer edging onto each piece in turn before you join the pieces together, omitting any edges which will be hidden.

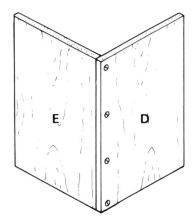

Start by joining the two backs D and E. Glue and screw them together using the 38mm long screws.

Prepare the two side panels F by sawing or planing off one long side so that the edge forms a 45° angle. To do this by hand, draw the 45° angle on each end, then draw the line along the side as a guide line for planing.

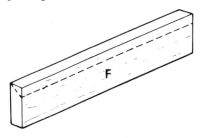

Since you are dealing with triangular-shaped pieces it is rather difficult to cut the shapes absolutely correctly. To make it easier to get the top and bottom and the two shelves identical, make a template out of cardboard. Place the joined back pieces D and E on a piece of cardboard or paper and use a try square to make sure they form a 90° angle. Hold them firmly in place while you trace along the inside edges (lines X) on the cardboard. Then hold the side panels F in place

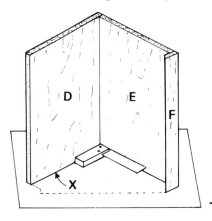

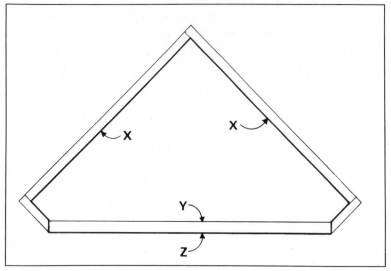

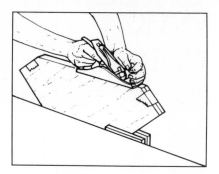

are the same. The top and base are easy to locate since they are flush with the sides but, before attaching the shelves, measure and mark the spaces along the inside of the backs D and E using a try square. Draw lines 19mm apart to give an exact location for the shelves.

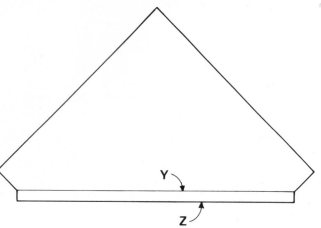

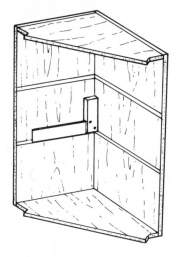

one at a time as shown and trace the insides of those as well. Finally take away the pieces and draw lines Y and Z.

The top and bottom pieces A and B are larger than the shelves C so first cut out the template along lines X and Z. Then use this template to trace two outlines on the 610 × 610mm piece for the top A and base B.

Cut the template along line Y and trace this shape on the other 610 × 610mm piece for the two shelves C.

All this template cutting and tracing sounds complicated but it is really the simplest way to get the shapes right. Triangular pieces are always tricky to cut so by getting the shapes directly from the cabinet you shouldn't go wrong.

Score the veneer along the pencilled cutting lines and then cut out the four pieces. To make the two pairs identical, hold them in pairs in a vice and plane the edges until both pieces

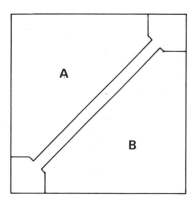

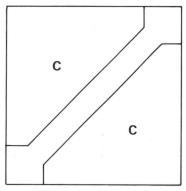

Glue and screw first the top and bottom and then the two shelves in place. Notice the two C clamps which hold the shelf in position.

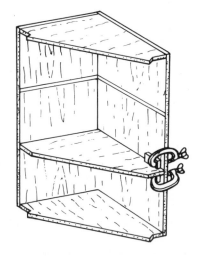

It is useful to drill the screw clearance holes for the shelves from the inside through the backs before the shelves are added so that you can centre the holes between the

lines. To finish the assembly, attach the side panels F by dowel jointing them to the main frame with six 25mm long dowels per side (page 232).

the pieces G and H to the exact size before dowel jointing them with 10mm diameter dowels, 50mm long to make the door frame. The door on this cupboard was mitred at the corners and then dowel jointed but this is much more difficult than a straight butt joint.

Before fitting the door, glue and pin 6 × 10mm stripping along the back edge of the door opening so that the strip just overhangs.

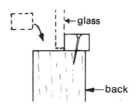

Screw the continuous hinge to the door. Then hang the door in place by screwing the other side of the hinge to the frame.

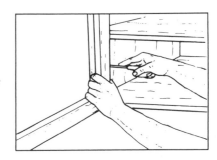

Finally buy a piece of glass to fit inside this frame, and after finishing, install the glass, holding it in place with 6 × 10mm stripping.

Making the door

Measure the opening and make the door to fit it, subtracting 3mm along the width for the hinge and 1.5mm along the height for clearance.

Then follow these dimensions to cut

Finishing the cupboard

Finish the cupboard by leaving it natural or by giving it a coat of oak stain to make it look antique. In either case, seal the surface with two or three coats of clear polyurethane.

Finally add the door pull and the two mirror brackets, and hang the cupboard in a corner, fixing a batten to the wall underneath for additional support if it is to hold a heavy weight like china, bottles or metal ornaments.

FLOOR LAMP

This elegant floor lamp, similar in design to the table lamp, consists simply of six dowels glued together and screwed to a plywood base. The thin electrical wire just fits into the space between the three large dowels. The larger the dowel you use, the easier it will be to pull the wire through the hole. Use a minimum diameter of 32mm dowel.

SHOPPING LIST

wood	three 1.2m lengths of 32mm diameter dowel
	three 1.2m lengths of 6mm diameter dowel
	300 × 300mm piece of plywood, 19mm thick
hardware	3 no.10 countersunk steel screws, 57mm long
	3 no.10 fibre wall plugs, 38mm long
plus	3m of fine electrical wire
	bulb holder and small switch
	contact adhesive / dark brown matt paint

To make the floor lamp

Glue the three large dowels together, tying them tightly with tape or string until the glue sets. Be careful not to use too much glue as it may block the central hole through which the electric wire will run.

Cut out the base from 19mm plywood. You can cut the base into a shape as shown or, if you prefer, just leave the shape square and round the corners slightly with a rasp or Surform.

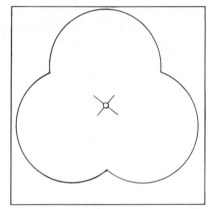

Drill a 12mm diameter hole in the centre to allow the electric wire to be threaded through.

Hold the dowels in a vice and pin the base onto them, then drill three 5mm diameter holes through the base, one into the end of each dowel. Drill deep enough so that you can insert the 38mm long fibre wall plugs into the dowels, then screw the no.10 screws in tightly.

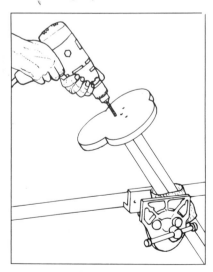

Paint the dowels and the base with two coats of dark, matt brown paint. Then, when the paint is dry, glue the natural coloured 6mm diameter dowels in place using contact adhesive.

Cut three small pieces from the waste plywood and glue them under the base to serve as feet. They don't have to be perfect circles; three small disks will give the base stability and provide a space for the wire which has to run from the lamp to an electric socket.

Finally attach the electric fittings. First pass the wire through the centre of the dowels, using a piece of sturdy wire to pull it through if necessary. Then connect the wires and screw the bulb holder to the tops of the dowels, attach the switch and connect the plug.

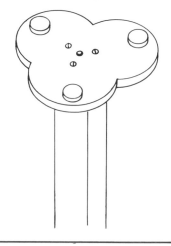

TABLE LAMP

This lamp is made from black walnut and maple. If you don't have access to these planed hardwoods, use a softwood, preferably pine, and colour all but the thin strips with several coats of a dark stain.

Start by cutting the 6 × 50mm section into two 1.4m lengths. Then glue these to the length of 25 × 50mm, one on either side. It helps to pin them in a few places to keep them from slipping while you clamp them.

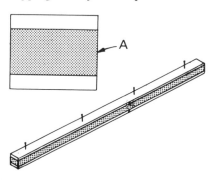

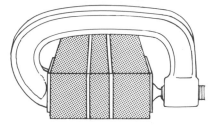

After the glue has set, cut the resulting section into four pieces each exactly 300mm long A. Then glue one of these between two pieces of 50 × 50mm. Make two of these sandwich constructions B. Finally glue the other two pieces A between these two B pieces, pinning and then clamping them together.

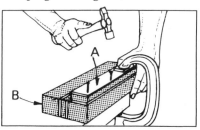

Trim the ends square, plane and sand the lamp base and, before connecting the wiring, finish with polyurethane. Cut a groove in the

SHOPPING LIST	
wood	4 pieces 50 × 50mm dark wood, 300mm long 1.4m of 25 × 50mm dark wood 3m of 6 × 50mm light wood
hardware	about 30 finishing nails or panel pins, 19mm long about 10 finishing nails or panel pins, 38mm long
plus	2.5m of electrical wire bulb holder and small switch lampshade clear polyurethane piece of felt for base

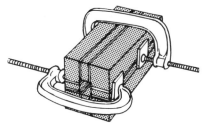

bottom as a channel for the wire. Glue on a piece of felt and finally fit the bulb and shade.

CONVERTIBLE SOFA

This delightful sofa design is just nailed together. It is designed to be a generous three seater that you can turn into a full sized double bed in seconds. You simply pull out the front panel and spread out the seat cushion which unfolds to become a 1370mm wide mattress. The main frame is made up of five flat panels, the two ends, front and back and the slat unit which supports the mattress. If you don't want to spend the time cutting and nailing all the diagonal slats – there are about 70 of them – you can make the four sides out of plywood or even chipboard, like the sofa on page 148. You can also simplify the job slightly by positioning the slats vertically or horizontally rather than diagonally. You should be able to make this good looking and versatile sofa over a single weekend.

The doubled-over mattress is made from two pieces of 75mm thick foam. The five back cushions should be filled with foam chips, kapok or feathers so that they will be rounded and soften the look of the sofa. Check the telephone book for specialist firms which make cushions to order. Choose a hard wearing furnishing fabric for the cushion covers. Bright basic colours like green, orange and red contrast attractively with the natural shade of the wood, but your choice will of course depend on your decorating scheme.

of the frames. The slats are attached at a 45° angle; however, the angle is not crucial so long as you attach all the slats parallel to each other and evenly spaced out across the frame.

Start by measuring one of the centre diagonal slats. Mark it so that it will overhang the frame by about 50mm at each end. Then cut it to length and glue and nail it to the frame using two 32mm pins per end, nailed from the frame side. Use a try square to check that the frame is kept square as you glue and nail the first slat in place. Notice that you nail through the 25 × 50mm frame into the slat, so that the nail heads will be hidden later by the cushions.

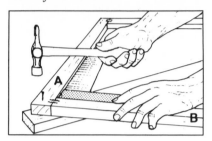

Continue with the rest of the slats, measuring and cutting them to length and then gluing and nailing them in position. Leave a narrow, evenly spaced gap between the slats.

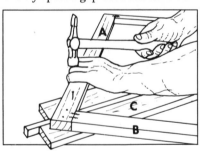

Making the sofa ends

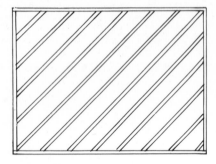
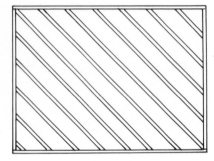

CUTTING LIST
25 × 50mm
    4 pieces 865mm long, A
    for end frames
    4 pieces 595mm long, B
    for end frames
19 × 75mm
    about 23m cut into slats
    as required C
19 × 50mm
    4 pieces 965mm long, for
    top and bottom edging
    strips D (to be trimmed)
    4 pieces 710mm long, for
    upright edging strips E
    (to be trimmed)

Start by making the two 25 × 50mm frames for the ends. Use two A and two B pieces for each frame, connecting the corners by nailing in two corrugated fasteners at each

corner (page 224). The frame does not have to be very rigid at this point as the slats, once they have been attached, will hold if firmly together.

The next step is to cut the 19 × 75mm slats C and nail them onto each one

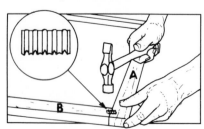

SHOPPING LIST

softwood	2.1m of 25 × 150mm / about 50m of 25 × 50mm
	55m of 19 × 75mm / 17m of 19 × 50mm / 2.5m of 19 × 25mm
	1m of 12mm wide stripping for spacer
hardware	4 no.10 countersunk steel screws, 38mm long
	12 no.10 countersunk steel screws, 32mm long
	6 no.10 countersunk brass screws, 65mm long
	about 400 finishing nails or panel pins, 32mm long
	about 75 oval wire nails, 38mm long
	32 corrugated fasteners, 50mm long
	3 metal L-brackets with 12mm screws
plus	wood filler / clear polyurethane
	2 pieces medium density foam, 685 × 1905mm
	for seat/mattress, 75mm thick
	filling for five pillows, three 460 × 635mm
	and two 305 × 635mm, all 150mm thick
	firm cotton fabric for pillow linings
	about 10m upholstery fabric, 1375mm wide for cushion/mattress covers
	zippers or snaps for cushion covers

Use a 12mm wide batten 1m long as a spacer between the slats to ensure that they are an even distance apart. If the amount of space left over for the last few slats is a little larger, space the slats out evenly by eye.

After you have filled the whole side frame, including the small corner pieces, trim the slats flush with the frame using a circular or panel saw.

It is best first to clamp a straight board on top of the frame as a guide

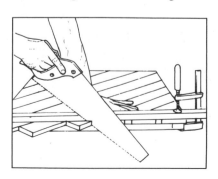

for the saw so that you make a perfectly straight cut. If you use a circular saw, it will be essential to clamp a straight edge to the top as a guide for the saw, as shown.

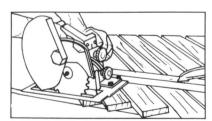

After trimming the edges, it will probably be necessary to run over them with a plane to make them even and smooth. Next glue and pin the 19 × 50mm edging to all four sides of the frame. Start by trimming the two upright edging strips E to the exact height of the finished end panel. Glue and pin these in place, then trim the two long pieces D to length and glue and pin them to the top and bottom.

Use five or six 32mm long pins for each edge. Set the heads with a nail punch and fill the holes carefully before sanding the surface smooth. You can round off the edges of the frame slightly with sandpaper or a file or bevel the edges with a block plane to make the sofa arms smooth to the touch.

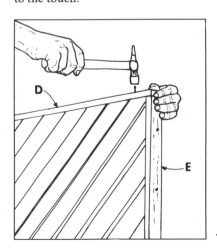

161

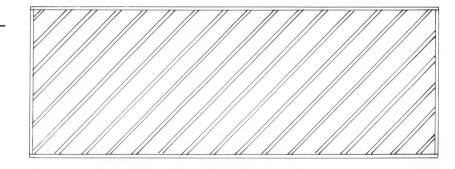

Making the front and back of the sofa

CUTTING LIST
25 × 50mm
   2 pieces 1880mm long F,
   for back frame
   2 pieces 1875mm long G,
   for front frame
   2 pieces 595mm long H,
   for back frame
   2 pieces 160mm long I,
   for front frame
19 × 75mm
   about 30m cut into slats
   as required J
19 × 50mm
   3 pieces 1930mm long K
   (to be trimmed)
   2 pieces 710mm long L
   (to be trimmed)
   2 pieces 330mm long M
   (to be trimmed)
19 × 25mm
   1 piece 1930mm long N
   (to be trimmed)

Make the front and back panels of
the sofa in exactly the same way as
the ends, by first joining the large
685 × 1905mm back frame with two F and
two H, 25 × 50mm pieces and then the
small 260 × 1900mm front frame with
two G and two I, 25 × 50mm pieces.
Notice that the front frame is 5mm
shorter than the back so that it can be
moved in and out easily when the sofa is
being converted to a bed.

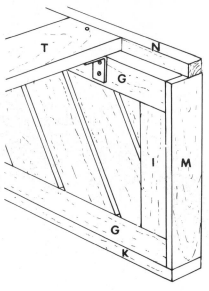

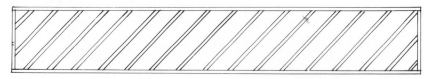

Cut and attach the diagonal slats J,
using a batten as a spacer to arrange
the slats evenly on the framework as
before. Also attach the 19 × 50mm
edging strips. Notice that the top
edge of the small front frame is a
19 × 25mm N piece and not the usual
19 × 50mm. This is to allow the bed
slats to sit on top of the frame behind
the narrow 19 × 25mm edging.

You will need a lot of space for the
next stage of the project so, before
continuing, clear a large work area.
Referring to the drawings below, then
temporarily assemble the back and
two ends by clamping or nailing
them together.

Attaching the bearers for the slat bottom

CUTTING LIST
25 × 150mm
   1 piece 1950mm long O
25 × 50mm
   1 piece 1790 long P
   (to be trimmed)
   2 pieces 815mm long Q
   (to be trimmed)

Remove the front panel then start by
screwing the 25 × 150mm piece O
along the front so that the top edge is

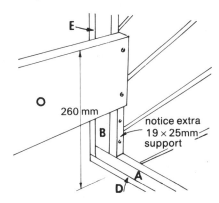

Making the slat base

CUTTING LIST
25 × 50mm
1 piece 1945mm long R
16 pieces 815mm long S
17 pieces 635mm long T

Start by gluing and nailing slats T to piece R. Position the slats by using a scrap of 19 × 75mm as a spacer so that the gap between each slat is about 70mm wide.

Place the first and last slats 25mm from the ends of R and attach them with the 38mm oval wire nails – spread the glue then use one nail in each end. You should now have seventeen pieces of 25 × 50mm attached at one end to piece R. The other ends of the slats will be attached next.

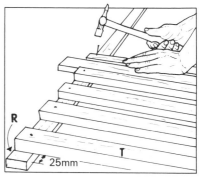

Then gently carry this assembly over to the sofa and position it so that the ends of the back piece R rest on the end supports Q, which have been screwed to the sides.

Place the short front panel of the sofa so that the other end of the seventeen slats T rests on the 25 × 50mm piece G behind the 19 × 25mm strip nailed on earlier.

exactly 260mm from the floor. Secure it to the inside edge of the end frame uprights B with two 38mm no. 10 screws per end. Notice that a short piece of 19 × 25mm pinned in place beneath the 25 × 150mm helps to position and support it.

Trim to length and then glue and

screw the 25 × 50mm slat bearers P and Q to the two sides and back. These will support the bottom slat structure. Screw the long piece P to the back diagonal slats with five 32mm no.10 screws so that the top edge is exactly 260mm from the floor. Attach the end supports Q 240mm off the floor with three 32mm screws each.

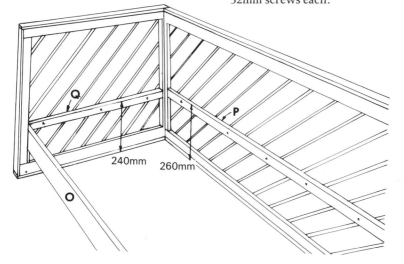

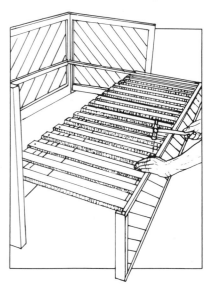

The slat assembly should now be positioned so that it can be pulled out easily. It may be necessary to re-position the outside slats slightly if they rub on the sides as you pull out the front.

Now screw three metal brackets underneath, one at each end and one in the centre. Screw them to the slats T and to the frame G as shown earlier to keep the front rigidly attached to the slats.

This is the first stage in making the slatted base which forms the convertible part of the sofa. Notice that by lifting the front slightly you can slide the slatted base structure in and out quite easily.

Pull the front out to get inside the sofa and then glue and nail the longer slats S in place between the short slats T, using one 38mm nail per end. Glue and nail the back ends to the bearer P and the front ends to the 25 × 150mm piece O. Space them out so that they are parallel to the short slats T, with equal spaces between them to allow the short slats to move smoothly back and forth without rubbing.

Assembling and finishing the sofa

To fix the sofa ends rigidly to the back, drill three holes through the end frames into each end of the back frame and insert three 65mm no.10 brass screws in each end.

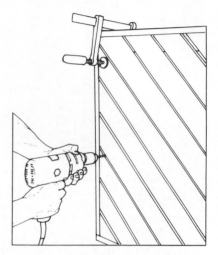

Sand off all marks and scratches and set the nail heads. Then carefully fill all the nail holes with wood filler, sanding them smooth when dry.

You can leave the wood unfinished, or, for a more durable surface which is easier to wipe clean, apply a couple of coats of thinned clear polyurethane finishing with a matt coat. Alternatively you can paint the wood any colour after first applying a coat of sealer, or you could stain the sofa in a darker wood tone to match your other furniture.

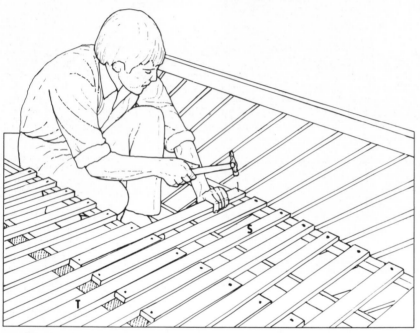

Making the cushions

The sofa seat unfolds to become the mattress and is made up of two layers of 75mm thick foam, so the seat is 150mm thick and measures 685 × 1905mm. When it is folded out, it becomes a standard double sized mattress 75mm thick and measuring 1370 × 1905mm.

A specialist store is probably the best place to buy the foam as it will have the facilities for cutting the foam exactly to the required size. You can usually find a supplier in the telephone book.

The sofa has five back cushions: two 305 × 635mm cushions, 150mm thick for the sides and three 460 × 635mm cushions, 150mm thick for the back. Soft, round, well-filled cushions look especially attractive because of the way they contrast with the simple,

straight lines of the ends of the sofa. So instead of using foam blocks for the cushions, sew a cotton lining for each cushion and fill it either with foam chips or with kapok.

Alternatively, to make the sofa really luxurious, you can use feather filled cushions. You will probably have to have cushions like these made up to size by a specialist supplier.

The cushion covers should be fastened with a zipper, buttons or snaps along one edge for easy removal when you want to clean them. You could also use decorative piping along the edges of the cushion covers as an attractive contrast with the main fabric, particularly if you decide to use unpatterned fabric for the cushions.

The pieces of foam used for the

seat/mattress do not need a lining. Just make up two large cushion covers to size and connect them along the long front edge so that you can unfold the double thickness to convert the seat into a mattress.

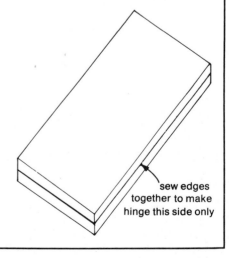

sew edges together to make hinge this side only

PLYWOOD END GRAIN COFFEE TABLES

The effect of cutting plywood into strips and then gluing all the strips together on edge is stunning. It is hard to believe that it is really plywood. These instructions are for a luxurious coffee table 1.22m square, but the instructions can just as easily be adapted to make a rectangular coffee table measuring 600 × 1220mm. The alternative table shown here has turned beech legs attached with metal brackets.

Preparing the plywood

Cutting plywood strips accurately should ideally be done on a table saw (page 210). It can also be done with a portable circular saw with a rip fence (page 208), using a fine blade.

CUTTING LIST
19mm plywood
    64 strips 50 × 1220mm A
    8 strips 125 × 1220mm, for legs B
    (to be divided)
    4 strips 75 × 1170mm, for rails C

Making the top

The 64 strips A have to be glued together to make up the top. It is best to divide the work up into eight sections each containing eight strips, which makes it easier to handle.

Apply glue to each strip in turn and spread it with a brush in a thin even layer. Then pin the strip to its neighbour with six pins, keeping the edges lined up. Glue and pin one strip at a time. Finish one eight piece section, put it aside and begin on the next section.

Be very careful to line up the top and edges of the strips exactly. The more even you make the surface at this stage, the less sanding you will have to do later.

If possible, use clamps to hold the eight pieces together until the glue sets. Clamping isn't absolutely essential however, as the pins should hold the sections firmly enough. Remember to clean off the excess

glue with a damp rag before it sets. After the glue has set, lightly plane off the surface of each 150mm section.

After planing off all eight sections, glue them together to make the table top. Use bar clamps, again making sure that the top edges line up.

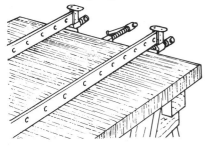

Making the legs and rails

Cut the eight 125mm strips B into 32 lengths, each 300mm long. Use eight of these pieces per leg. Glue and pin as for the top, but remember not to pin the last piece so that no nail heads will show on the outside. Instead, clamp the last piece on to hold it until the glue sets. After the glue has set, plane and sand until the legs are smooth.

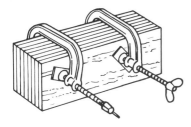

The rails C are quite easy to make. Simply notch the four identical pieces as shown so that they slot together snugly. Mark out the width of each notch using a scrap of plywood. Saw on the waste side of the line and then chisel out the waste to the marked line.

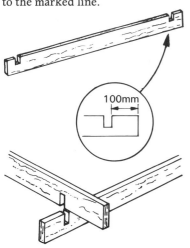

100mm

SHOPPING LIST *to make a table 1.22m square*

birch plywood	2 standard sheets, 19mm thick
hardware	16 no.10 countersunk steel screws, 50mm long 12 no.8 round head steel screws, 25mm long 12 no.8 fibre wall plugs, 25mm long 12 metal shrinkage brackets 24 no.8 round head screws, 12mm long for brackets about 400 finishing nails or panel pins, 32mm long
plus	wood filler clear polyurethane

Assembling the table

First trim the edges of the top with a circular saw then round the edges and corners with a file, sabre saw or router. Make up the leg and rail assembly. Slot the rails together, then screw them to the legs with the 50mm screws, using two per rail end.

Screw the metal shrinkage brackets to the rails, three per rail, with two 12mm screws per bracket.

Finally, place the top upside down on the bench or floor putting a blanket underneath to protect the surface and attach the rails and legs with the 25mm screws.

Since the screws don't hold well in the end grain of the plywood, first fit a fibre wall plug into the plywood and then insert the screw.

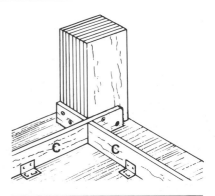

Finishing

Sand thoroughly with a belt sander to get a good, smooth finish. Then rub in a clear filler (page 248) to seal the grain before applying four or five coats of clear polyurethane, rubbing with fine sandpaper or steel wool between coats.

VENEER LAMPSHADES

Both these lampshades are made from Oregon pine veneer, available in strips of varying width and length. Most veneer merchants who advertise in the telephone book sell Oregon pine. If you have trouble finding it, use any other light coloured veneer, preferably with a grain pattern to make the lamps more interesting. There are also mail order firms which sell various tools and supplies and a good selection of veneers. These companies are listed in hobby or woodworking magazines.

Round lampshade

Cutting the veneer strips

Lay the lengths of veneer on a cutting surface, such as a piece of hardboard, plywood or another piece of scrap sheet material, so that you do not score the top of the workbench. Then measure and cut the six strips with a sharp knife against a steel ruler. The secret of success is to score the veneer with a couple of light strokes first, then cut through firmly.

After cutting all the pieces to length, trim them so that they are all exactly 150mm wide.

Assembling the lampshade

With a coping saw, cut two plywood disks 190mm in diameter. Drill a 12mm

SHOPPING LIST	
Oregon pine veneer	about 10m of 150mm wide, cut into 3 strips 1.5m long A and 3 strips 1.3m long B
plywood	200 × 400mm, 6.5mm thick
plus	contact adhesive / bulb holder with electric wire

hole in the centre of one and in the other cut a 125mm diameter hole. These will form the top and bottom of the lampshade respectively.

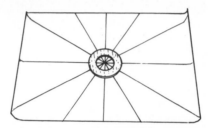

Lay the second disk in the centre of a piece of paper or cardboard on which you have drawn six lines 30° apart, as a guide for the strips.

Start with the three short strips B. Glue the first strip to the disk and then glue each in turn on top of the last, so that the strips are centred along every other line. Spread contact adhesive on both surfaces and allow it to become dry to the touch before bringing the pieces together carefully and pressing down firmly.

After gluing down the three short pieces B, continue with the three long pieces A, gluing each along the lines between two short pieces.

Turn the whole assembly over and, before gluing to the top disk, cut through the veneers around the 125mm

hole to make a hole in the base so that you can change the bulb.

Cut through the veneer carefully with a sharp trimming knife, and then sand around the edges of the hole using fine sandpaper to make the opening smooth and even.

For the next stage of the work, bend and glue all the lengths to the top plywood disk. Glue each end in turn, holding the underside of the disk with one hand while you press the end of the veneer strip down firmly with the other. The strips should be glued down in the same order as before, first the three short lengths and then the three long lengths.

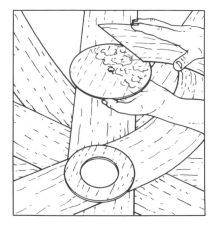

To hold the lampshade firmly while gluing the last two ends, put your hand through the hole in the bottom.

If you have any difficulty in getting the last few strips to stay glued down, it may be necessary to put in a few staples or nail in a few small pins to secure them.

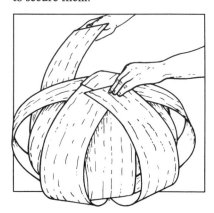

Finally, cut through the layers of veneer to make the 12mm hole in the top of the lampshade. Then push the electric wire through this hole and connect the bulb holder. After attaching the holder and putting in the bulb, simply let the lampshade hang from the bulb holder.

Slot together lampshade

Make this attractive, slot together shade out of the same Oregon pine or any similar veneer. If possible, buy a thick grade of veneer, but if this is not available, buy twice as much and glue two pieces together with contact adhesive.

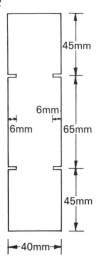

Cut 60 pieces of veneer 40 × 155mm, then cut four slots 6mm deep in each piece with a tenon saw. To make this easier, make a template by cutting slots in two pieces of 4mm plywood, 40 × 155mm as shown. Then sandwich

SHOPPING LIST	
Oregon pine veneer	about 3m of thick veneer, 150mm wide (or 6m of thin veneer)
plywood	155 × 155mm, 4mm thick
plus	bulb holder with electric wire

ten to fifteen strips of veneer between the plywood templates in a vice and use the slots in the plywood as a guide for sawing.

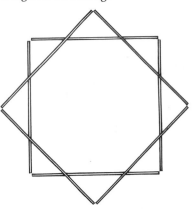

Slot the pieces together so that each 155mm square is diagonally above the next. Add a dab of glue to each joint as you go along.

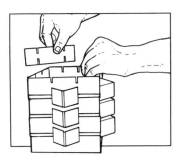

To support the bulb holder, slot a 155mm square of 4mm plywood between layers near the top and drill a 12mm hole for the wire.

OUTDOOR PROJECTS

The selection of outdoor furniture in this final projects section includes a good looking, fold-down picnic table and benches to make in weather resistant teak or cedar, an outdoor lounge chair that folds down for sun bathing, a barbecue trolley handsome enough to use as a serving cart in the dining room and planters to be used indoors or out.

Picnic bench

Parquet planter

Barbecue trolley, picnic table and benches

Outdoor lounge seat

Barbecue trolley

Slat plant stand

Bench planter

Pine plant container

Outdoor lounge seat

PICNIC TABLE AND BENCHES

This luxurious picnic table measures a full 915 × 1525mm yet, like the benches which accompany it, it folds up flat in seconds for easy carrying, or for storing when not in use. It is also attractive enough to be used as a spare table indoors.

If possible use a wood like cedar, teak or the teak substitute called iroko which was used here, all of which are weather resistant. This means that you can leave the table outdoors without damaging the wood. The natural oils or resins in the wood provide enough protection from the elements. With the exception of the bench legs, which are made of 25 × 75mm section, all the wood is conveniently of one section, 25 × 100mm, which ensures that it is a

sturdy table. If you are unable to find a supplier of one of these weather resistant woods, use pine instead and make sure to protect it well with several coats of clear polyurethane. Also make sure to finish the edges between the slats well with several thin coats to prevent dripping. The slatted construction is very straightforward. The top of the table is made up of nine boards screwed to the rails underneath, one located at each end. Notice that the screws are hidden by plugs cut from another, contrasting dark wood which adds a nice decorative touch. The plugs shown here are made of American walnut.

The legs require accurate marking and cutting. It is particularly important to locate the holes correctly so that the table will fold up easily.

Study the diagrams and make sure to double check all the measuring and marking before you drill the holes. You will need a 25mm diameter drill bit, either a flat bit for the electric drill or an auger bit for the brace, to countersink the bolt heads so that they don't protrude and interfere with the mechanism when the legs

are folded up. The instructions require the drill to be set up in a drill stand which is very convenient for getting the holes located correctly, but the drilling can also be done carefully freehand.

Making the table-top

CUTTING LIST
25 × 100mm

    9 pieces 1525mm long, for slats A
    5 pieces 890mm long, for rails B

First make two thick rails by gluing four of the 890mm long pieces B together in pairs. Save the last piece B for later use. Make sure to use

SHOPPING LIST	
to make a table 915mm × 1525mm and two benches 1525mm long	
teak, cedar or pine	45m of 25 × 100mm 4.5m of 25 × 75mm
hardware	84 no.8 countersunk steel screws, 38mm long 15 no.8 countersunk brass screws, 38mm long 12 machine bolts 10mm diameter, two 60mm long and ten 38mm long with nuts and washers
plus	polyurethane or teak oil

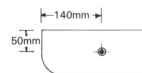

waterproof resin glue as the table will need to withstand the elements when used outdoors. Clamp the pieces together in pairs until the glue sets, then follow the diagram to round the ends and to locate the hole in each rail.

To drill the holes, mount the drill in a drill stand if possible. First drill a 25mm diameter hole 10mm deep to take the washer and the bolt head and then drill straight through the rest of the way with a 10mm diameter drill bit for the bolt. Drill from one side, then turn the piece over and finish the

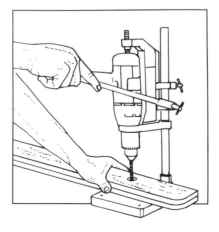

hole from the other side to avoid having the wood break out around the hole. Notice that the 25mm counterbore is on the opposite side on the second piece.

Before screwing the slats A to the rails B, round the edges with a file, a plane or, most easily, with a rounding-over bit fitted into a router (page 216). Then sand the slats well. It is much easier to do this now rather than after they have been screwed down when they will be too closely spaced for you to be able to sand between them.

After sanding smooth remember to handle the pieces carefully to avoid marking them during assembly. It is a good idea to lay an old blanket on the bench to protect the wood. Start by drilling holes in the slats A, two per end, placed 75mm from the ends of the boards. Mark and punch the hole centres, then counterbore the holes with a 10mm drill bit about 6mm deep for the wood plugs. Then drill the screw clearance holes with a 5mm diameter drill bit, straight through the board.

Place the two rails at either end of the bench so that the 25mm countersunk holes face away from each other.

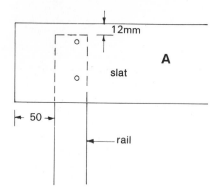

To make the slatted table top, screw the first of the nine top slats A to the rails. Place it so that it extends 12mm and 50mm beyond the rail as shown. Hold it in position and check with a square before you mark through with an awl or nail to locate the screw holes.

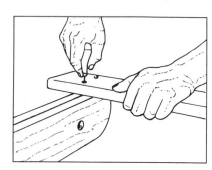

Drill pilot holes for the 38mm steel screws. Then screw down the slat at one end.
Before screwing down the other end, check with a try square and make sure that the distance between the rails is exactly 1345mm as shown.

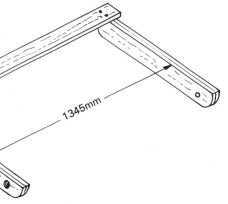

Following the same procedure now screw down a second slat at the other end of the rails. Again check with a try square and measure the distance between rails to make sure that it is assembled correctly.

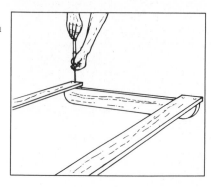

Lay the other seven slats down in between these two, spacing them out evenly with about 6mm between each one. Use a 6mm thick board as a spacer if you find that it is necessary. It helps to pin a small board to the end of the first and last slat so that you can automatically line up all the ends.

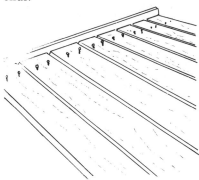

After screwing down all the slats, make 10mm diameter plugs out of a scrap of a contrasting wood and glue them into the holes over the screws with waterproof glue. In this case walnut was used for the plugs to contrast with the iroko table. After the glue has set, carefully cut the plugs off flush with a chisel and sand the surface smooth.

Turn the top over onto a blanket laid on the bench to protect the surface.

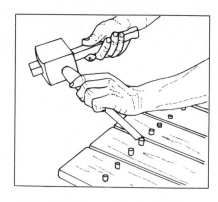

Screw the remaining 890mm long 25 × 100mm B piece across the middle using one brass screw per slat placing it centrally.

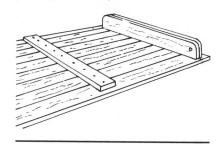

Making the underframe

CUTTING LIST
25 × 100mm
    4 pieces 990mm long, for legs C and D
    2 pieces 1343mm long, for braces E

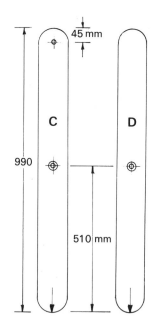

After cutting the pieces to length mark the rounded ends of the legs C and D with a compass, or a jar or

centre counterbores face outwards
on both C and D so that the bolt head
and nut are flush with the surface.

Hold the bolted frame against a try
square so that the legs are exactly
square with one another. Then mark
the bottom edge of one leg as shown.
Turn the bolted frame over and mark
the bottom edge of the other leg. The
braces E will line up against these
marks later.

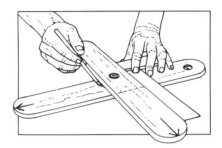

Lay each frame on the bench with
the marked bottom ends pointing in
opposite directions and legs C on the
outside. Place one of the 1343mm long
braces E so that each end rests on a
leg C. Place it so that its top edge is
exactly along the mark made earlier
and is flush with the end. Then drill
holes and glue and screw it to C,
using two 38mm steel screws per end.
Counterbore the holes and cut 10mm
diameter plugs from a darker
coloured wood. Glue them in place
with waterproof glue, chisel them off
flush and sand them smooth when
the glue is dry, exactly as for the
table top.

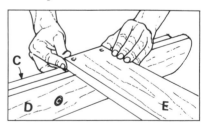

Place the other 1343mm brace E across
the two ends in exactly the same
way against the marks. The ends of
this brace should also line up flush
with the edge of leg C as shown. Glue
and screw it to legs D, again using
two hidden 38mm screws per end,
hidden by plugs as before.

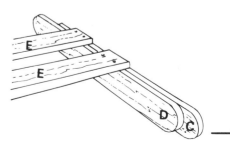

can of approximately the right
diameter. Also carefully mark the
bolt hole locations as shown. Notice
that two legs C have two holes
whereas each leg D has only one hole.

Drill the holes as before; first 10mm
deep with a 25mm diameter bit and
then straight through with the 10mm
diameter bit.

The two holes on each leg C are
countersunk on opposite sides. Cut
the rounded end shapes with a sabre
saw or, if necessary, with a coping
saw. Sand the pieces well and then
lightly mark the bottom ends as
shown, above right.

Temporarily bolt legs C to legs D to
make two X-shaped end frames. The

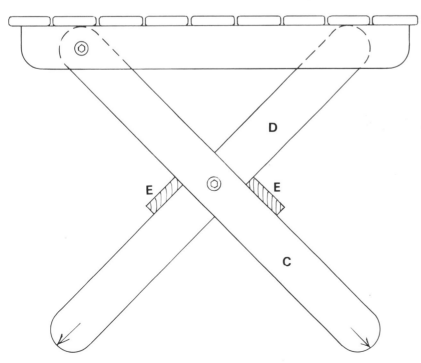

175

Assembling the table

Take out the bolts in the legs to separate the two halves of the underframe and, after re-positioning the frame into its final position as shown, put the 38mm bolts back in with washers under the bolt head and nut.

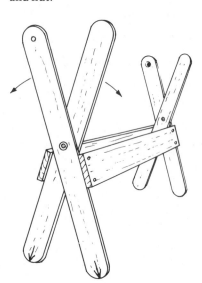

Lay the table top upside down on the bench once again, spreading a blanket to protect the sanded top. Get someone to help you support the underframe while you bolt through leg A and the rails with the 60mm bolts to complete the table.

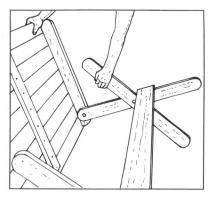

To fold it flat, lay the table on its side and tilt the top over sufficiently to allow enough space to push the legs together. Then lay the top down gently on top of the folded leg structure. The table takes up very little storage space once it has been folded.

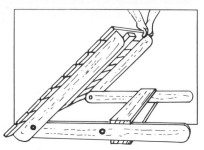

Finishing the table

For teak or iroko, rub several coats of teak oil into the wood making sure to oil all the crevices between the slats. Buff each coat with a soft cloth after allowing the oil to dry for about twenty to thirty minutes. Cedar can be left completely untreated and will age a pleasant silver grey colour as it weathers. If you use pine, the table and benches will have to be carefully finished with several coats of clear polyurethane to make them weather resistant. The bolts should also be painted, oiled or varnished to prevent them from rusting or alternatively, they can be stove enamelled.

Making the two benches

CUTTING LIST

25 × 100mm
    6 pieces 1525mm long,
    for slats A
    6 pieces 280mm long,
    for rails and
    battens B
    4 pieces 1343mm long,
    for braces C

25 × 75mm
    8 pieces 480mm long,
    for legs D and E

Cut all the pieces to length. Before assembly, round the edges with a file, plane or a router with a rounding-over bit. Sand all the pieces well. Then assemble the two bench tops, using three slats A and two 280mm long shaped rails B per top.

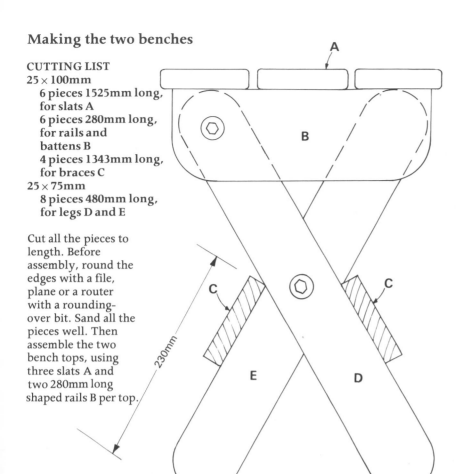

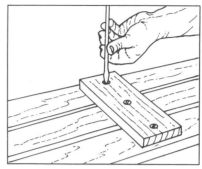

brass screw to each slat. Bevel the edge of batten B before you fix it in place.

To make the legs, proceed exactly as for the table. First mark the ends and hole centres for the legs D and E, then round the ends, drill the holes and bolt them together while you attach the cross braces C. Notice that the top edges of the braces C are placed 230mm from the bottom edge of the legs, so the legs do not form a right angle when opened. Use four 38mm bolts per bench, one to bolt each pair of legs together and two to bolt the legs to the rails. Finish in the same way as the table.

Space the rails 1345mm apart as for the table. Then screw down the top slats A, again hiding the 38mm screws with plugs of a contrasting wood.

To finish the bench tops, screw a single 280mm long 25 × 100mm batten B flat to the underside of each bench. Position the batten in the centre to hold the top slats in place, using one

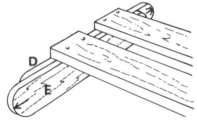

SLAT PLANT STAND

This simple plant stand is quick to make and adds a decorative touch to a large plant standing on the floor, as well as protecting the carpet and allowing air to circulate beneath the pot.

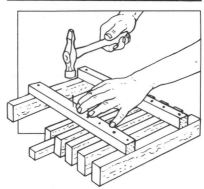

SHOPPING LIST	
softwood	3.4m of 25 × 50mm cut into nine 330mm strips 2 pieces of 25 × 25mm 330mm long
plus	18 finishing nails or panel pins, 38mm long

After cutting the pieces to length, sand them and slightly round the edges. Use the two 25 × 25mm slats as the base. Glue and nail these to the nine 12 × 50mm slats starting with one at each end and spacing the others out evenly in between. Use a piece of 25 × 25mm scrap as a spacer. Finish the plant stand with two coats of clear polyurethane or oil-based paint over a sealer coat.

PLANTER WITH PARQUET INLAY

The dimensions given here are for parquet with 115mm square sections. Before cutting the hardwood frame, check the size of the parquet. If it is a different size, work out another cutting list.

Making the sides and ends

CUTTING LIST
25 × 50mm
4 pieces 825mm long A
10 pieces 117mm long B
4 pieces 206mm long C

Assemble each of the two identical sides by clamping two A and three B

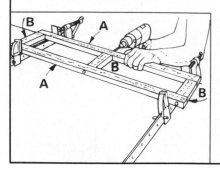

SHOPPING LIST	
hardwood	5.8m of 25 × 50mm mahogany or teak (planed size about 20 × 45mm) about 7.3m of 10 × 10mm beading in the same hardwood
plywood	200 × 815mm, 12mm thick (trimmed to size at assembly)
dowel	1.2m of 6mm diameter for pegs
hardware	about 70 finishing nails or panel pins, 19mm long
plus	parquet flooring, one piece about 460 × 460mm consisting of at least fourteen 115mm squares clear polyurethane

pieces together while drilling and through dowelling (page 232). Place the third piece exactly central to leave two identical windows for the parquet.

For an interesting effect, hide the dowel by inserting a short plug cut from a matching piece of waste wood (page 214).

To assemble the two ends, use the 206mm pieces C on top and bottom with the 117mm pieces B in between. Clamp, drill and dowel them exactly as for the sides.

SLOT TOGETHER PLANTER

The bottom panel of this planter can be slotted in at any level to accommodate a small or a large plant. To make a larger or smaller sized planter, change the length of the sides keeping the slots exactly the same.

SHOPPING LIST	
plywood	710 × 915mm, 12mm thick
	325 × 380mm, 12mm thick, for bottom
plus	green stain polyurethane

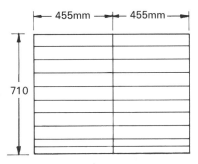

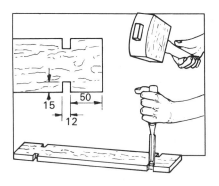

Follow the diagram (right) in cutting the plywood into sixteen strips, 75 × 455mm long and four strips, 38 × 455mm long.

The sixteen 75mm strips are marked identically. Mark lines for the 15mm

deep slots, 50mm from the ends, using a piece of 12mm plywood to get the width right so the pieces will fit together snugly. Saw on the waste side of the lines and chisel out the waste. Make one slot and test for fit

before cutting the rest to be sure they are right. The 38mm strips have slots on one edge only.

Finish the pieces by sanding smooth and applying green stain and then two coats of clear polyurethane.

To assemble the planter, start with two 38mm strips and build up the sides by simply slotting the pieces together. The two remaining 38mm strips go on top. Slide the base in at the desired height.

The parquet is held in place by pieces of beading nailed around the openings. Cut one strip at a time, then glue and nail it flush with the front edge. These beads may be mitred or butt jointed.

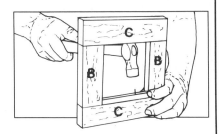

To secure the parquet, cut off a row of three squares for each wide opening and one square for each of the ends. Lay it in the window against the beading and pin it carefully to the beading from the back.

Assembly

Before assembling, glue and nail beading at the bottom of each side to hold the plywood base. Join the four sides with through dowels and cover with a plug. Drill 20mm holes in the base for drainage before trimming it and dropping it in position.

Finishing

Sand the sides smooth and finish with several coats of clear polyurethane.

OUTDOOR PLANTERS

Attractive plant containers are surprisingly expensive to buy, but in fact they are easy to make yourself. These two planters have been designed to be used outdoors, but they could just as easily be made smaller and used for indoor plants. Try to use a wood which will stand up to the weather like cedar, teak or mahogany. If you use pine, seal it well with several coats of clear polyurethane.

Bench plant holder

Making the planter

Cut the 38 × 150mm into two 1050mm lengths for the top and four 330mm lengths for the legs. Save the remaining piece for the cross braces, which are measured and cut after the legs are attached.

First bevel or round the edges with a plane or with coarse sandpaper and then sand the face of the pieces well.

Assemble the pieces first by drilling the holes and then screwing the legs to the top pieces, holding them with a clamp to leave your hands free. Notice that the legs extend about 25mm above the top boards. The screws are set into 10mm diameter holes drilled about 10mm deep. The countersunk screws are hidden by filling the holes with plugs cut from a matching wood (page 214). This means that the screws will not rust.

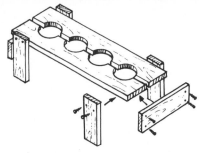

It is easier when clamping the legs to the top to place a 25mm strip between the two top boards to space them evenly apart. After attaching the four legs, cut off two lengths for end braces so that they extend about 6mm beyond

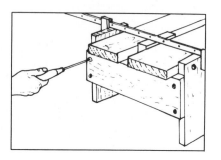

the legs. Then screw these in place, making sure the legs are square. Glue the matching wooden plugs into the holes and carefully sand off any marks which were made during assembly.

Measure the neck of the flower pots you are using. Mark the circles and cut them out with a sabre saw. Four pots is a good number for a planter of this length, but you can of course make a longer one or use small diameter pots. You could also make a matching bench.

Leave the wood unfinished if you have used a wood that will withstand the weather. Otherwise, protect it with several coats of clear polyurethane.

SHOPPING LIST	
wood	4.5m of 38 × 150mm (mahogany, teak or cedar)
hardware	16 no.10 countersunk steel screws, 50mm long

Pine plant
container

CUTTING LIST
25 × 125mm
    16 pieces 380mm long A
25 × 50mm
    4 pieces 520mm long B
    4 pieces 480mm long C
    4 pieces 610mm long D
    (to be trimmed)
12mm plywood
    1 piece 520 × 520mm
    4 pieces 75 × 430mm

After cutting the boards to length, make each of the four sides by laying out four boards A, spacing them about 12mm apart and nailing the 25 × 50mm pieces to them as shown with a 12mm overhang at the bottom. On two panels the 25 × 50mm pieces B are flush with the edge, and on the other two, the 25 × 50mm pieces C are nailed on leaving a 19mm gap at each end.

To make the planter more decorative, draw heart shapes on the boards and cut them out with a sabre saw. Sand the edges well.

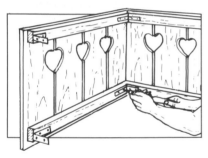

Then join the sides together using two metal brackets at each corner. To finish off the sides, trim the edging D to length and then nail the pieces to the top edges of the four sides so that the ends of the boards will not be exposed to the weather. Set the nails and fill the holes to keep the nails from rusting.

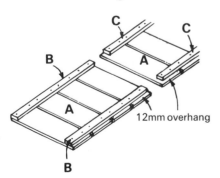

To make the base, nail the four small pieces of plywood together to form a square, then nail the large piece onto

the square. The sides of the planter simply rest on the base. The planter is thereby raised off the ground to protect the wood from moisture.

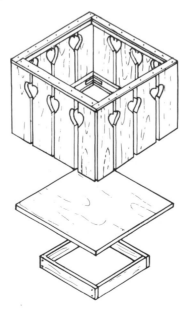

SHOPPING LIST	
softwood	6.7m of 25 × 125mm 7.3m of 25 × 50mm
plywood	600 × 900mm, 12mm thick
hardware	8 metal corner brackets with 12mm screws about 90 oval wire nails, 38mm long
plus	clear polyurethane

Finishing the planter

Seal all the pieces of the planter with several coats of clear polyurethane if you have used pine, paying special attention to the inside edges, end grain and the base pieces to keep the weather from spoiling the wood. You can stain pine with a coloured or wood tone polyurethane first. If you use mahogany or teak for the planter, finish it with linseed or teak oil.

OUTDOOR LOUNGE SEAT AND TABLE

This adjustable lounge seat is both a stylish and practical design. The pine battens are simply screwed to two supports to make a chair with a backrest that can be adjusted for sitting upright or for lying down. The small wheels at the back make it easy to move. You simply lift the front and roll it away. Instead of finishing with clear polyurethane as shown here, you could paint the chair and its matching table in shiny white or in a bright colour to cheer up a patio or garden. The construction is quite easy. The only part which is tricky is fitting the backrest but, as always, if you read the instructions and study the diagrams carefully before beginning, you shouldn't have any difficulties. The two small wheels should be quite easy to find. Large hardware stores usually sell wheels like this. Alternatively, buy large toy wheels such as those used for the truck on page 94. As a last resort, use a couple of wheels from an old baby carriage.

SHOPPING LIST

softwood	6.1m of 38 × 200mm for supports 29m of 19 × 100mm for slats 7.6m of 38 × 38mm
plywood	2 pieces 75 × 600mm, 19mm thick
dowel	two 600mm lengths, 12mm diameter
hardware	125 no.8 countersunk brass screws, 32mm long 125 no.8 brass screw cup washers 22 no.8 countersunk steel screws, 38mm long 30 finishing nails or panel pins, 38mm long 3 brass hinges 38mm long with matching 12mm long screws two 100–125mm diameter wheels or castors with fittings
plus	1 piece of 50mm thick foam, 585 × 2035mm 2.5 metres of heavy cotton fabric, 1375mm wide

Preparing the supports for the lounge seat

CUTTING LIST
38 × 200mm
   2 pieces 1950mm long, for supports A
38 × 38mm
   2 pieces 1950mm long B
   1 piece 1065mm long C

After cutting the pieces exactly to length, sand them well as it is easier to do now than when the pieces have been joined. Use a sanding block and medium then fine sandpaper to make the wood smooth and pleasant to touch. Temporarily nail one 38 × 38mm piece B to the edge of one support A, and the second piece B to the second support A. Nail each piece with five or six 38mm pins avoiding placing the pins near the ends as you will be making a saw cut later. Make sure not to add any glue at this stage.

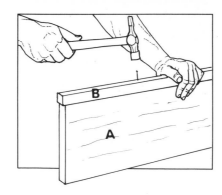

mark and cut the remaining 38 × 38mm C into six mitred pieces as shown.

Screw one of these to one end of each support as shown. This becomes the front end of the chair. Use two 38mm long screws per piece, counterboring the hole about 12mm into the piece and then hiding the screw with a plug or with wood filler. Save the other four pieces as they will be of use for making the table.

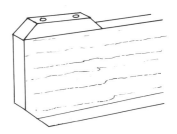

The top slats will be screwed into the 38 × 38mm pieces B attached to the supports. Part of piece B will be cut off so that it can be attached rigidly to the support, but the remaining part which holds the slats for the adjustable backrest will not be fixed down, to allow it to be lifted up and down.

Measure exactly 1120mm from the front end of the support as shown, then cut the 38 × 38mm at this point. Also

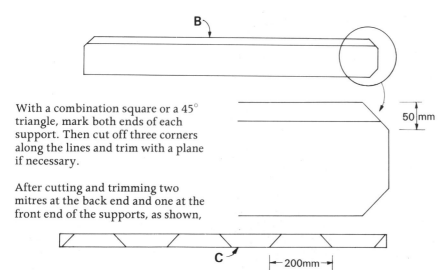

With a combination square or a 45° triangle, mark both ends of each support. Then cut off three corners along the lines and trim with a plane if necessary.

After cutting and trimming two mitres at the back end and one at the front end of the supports, as shown,

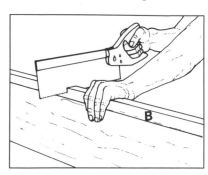

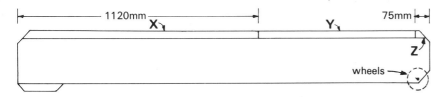

make a cut 75mm from the back end as shown. The middle piece Y will form the adjustable backrest. Screw the pieces X and Z down rigidly, using four 38mm long screws on piece X and one on piece Z. Sink the screws about 12mm into the wood and hide each screw with filler or with a matching wood plug. As well as hiding the screws, this also seals them from the weather and prevents them from rusting.

The next step is to glue and nail the plywood pieces in place, one to the inside of each support near the back to hold the adjustable prop. Start by cutting out the shapes shown with a sabre saw or a coping saw. Notice that the top edge of the plywood piece is lined up with the joint between the 38 × 38mm B and the 38 × 200mm support A. Spread glue over the plywood, then hammer in six 38mm pins per side.

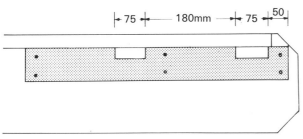

Attaching the slats

CUTTING LIST
19 × 100mm
   20 pieces 840mm long
   1 piece 600mm long A
   (to be trimmed)

Cut all the slats, then sand them making sure to round the edges and ends so that there will be no sharp edges to catch on clothes.

Drill two 4.5mm diameter screw clearance holes at both ends of each

slat. It is a tedious job drilling 80 holes so it would be a good idea to speed up the job by making a drilling guide out of a scrap piece of 19 × 100mm with three battens on the

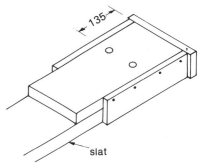

sides. Drill two 4.5mm diameter holes, 135mm from the end. Hold this jig over the end of each slat in turn and drill straight through the guide holes into the slat.

Place the two supports on the floor about 535mm apart and attach one slat at each end placed at a 45° angle as shown. Use a combination square set at 115mm as a gauge to get an equal overhang on both sides of the supports. Screw the slats down using 32mm brass screws with cup washers. Make sure the overhang is equal on all sides so that the supports are parallel.

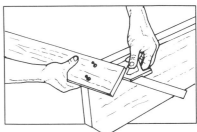

On one side pin a small board to the ends of these two slats so that it forms a guide for lining up the rest of the slats.

Now screw down one slat near the middle so that it lines up on the X side of the saw cut in the 38 × 38mm. Trim the 600mm slat A so that it fits tightly between the supports and screw it

183

under the middle slat aligned with the edge with three brass screws, as shown.

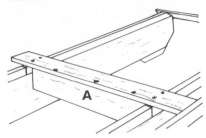

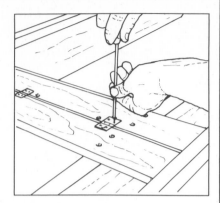

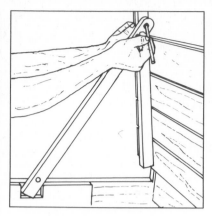

Screw down another slat directly behind with the edges touching and attach the three hinges to the two slats. Don't cut recesses for the hinge flaps. Simply hold them in place, centred between the two slats and make screw holes with a bradawl. Then screw down the hinges with the 12mm long screws.

Now screw down the rest of the slats in between, spacing them out evenly.

Finally screw one slat vertically to the end at the front and one at the back and remove the strip which was pinned on as a guide.

the batten. Repeat this for the other side using the other prop.

Flip the backrest over completely so that it lies flat. Lay the props inside the battens B with the holes lined up and push one of the 12mm diameter dowels straight through the holes so that it goes through all four battens.

Constructing the adjustable back rest

CUTTING LIST
38 × 38mm
    2 pieces 600mm long as props

The backrest, which is hinged to the front, can now be lifted up. It is only held down to the support with a few temporary nails. Lift it up and try to pull out the temporary nails from the back with a pair of pliers. If it is too difficult to pull the pin heads straight through the wood, just hammer them over, punch them below the surface with a nail punch,

and fill the holes with matching wood filler.

Round one end of both the 38 × 38mm props with a file and smooth off the wood with fine sandpaper. Drill a 12mm diameter hole in each end of both props exactly as shown. Hold one prop in position with the bottom square end resting in the plywood cut-out and tilt the backrest until the prop just touches the slat. Copy the outline of the 12mm diameter hole onto the 38 × 38mm batten Y which is screwed to the slats, then drill a 12mm diameter hole where marked, straight through

Trim the other dowel so that it fits loosely between the two supports, then push it through the bottom holes of the two props.

The backrest should now fold flat with the prop resting flat on the inside. Check to make sure it works all right and make any adjustments if necessary.

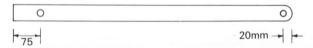

┝—┥
75   20mm →┥ ┝—

Finally fit one wheel to each back end of the support so that it extends about 40mm below the support.

Making the table

CUTTING LIST
38 × 200mm
    2 pieces 840mm long
19 × 100mm
    10 pieces 840mm long

Start by adding the four 38 × 38mm feet cut out earlier when making the chair. Screw them to the bottom ends of the 38 × 200mm pieces with two 38mm long screws. On the top corner of each end of the two pieces, cut off

the corner at a 45° angle in the same way as for the chair. Drill the two 4.5mm diameter holes at the end of each slat using the drilling guide made for the chair. Then screw down the ten slats, starting with the two angled ones at either end and spacing the others out evenly against a guide temporarily pinned to the two end slats.

Finishing the chair and table

Sand off any marks made during assembly and then apply about three coats of clear polyurethane to the entire chair and table. Pay particular attention to the ends of all the boards and slats, making sure that they are thoroughly finished to prevent damage by the weather.

Making the cushion

The bold stripes used here are an attractive pattern for the lounge seat. You can make the cover for the cushion with the pattern running up and down or across the cushion or, if you don't mind using about 50 per cent more fabric, you can have the pattern running diagonally, as shown here.

Cut out the fabric to match the piece of foam exactly allowing for a 12mm seam all round. Sew a full length zipper down one side so that the cover can be removed for washing. Make eight 150mm long ties from the same fabric as the cover and sew them to the underside of the cushion, two to each corner. Use these to tie the cushion down firmly to the slats.

BARBECUE TROLLEY

This trolley with four interchangeable trays is an ingenious design and is very easy to make. One tray houses a built-in double hibachi or brazier with a tile surround so that you can barbecue right on the trolley wheeled close to a picnic table. The barbecue tray lifts out so that you can barbecue wherever you want and place it on the table for serving if you like. The second tray holds bottles and glasses firmly in cut-out holes, a third is a large chopping board and the fourth is a flat tray for stacking plates and cutlery. You can make one each of the trays as shown here or, if you prefer, make two trays for glasses or two plain trays depending on how you want to use your trolley. When the hibachi is not in use, you can move it to the bottom shelf of the trolley or put it away completely. For indoor use, you can remove the barbecue tray and use the trolley as a serving cart. The large castors ensure that it is steady and sturdy enough to bring dishes to the table.

The trolley is remarkably easy to make. The basic framework screws together very simply and the built-in barbecue is the only section which requires extra care. Buy a standard sized double hibachi measuring about 250 × 430mm. It comes with a handle which can be screwed to the tray to make it easy to carry.

Making the trolley framework

CUTTING LIST

25 × 50mm
  4 pieces 685mm long, for legs A

19 × 50mm
  2 pieces 1090mm long, for rails B
  2 pieces 890mm long, for rails C
  3 pieces 535mm long, for cross rails D
  1 piece 430mm long, for cross rail E

19 × 19mm
  4 pieces 890mm long, for battens F
  4 pieces 460mm long, for battens G (to be trimmed)

6.5mm plywood
  2 pieces 430 × 890mm

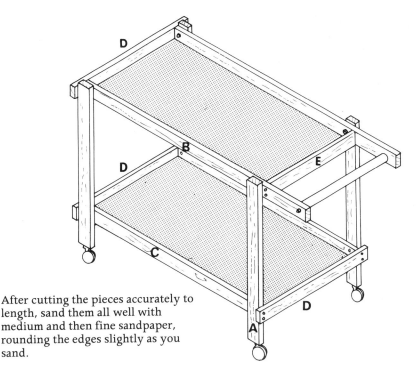

After cutting the pieces accurately to length, sand them all well with medium and then fine sandpaper, rounding the edges slightly as you sand.

Start by drilling holes in the exact centre in the bottom of the four legs to take the castor sockets. Tap a socket into each hole with a hammer, but be careful not to split the wood. The castor manufacturer will usually supply instructions for installing the castors with the diameter and depth of holes required.

On the inside of each leg, mark two lines, one 100mm up from the bottom and one 6mm down from the top as guide marks for the rails.

Lay two legs on the bench about 1m apart with the marks facing up. First glue and pin one bottom rail C so that the bottom edge is against the marks on A and the ends of the rail are exactly flush with the legs. Use two

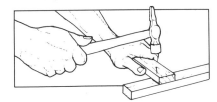

32mm pins per end, and check with a try square before pinning.

Next pin and glue the top rail B, 6mm from the top of the leg. Attach one end first, flush with the leg, then glue and pin to the other leg making the frame square. Notice that the other end of B extends about 200mm beyond the leg.

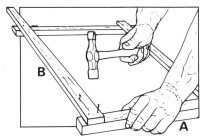

After attaching the two rails to the two legs to form one side frame, reinforce each glued and pinned joint with one 32mm brass screw, countersunk flush with the surface.

Make another side frame identical to the first except that the top rail extends 200mm in the opposite direction to that of the first frame. This way you will have one left-hand and one right-hand frame to form the two sides of the trolley.

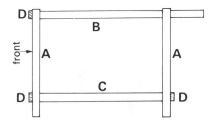

Prepare the three cross rails D by drilling two 4.5mm diameter screw clearance holes 28mm from the ends and about 10mm from each edge.

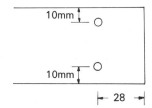

Lay the side frame on the bench and glue and screw two of the cross rails

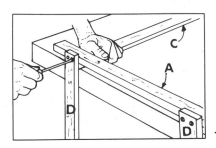

SHOPPING LIST

pine	2.1m of 12 × 125mm / 3m of 25 × 50mm / 10m of 19 × 50mm 3.4m of 25 × 25mm / 6.7m of 19 × 19mm
plywood	460 × 460mm, 10mm thick 915 × 1370mm, 6.5mm thick
dowel	430mm of 38mm diameter 460mm of 10mm diameter
hardware	6 no.8 brass screws, 38mm long 24 no.8 countersunk brass screws, 32mm long 18 no.8 brass screw cup washers 26 no.6 countersunk brass screws, 19mm long 50 finishing nails or panel pins, 32mm long 100 finishing nails or panel pins, 25mm long 4 castors with socket type fittings 6 no.8 fibre wall plugs, 25mm long
plus	3 pieces of bright red plastic laminate, 2 pieces 440 × 895mm one piece 430 × 430mm contact adhesive 8 tiles 110mm square (or trim 115mm tiles) tile cement hibachi measuring 250 × 430mm clear polyurethane

D to the front legs using two 32mm screws with cup washers for each end.

Locate the rails so that they line up exactly with the long rails B and C, covering their ends.

Stand both side frames upside down on the bench and attach the other ends of the cross rails D to the front legs.

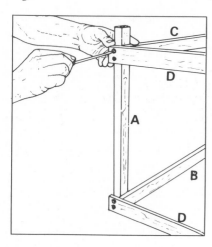

It is important that the distance between the insides of the rails B at the top and rails C at the bottom is exactly 430mm. To get this right, hold the 430mm long cross rail E tight between the long rails as you screw on the cross rails D.

Screw the third cross rail D to the back legs in exactly the same way. Line up with the bottom rails C, again making sure the distance between the long rails is 430mm by holding rail E in between.

Glue and screw rail E between the top rails. Locate it so that it lines up with rail D below, making the distance between it and the front cross rail exactly 890mm. Use two 38mm long brass screws with washers per end and screw them into fibre plugs.

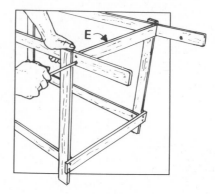

Next turn the assembly on its side and glue and pin two of the 19 × 19mm battens F to the insides of the long rails flush with the bottom edges. Use about five 25mm pins per batten.

Turn it over on its other side to attach the other two battens F in the same way. Then trim the battens G to fit along the cross battens and glue and pin them in place, three pins per batten.

This forms a ledge at the top and bottom of the trolley to hold 6.5mm

plywood panels. Trim these with a plane if necessary and drop in place. Remove the panels and glue the laminate to each of them leaving a 3mm overhang on all sides for trimming with a sharp block plane. See page 46 for instructions for gluing down the laminate.

After trimming the edges flush with the plywood on both panels, spread glue on the 19 × 19mm battens and drop the panels in place securing each from underneath with eight 19mm brass screws through the battens.
To finish off the trolley, glue and screw the 38mm diameter dowel handle between the long rails B. Spread glue on the ends of the dowel and then screw one 38mm long brass screw with washer through the rail into a fibre plug. Finally, push the castors into their sockets at the bottom of each leg.

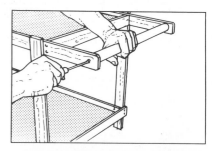

Making the barbecue tray

CUTTING LIST
12 × 125mm
   2 pieces 460mm long A
   2 pieces 430mm long B
19 × 50mm
   2 pieces 430mm long C
25 × 25mm
   2 pieces 430mm long D
   2 pieces 460mm long E
   (to be trimmed)
6.5mm plywood
   1 piece 215 × 440mm F
10mm dowel
   6 pieces 65mm long

Prepare the sides by gluing and pinning the battens C and D to the sides. Attach one batten C

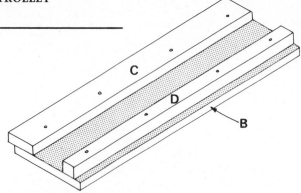

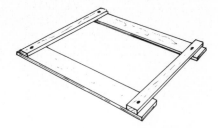

along the bottom of each side B so that about 12mm of batten extends below the edge. Use four 25mm pins per batten. Then glue and pin a 25 × 25mm batten D near the top edge of the same sides, 12mm down from the top edge. Use four 32mm pins per batten.

To assemble the tray, glue and pin the sides A to the sides B using four 32mm pins per corner. Then trim the 25 × 25mm battens E so that they fit in between the battens D which are attached to the sides B.

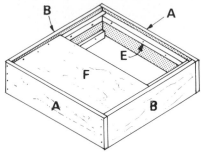

Turn the tray on its side and glue and pin these battens E to sides A, placing them 12mm from the top edge to line up with the other battens.

Trim the 6.5mm plywood piece F to fit, and pin and glue it in place with eight 25mm pins.

To protect the box from the heat, the hibachi is perched on six small dowels which are attached to the 25 × 25mm battens.

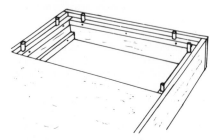

Hold the hibachi in place to determine the dowel locations and then drill six 10mm diameter holes in

the 25 × 25mm battens. Cut six dowel pegs, 65mm long and glue them into the holes. Then place the hibachi on the pegs to be sure that it fits securely. Make adjustments, re-locating the pegs if necessary.

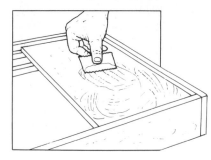

Glue the tiles to the plywood by first spreading a thin layer of tile cement on the surface using a serrated spreader. Then place the tiles in position, pressing down firmly to make them even. Trim the last tile with a tile cutter if necessary, or gently sand off the edge if the fit is snug. Allow the tile cement to set for 24 hours before using the barbecue.

Making the drinks tray

CUTTING LIST
19 × 50mm
  2 pieces 445mm long
10mm plywood
  5 strips, 75 × 460mm

Start by gluing the 19 × 50mm battens to the two end plywood strips so that 12mm of plywood extends beyond

the batten. Simply spread glue along the full length of the batten and then place it on the strips. Fix the other three strips in between, spacing them about 20mm apart, and allow the glue to set. After it has set, reinforce the joints 19mm with one 25mm brass screw per end.

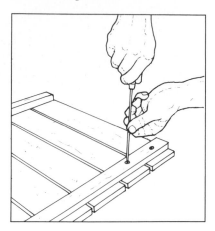

Without turning it over, draw the circles for the glasses, bottles and perhaps small bowls to fit into the tray. Trace around the glasses and bottles themselves to make sure to get a tight fit. Centre each circle around the 20mm space between the strips.

Then cut out all the circles using a sabre saw and clean up the edges with sandpaper. Sawing from the bottom means that the top edges of the holes will be neat and free from splinters.

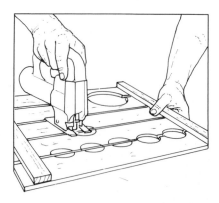

The tray drops onto the sides of the trolley with the plywood ends sitting on the long rails.

Making the chopping board

It is easiest to buy a maple or beech chopping board, 460 × 460mm, but if one isn't available follow the instructions on page 231 for gluing together planed boards to make one. Glue a short piece of 19 × 50mm underneath near each corner to hold the chopping board within the rails on the trolley.

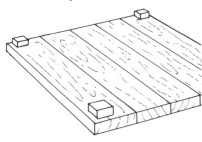

Making the tray

CUTTING LIST

19 × 50mm
   2 pieces 460mm long A
   2 pieces 430mm long B
   4 pieces 50mm long C
19 × 19mm
   2 pieces 460mm long D
6.5mm plywood
   1 piece 460 × 460mm

Glue and nail the sides A to sides B as shown, using two 32mm pins at each corner. Then glue and pin the 6.5mm plywood panel to the bottom edges, using four 25mm pins per side. Trim any protruding edges of plywood with a block plane. Trim the 430 × 430mm laminate panel to fit inside the wooden frame and glue it to the plywood with contact adhesive. Glue and screw the two 19 × 19mm battens D to the sides, flush with the top, to serve as handles. Use two 32mm brass screws and cup washers for each handle. Finally glue the four small 19 × 50mm blocks at the corners

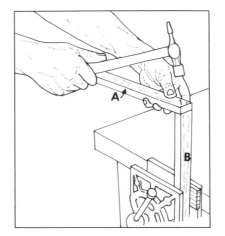

placing them so that they fit within the rails with the tray in place, exactly as for the chopping board.

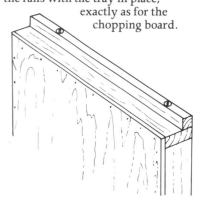

Finishing the trolley

Oil the chopping board with one or two coats of salad or olive oil and renew the oil finish from time to time. Finish the rest of the pine pieces of the trolley and trays with at least two coats of clear polyurethane. Rub down all the surfaces with fine sandpaper or steel wool between each coat to achieve a really smooth finish. If you plan to use the trolley outdoors a lot, it will be a good idea to give the wood a third coat of polyurethane so that it is really well sealed against the weather.

WOODWORKING TECHNIQUES

This section is really a book in itself with a tremendous amount of information packed into 64 pages.

It can be used as a general reference book on woodworking techniques, for detailed instructions on using machines, hand tools and on making joints, and for buying, cutting and finishing the wood. Also included are detailed directions for making jigs and other devices to make your tools more versatile. There is no reason, for example, to buy a table saw since you can make one out of the portable circular saw following the instructions on page 209. But this section has also been designed to be used in conjunction with the projects with frequent cross references between the two to make it easy to check from one to the other for additional information. So it is a good idea when planning out a project to read through the instructions and make a note of the various techniques you may want to refer to before starting work.

measuring and marking

Measuring, marking and squaring off happens constantly in woodworking. In many ways, it is the most important step of all. Without accurate marking, it doesn't matter how well you saw, the measurements will not be exact. The dimensions of a project must be accurate for a good fit.

TAPES AND RULES
A tape measure is adequate for most measurements. For very accurate dimensions use a good quality boxwood rule for long lengths and a steel rule for short lengths. Always hold the rule with the marked edge against the wood for greater accuracy.

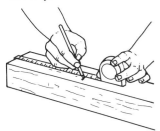

Use a sharp, fine pencil for most marking but, again, take more care and use a marking knife when really accurate marking is required. A marking knife or a trimming knife is particularly useful for marking chisel lines because the score in the wood serves as an accurate guide for the chisel blade.

CALIPERS
Calipers are essential for measuring thicknesses accurately. It isn't necessary to buy an expensive engineer's precision pattern – the cheapest one available is adequate for woodworking. Most calipers have arms for both interior and exterior measurements and a vernier scale for greater accuracy when making precise measurements.

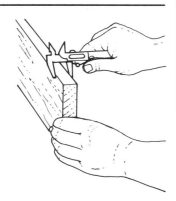

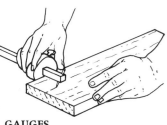

GAUGES
The simplest way to mark lines parallel to the edges of boards is to use marking or cutting gauges. A marking gauge scores a line parallel to the grain. Hold the marking gauge with the body firmly against the edge. Pull the gauge toward you with the point sloping away as shown.

When marking across the grain

at the end of a board, use a cutting gauge which is exactly like the marking gauge except that it has a small knife blade instead of a point for easier marking across a board.

The marking gauge can be used for marking mortise slots but it must be set twice. Using a special mortise gauge with two adjustable points, this operation is done more accurately and in one stroke.

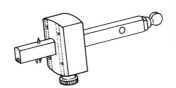

SQUARES AND BEVELS
The try square is used constantly in the workshop to draw square lines across boards, to transfer lines from one face to another and to check the square of saw cuts and of planed surfaces.

Buy two good quality try squares, one 100 or 150mm long and the other 300mm. On most squares, the blade is set in a hardwood handle with brass studs, but plastic handles are actually better since they will not warp.

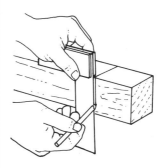

The combination try and mitre square is extremely useful. Besides its use as both try and mitre square, it also serves as a useful depth gauge and the

blade can be removed to be used alone as a rule or straight cutting edge when necessary.

For marking any angle, use a sliding bevel. Set the angle of the blade against a protractor, then tighten the wing nut and use it like an ordinary try square. If you are marking several pieces at the same angle, it is best to check the angle on a piece of scrap or against a protractor before final marking to be sure it is correct.

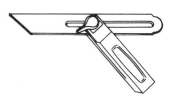

MISCELLANEOUS MARKING TOOLS

The panel gauge is used for marking parallel lines on wide boards or on sheets of plywood. You can easily make your own out of good quality hardwood. Cut a slot in the head to take the arm. This is adjustable and is held in place with a peg. A hole drilled in the end of the arm holds a

pencil which is held in place by a screw fixed from the side of the arm.

To mark large circles, either make a homemade jig from a strip of wood with a nail for the centre, or buy two trammel points which adjust along the strip for any size of circle.

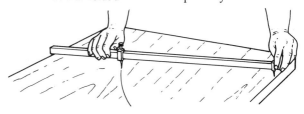

hammers and mallets

Hammers most often used in furniture making are the Warrington hammer for driving pins and the claw hammer, used for driving larger nails and for pulling out nails. The lighter pin hammer has a smaller head for use in fine work, as, for example, with veneer pins.

Striking tools used in woodworking. Left to right : pin, Warrington, claw hammers and wooden mallet.

For general work buy a 280g Warrington hammer and a 454g or 560g claw hammer, whichever you find most comfortable to use. The ash handles, which are replaceable, are held in the head with two metal wedges. It is important to keep the face of the hammer clean and polished by rubbing it periodically on emery cloth.

The pin push is used instead of a hammer for holding and driving small pins and for nailing thin plywood. The pins, which fit into the tube, are driven by pushing hard on the handle, or if necessary driving with a hammer.

NAIL PUNCHES AND CENTRE PUNCHES

Nail and pin punches are used to drive nails below the surface. The square shanked type are best since they are easier to hit with a hammer. Nail and pin punches are available in sets to suit varying sizes of nail heads, but two or three sizes are enough for

general use. Centre punches should always be used before drilling to make a centre mark as a starting guide for the drill bit.

It is impossible to give instructions for using a hammer. After a little practice and a few bent nails, you will soon acquire the knack.

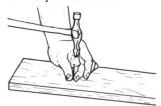

Start very small pins with the cross pein and if you are going to hide the nails by driving them below the surface, stop nailing when the pin head is just proud of the surface. Then use a nail punch of the correct size to drive the nail below the surface. Finally, fill the hole with filler to hide the nail.

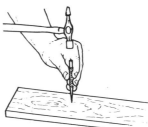

Pull nails out with the claw hammer, using a block of waste

wood to prevent marking the workpiece. You can also use a pair of pincers which have a fine claw on one end of the handle for getting under nail heads.

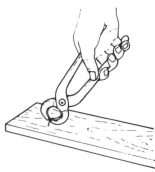

The beech wooden mallet should always be used for striking chisels, for tapping in dowels and generally for adjusting pieces of wood and knocking together joints. To prevent damage to valuable pieces of wood, cabinetmakers tape layers of cardboard over the face of the mallet and use it as a substitute for a soft-faced mallet which is made with a soft nylon head.

drills

For hand drilling use either a hand brace or a hand drill.

The brace is available with a ratchet mechanism and with several sizes of handle. The 200mm and 250mm sweep handles are the most common, and they are manufactured in a range of sizes for special applications

such as drilling between joists. The brace is used mostly with auger type bits with square tapered shanks, but it will take

straight shanked twist drills up to 12mm diameter.

To fix the bit into the chuck, first open the chuck jaws by

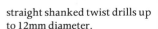

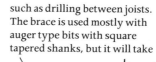

turning the handle with one hand, holding the chuck fixed with the other. Insert the bit, and tighten the jaws by turning the handle the other way.

DRILL BITS USED IN A BRACE

1. Jennings pattern auger bits, for general cabinetmaking. From 6 to 25mm diameter.

2. Solid centre auger bit. Similar to Jennings but with extra strength and faster chip clearance.

3. Single spur solid centre bit. Primarily for deep boring in harder wood.

4. Forstner bit, used either in a drill press or brace. Does not split wood and is useful for thinner pieces like plywood

and for drilling shallow holes.

5. Expansion bit. Variable diameters for drilling shallow holes in softwood. Two sizes: 12mm to 38mm and 22 to 75mm diameter.

6. Centre bit. Less expensive than auger bits, cuts shallow holes efficiently.

7. Jennings pattern dowel bit.

8. Countersink bit.

9. Screwdriver bit for turning screws in quickly.

Use bits with a tapered square section tang for a firm grip in the brace. From left to right: centre bits and two sizes of solid centre bits.

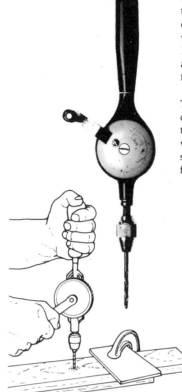

The hand drill is used with twist drills up to 8mm diameter, with dowel bits which are available up to 12mm diameter and can also be fitted with a useful bit for countersinking screw holes.

Twist drills are intended for drilling metal, but nonetheless, they are universally used in woodworking for general work such as drilling clearance holes for screws.

The bit is mounted in the chuck in the same way as in the brace, by turning the handle while holding the chuck.

It is a common fault to inadvertently lean the brace over when drilling which results in a hole that is not vertical. Drilling vertically comes with practice. On occasions when it is important that the holes are absolutely vertical, such as for dowel joints, check the alignment either by standing a try square on the bench or by having someone else sight along the drill to guide you.

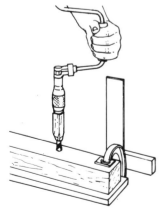

When drilling to a required depth, for instance in dowelling work, use a depth stop, either bought from a shop or made from a scrap of waste wood.

SHARPENING DRILL BITS

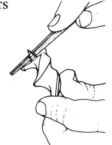

Sharpen auger bits with a special smooth file, making sure to file lightly and remove as little metal as possible.

First file the spurs. Lean the bit against the bench and file the *inside* of the spurs. Never file the outside as this reduces the cutting diameter. Then hold the bit against the top of the bench to sharpen the cutters. File only the underside of the cutters, i.e. the tapered side.

MAKING A DEPTH STOP

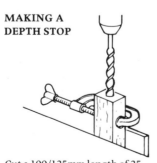

Cut a 100/125mm length of 25 or 38mm square scrap wood,

depending on the diameter of the drill bit. Fasten it in the vice with an extra clamp to prevent splitting, and carefully drill a hole down the centre. Then work out the exact length required for the depth stop, cut off that length, and slide it on the drill bit.

Taper the end slightly with a knife or chisel to prevent it from marking the wood.

For more accurate work use dowel or brad point bits available for use in the hand drill in 6/8/10/12mm diameters.

Another extremely useful tool, for making small clearance holes for nails and screws, is the bradawl. Use it so that the edge cuts across the grain to avoid splitting the wood, twisting back and forth into the wood to make a small hole. Sharpen the bradawl with a fine file and finish by rubbing on an oilstone.

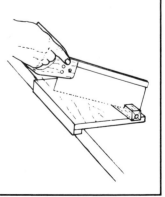

handsaws

Sawing is the most basic operation involved in making any project. You will have to cut long boards to rough length then trim them square and to length before beginning the work of cutting joints or assembling pieces.

Even though the portable circular saw does the job much quicker, handsaws are still indispensable to the woodworker.

The teeth of the saw, which are bent or 'set' out from the blade alternately to the right and left, score two parallel lines along the wood and the waste in between crumbles away as sawdust, leaving a space called the kerf.

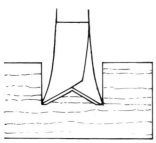

The use of the saw depends on the fineness of the teeth. The more teeth or 'points' per 25mm, the finer the cut. A large ripsaw for example may have only six points per 25mm, whereas a dovetail saw can have as many as twenty two points per 25mm for especially fine cuts.

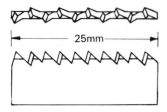

Handsaws are divided into three main types.

1. Large saws such as rip, crosscut and panel saws for rough work.

2. Backsaws such as tenon, dovetail and gent's saw for fine work.

3. Fine saws with narrow replaceable blades such as bow, keyhole, coping and fretsaws for cutting curves.

THE RIP, CROSSCUT AND PANEL SAWS

The ripsaw, about 660mm long with four and a half to six points per 25mm, is used for cutting along the grain, called 'ripping', for example to cut a 150mm wide board into two 75mm boards.

The crosscut saw is also about 660mm long but has seven or eight points per 25mm and is used for cutting across the grain, to cut boards roughly to length.

The panel saw, about 560mm long, is a smaller crosscut saw with about ten points per 25mm. If it is kept well sharpened, it is an extremely versatile hand saw because it is small enough to handle well and the teeth are just fine enough to give a fairly smooth cut.

When sawing, hold the handle with the index finger pointing along the blade for better control. Using your thumb as a guide, start the saw cut at a low angle, then raise the saw to about 45°

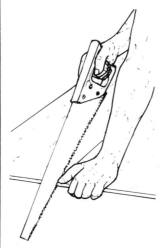

The work should always be well supported on trestles, clamped to the bench or held in a vice. During ripping, some boards have a tendency to spring together as you cut,

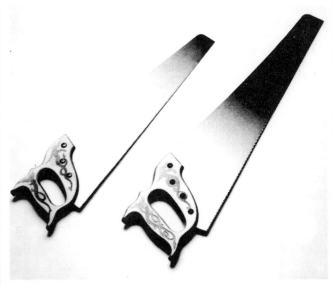

Panel crosscut saw, left ; ripsaw, right.

jamming the saw blade. The easiest remedy is to place a short wedge or a nail in the cut to keep the edges apart.

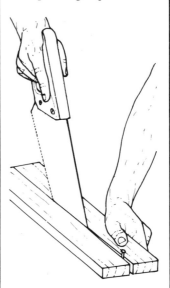

When crosscutting it is important to prevent the end

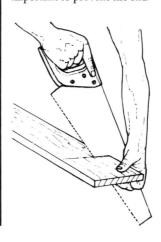

from splitting off before you finish the cut. Either support both sides of the cut as you finish, or as experienced woodworkers do, finish the cut with one smooth powerful motion to leave a clean finish.

When ripping or crosscutting with a large saw, it is a good idea to saw about 1mm away from the marked line, leaving enough waste to allow you to plane smoothly down to the line.

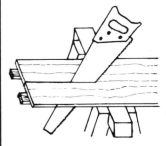

Cutting large sheet materials by hand is hard work but, in the absence of a power saw, it can of course be done. Support the sheet on two or three boards laid on trestles, with one board on each side of the cut. Use boards sturdy enough to allow you to climb on top to saw near the centre of a large sheet. On very thin sheets such as 4mm hardboard, it helps if you hold the saw at a very low angle. Remember to move the sheet over when you get near the trestle to avoid cutting into it.

BACKSAWS

The blades of the smaller crosscut saws are stiffened across the top with a rib or 'back' of steel or brass. The tenon saw, which is about the most useful of all the handsaws, is about 300mm long with twelve to fourteen points per 25mm. It is used for most fine crosscuts such as trimming off small boards to exact length, cutting joints such as halving joints or tenons, and for other small sawing jobs.

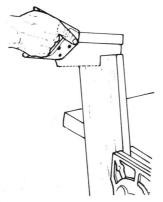

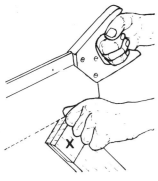

The 200mm dovetail saw, with eighteen to twenty two points, produces a finer cut and should be reserved for cutting

dovetails and other fine cuts only. It should not be used instead of the tenon saw for general work.

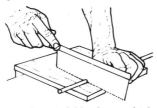

Another useful backsaw which is even finer than the dovetail saw, is the bead or gent's saw. It is convenient for cutting off small sections like dowels or beadings, using a bench hook.

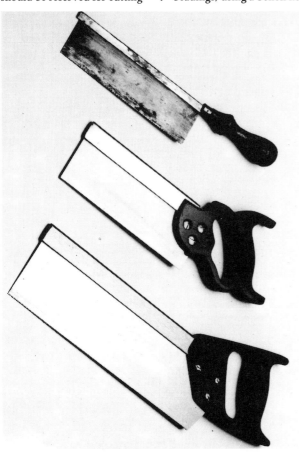

Top to bottom: gent's saw, dovetail saw, tenon saw.

MAKING A BENCH HOOK

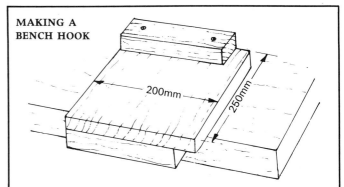

The bench hook is a simple and ingenious device which helps you to hold small pieces like dowels and mouldings during sawing.

Make it from a piece of 19mm thick plywood or hardwood, about 200 × 250mm, with two 150mm long 25 × 50mm hardwood battens screwed on as shown to the top and bottom. You can hide the

screws with wood plugs (page 214) to avoid harming the saw.

Hold the bench hook with the bottom batten against the edge of the bench and support the work against the top batten as you cut.

When the top surface gets worn, turn the bench hook over and use the other side.

CUTTING SHAPES

There are several purpose-made handsaws for cutting irregular shapes in wood. If you do a lot of work in wood which requires irregular cuts, a good sabre saw or jigsaw is very convenient because it will cut easily through solid wood as well as sheets of plywood and chipboard (page 215).

The most useful handsaw for cutting curves is the coping saw which uses easily mounted, disposable blades. The direction of the blade can be altered to make it easier to guide the saw along a curve.

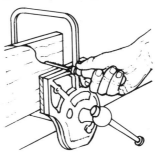

It is important to support the work well when using a coping saw. Either clamp the work in a vice and use it like an ordinary saw with the blade mounted so that the teeth point away from the handle, or support the work on a home-

made jig with a V-shaped top and use the saw vertically with the teeth pointing downwards.

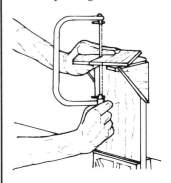

Use the coping saw to cut wood up to about 25mm in thickness. To replace the blades, first unscrew the handle a few turns, then hold the saw between your body and the bench to reduce the tension as you take out the old blade. Insert the new blade top first into the slots at each end before tightening the handle to increase the tension.

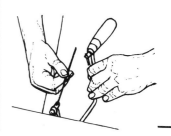

handsaws

continued from page 197

The coping saw has a narrow 'neck' which limits its use to short distances in from the edge of the wood. The fretsaw which is used with finer replaceable blades, has a longer neck and can therefore cut further in from the edge. It is used in the same way as a coping saw, with various grades of blade to make fine cuts in thinner wood.

Use the fretsaw for cutting out intricate shapes such as in decorative fretwork. To make jigsaw puzzles, glue a picture or drawing to a piece of 4mm thick plywood with contact adhesive, draw the shapes of the jigsaw pieces and cut them out with a fretsaw.

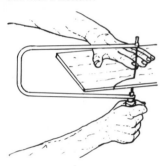

The bow saw is an old-fashioned saw which is still popular for cutting shapes. Although it is quicker to use and will cut through much thicker material than the coping saw, the bow saw will not cut such intricate shapes with sharp curves.

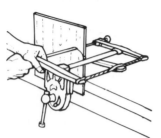

Replaceable blades for the bow saw are held, teeth pointing away from the handle, with tapered pins at each end. Tension the blade by winding the wedge around until the twine is taut, then keep it from unwinding by holding the wedge against the crossbar.

As with the coping saw and fretsaw, it is important to hold the work firmly clamped to the bench or in a vice as you use the bow saw.

SHARPENING SAWS

It is difficult as well as dangerous to cut with blunt saws. It is therefore very important to keep your saws sharp and in good condition at all times. When storing the saws wipe a light coating of oil over the blades to prevent rusting.

As soon as a saw loses its sharpness, before it is dull, either take it to a large hardware store for a 'saw doctor' to deal with it or sharpen it yourself.

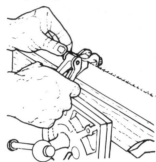

INTERIOR HOLES

To make an interior hole, such as a cut-out drawer handle, first drill a hole in the waste area. Remove one end of the

To sharpen a saw, first set the teeth to the required angle, alternately left and right, using a special saw set which adjusts according to the fineness of the teeth. Then sharpen the edges of the teeth with a fine triangular file, removing as little metal as possible. Clamp the saw in a vice between two pieces of wood then file the tips of the blades, holding the file horizontally.

To sharpen the crosscut saw, file at a 60° angle following the original sharpened angle of the teeth. For a ripsaw, file at a 90° angle straight across the saw blade.

blade of the coping saw or fretsaw from its fixing and thread it through the hole before re-fitting the blade to cut the interior shape.

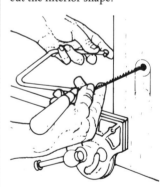

The keyhole saw or padsaw, with a small narrow blade, is easier to use for cutting interior shapes because there is no need to undo the blade as with frame saws. It can also be used as a substitute for the sabre saw for cutting openings in plywood, as for example in the captain's bed project on page 60.

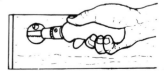

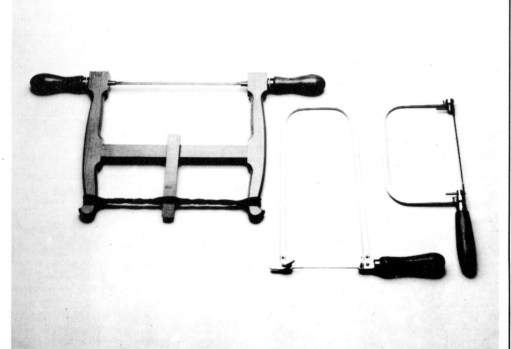

Frame saws for cutting curves. Left to right: bow saw, fret saw and coping saw.

chisels and gouges

There are various types of chisels such as bevel edge, firmer and mortise chisels for use on particular types of work. The mortise chisel for example has a stout, heavy blade for cutting out mortise slots. For most jobs only bevel edge chisels will be needed. Buy the 6, 12 and 19mm sizes first, adding wider chisels as you need them.

The handles are made either from a hardwood such as boxwood or ash, or from shock resistant plastic. The wooden handles may feel and look better, but the plastic ones last longer.

Gouges, in widths from 6 to 38mm, have curved blades for cutting rounded shapes or grooves. There are two types of gouge. The firmer gouge, used for cutting grooves, has the ground bevel on the underside and the scribing gouge has the bevel on the inside.

USING CHISELS

Chisels cut with a wedge-like action so they tend to split the wood fibres apart as they go into the wood. When cutting along the grain be sure to cut in the right direction to prevent the point from digging into and splitting the wood.

Chisels are used mainly for paring away wood both horizontally and vertically for joints and shaping.

Always support the work well, hold it in a vice for horizontal paring and on a waste board for vertical chiselling. When cutting a halving joint, pare away slices from both sides with the cuts slanting upwards before final levelling. This reduces the risk of splits caused by cutting straight through from one side only. Guide the chisel with one hand while you provide the force with the other hand, or with a mallet.

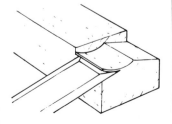

Vertical chiselling is very similar. Clamp the wood onto a flat piece of waste wood and with your hand over the chisel, firmly pare away small slices at a time. When cutting across end grain like this, there is of course no danger of the chisel digging into the wood. At the same time, cutting across the grain requires more force so remove a small amount of wood at a time so that the chisel does not slip.

To cut a mortise joint, use a mallet for greater driving power. Using a chisel the exact width of the mortise slot, carefully chisel away the wood with firm taps from the mallet. Remove the bulk of the wood first by drilling holes within the waste area to the correct

SHARPENING CHISELS AND GOUGES

Chisels should always be kept razor sharp by frequent honing on an oilstone. Most chisels are ground at an angle of 22° to 25° by the manufacturer and usually honed on an oilstone to a second cutting bevel of 30°.

However, for all but the most heavy work, one long bevel at 25° for bevel edge chisels gives much better results. It takes practice to rub the chisel back and forth at a constant angle to get a flat bevel, so invest in a honing guide which holds the blade at the correct angle.

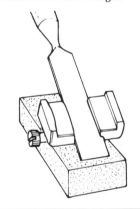

depth and then cleaning out the slot with a chisel.

When cutting out waste to a marked or gauged line, remember that the bevel on the chisel forces the blade in at an angle away from the direction of cut. Always cut away a recess within the waste area first, then pare away gradually up to the line.

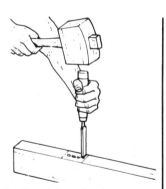

When sharpening all cutting irons for chisels, planes and spokeshaves, first hone the bevel side, then turn the blade over and rub back and forth a few times across the stone to remove the burr of metal that will have formed.

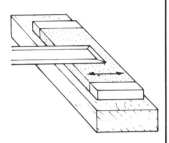

Firmer gouges are sharpened in a similar way, first by honing on the rounded edge of a special oilstone and then removing the burr on the inside with a curved slipstone.

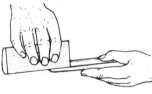

Chisel points which are nicked or very worn must be re-ground on a grinding wheel. Grinding on a wheel leaves a curved, slightly hollow shape which must be honed flat on an oilstone.

Use a gouge in the same way as a chisel, either using hand force or a mallet to cut away curved shapes.

To cut a curved groove use the correct width gouge and make successively deeper cuts until you can pare away the final layer in long, smooth cuts.

planes

In a furniture workshop, most planing is done by machine. The sawn planks are run over a surface planer or jointer to get one good face and a square edge from which all measurements are taken.

Hand planing requires considerably more skill and hard work but it is infinitely more enjoyable and rewarding. Several of the projects in this book are made from hardwoods like beech or maple which are usually available only in a rough sawn state and it requires a great deal of hard work to plane them smooth by hand. In this case it is probably best to have the boards planed by a woodworking shop or by the supplier.

Hand planes are nonetheless required for many jobs in the shop such as 'truing up' boards when joining several boards into a table top, for squaring off ends and for many other small jobs.

Left to right: try, jack, smoothing and block plane.

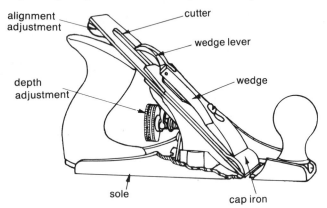

The cutting blade of a plane is usually either 50 or 60mm wide and must be kept sharp by rubbing on an oilstone. The blade can be adjusted for a finer or heavier cut by means of a knurled knob. There is usually a lever which is moved sideways to adjust the blade parallel with the base.

The blade is attached to a cap iron which is mounted about 1mm back from the tip of the blade depending on whether a fine or heavy cut is required.

The cap iron breaks up the wood shavings and prevents the wood underneath from splitting along the board.

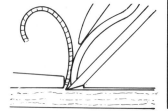

GENERAL PURPOSE PLANES

Modern metal planes are available in lengths from 200mm to 600mm. For most work only three or four planes will be needed. For 'truing up' boards and general levelling, buy a 550mm try plane. For rougher work a 350 to 375mm jack plane is very useful and for final surfacing the 200 or 225mm smoothing plane is a good size. The small block plane is also very handy for planing ends of boards. Before using any plane, make sure that the blade is razor sharp and that the cap iron is correctly set. Then sight along the bottom and adjust the lever to get the blade set parallel to the base. When planing, make sure the board is held on a firm, horizontal surface. For long pieces either use the bench stop mounted in the workbench top, or nail a batten to the bench as a stop

for the board. The plane will gradually take off high spots on the board until it is even. Remember that the longer the plane, the more accurate the work.

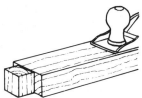

Work with a smooth motion applying even pressure along the whole length. Don't lift the plane up until the plane is beyond the end of the board.

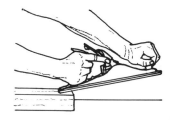

On narrow edges it is difficult to keep the plane square. To help support the plane, hold one hand along the edge as a guide. Check the work frequently for straightness by sighting along the length and for squareness by using a try square.

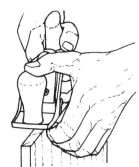

PLANING A TABLE TOP

Several of the projects in this book involve gluing up boards to make wide, solid surfaces. After the joints have been glued or dowelled, it is best to finish by making the top smooth and even using a long plane such as a jointer or try plane. Depending on how much wood will have to be removed to smooth the top, set the blade to take as fine a cut as possible. Then after scraping off any dried glue, start by planing the surface of the boards diagonally.

Plane in one direction then in the other, checking continually for high spots by holding the plane on edge or by using a straight edge.

After the top is fairly flat and even, plane along the length of the boards. Finish off the surface with a very fine setting to leave a smooth and even surface, ready for sanding.

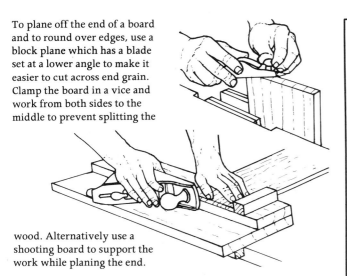

To plane off the end of a board and to round over edges, use a block plane which has a blade set at a lower angle to make it easier to cut across end grain. Clamp the board in a vice and work from both sides to the middle to prevent splitting the wood. Alternatively use a shooting board to support the work while planing the end.

MAKING A SHOOTING BOARD

The shooting board is a useful holding device for accurately planing the board ends or the edges of thin, awkward boards. Make the base from two 19mm thick hardwood boards or from plywood, 750mm long. The 150mm wide top board is glued and screwed to the 225mm wide base. The stop is made from a 32mm square section of hardwood and screwed absolutely square to a groove cut in the top. To use the shooting board, hold the wood firmly against the stop and run the plane on its side so that it takes off fine shavings.

SHOULDER PLANE

The shoulder plane is a small plane for cleaning up the shoulders of tenons and other joints.

Adjust the depth of the blade with the screw at the back. To remove the blade for sharpening, pass it through the bottom.

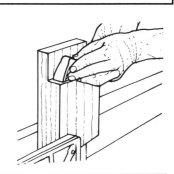

SPECIAL PURPOSE PLANES

Two kinds of plane which may come in handy in shop work are the combination plane and

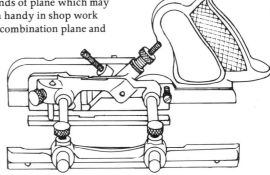

Clockwise from top right: rabbet, shoulder and combination plane with blades.

RABBET PLANE

The blades on ordinary planes don't extend the full width of the plane so they can't be used to cut rabbets.

The rabbet plane is extremely useful in cabinetwork. Many of the projects in this book require rabbets to hold back panels, for example the bookcase on page 114.

A portable router is the easiest way to cut a rabbet, but for the experienced woodworker the rabbet plane is just as quick. The rabbet plane has an adjustable fence for the width of the rabbet, and a gauge to set the depth. For through rabbets, which extend to the end of the board, use the blade in the normal position and run the plane along the wood, pressed firmly against the side.

It takes a little practice to get this right so make a few trial runs on scrap pieces before planing your piece of work.

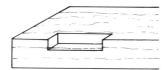

For stopped rabbets, chisel out the first inch or so, then place the blade in the forward or bull-nose position and cut the rabbet in stages beginning at the chiselled end and working gradually back toward the other end.

moulding plane. The combination plane is a multi-purpose plane which comes with interchangeable cutters for cutting grooves, rabbets, mouldings and even tongue-and-groove edges. It is rather expensive, but for a furniture maker who relies on hand tools it is a versatile plane.

There are various other planes used for special jobs, such as adjustable compass planes for planing along arcs, and plough planes for making grooves.

Moulding planes take the place of the router which is widely

used to cut decorative edges on furniture. Wooden moulding planes are still available with variously shaped blades to cut moulded edges by hand. Cabinetmakers once made their own moulding planes, grinding the cutters to shape from old files and fashioning the body of the plane in beech or similar hardwood.

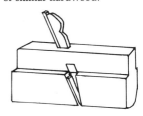

clamps

Clamps are essential for even the smallest woodworking jobs. They not only hold wood together tightly while glue sets to form a permanent bond, but clamps are frequently used to hold pieces leaving both hands free to work. They are also useful during assembly to pull and hold joints together and to straighten out framework constructions.

Probably the most frequent use of clamps is to hold work down securely to the bench while you saw, rout, drill or chisel it. A workshop can never have enough clamps of various sizes. You always seem to need one more at a critical moment. But it is best to start off with three or four clamps and then add to your collection as need arises rather than investing in expensive clamps before you know exactly what you require.

There are various types and sizes of clamp. The most common small clamp is the C or G-clamp which comes in sizes from 50mm to about 200mm maximum opening size. The basic tool kit should include at least two C-clamps, one 150 or 200mm and one about 100mm.

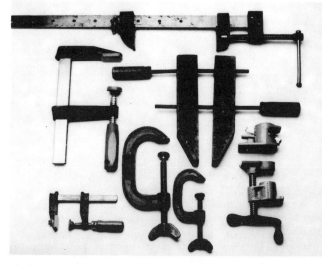

Clockwise from top: bar clamp, hand screw, pipe clamp heads, C-clamps, small and large fast action clamps.

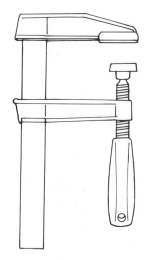

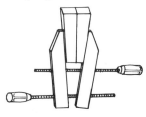

The two screws operate separately along the two wooden heads which can be set at any angle.

To clamp large pieces such as boards to make up table tops, bar clamps, also known as sash clamps, are required. The best type has an integral bar with holes to take a locking pin on the moveable head. As a less expensive substitute, buy separate components and make

Another useful type of clamp, in sizes from 100 to 600mm, is the fast action type which can be opened and closed in one movement. This type is fitted with plastic pads on the ends of the jaws so no additional padding is needed to protect the work. The handle can be given extra force by inserting a screwdriver or bar into a hole.

The old-fashioned wooden handscrew is particularly good for clamping at an angle.

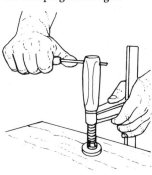

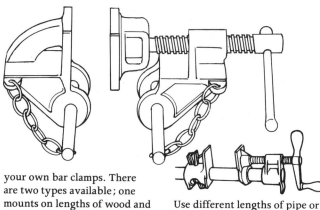

your own bar clamps. There are two types available; one mounts on lengths of wood and the other on lengths of plumbing pipe. The advantage of these clamps is that you can make them as long as you wish.

Use different lengths of pipe or wood and with just a few sets of clamp heads, you have a complete range of bar clamps from, say, 600 to 2100mm.

USING THE CLAMPS

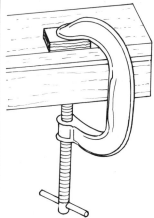

The most important rule about clamping is to always put a sturdy piece of waste wood under the clamp heads, unless they are

already protected with plastic pads, to avoid leaving indentations on your work. Do it automatically whether you are clamping a piece of plywood down as a guide for the saw, or holding two components together while glue sets. That way you will not mark the work.

Notice that the fast action clamps which are available in up to 600mm lengths do not require padding. They are often used to hold pieces firmly together leaving two hands free to do the work.

When gluing boards up into a single surface, use several bar clamps and alternate them under and over the surface to keep the boards flat. It is a good idea to use a stout batten under the clamp heads along each side, both as padding for the clamp heads and also to spread the clamping force evenly along the length.

Without dowel pegs in the edges the boards tend to slip

SPECIAL CLAMPS

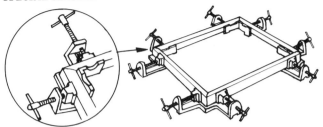

There are many special clamps such as mitre clamps and web clamps which are used for specific jobs. Mitre clamps are used in sets of four to clamp a mitred frame together. Alternatively, you can make a simple string device with cut corner blocks which makes the job even easier.

A web or band clamp is a special device which is convenient for gluing awkwardly shaped objects. It is often used when repairing broken chairs to hold the legs together until the glue sets.

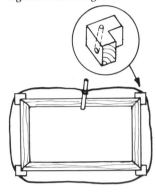

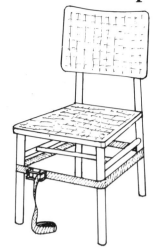

HOMEMADE CLAMPING DEVICES

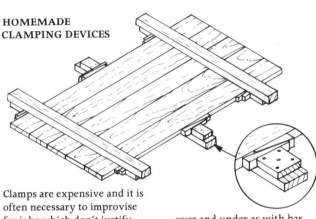

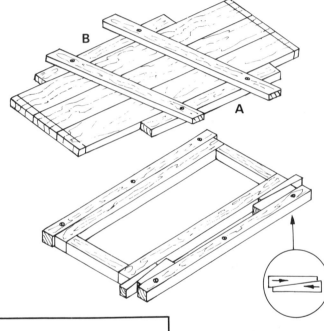

Clamps are expensive and it is often necessary to improvise for jobs which don't justify buying additional clamps for the workshop. Instead of bar clamps, you can screw stops onto stout battens, then tap pairs of hardwood wedges between to tighten up the boards. Place them alternately over and under as with bar clamps.

Another old-fashioned device suitable for light work is shown in the diagram. The battens A and B are moved sideways to bring them closer together. When they are tight enough, a nail or screw next to A and B holds them in place until the glue has set.

Another clever device uses wedges, again placed between two strong battens screwed to a base. Alternatively, screw one batten to the workbench and use the vice to tighten up against the other side.

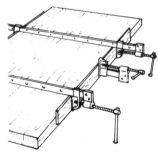

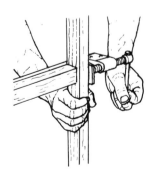

slightly as you apply clamping pressure. This results in an uneven surface which requires considerable work in planing flat. To minimize slipping, apply only modest pressure and pay close attention to the joints, gently tapping them flat with a rubber mallet if necessary as you tighten up the clamps.

Lay a straight edge across the boards as a final check for flatness when you tighten up the clamps.

Also use bar clamps to hold frameworks together until the glue sets. Clamp straight across the joints using softening to protect the wood and tighten slowly pulling the joint together gradually until it is tight. You may have to add a clamp from the other side to keep the joint tight on all sides. Put the clamps at a slight angle to correct the frame if it is not square.

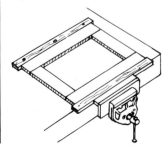

shaping tools

SPOKESHAVES AND DRAWKNIVES

For shaping irregular surfaces there is no substitute for hand tools. Even the most modern furniture factories employ craftsmen who are skilled with the spokeshave and drawknife and can use these tools quickly, with an experienced and accurate eye.

The drawknife is the most basic shaping tool and is used

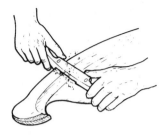

to remove large amounts of wood or to get a piece roughly to shape.

The spokeshave is a finer tool and if kept sharp and properly set, is capable of producing a finish on hardwoods which will require no sanding. There are several types of spokeshave with either wood or metal handles. The metal variety can be plain or adjustable. The blade on the adjustable type can be set by fine screws. It is a precision instrument well worth buying if you will be working with hardwoods.

USING A DRAWKNIFE

The drawknife is ideal for removing large amounts of wood in a short time. It must be kept razor sharp by honing the bevelled edge with a hand-held oilstone and then rubbing with the stone to remove the burr on the underside.

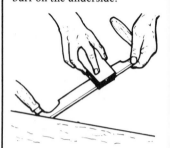

Always cut along the grain to avoid digging into the wood. Hold the tool with both hands and control the cutting angle with the thumbs. The drawknife can be used bevel downwards for light cuts or for cutting convex shapes, but it is usually used bevel up.

USING A SPOKESHAVE

As with all cutting tools, the success of working depends a great deal on keeping the blade very sharp. If you use the spokeshave frequently, sharpen the blade often as you work. The blades of metal-handled spokeshaves are flat so they can be sharpened just as plane irons, but those for wooden spokeshaves must be honed with a small hand-held slipstone.

Use the spokeshave with a light wrist action in a slight shearing or diagonal direction to give a smoother surface.

Work from the middle of the curve toward the ends. On the screw-adjustable types, adjust the set of the blade with both setting screws until you get just the right thickness of shaving.

On the wooden type, the tangs which protrude through the body must be tapped gently with a hammer to get the adjustment just right.

RASPS, FILES AND SURFORMS

You can also use rasps and files for shaping wood. The edges are rounded on many of the projects in this book to make them look softer. This can be done equally well with a Surform, rasp or a file. The rasp is a very coarse file used for preliminary shaping to remove a large amount of wood. Buy a 250mm long rasp with one side rounded and one side flat for all-purpose work.

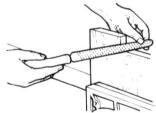

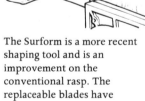

The Surform is a more recent shaping tool and is an improvement on the conventional rasp. The replaceable blades have perforated, raised teeth so that the sawdust can escape.

The variously sized blades are held in an array of handles to cut flat or round shapes. They are excellent for removing wood quickly but they must be used carefully.

Use Surforms with the blade set either for a pushing motion like a plane or for a pulling motion for rounded shapes.

Files give a smoother cut than rasps and Surforms and are used for finer work or for cleaning up after preliminary shaping. Various types are used but the most useful general file is the bastard double cut which gives a medium cut.

All files and rasps should be kept clean and hung up when not in use. To remove the clogged wood from the teeth, use a wire brush or a wire file card, or if the tool is especially clogged gently heat it over a flame to burn off the dust.

screwdrivers

Besides hammers and saws, the screwdriver seems to be the most frequently used tool in the workshop. It should of course be used only for turning screws and not used to prise open cans of paint and to do odd jobs. The main types of screwdriver are the standard screwdriver, the ratchet type, the spiral pump action ratchet or Yankee screwdriver, and the Phillips screwdriver.

All of these are available in different lengths from about 75 to 400mm long. It is important to notice that screwdriver tips also come in a range of widths and to choose a screwdriver to

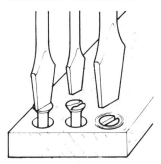

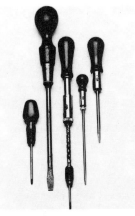

match the screw you are driving. For fine work, get into the habit of using the right sized tip for each job, to avoid damaging the screw or the wood, see left. The same is true of Phillips screwdrivers which are used for screws with cross slots in the head.

A few sizes of screwdrivers will be adequate for most work. It is always useful to have one really long screwdriver for large screws and one very small one.

A ratchet screwdriver allows you to set the blade for forward, normal or reverse action and allows you to turn the screw with one hand without having to change grip.

The pump action or Yankee screwdriver is very convenient. It comes in sizes up to 710mm long and each size has interchangeable blades for variously sized screws. It can be used closed like an ordinary screwdriver for better control or opened full length with

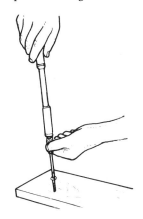

pump action. To use it this way, first put the screw in a few turns so that it is secure, then place the tip of the screwdriver in the slot and push down on the handle.

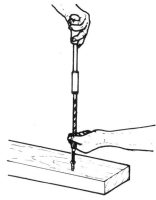

But be careful as the blade can easily slip and damage your work or injure you. Remember that after frequent use all screwdriver tips become rounded and dull, which increases their tendency to slip. Always keep the tips ground square and sharp to give a good grip.

miscellaneous hand tools

PLIERS AND PINCERS
There are many other hand tools and devices which are sometimes required in woodworking. Pliers and pincers for example will come in handy for a variety of jobs in the workshop from pulling out nails and staples to stripping wire for fitting a new plug.

An adjustable wrench is also indispensable in a workshop for tightening nuts on machines and for fixing bolts in wood. Buy a good quality adjustable wrench as it will last longer and give better service than a cheap one.

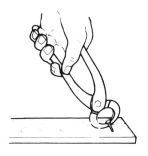

CABINET SCRAPER
Cabinet scrapers are pieces of thin, flat metal available in various sizes and used to give a very fine finish to hardwood surfaces. They are inexpensive to buy, but are very useful for fine work. They must be sharpened carefully with an oilstone file and burnisher to bring up a burr along the

bottom cutting edge. Use the scraper with both hands, curving it slightly as you push it along the grain. A sharp scraper should bring up a fine shaving of wood, not just dust.

WOOD SCREW AND TAP
Another interesting device which opens up all sorts of possibilities is the wood screw

box and the matching screw tap. Although it is available only from specialist suppliers and is quite expensive, it allows you to make threaded wooden screws and matching threaded holes. You could for example make wooden bolt connectors and matching nuts.

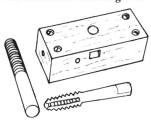

MITRE BOX AND MITRE BLOCK
There are various devices for cutting accurate mitres with a tenon saw. The mitre box is

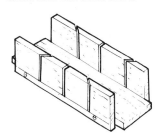

SANDING BLOCK

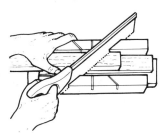

Sanding blocks are made of cork or felt-faced wood in a convenient size to fit the hand, using a quarter of a standard sheet of sandpaper. You should always use blocks rather than your bare hand to back up the sandpaper to apply even pressure. To get into moulded shapes, make up small sanding blocks using dowels or wood scraps.

inexpensive to buy and quite accurate to use. Screw a long base plate to the base of the box to support the work and to avoid marking the mitre box.

workbench and accessories

THE WORKBENCH AND SIMPLE SUBSTITUTES

Much of the furniture in this book can be made on a temporary work surface but it is much easier if you have a workbench set up in a spare room, garage, garden shed or basement. It is very convenient to have a workshop area, however humble, where you don't feel inhibited about sawdust and where you have enough space to work on large sheets of material.

A woodworking bench is important because it gives solid support and has a vice to hold work steady. There are complete instructions for making a solid screw-together workbench on page 136. The bench has a plywood top which can be replaced when it gets too worn. Alternatively, you can buy a bench made from a hardwood such as beech with a side vice for holding small pieces and also an end vice for holding longer pieces while planing.

VICES

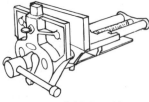

Vices are available in various weights and sizes. The woodworker's vice is a heavy-duty model which bolts or screws onto the bench from underneath. It is available with or without a quick release mechanism which allows you to open and close the vice by just pushing or pulling instead of turning the handle. The face plates should be fitted with pieces of plywood so that the work is not damaged.

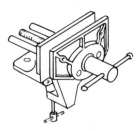

You can also buy vices which clamp onto the bench or table

top. These are not as strong but will hold light work very well. For planing, use a bench stop which fits into the bench top. The hardwood block is mounted from underneath and raised through a slot cut into the top of the bench to hold the work steady.

Woodworkers frequently use clamps to hold the work down on the bench. This is a good technique for large pieces which cannot be held by a vice. Benches and vices are expensive, but you can use substitutes such as trestles, Workmate or a sturdy table.

TRESTLES AND SAWHORSES

Trestles or sawhorses are indispensable in a workshop. They can be made the traditional way using softwood sections, or they can be put together quickly using two pieces of chipboard hinged together as shown on page 108.

Use the trestles or sawhorses in

THE WORKMATE

The Workmate is a fairly recent invention which is becoming extremely popular and for good reason. It is sturdy and has a built-in vice which grips work of most sizes while you work, leaving both hands free. When it is not in use, it folds flat so that it can be hung on the wall out of the way.

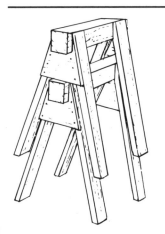

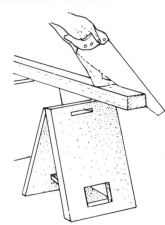

pairs to hold long pieces of wood for crosscutting or ripping.

When crosscutting long heavy pieces, it is a good idea to turn one trestle sideways along the wood and set the blade so that it just cuts through the wood. Position the cut so that both

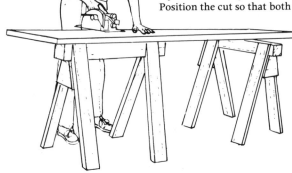

ends are supported to prevent the saw from jamming or the wood from splitting.

Use the trestles for working on large sheets. To saw a sheet of plywood or chipboard for example, lay a couple of stout boards on the trestles under the sheet on each side of the cut. Climb up on the surface if

necessary to reach the end of the cut.

To assemble work or for doing finishing work like sanding, lay a piece of plywood on the trestles and cover it with an old blanket to protect the surface of your work. A pair of trestles can also be used as a workbench. A solid door or 50mm thick boards can be screwed down to make the work surface.

STORING WOOD

Storing wood is always a problem. If you do work continuously, the scraps will accumulate very quickly. It is always difficult to throw pieces of wood away so the best method is to keep a cardboard box for scraps and to empty it and start again when it fills up.

For storing larger pieces, either make a rack on the wall for storing boards flat with enough supports to prevent sagging, or store the pieces

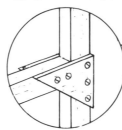

vertically against a wall, first sorting them into lengths.

Store large sheets in the same way, standing them on edge leaning against a wall. Be careful to store them so that they cannot fall over. It is a good idea to provide a stop to

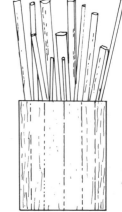

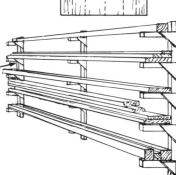

hold the sheets in place and to tie bundles of wood to the wall. Blockboard must be stored flat.

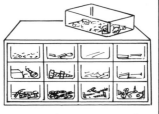

Overhead racks can be a nuisance because the wood is hard to reach and pieces tend to get buried. They can also be dangerous unless they are strong enough to take the full weight of a load of wood.

Dowels, mouldings and other pieces of hardwood should be stored in a warm, dry place and should not be subjected to changes in temperature and moisture or they may warp.

STORAGE IN THE WORKSHOP

All tools are better hung up within reach rather than slung in drawers where they are easily blunted or damaged. Pegboard is the best material to use as a base for hanging tools.

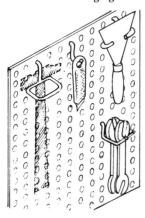

Draw the outline of each tool on the pegboard and screw in hooks or nails before hanging it, so that you can replace tools in the right place.

You can also make a slat wall unit similar to the one shown on page 22 for hanging up your tools. For chisels and screwdrivers make a simple rack from lengths of wood

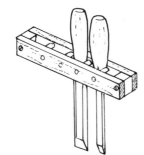

with dowel dividers as on the workbench on page 136.

For those tools which you want to keep locked up or away from dust, make a wall-hung tool cabinet such as the one shown on page 140.

There are also numerous racks and plastic drawer systems which you can buy to house screws and hardware and all the other small bits which inevitably accumulate in a workshop.

the circular saw

The portable circular saw is a worthwhile investment for anyone who does a lot of woodworking. You can fit a saw attachment to the electric drill, but it isn't very powerful and it's time-consuming to switch back and forth from saw to drill while you are working. The best answer is a 125mm or preferably a 185mm circular saw. The 185mm diameter model is powerful enough to cut cleanly through fairly thick softwood and hardwood and through heavy plywood sheets. Also with more power you get greater accuracy and safety. The more powerful saw will cut straight and clean and has less tendency to bind in the wood or kick back.

The essential features of the circular saw are the **1.** motor, **2.** blade, **3.** guard, **4.** adjustment knobs, **5.** base plates and **6.** detachable rip fence.

CHOOSING THE RIGHT BLADE
Blades are available in various diameters to suit specific saws and in various types for specific uses.

The rip blade and crosscut blade are used for the two basic functions, cutting along and cutting across the grain of the wood. The combination blade both rips and crosscuts.

The planer blade is also a combination blade but it is hollow ground to leave a very smooth finish. Carbide tipped blades can also be used for both ripping and crosscutting. The hard tips stay sharp much longer than ordinary blades and cut more cleanly, even in harder woods. These are much more expensive than the ordinary blades but they soon pay for themselves.

You can also buy special blades for cutting through floorboards and the occasional nail, and blades which cut non-ferrous metals. Refer to a manufacturer's catalogue for a complete list of available blades.

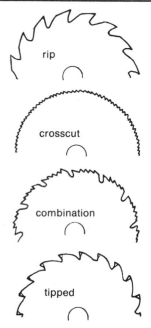

1. The motor should be at least 0.5kw to do most medium work. For heavier construction work a larger, 1.5kw model will be necessary.

2. The blade is locked on the shaft or arbour. There are various types of blades available for different jobs.

3. The spring-loaded guard is an important safety feature. It comes down automatically to cover the blade as soon as you move the saw away from the work. It is also raised automatically when you start a cut.

4. There is a knob for adjusting the depth of the cut indicated on a scale on the side of the saw. On some saws there is a second knob for locking the blade at any angle up to 45° to allow for bevel cuts.

5. The base plate rests on the wood as you push the saw along. Keep the base plate clean and rub a hard wax candle over it occasionally to reduce the friction. Notice the small notch at the front of the base plate ahead of the blade which is used as a guide when you are using the saw to cut freehand.

6. The rip fence is adjusted and locked in position for use in guiding the saw parallel to the edge of the work.

USING THE SAW
You can use the circular saw in various ways; freehand or with guides for ripping or crosscutting, with the blade tilted for angled cuts or with a shallow set to make grooves or saw kerfs. You can also mount the saw in a stand to make a very useful table saw.

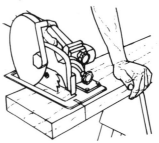

For quick crosscuts, for example to cut a board into

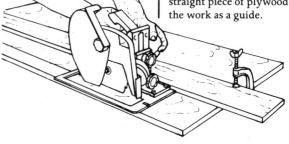

rough lengths, use the saw freehand with the notch at the front of the base plate as a guide. You can also rip freehand but it is more accurate to fit the rip fence as a guide for cutting parallel to the edge. Notice the strip of hardwood screwed to the fence.

If the cut is too far in from the edge for the rip fence to reach, clamp a straight edge or a straight piece of plywood to the work as a guide.

MAKING OTHER CUTS

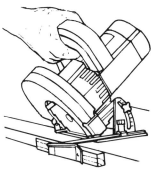

Make angled cuts in the same way, running the saw against a guide. To make grooves, set the blade to the required depth and make a series of cuts moving the fence a short distance for each cut.

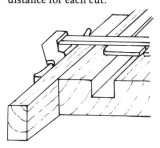

You can bend wood by first cutting a series of closely spaced grooves called kerfs, along the inside to within about 3mm of the bottom face. Test for depth of cut and for spacing of kerfs to get it right.

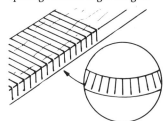

CONVERTING TO A TABLE SAW

To make the portable saw into a table saw, you can buy a special metal table sold by the manufacturer, but this table is quite small and is not adequate for cutting large sheets.

Make a table out of a piece of 750 × 1000mm plywood 19mm thick, with stiffening battens screwed underneath. It can be nailed or screwed to a pair of sawhorses or placed on its own structure. Cut a hole in the plywood top to allow the saw blade and guard to pass through, then bolt the saw to the underside with

countersunk machine screws. To make a crosscut fence, cut a 50mm wide groove exactly parallel to the blade about 300mm away, then make an absolutely square fence with a batten underneath which fits

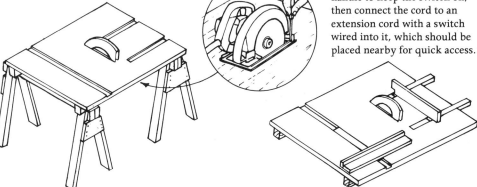

CHANGING A BLADE

Always disconnect the power before changing blades. Then remove the locking nut with the wrench or Allen key provided with the saw. If necessary hold the blade stationary against a block of wood or the edge of the bench when undoing the nut.

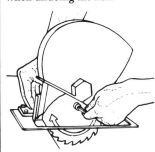

Refit the new blade so that the arrow printed on the side of the blade is pointing in the correct direction. Then tighten the locking nut with the wrench provided. The thread of the tightening nut is reversed so that it will tend to tighten when the saw is working.

snugly in the groove to allow it to run back and forth.

The rip fence can be set by measuring for parallel each time, or it can be made to run in two grooves cut square to the blade. When using the saw, wedge a block of wood into the handle to keep the switch on, then connect the cord to an extension cord with a switch wired into it, which should be placed nearby for quick access.

MAKING A 2.44m LONG STRAIGHT EDGE GUIDE

Screw a 300mm wide strip of 4mm thick plywood to a 125mm wide board of 19mm plywood. Screw from underneath and countersink the 12mm no.6 screws to leave a smooth surface.

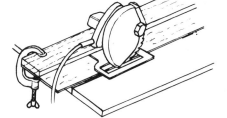

Then clamp this over the edge of the bench and run the saw along the 19mm board, cutting off the 4mm piece.

To use the guide, clamp it to the work with the edge of the 4mm plywood flush against the measured marks.

To make a shorter version of the guide for crosscutting and

cutting smaller panels of plywood, screw a 75mm piece of plywood underneath, positioned absolutely square. This is then used like a try square against one mark to make square cuts.

table saw

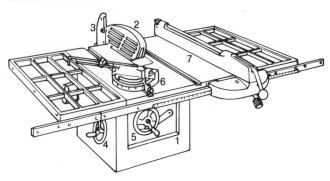

Whether you buy a table saw, or improvise with a plywood stand and a circular saw (see page 209). it will prove to be the most valuable tool in the workshop. Almost all the cutting work can be done on it, not just crosscuts and rips, but with a little ingenuity you can also cut bevels, tongues-and-grooves, rabbets, tapers and so on.

For most people the job of cutting boards accurately to length so that they are truly square isn't as easy as it sounds, and yet the success of every project depends on it. With a table saw, you can do it easily and automatically.

The main features of the table saw are 1. motor assembly, 2. blade guard, 3. splitter and anti-kickback fingers, 4. rise and fall control, 5. tilt control and of course the table

itself with 6. sliding crosscut and mitre fence, and 7. rip fence.

It is important to select a table saw which is sturdy and robust, and which has all the necessary safety features. Don't buy a cheap saw, it isn't worth it, because the resulting inaccuracies in your work will waste more wood than it would cost to buy a good saw.

The more power a saw has, the better. You should avoid one with less than 0.5 kw. The effective cut of a saw blade is roughly $\frac{1}{3}$ its diameter, so a 200mm blade will cut 67mm material.

It is important that the area of the table around the saw blade is filled in with a metal or wooden insert, to prevent small pieces of wood from getting wedged next to the saw blade. The saw should have

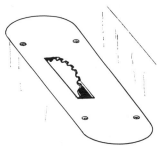

easily operated controls for raising and lowering the saw blade and a separate control and indicator for tilting the blade.

Most good saws have all these features and more and it's a good idea, as with all tools, but particularly with this one, to buy the best you can afford.

SAFETY
The table saw is a dangerous tool and is always treated with respect and a small measure of fear even by professionals who have been in the trade all their lives. Many of the serious accidents happen on the table saw.

It is very important to develop the right habits and never to take chances with the saw.

Safety laws vary from country to country but it's always wise to have a guard and splitter and anti-kickback fingers fitted. During ripping some boards release their built-in tension and spring together closing up on the blade. This causes the saw blade to throw the piece of wood backwards towards the operator with tremendous force. This is prevented by the splitter and anti-kickback fingers.

The best way to prevent accidents is to keep your hands away from the blade. Use a push stick every time you rip a board and when you are cutting small pieces, clamp them to the fence rather than gripping them dangerously close to the blade.

Another safety point worth noting is the use of a support behind the saw to prevent long boards which are being ripped from tipping down and lifting the other end up into the saw blade. Make a table to stand behind the saw or, even better, a roller on a trestle as shown.

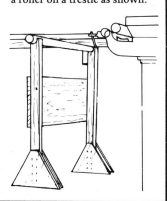

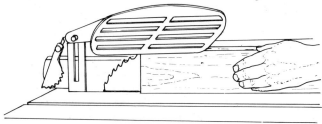

SAW BLADES

The saw blades used in the table saw are basically the same as those used in the portable circular saw. The crosscut, rip, combination, and carbide tipped blades are shown on page 208. In addition, you can use a marking head and also a dado head blade for cutting grooves and dados. It has two outside cutters and inside blades of different thicknesses to cut grooves of varying widths.

USING THE TABLE SAW

Crosscutting

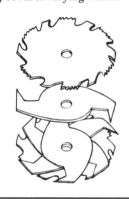

The main function of a table saw is to crosscut boards accurately and squarely. Hold the work firmly against the crosscut or mitre fence as you push it slowly through the saw. It's a good idea to attach a board to the mitre fence to give better support. Always

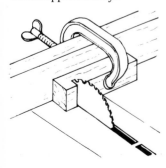

support small, difficult to hold pieces with a stick or by clamping them to the fence.

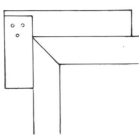

To cut off several identical lengths, clamp a stop to the crosscut fence as a guide. For shorter pieces, clamp the stop to the rip fence instead. Place the stop well in front of the saw blade so that the scrap pieces will not bind between the stop and the blade.

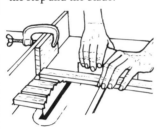

It's quite easy to make tenons, housings and halving joints on the table saw. Use a piece of scrap as a trial piece to set the saw blade at the required depth. Make a cut and measure it to make sure it's the correct depth. Then set one stop on the crosscut fence and the other on the rip fence as guides for the first and last cuts. Remove the waste as shown below with successive runs of the saw. Again use a piece of scrap to make sure the width of the halving notch or the tenon is exactly right and make any fine adjustments necessary before cutting the pieces.

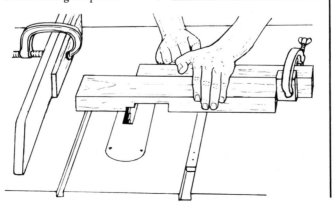

Cutting mitres

To cut mitres, set the fence at 45°. Test by cutting two mitres and holding them together against a try square. They should make an exact 90° angle.

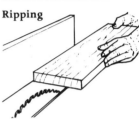

In cutting mitres, the work tends to move or creep slightly if not held firmly. To prevent this, either clamp a small scrap to the fence as a stop, or alternatively hammer a couple of pins from the back of the wood fence so that their heads just protrude to keep the work from moving.

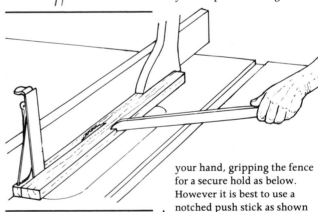

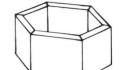

You can cut mitres to make picture frames or doors (see cupboard on page 155). For hexagonal or other shapes, set the mitre gauge to the appropriate angle and use a stop to make all the pieces identical.

Ripping

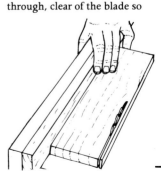

To cut boards along their length use the rip fence. Adjust it for each cut by checking the scale indicator or by trial and error against a mark on the piece to be cut. When ripping, always push the wood firmly at a slow constant rate, guiding firmly against the fence with the left hand or a push stick.

If the board is wide enough, you can push it through with your hand, gripping the fence for a secure hold as below. However it is best to use a notched push stick as shown above to guide the piece through. Push it straight through, clear of the blade so

table saw

continued from page 211

that it won't bind against the fence and get thrown back. For smaller pieces, use two push sticks; one to push from behind and one to keep the piece down and against the fence.

Remember when ripping long boards to support the end behind the saw to keep it from dropping down which would result in the front end jamming against the blade.

When ripping boards on their edge into thinner boards, called resawing, it may be necessary to make two runs if the sawblade isn't large

enough to cut it in one. Make the first cut then turn the board over, keeping the same side against the fence, to make the second cut.

When resawing it is a good idea to hold the work down with a special board clamped to the fence. Cut the board with a coping saw or sabre saw to produce feathers. With the board clamped at the right height, the feathers allow work to be pushed through but prevent it from being thrown back.

Cutting bevels and mitred edges

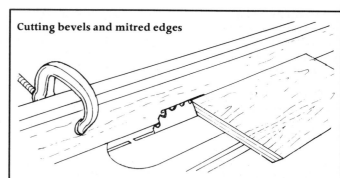

Make bevels and mitred edges simply by tilting the blade. When making mitre cuts it's a good idea to clamp a piece of wood to the rip fence and raise the blade so that it just cuts into it. Then rip the piece as usual.

To cut mitre joints reinforced with a plywood spline, first cut all the pieces of wood at 45° as shown, then lower the blade to cut the groove the width of the sawblade. The groove should extend about 6mm into each side.

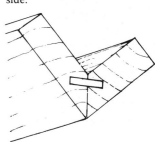

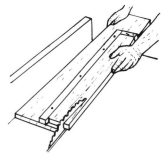

MAKING A PUSH STICK

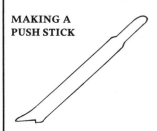

Make the push stick out of a piece of straight hardwood or good quality 19mm plywood. Follow the diagram to cut out the shape, then round the

handle with a file to give a better grip.

Make another push stick with a more delicate tip for guiding the work against the fence when ripping small pieces.

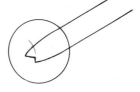

Cutting tapers
To cut tapers to make tapered pieces for this trestle table base for example, make a jig out of 19mm plywood which holds the piece at an angle while you push it through the saw against the rip fence.

There are many other possibilities for using the

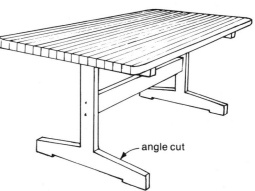

Cutting wedges
Wedges have many uses in the workshop, such as for making the homemade clamping jigs on page 203. To cut wedges,

hold the wood in a jig or holder made from a piece of 19mm plywood.

Cutting rabbets

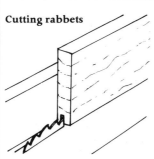

To cut rabbets, set the saw blade to the required depth and cut along the edge of the board first. Make the second cut with the board flat.

— angle cut

versatile table saw. Jigs can be improvised as the need arises. You should always save a jig for another occasion, marking it and hanging it in a place reserved for jigs. Every workshop accumulates many of these jigs to make the next job quick and easy.

Many other cutters can be fitted to the saw, such as dado heads, shaped moulding cutters and sanding disks to extend the use of the table saw, making it an extremely adaptable piece of equipment. Check manufacturers' catalogues for accessories.

radial arm saw

The radial arm saw is an extremely useful and versatile machine. With the right attachments it can become an entire workshop. It will crosscut and rip at various angles doing away with the need for a table saw and because the blade can be rotated to almost any position, it will cut grooves, circular shapes, rabbets, finger joints and a wide variety of other shapes.

You can buy attachments to make it into a shaper, a sander, a planer, a drill or a jigsaw. But keep in mind as with all types of multi-purpose tools, that it takes time to change over from one function to another. So if you use the machine frequently, it is best to use it mostly for crosscutting for which it is best suited and buy other tools to do shaping, sanding and so forth.

Crosscutting

The radial arm saw is easier to use to make crosscuts than the table saw, since the work remains stationary. The saw rides on an overhead arm and when making crosscuts it is pulled towards the operator over the work which is held firmly against the fence.

Ripping

The motor and saw blade are rotated in a number of ways to make different cuts. For ripping, the saw is rotated 90° and clamped firmly. The work is fed into the blade against the rotation, with the kickback fingers against the blade to prevent the work from being thrown back.

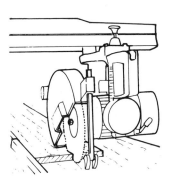

The saw can be set in two different positions for ripping. To cut narrow pieces, set it so that the blade faces back toward the column. For wider cuts, up to about 460mm, set the saw in the other direction with the blade facing outwards. To cut even wider pieces it is necessary to move the wooden fence further back to gain slightly more space for maximum clearance.

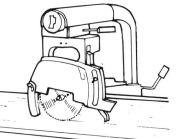

OTHER RADIAL ARM SAW CUTS

Halving joints
Both pieces are cut at the same time. Use stops to the left and right as guides.

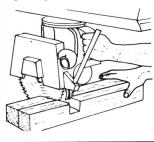

Grooves and housings

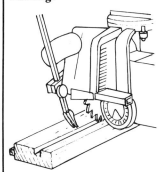

Cut grooves and housings with successive cuts using an ordinary blade, or with one cut using a dado blade.

Mitres
Mitres are easily cut by setting the crosscut to 45°. Use a 45° scrap as a stop to get all the pieces the same

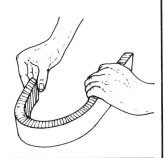

Kerfing
To bend wood, make close crosscuts to within about 4mm of the bottom face.

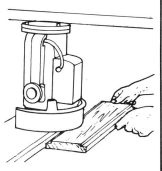

Rabbets
Rabbets are cut with the ordinary saw blade, or better yet, with a dado blade, set horizontally.

Bevel cuts
With the radial arm saw it is also easy to make bevel cuts both in crosscutting and in ripping. Tilt the blade to the required angle indicated on the bevel scale and lock the saw firmly in position before making the cuts.

To make horizontal cuts such as grooves, finger joints and rabbets, swivel the saw so that the blade is horizontal.

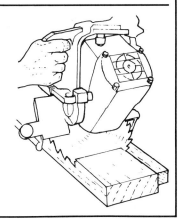

electric drill

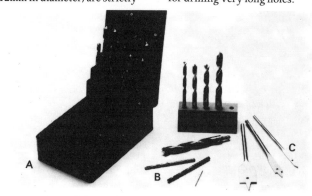

For the occasional drilling job a hand drill or brace and bit will be sufficient. But most woodworking projects require a fair amount of drilling and an electric drill will do the job faster and more easily.

There are several types of drill available. The basic single speed drill is adequate for most woodworking and household jobs but the two or four speed drill gives more flexibility in drilling different materials.

Some drills have a hammer action which causes the drill to hammer back and forth as it rotates, making it go through hard masonry materials much more easily.

You can extend the use of a drill into a mini-workshop by fitting it with many different attachments. For example, the drill can power a circular saw, sabre saw, lathe or mortise attachment, or it can be fitted to a horizontal drill stand with a sanding disk, wire brush, or grinding wheel.

Keep in mind though that it takes time to change the drill from one use to another. For frequent use it may be better to buy integral tools like a portable circular saw or a sabre saw as they are more powerful than the drill attachments.

DRILL BITS
Several types of drill bit are used in power drills. The shanks are usually round although flat bits for drilling large holes have triangular sides for a better grip.

Drill chucks come in three sizes – 8, 10 and 12mm. Check the capacity of the chuck on your drill before you buy a bit or attachment. Taper shanked auger bits are intended only for use in a brace, never try to fit them into a power drill.

A. Twist drills
Twist drills, available individually or in sets up to 12mm in diameter, are strictly intended for metalwork but they are used extensively in woodworking, particularly for drilling small holes such as screw clearance holes.

B. Dowel bits or machine bits
These are special wood drilling bits available in diameters from 6 to 12mm. They are used for drilling clean, accurate holes for general work, but particularly for dowel jointing.

C. Flat bits
Flat bits are only for use in power drills. They are inexpensive and available in sizes from 6 to about 38mm in diameter with extension shafts for drilling very long holes.

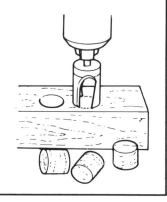

USING THE DRILL
To fit a drill bit, open the jaws of the chuck, insert the bit then lock the jaws with the chuck key.

Always centre punch holes to give an accurate guide for the drill bit. Holding the drill upright requires practice. You can stand a try square beside the drill as a guide, but a more accurate method is to get a second person to sight in one direction while you check the other.

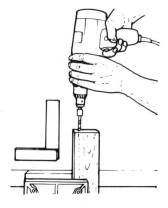

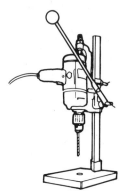

The best way to use the drill is to mount it in a vertical stand. The stand holds the drill firmly and absolutely vertical. It also allows you to hold the work with one hand while you lower the handle to bring the drill down to the work. The adjustable depth stop allows you to drill holes to a predetermined depth.

PLUG CUTTER
Plug cutters are used to cut small plugs which can then be prised out of the wood with a screwdriver and used to fill counterbored holes over screw heads. They are available in various sizes up to 12mm in diameter. You can use plugs in a contrasting wood for a decorative effect or a matching plug which will be hardly noticeable.

When drilling holes to a specific depth, you can also use a depth stop made from a piece of dowel or 25 × 25mm scrap, cut to length to suit the required depth (page 195).

The drill stand is also useful for drilling out the waste in mortise slots before cleaning out with a chisel. Hold the work by hand or in a special vice if it is too small. Alternatively, use a C-clamp.

To drill holes in dowels, cut a V-shaped notch in a small block and drive in a couple of pins leaving the heads protruding to hold the dowel.

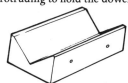

To drill at a 45° angle, make a jig as shown on page 24 for the kitchen work island.

sabre saw

The sabre saw or power jigsaw is a versatile portable tool. It is primarily used for cutting out irregular shapes in solid wood and in plywood.

The blade cuts at speeds which vary from 2500 to 4500 strokes a minute. It cuts on the upstroke so cutting should always be done with the less attractive face of the wood facing upwards so that the ragged edges formed by the exit of the blade will not show.

Some saws have variable speed controls and bases which tilt for making bevel cuts. However, the most important

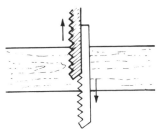

characteristic to look for is an orbital cutting action which is preferable to the straight up and down action. It produces a cleaner cut with less blade wear.

USING THE SAW
Hold the saw firmly when sawing freehand to cut circular or irregular shapes, guiding the saw by eye along a marked line.

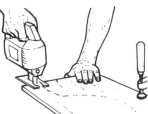

A good saw will handle plywood 19mm thick and hardwoods up to 38mm thick.

To make straight cuts, use the rip fence or clamp a straight edge to the work as a guide.

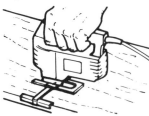

For crosscutting, make a T-square guide out of two pieces of wood glued and screwed exactly at right angles. Leave the end overlong as shown then cut it off with the saw. The cut end can then be quickly located against a mark on the board.

MAKING AN INTERIOR CUT
To make an interior cut, start by drilling one or more holes in the waste area. Alternatively, start the cut by tilting the saw forward, holding it very firmly while the blade cuts through the line.

CHOOSING BLADES
Use coarse blades with fewer teeth for rough work, but change to finer blades for more delicate work. Special hollow ground blades with no set give a very smooth cut but are not intended for constant use. There are also blades for cutting metal, linoleum and a variety of other material. Refer to manufacturers' catalogues for complete details of blades to fit your saw.

sanders

Use a power sander to make the laborious work of sanding easier. There are several types intended for different jobs and suitable for all but the most delicate work.

ORBITAL SANDER
The most useful sander is the orbital type. It works with an oscillating motion so it can be used equally well with or across the grain.

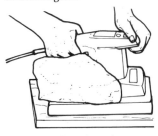

Special sized sanding sheets can be bought in various grades, or cut from ordinary sheets of good quality sandpaper. The paper is mounted in grooves at each end of the sander. The bottom of the sander is covered with a replaceable rubber pad which

provides a soft base, convenient for sanding corners and edges.

If the paper becomes clogged the orbital sander can leave small circular marks on the surface of the wood which are difficult to remove, so always replace the sandpaper as soon as it is necessary.

BELT SANDER
The belt sander is intended for rougher work such as stripping paintwork. It can also be used, instead of a plane, to level off boards which have been glued together to make a table top, such as the pine table on page 12, providing not too much wood needs to be removed.

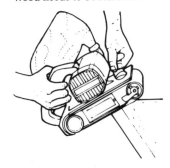

Work diagonally at first, then along the boards using a coarse paper. Finish off with a smooth belt along the grain. It takes practice to use this heavy machine on delicate tops without digging in. Keep it moving around with the weight evenly distributed.

To sand smaller pieces, you can clamp the sander upside down in the vice and hold the work against the moving belt. To change the belt, push down on the front wheel to release the old belt, fit the new belt, then force the wheel back in position to tighten the belt.

router

The router is probably the least understood of all the power tools, which is strange because it is so versatile and is certainly the most enjoyable tool to use. Fitted with different cutters it will cut grooves and housings, make circular shapes, mould edges, cut rabbets and dovetails and even trim plastic laminates.

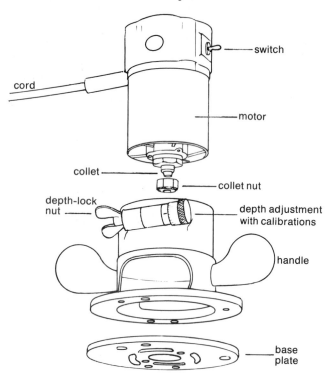

The router is basically a motor with a vertical shaft that holds the cutter. The base plate adjusts up and down to expose more or less of the cutter so that you can vary the depth of the cut.

The cutter rotates at very high speeds producing a fine, smooth finish. You can buy a low priced, lightweight router which will do most jobs very well, but for frequent use buy a commercial model with at least 0.5 kw motor. Buying a router is a compromise between the weight, which should be as light as possible, and the price, which varies enormously from one end of the range to the other.

MOUNTING THE CUTTERS
Mounting the cutters is easy. First shut off the power and unplug the machine. Then remove the base plate and with the wrench provided, loosen the locking nut. Some routers have removable collets in the shaft so that they can take shafts of both 6.5 and 10mm diameter.

Push the cutter in all the way then tighten the locking nut before finally replacing the base plate.

USING THE ROUTER
The router is often used to make grooves or dados like the housing grooves for the roll top desk on page 128.

To make grooves, fit the router with a straight cutter preferably of the same diameter as the width of the groove. To make grooves across a board, use a homemade straight edge guide which is clamped to the work. Make it out of two pieces of 19mm plywood, then try it on a piece of scrap wood. The groove made in the front piece can then be used to line up all subsequent cuts.

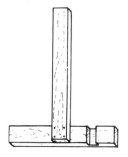

If you are using a smaller bit than required, say a 12mm diameter bit for a 19mm groove, add a second straight edge as a guide for the other side.

The cutter rotates clockwise and it should always be fed 'into' the work or it will tend to pull away.

CUTTERS
You can buy a wide variety of cutters for specific jobs, but they are quite expensive so it's best to buy them as you need them and build up a supply over the years.

Cutters are usually made of high speed steel which can be re-sharpened. They are also available with tungsten carbide tips to give an even cleaner cut and a longer life. Carbide tipped cutters, however, are much more expensive.

Cutters are available with shafts of 6, 10 or 12mm diameter, but most of the light models take a 6 or 6.5mm shaft.

1. Straight bit for cutting grooves, rabbets and trimming edges. In sizes from 4 to 19mm diameter.

2. V-grooving bit

3. Core box bit for making rounded grooves as for the draining board on page 20.

4. Rabbeting bit

5. Chamfering bit

6. Beading bit

7. Rounding-over bit for cutting decorative edges as for

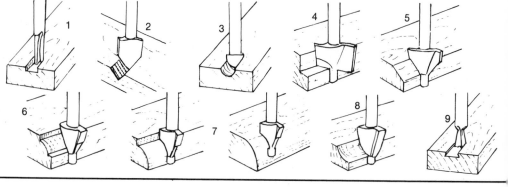

For stopped grooves, attach a small stop onto the straight edge then square off the rounded end of the groove with a chisel.

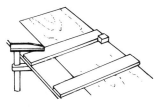

To make grooves along a board, clamp a straight edge to the board as a guide. Alternatively, use the adjustable fence provided with the router for making cuts parallel to the edge.

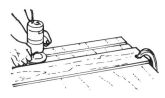

To make grooves in drawer sides to take a 6.5mm plywood bottom, for example, use a 6.5mm straight cutter and adjust the fence so that the cut

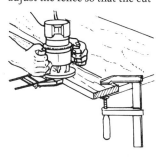

the drawer front on page 26, or for simply rounding edges.

8. Cove bit

9. Dovetail bit for cutting dovetails slots as shown, and for use with the dovetail jig.

10. Laminate trimming bit is tungsten carbide tipped with ball bearing guide.

You can also have cutters made to your exact specifications by specialist machine toolmakers. Provide an accurate full sized drawing of the cutter required and allow several weeks for delivery.

CUTTING CIRCLES
Fitted with a simple circle cutting attachment, the router can cut disks and make circular cut-outs with decorative edges.

Drill a 6.5mm diameter hole to take the guide pin, then simply run the router in a circle to make the cut.

For cutting straight through heavy material make several passes, lowering the cutter about 6.5mm each time. You can

is 10 to 12mm from the edge as required. The cuts can be made to an exact depth in one run and stopped, or run through to the end.

Cutting decorative moulded edges for table tops, drawer fronts, shelves and so on, is very simple with the router. Notice that all the moulding cutters including the rabbet cutter, have a guide pin which extends below the cutter. This pin runs along the edge of the work to guide the cutter along an even path. Any irregularities in the edge will be reproduced in the cutting.

The guide pins tend to overheat and burn the wood. To prevent this from happening use the fence as a guide instead, setting it so that the pin just misses the wood. This method will work only for straight runs. For curved and circular shaped edges, such as

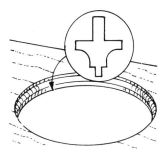

then decorate the edges of the cut-out by running a moulding cutter around the inside.

a round table top, use the circular guide instead. On some machines the same guide performs both functions by means of a simple adjustment.

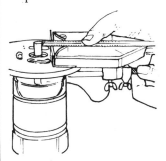

To cut moulded shapes on curved edges, adjust the circular guide by trial and error to get the exact setting required. Then simply run this along the edge as you cut the shape.

Another advantage of the router is that it can get into corners to cut moulded shapes, around the inside edge of a door frame for example. The

To cut out large circles, to make round table tops for example, make your own guide out of a piece of 6.5mm plywood, about 150mm wide, attached with two small machine screws bolted through the base of the router. Then drill a small hole at the circle centre. To use the guide simply pin through the plywood at the centre and cut along the perimeter for perfect circles. Use the same board with holes for various radii to cut out circles of different sizes.

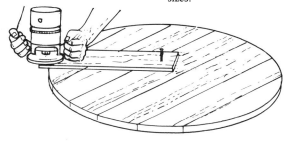

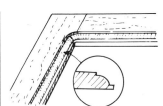

door frames on page 70 were decorated by running the beading bit around the insides. It leaves an attractive curved shape in the corners.

When putting a decorative edge on the end of a board the wood tends to split when the router reaches the end. To prevent this, clamp a piece of scrap wood at the end. If all four sides are to be shaped, for example to decorate a drawer front like the one on the kitchen work island shown on page 24, cut across the ends first. The subsequent cuts along the sides will then remove the split sections.

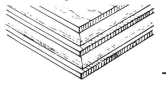

router

continued from page 217

CUTTING DOVETAILS

The dovetail cutter can be used not only to make dovetail joints but also to cut dovetail dado grooves. This makes an extremely strong and durable joint and is useful for projects like bookcases. The dovetail shape at each end of the shelf fits exactly into the dovetail groove or dado in the upright. It is a particularly useful joint because it locks the verticals in position so that unlike an ordinary housing joint, the sides can't come apart.

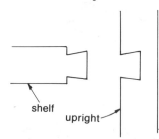

shelf
upright

Cut the end of the shelf first. Clamp it in a vice with identical blocks of wood on each side located exactly flush with the end of the board. Set the fence to give just the right depth of cut, then run the cutter first along one side then the other to leave a male dovetail section.

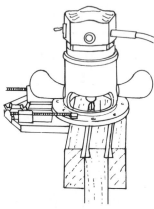

Next cut the matching groove in the upright. Mark the exact area to be cut. Before cutting with the dovetail cutter, make a cut with a straight cutter to the required depth along the centre line of the cut to remove most of the waste. This makes

it easier for the dovetail cutter to cut through in one run. Use the try square guide shown clamped to the board, set to make the right size of groove.

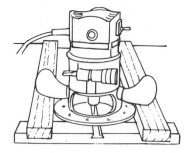

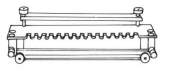

Making perfect dovetail joints is straightforward with the dovetail accessory. You cut both members of the joint at the same time. Clamp them together in the jig, one piece vertically, the other horizontally, then cut each dovetail shape in turn.

There are two sizes of template available for use

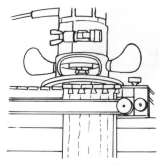

with the dovetail attachment. One is for use on wood from 22mm to 25mm thick, the other is for thinner pieces, from 8 to 15mm thick.

MAKING A SHAPER OUT OF THE ROUTER

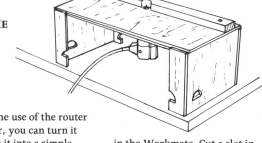

To extend the use of the router even further, you can turn it over and fix it into a simple homemade table to make it into a very useful shaper or spindle moulder.

Make the table of 19mm plywood. Cut semi-circular slots in the sides to take the clamp heads which hold it to the bench. You can also screw a board underneath to clamp the table

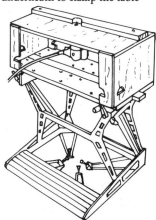

in the Workmate. Cut a slot in the top large enough to get the router through, then fit a 6.5mm plywood top over it, cutting out a rectangular opening which is bolted to the router base with two or three machine screws countersunk flush. The plywood top is held in place flush with the top by the fence.

The fence is pivoted at one end with a bolt fixing and moves back and forth at the other end in a slot cut in the base. After adjustment, fix the fence in place by tightening the bolt. The slot cut in the fence

behind the cutter allows the shavings to fall clear.

USING THE SHAPER

You can now cut grooves and moulded edges with accuracy. The rounded edges on the dining chairs on page 32 were cut in exactly this way.

To cut the dovetail ends on the shelf mentioned earlier, you could make a simple holder which clamps to the work and holds it square and straight as you push it by the cutter, as above. When cutting across the end of a board use a push stick behind for safety.

other woodworking machines

PLANER

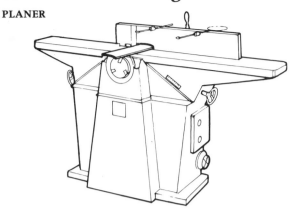

When working in hardwoods which are usually only available rough sawn, you can as suggested in this book, take your boards to a nearby woodworking shop, but eventually it may be necessary to buy a planer. A jointer or surface planer is used to plane first one face side smooth and straight, and then the face edge square with the face side. A thicknessing planer is then used to plane the other sides parallel. A combination planer/thicknesser can do both jobs.

BANDSAW

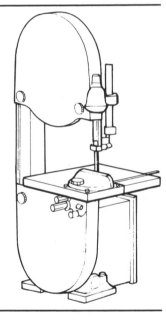

The bandsaw is another useful machine which can be used not only to cut curves and irregular shapes but, if the motor is powerful enough, to make fairly accurate crosscuts and ripcuts, which are cleaned up with a plane.

It can be fitted with home-made crosscut and ripping fences to make this process easier. With the larger, heavy-duty models available you can even rip logs down into boards. The first cut is made by eye against a chalked line and each successive cut is then made against a rip fence.

JIGSAW

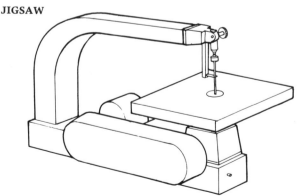

The table jigsaw cuts delicate shapes in thin wood. It is primarily a hobbyist's tool, used for making jigsaw puzzles and other fine work, but it has its place in the workshop too for model making and small, accurate work.

LATHE

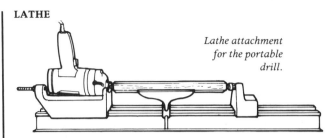

Lathe attachment for the portable drill.

The lathe attachment for the drill consists of a bed fixed to a base, a horizontal fixing for the drill, a tool rest and an adjustable tailstock. Alternatively, buy an integral lathe with a more powerful motor for turning larger and more ambitious pieces. You will also need special turning tools such as gouges, chisels and parting tools.

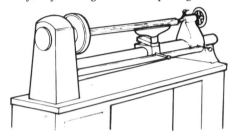

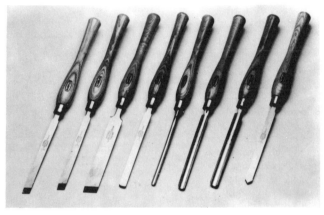

GRINDER

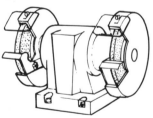

A grinder is almost essential for sharpening tools. It should be bolted to a bench at a comfortable height and fitted with tool rests and eye shields. Ideally there should be a light just above it to avoid shadows.

Larger grinding wheels have a coarse stone wheel at one end and a fine wheel at the other end. Alternatively you can fit a grinding attachment to the electric drill and mount it in a horizontal stand. Use the grinder to re-grind and sharpen chisels, plane irons and spokeshaves and to re-point screwdrivers and drill bits.

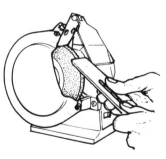

Stand a bucketful of cold water beside the machine and dip the tip of the tool in it occasionally to prevent overheating the metal and ruining the cutting edge.

wood characteristics

STRUCTURE OF WOOD

As a simplified model, the tree's cells resemble bunches of drinking straws. The walls are composed of cellulose and are bonded together by a natural substance called lignin. The sap, made up of water and minerals and collected by the roots, is carried up to the leaves through the hollow cells. In turn, the leaves convert the sap through photosynthesis into starches which travel down the tree just inside the bark. They are distributed to the inner parts of the tree through another network of tubular pores called medullary rays. These rays which run radially across the annual rings from the bark to the heartwood are clearly visible in some species of wood.

This structure of fibres and hollow cells gives wood its strength and relatively light weight. But the porous structure also means that all wood, even wood in a piece of antique furniture, constantly absorbs and gives off moisture from the atmosphere. When the wood picks up moisture, it expands and this must be allowed for. A solid table top for example, may be up to 6mm wider at one time of the year than at another.

To allow for this seasonal expansion and contraction to take place, you can use various

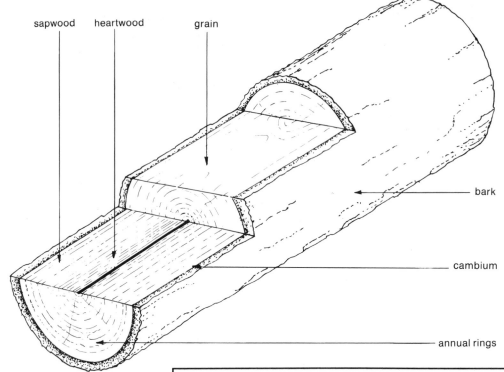

sapwood   heartwood   grain

bark

cambium

annual rings

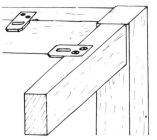

devices such as slotted brackets as shown above, to connect a table top to the rails. The screws hold the top in place but are allowed to slide in the slots which are always aligned across the grain.

WOOD GROWTH

The growth of a tree takes place in a thin, sensitive layer inside the bark called the cambium. Each spring there is a time of new growth and the resulting 'spring wood' is formed with large pores to carry all the sap.

During the slower summer growing season, the pores created are smaller and the cell walls are thicker. This results in stronger summer wood. It is this variation in spring and summer growth which gives the tree its characteristic annual rings which enable you to count the age of the tree from a cross section of the log.

The layer of live, sap-carrying wood is called the sapwood. As the sapwood ages, it becomes inactive and turns into heartwood. It is the heartwood, which is denser and therefore harder and stronger, which forms the structural rib or backbone of the tree.

SOFTWOODS AND HARDWOODS

Wood is classified in two groups, hardwoods and softwoods. Hardwoods, which may actually be quite soft, are those from deciduous trees, that is those which shed their leaves in winter. Softwoods such as pine, Douglas fir and cedar come from evergreen, cone bearing trees with needle

pointed leaves. Softwood species grow faster and have larger cells, and are therefore less expensive than hardwoods. Softwoods are generally available ready planed up in a wide variety of standard sizes.

Hardwoods such as ash, beech, oak, mahogany, walnut and maple must usually be bought from specialist suppliers. Hardwoods normally come in sawn planks either with square sawn edges or sometimes with 'wany edges', with the bark

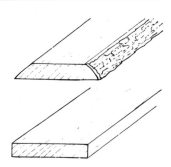

still on. The planed and polished colour of the wood bears little resemblance to the rough unfinished surface of the sawn boards.

SEASONING AND MOVEMENT IN WOOD

When a tree is felled, its pores are full of water which must be removed before the wood is stable and usable, and safe from fungal attack. A felled tree would eventually lose much of the moisture naturally but this could take many years and is therefore not commercially viable. To speed up the drying process, the wood is either air or kiln dried.

AIR DRYING

In air drying, the tree is cut through and through into planks which are then piled up outdoors under cover with sticks in between each plank to allow circulating air to dry out the wood over a year or two depending on the thickness of the planks and the species of wood. The advantage of air drying is that the moisture evaporates slowly minimizing shrinkage and distortion.

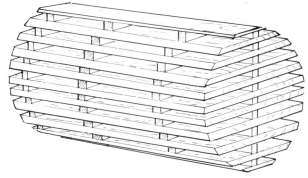

KILN DRYING

Kiln drying is an artificial process which reduces the drying time to a few weeks. The wood is placed in closed compartments much like ovens and moist, heated air is passed through to dry the wood at a controlled rate to a specified moisture content.

MOISTURE CONTENT

Moisture content which is the percentage of water to dry weight of wood varies from about 60 per cent in newly felled wood to about eight per cent in very dry wood.

All wood used in furniture making must be dried to a moisture content which does not exceed twenty per cent. Below that level, the wood is fairly immune to dry rot and other fungal attack. The moisture content required will depend on the eventual use of the wood. Outdoor furniture and construction grade boards can be up to fifteen per cent, whereas wood to be used for furniture should be between nine and twelve per cent. For most woodworkers, it is not possible to control the moisture content of the wood with any accuracy. The wood you buy may have been standing in open sheds and your workshop may not be heated at all times.

When making a fine piece of furniture, it is important to keep the wood in a warm dry place for a month or so before beginning work and to see that it is not exposed to fluctuations in heat and moisture.

If possible, try to accumulate a supply of wood which can be stacked horizontally off the floor with spacer sticks placed about 300mm apart along the boards to allow air to circulate. You will have to keep the storage area at a constant temperature for this seasoning to be effective.

MOVEMENT IN WOOD

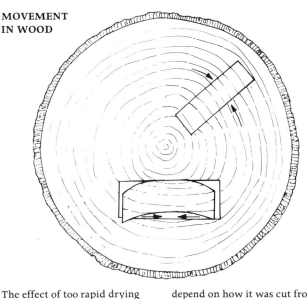

The effect of too rapid drying of a board is distortion of the shape. As it dries out, it shrinks in every direction except length and too rapid drying will result in shrinkage that is not uniform in all directions. The direction in which the plank distorts will depend on how it was cut from the log. A tangentially cut plank will pull in on the underside away from the heart where the rings are longer. A radially cut plank is more stable as most of the shrinkage is across the thickness which will not affect the shape.

DISEASES AND PESTS

Wood decay caused by fungal attack is a serious problem and must be treated when it occurs. Dry wood is relatively safe as fungal attack usually only occurs in wood that is over twenty per cent in moisture content.

Dry rot is the most serious wood disease. It starts when the wood is in a damp, badly ventilated condition and spreads over wide areas while these conditions exist. The affected wood must be removed and burned and all nearby wood must be treated with a suitable fungicide to prevent spreading.

Insect pests such as death-watch A, lyctus B, and furniture beetles C, which are collectively known as woodworm, usually attack the softer sapwood species.

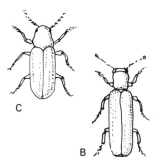

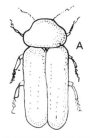

Wood should be inspected periodically, particularly the unfinished backs of furniture and should be treated immediately if found to be infested.

Vacuum off the surface to remove the dust from the insect holes. Then brush the surface liberally with a suitable insecticide or preservative.

wood characteristics

continued from page 221

DEFECTS IN WOOD

Natural defects
The most common defect, found in most softwoods, is knots, the result of branches going through the wood.

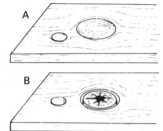

Branches which fell off or were cut early in the life of the tree will be healed by the tree to form a live knot, A. Where a mature branch is broken, the stump dries and shrinks resulting in a dead knot, B. Live knots may be acceptable in the wood, but dead knots, which tend to fall out leaving a hole, should be avoided.

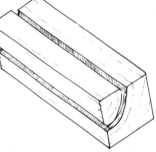

Splits along the grain resulting from weaknesses between the spring and summer wood layers are called shakes. This splitting usually occurs during the seasoning process.

Artificial defects
Artificial defects are those which result from too rapid or uneven seasoning of the wood. Warping occurs when the

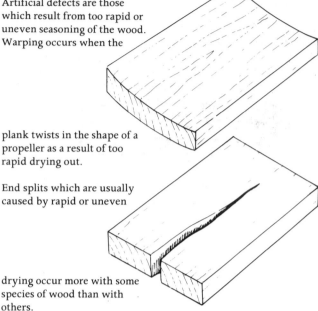

plank twists in the shape of a propeller as a result of too rapid drying out.

End splits which are usually caused by rapid or uneven drying occur more with some species of wood than with others.

BUYING WOOD
Wood can be bought either sawn or planed. Softwoods are usually bought planed whereas hardwoods are most often available only as sawn planks which must be planed before use. Softwoods are available in many standard sized sections. The size of the board is stated as nominal even though the planed size is actually somewhat smaller. Thus a 50 × 100mm is actually about 45 × 95mm once it has been planed although it is still referred to as a 50 × 100mm. In some cases the letters PAR are added to the size to indicate that the board has been planed all round.

The instructions and cutting lists throughout this book have allowed for the planed sizes of wood. When buying softwoods, try to select the boards yourself if the supplier will allow you to. Wood is expensive so it is not unreasonable to insist on buying straight, clear boards, fairly free from knots and splits. Don't accept any boards which are warped or twisted as they are not usable.

Avoid wood which has been stored outdoors. Even in open sheds, the wood picks up a lot of moisture and this wood will be prone to warping and splits as it dries in your workshop.

Many wood dealers will cut the boards to length for you for a nominal extra charge. This is a very convenient service for people with limited workshop facilities or who have no facilities for transporting long boards or large sheets.

Bring along a cutting list of the lengths needed and be sure to check the boards for length and square to be sure that they are cut accurately.

It may be difficult to find a good selection of hardwoods at a local supplier. Look in the telephone book for large wood yards or check specialist magazines for suppliers in your area. Then phone up to check that they will sell small amounts.

	characteristics	uses
SOFTWOODS **Douglas fir**	resinous with pronounced attractive straight grain	construction and furniture
Red Baltic pine	fairly stable and straight-grained with frequent knots	widely available for construction and furniture
Western red cedar	contains oils which prevent insect and fungus attack	used as cladding for walls and ceilings, also outdoor furniture
HARDWOODS **Mahogany**	African and South American, wide straight boards	furniture as veneers or as solid boards
Oak	English, Japanese and American, stable and easily worked	ideal for furniture, both indoor and outdoor
Maple	hard and close-grained, takes finish well	used for furniture
Beech	European and American, close even-grained, relatively unstable	widely used for furniture particularly bentwood
Walnut	European and American, straight, close grain	valued for veneer, ideal for furniture

sheet materials

Solid wood is expensive and is subject to defects and to expansion and contraction with changes in the weather. It is therefore not always the best choice of material for a project. Manufactured boards such as plywood, blockboard and chipboard have many advantages over wood. Although they are not as attractive and possibly not as rewarding to work with, they are stable and available in large sheets which makes it easy to make up large surfaces with a minimum of waste and with no gluing up of boards.

PLYWOOD

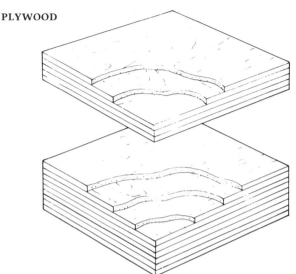

Plywood is made up of layers of veneer glued together to form sheets of standard sizes and thicknesses. The successive layers, called plies, are glued with the grain of the layers at right angles to one another, effectively locking the grain together to keep the sheet from expanding or warping.

The more veneer layers, the greater the strength of the plywood. Good quality plywoods like Finnish birch plywood have many thin layers with an exterior surface of birch veneer making a board which finishes well and is ideal for furniture. Other types of plywood are faced with wood such as Douglas fir, redwood or beech veneer. You can buy sheets with decorative veneered surfaces in finishes of oak, mahogany and teak.

The edges of the plywood can be covered to match the surface with special iron-on veneer edging usually available in two widths from specialist suppliers. It has a Scotch glue backing which melts when you pass a medium-hot iron over it and then quickly sets giving a firm bond.

The type of glue used in manufacture determines whether the plywood is suitable for exterior use or only for interior work. Make sure to specify which you require when you buy plywood.

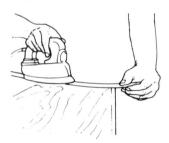

You can buy plywood sheets in various grades and sizes. The most common size is 1220 × 2440mm which we have used as the standard size for the projects throughout this book. Other sizes sometimes available are half sheets, 1220 × 1220mm, or 1500 × 1500mm and larger 1220 × 2700mm, 1220 × 3050mm or 1525 × 3050mm sheets.

Thicknesses range from 4mm to 25mm in 4mm graduations. The most commonly available thicknesses are 12mm and 19mm. Thinner sheets are used primarily for drawer bottoms, cabinet backs, jigs and templates.

BLOCKBOARD

Blockboard is made up of a core of wood strips glued together between outer layers of veneer. The surface veneers are either single or double layers of such woods as birch, beech or Douglas fir. Blockboard like plywood can be bought with decorative veneered surfaces in teak, oak and mahogany. These are either on one face of the sheet with a less expensive 'balancer' veneer on the other side, or applied to both faces.

Blockboard is ideal for use in furniture making because it has many of the characteristics of solid wood without some of the disadvantages. The core of wood strips means that it can be joined by traditional joints.

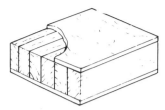

But remember that blockboard is much stronger in the direction of the core strips than across the sheet. Shelves made of blockboard must be cut from the length of the sheet.

Sizes commonly available are the standard 1220 × 2440mm sheet and also 1220 × 2700mm, 1200 × 3050mm and 1500 × 3050mm sheets. It is sometimes available in sheets up to 1500 × 4880mm from specialist suppliers. The common thicknesses are 12, 15, 19 and 25mm.

PARTICLEBOARD AND CHIPBOARD

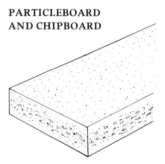

Particleboard or chipboard is made by mixing wood chips with resin glue and then pressing it into rigid sheets in standard sizes. It is inexpensive and widely used in the furniture industry as a stable base for veneers. It can be bought unfinished, or ready primed with paint, or veneered on one or both faces with a variety of woods. Chipboard is sold in do-it-yourself stores in panels of various widths, usually in 2440mm lengths.

Plastic laminate-covered chipboard in various colours is also sold in standard sheets and in special time-saving panel sizes. These are especially useful, particularly in making kitchen and bathroom units.

Both plastic laminated and veneered chipboards can be edged with matching iron-on trim backed with Scotch glue.

Standard sheets are the same as for plywood and thicknesses range from 12mm to 25mm with 19mm a versatile thickness for most work.

HARDBOARD

Hardboard, made from wood fibres mixed with glues and pressed into sheets under heat, is also sold in the standard 1220 × 2440mm sheet size in 3mm and 6mm thicknesses. It is available in standard grade and in a harder and more durable tem-

pered grade. It is used for drawer bottoms and cabinet backs.

It is also sold in a variety of decorative cut-out patterns such as the perforated pattern known as pegboard, which is useful for hanging tools.

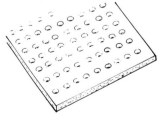

nails

Nails, which are sold by weight, are available with different shaped heads and cross section of shank and in lengths from 12mm to about 150mm When driven into the wood, the nails separate the fibres and hold by friction. Since they tend to split the wood, nails shouldn't be placed near the end of a board. Use two or three nails per joint, spacing them out evenly.

TYPICAL APPLICATIONS

Nailing corner joints. Nail at alternating angles for more strength. Skew or toe nailing for butt joints.

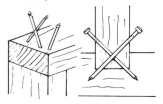

To strengthen joints that do not show, bend nails over on the other side.

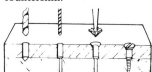

TABLE OF NAILS

Common or round wire nails 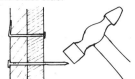	General purpose nail used in construction. Length 25 to 150mm.
Oval wire nail	General purpose nail, more often used in joinery work as less likely to split wood than the round nail. Length: 25 to 150mm
Flooring or lost head nail	Has a tapered head which is easily driven flush with or below the floor surface. Length: 25 to 150mm.
Finishing nails, panel pins or brads	Thin nails with a small head, ideal for use in joinery and furniture making to avoid splitting the wood. Head is usually punched below the surface. Length: 12 to 38mm.
Deformed nails	spiral nail or annular rings for better holding power. Used in construction work. Length: 25 to 75mm.
Upholstery	Domed heads available in decorative finishes like copper, bronze, chrome. Used in upholstery work. Length: 6 to 25mm.
Corrugated fasteners	Used for quick framing joints where strength is not important. Sizes: 6 to 25mm deep, 25 to 38mm long.
Staples	Applied with a hammer or a staple gun. Used in upholstery work and to fix thin hardboard.

Hide nails by using a nail punch (page 194), or lift a

sliver of wood with a chisel and insert the nail. Glue the sliver back in place to hide the nail head.

In rough work, hold joints together with nails while glue sets. Then either remove the

nails or leave them in for added strength.

---

screws

Screws are sold by length and a gauge number which is a measure of the diameter. Countersunk steel screws which are the type most frequently used are available in lengths from about 10mm to 150mm and gauges from 0 to 20.

TYPICAL APPLICATIONS

To fix a screw, first drill the shank hole, then the clearance hole, the pilot hole and the countersink.

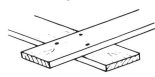

To hide the screw, counterbore the hole 10mm deep then drill the clearance and pilot holes. Fill the hole with a wood plug, see A.

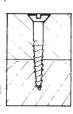

TABLE OF SCREW TYPES

Countersunk	For general work. Flat head is driven flush with, or slightly below, the surface. Available in steel and brass.
Round head	Used for fixing hardware or for decorative uses. Available in steel, brass and black japanned finish.
Oval or raised head	Decorative head, used for fixing hardware. Usually chrome plated.
Phillips head	Cross slotted heads are driven by special screwdrivers fitting only these heads. Less likely to slip than ordinary straight slotted screws.

SCREW GAUGE NUMBERS

	1	2	3	4	5	6	8	10	12	14	16	18	20
Clearance hole	2	2.5	3	3	3.5	4	4.5	5	5.5	6.5	7	8	8.5
Pilot hole softwood	1.0	1.0	1.0	1.0	1.5	1.5	1.5	2.0	3.0	3.0	3.0	3.5	4.5
Pilot hole hardwood	1.0	1.5	1.5	2.0	2.0	2.0	2.5	3	3	4.0	5.0	5.0	5.5

The table above gives drill sizes for screws. Notice that the pilot holes for softwood and hardwoods are different. In softwood, pilot holes for

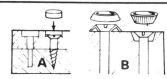

small screws can be made with a bradawl. For a decorative finish, use either type of screw cup under the countersunk heads as shown in B.

adhesives

Good gluing habits are essential in woodworking. You must use the correct type of glue, chosen for its strength, resistance to heat and water and its gap filling properties.

Gap filling properties are important in some applications particularly in woodworking joints where the pieces being joined may not be a perfect fit. For example, when gluing up mortise and tenon joints where the sides are not smooth, a gap filling glue such as synthetic resin glue is ideal.

Most woodworkers use mainly two types of adhesive: PVA white woodworking glue available in plastic squeeze bottles for general work, and synthetic resin glue which is sold in powder form to be mixed with water, for joints and waterproof work. In addition it is a good idea to have quantities of contact adhesive on hand for gluing down plastic laminates and tubes of epoxy for special jobs.

Scotch glue, the traditional woodworking adhesive, is an animal glue and comes in the form of sticky sheets or in granules. It is dissolved in warm water in a glue pot and must be used while it is still warm. For maximum strength, the joint being glued should be warmed too, so that the glue doesn't set too quickly.

Scotch glue is brushed on and the joint is clamped until the glue sets. It has the advantage that the joint can be unmade again simply by heating until the glue melts. It is therefore the ideal glue to use for veneer

type of glue	description and uses	strength	water resistance	gap filling	setting time	preparation	cleaning method
animal glue Scotch glue	general woodworking glue, widely used for veneering since re-heating allows lifting of veneers. Applied to back of iron-on edgings	good	poor	poor	2–4hrs	melt under heat	warm water on cloth
casein glues	general woodworking glue for indoor work	excellent	poor	poor	4–6hrs	mix powder with cold water	water on cloth
PVA white glue	general indoor work	good	poor	poor	20–40min	ready mixed	water on cloth
synthetic resin	excellent for all work, including outdoors	excellent	excellent	excellent	4–6hrs	mix powder with cold water	warm, soapy water
contact adhesives	rubber based, used mostly for laying plastic laminates. Applied to both surfaces, leave to touch dry before bringing in contact. No clamping required.	poor	good	poor	on contact	ready mixed	acetone nail polish remover
epoxy resin	glues almost anything well	excellent	excellent	excellent	½–6hrs depending on type	two parts are mixed together	methylated spirits, denatured alcohol

work so that the veneer sheet can be moved. Scotch glue is applied to the back of ready to use iron-on veneer and plastic edgings which are used to cover the edges of sheet materials.

Most joints require clamping until the glue sets, so if several components have to be glued together such as in carcass work, it is an advantage to use a glue like PVA which sets quite quickly so that the clamps can be used for the next job. Instead of clamping, the joint can be held together with nails or screws which can be removed or left in place for added strength after the glue has set.

GLUING PROCEDURE

1. Make sure both surfaces are straight and true and free from dirt, oil and dust. Test the joints for fit.

2. If mixing glue, mix only as much as is required and use it as soon as it is mixed.

3. Spread adhesive evenly on joint with brush, stick or glue spreader.

4. Bring joint together, clamp or fix with nails or screws, but do not clamp so tight that all the glue is squeezed out.

5. Check that the work is held correctly; that frameworks are square, surfaces are straight, joints are flush.

6. Clean off excess glue on work and from work surfaces. Then clean applicators and glue containers.

MIXING AND APPLYING

If you use synthetic resin glue regularly you can speed up the mixing by making a beater to fit your drill by bending a rod as shown. Put the correct proportions of glue powder and cold water in a plastic container. Use the drill at slow speed to mix the glue. Clean the beater after each use.

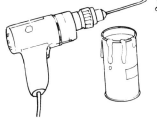

Keep a selection of different sized containers for mixing glues in the workshop. For resin glues, use plastic containers with fairly high sides. You can then let the remaining glue set and simply flex the sides of the container to remove the glue once it has hardened.

Keep mixing sticks, spreaders and brushes clean between applications and be sure to close all tubes and bottles well after use so that the glue does not harden in the container.

The glue spreader is a very convenient but expensive tool, for applying synthetic resin glue to even surfaces such as boards being glued up. If you do a lot of work of this kind it is a good investment. Pour the mixed glue into the container. The rubber roller spreads it evenly over the surface. The only difficulty is that it must be cleaned immediately after use or the glue will be very

difficult to remove. Take the spreader apart and soak all the pieces in warm soapy water.

connectors

Using hardware like screws or brackets to join wood is more common today both in manufactured and in homemade furniture than the traditional woodworking joints.

Sheet materials like plywood and chipboard are much more easily joined using the special connectors as shown on page 240. Most fittings such as bolts, brackets and plates are easily obtainable from hardware stores, but you may have to find specialist or mail order suppliers for some of the less common ones such as the bolt and cross dowel fitting for example.

BOLTS AND NUTS

Bolts, nuts and machine screws are frequently used in furniture construction, particularly for rough work requiring strong, easily made fittings. Bolts are easy to fit since the only preparation required is a hole drilled through both pieces.

Carriage bolts

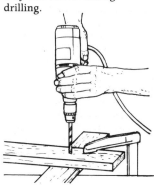

Carriage or coach bolts, such as those used on the bathroom bench on page 74, have domed heads. Insert the bolt into a hole drilled slightly larger than the shank. Place the washer and nut on the threaded end and tighten with a wrench to pull the square shank under the domed head tight into the wood so that the surface is flush.

Machine bolts

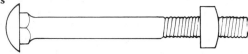

Machine bolts are not very common in woodwork but they provide a sturdy fixing and can be painted bright colours as a decorative touch. The hexagonal bolt head and nut can be left on the surface or they can be set into a counterbored hole so that they are flush with the surface as on the folding picnic table and benches shown on page 172.

Machine screws

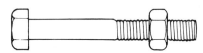

Machine screws are small bolts with round or countersunk heads. They are available in diameters from about 4mm to 8mm. They are frequently used in woodworking particularly to attach wood to metal. For example, the metal router base was bolted to the plywood strip to make the circle template which is shown on page 216.

Dowel screws

Dowel screws have threads on both ends to provide a secret fixing for attaching wooden knobs such as those used on the kitchen work island on page 24. Drill clearance holes in both pieces and attach the dowel screw to one piece before tightening it into the second hole.

FIXING BOLTS

Bolts are not only extremely strong but they are also very easy to fix.

1. First hold the two (or three) pieces to be joined together either by clamping or temporarily nailing. Make sure to hold them firmly so that they don't move during drilling.

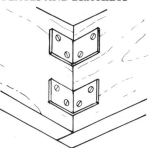

2. Drill straight through with the correct sized drill bit. The hole should be slightly larger than the shank diameter so that the bolt can be pushed right through the hole without any difficulty.

3. Fit the nuts and washers and tighten up using a wrench. The advantage of bolted connections is that they can be easily unbolted and reassembled again so furniture can be moved or stored.

PLATES AND BRACKETS

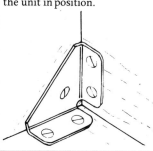

Metal brackets are very useful for making or strengthening corner and T-joints. The corner bracket is used inside on the corners of structures like drawers or children's toy boxes, whereas the L and T-plates are used on front or back edges to reinforce a joint. These metal plates are also available with attractive finishes such as brass or chrome for the construction of wall units.

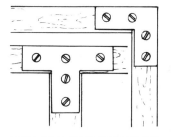

Corner bracket

The corner bracket is used inside cabinets, such as kitchen cabinets, to fix units to a wall. First screw the bracket to the cabinet, then drill through the back hole into the wall to fix the unit in position.

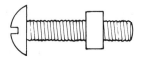

Mirror plates

Mirror plates are thin brass plates with round or key shaped holes for hanging mirrors, lightweight frames or small cabinets such as the bathroom unit on page 76.

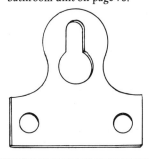

connectors

KNOCK-DOWN FITTINGS

Knock-down fittings are a recent development which allow furniture to be assembled and taken apart easily. They are particularly convenient for mass production because furniture can be shipped flat in narrow cardboard boxes, making large savings in shipping and storage costs. Knock-down fittings are easy to install and mean that you build furniture which is easy to ship or store when not in use.

Many knock-down fittings are only available through the trade, but a few, like the block joint and cross dowels, are more generally available in hardware stores or through mail order firms.

Block joint

Block joints are an easy to install method for joining

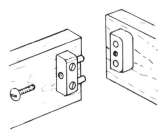

panels to make cabinets, wall units and even built-in closets. Each half of the joint is screwed to a piece being joined and these are brought together and fastened by a machine screw (see honeycomb wall unit page 110). The two halves of the block have to be very accurately positioned for this method of joining to be successful. Block joints come in brown or white plastic.

Corner table plate

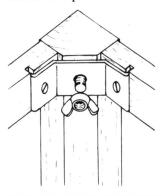

This is a very strong and efficient fitting for fixing the two rails to each leg at the corner of a table. The bolt has a wood thread on one half for fixing into the leg and a machine thread on the other half to take the wing nut. The bracket is held in narrow slots which are cut in the rails with a saw, and it is fixed to the rails with screws. The legs can therefore be removed for easy transporting (see kitchen work island, page 24).

Shrinkage plates and angles

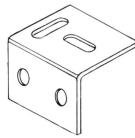 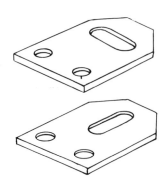

These fittings are used to fix solid wood panels to a rigid framework, such as table tops to the rails underneath. Because wood expands and contracts across its width, it would crack or split if it was fixed rigidly with glue or screws. Shrinkage brackets allow the screw fixing to move back and forth with the wood. Use round head screws with small washers under the head. Always fix the screw to the slot that is perpendicular to the grain.

Flush mounts

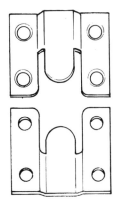

Flush mounts make a convenient knock-down fitting. They consist of two interlocking plates. One is fixed to a wall, the other to the back of a mirror or a cupboard for example, which can then be lifted on or off the wall quite easily.

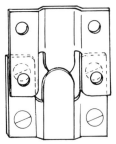

Bolt and cross dowel

The bolt and cross dowel is an ingenious fitting, widely used in manufactured furniture, not just for panels but for solid wood joints. The bolt has an attractive round head with a hexagonal recess which is turned by an Allen key.

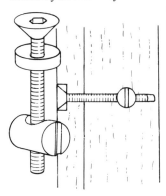

The cross dowel is inserted into a hole drilled in one piece and the bolt is screwed into the dowel. Use at least two bolts for each joint to make it rigid.

Plastic dowel plugs

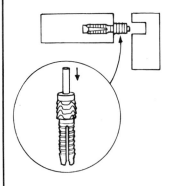

Plastic dowel plugs are an ingenious hidden fixing often used in chipboard furniture. One end of the dowel is fitted into a drilled hole in the edge of the chipboard before a peg is inserted to hold it tight. The hole in the other piece fits onto a projecting part of the dowel, the pieces are brought firmly together, the plug expands to hold the joint securely.

Corner plates and knock-down plates

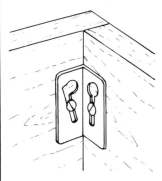

Round head screws are placed in slanted slots which pull the work together to tighten the joint. There are two types. The L-shaped plate is used at corners to join two pieces at right angles. It is made in left and right-hand versions.

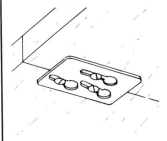

The flat plates are used in the same way to join two boards together edge to edge.

hinges

BUTT HINGE
The butt hinge is the most common type of hinge and is used for all kinds of doors. The hinge leaves are set flush into recesses.

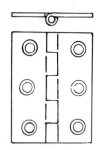

The fixed pin butt hinge is used in general work for hanging large doors and also in furniture making for smaller, more delicate doors. Butt hinges are available in steel and brass in various sizes from about 25mm to 150mm. They are also available in plastic to be used in light work where appearance is not important.

LIFT-OFF HINGE
The lift-off hinge makes fitting easier because the two halves can be screwed on separately and then the door lifted onto its mating fitting. The door can then be lifted off without removing the hinge. The lift-off hinge is available in brass or steel finish in a range of sizes.

FACE FIXING HINGE

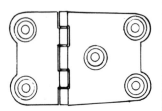

This type of hinge is most commonly used for fitting lightweight doors, such as those used for kitchen cupboards or closets. It fixes flat onto the door and frame.

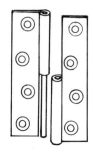

PIVOT HINGE
Like the cranked hinge, the pivot hinge also called the centre hinge, opens 180° and clears the adjacent door. It is fixed at the top and bottom edges of the door.

CONCEALED HINGE
Used with lay-on doors which overlap the cabinet opening, this hinge opens 90° or 180°. It is fitted by drilling a hole in the door with a special drill bit.

BACK FLAP HINGE

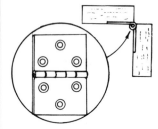

The back flap hinge is a butt hinge with oversized leaves making it a stronger fixing than the standard butt hinge. It is used on the gate leg table on page 280.

FITTING A BUTT HINGE
First decide on the position of the hinges using two for light cabinet doors, three for heavy room doors.

1. Clamp the door to a bench or place it in the Workmate. Mark the outline of the hinge with a knife. Notice that the hinge knuckle should extend halfway beyond the face.

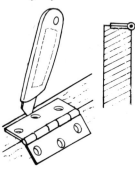

2. Using a sharp chisel, cut along the scored line to the

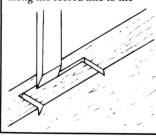

depth required to set the leaves of the hinge flush with the door.

3. Clean out the waste with the chisel by first making several cuts in the middle, then paring down from the side.

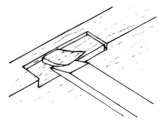

4. Rest the door on two wedges, attach the centre screws and check the hang of the door. If the hinge recess is too deep, pack it with cardboard, if it is too shallow, remove the hinge and shave off more wood. Then fix the remaining screws.

CRANKED HINGE

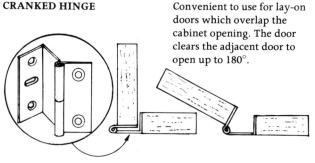

Convenient to use for lay-on doors which overlap the cabinet opening. The door clears the adjacent door to open up to 180°.

TABLE HINGE

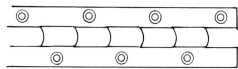

The table hinge has one leaf longer than the other for a strong fixing into the table leaf. The flap is mated to the table top with a special joint, as shown.

CONTINUOUS HINGE

Also known as the piano hinge, this hinge is sold in long lengths in either chrome or brass finish, which are cut to the required length. The hinge is screwed directly to the surface and is excellent for long edges requiring a strong fixing. It is used for the corner cupboard on page 155.

miscellaneous fittings

Locks, catches and other hardware are an important consideration for every piece of furniture. They must function smoothly and correctly and should also match the furniture in style and in weight. It is no use installing a heavy catch to a small delicate cabinet for example, nor a small barrel lock in a domestic door where a heavy duty one is required.

LOCKS

Cupboard lock

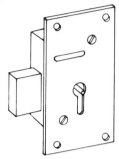

These are widely used for all sizes of cupboard and closet doors. There are several types of cupboard locks available. The straight cupboard lock, left, screws directly into the inside face of the door. The cut cupboard lock is mounted in a recess cut in the door and is bought in left or right-hand versions. The mortise cupboard lock is fitted in a slot in the edge of the door.

Barrel lock

This lock is easy to fit into a drilled hole and is therefore used in production furniture for both doors and drawers.

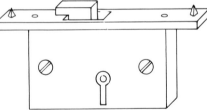

Piano mortise lock

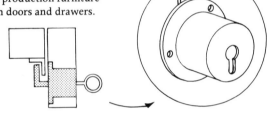

This lock is used for the roll-top desk on page 128. It is fitted into a slot or mortise in the front rail of the desk and a matching plate is fitted to the sliding tambour. The keyhole is drilled from the front after the mortise is cut.

CASTORS

Castors are available in various types and styles. They are quite simple to fit. A hole can be drilled into the bottom of the piece of furniture to take a pin from the castor. The other type of castor has a plate which screws to the underside of the furniture with four screws. Choose light, medium or heavy duty castors depending on the amount of use the piece will get and its weight.

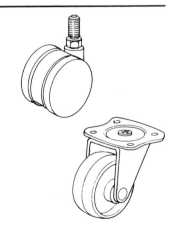

CATCHES

Ball catch

The ball is spring loaded and mounted either on the inside of the door or in a hole drilled in the door edge. The ball catches in the hole in the plate which is screwed to the frame. This catch is available in various sizes depending on the weight of the door.

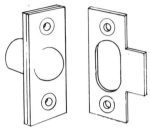

Push-pull latch

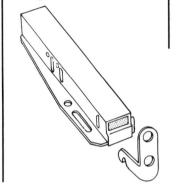

Magnetic catch

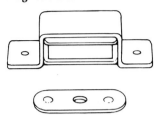

These catches come in two pieces. The magnet part is screwed to the cabinet and the matching plate to the door. Fine adjustments are made by sliding the magnet part

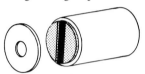

backwards or forwards. A cylindrical type is used for small delicate cabinetwork and works on the same principle but the cylinder is placed in a hole drilled in the edge of the frame.

This catch is screwed to the inside of the cupboard door and allows you to open the door without a handle. The latch, which must be accurately mounted, swings the door open automatically when you press on the door.

STAYS

Cranked stay

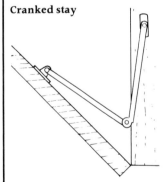

Available in chrome or brass finish, the stay is widely used for all types of drop doors. The stay folds in half as you close the door and folds up neatly. Only one stay per door is required mounted on the right or left side. This type of stay was used for the cocktail cabinet on page 124.

Sliding flap stay

This stay is also commonly used for light drop doors and has become more popular than the cranked stay. Instead of folding up at the middle one end of the stay pivots and slides on a track. The track can be vertically, horizontally or even diagonally mounted inside the cabinet as is required. The other end which is also pivoted simply screws onto the face of the flap.

preparing the wood

The most crucial part of any job is the preparation. When working in solid wood, each piece must be sawn and planed so that it is accurate and square. Softwoods such as Douglas fir and pine are available with the four sides already planed up and these present less of a problem than hardwoods which are usually bought in the sawn state. But softwood boards, once brought into a heated house, often warp and bend just enough to require a few strokes with the plane to make them straight enough to use.

SELECTING AND CUTTING TO LENGTH

Always buy boards long enough to allow for cutting off the ends which are often split or damaged. Lay the boards out and select the lengths by first examining both sides for knots, splits and other defects.

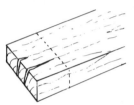

This step is more important than most people realize because you are deciding on the location of the boards, using the best ones for fronts and tops. Plan out the cutting carefully so that you have as little waste as possible. Always cut the longest lengths first so that if you make a mistake there is enough wood to cut another one.

Cut the boards about 50 to 75mm overlength to allow for final trimming. Label each piece according to the cutting list.

THICKNESSING

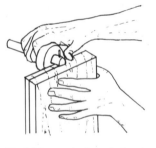

To thickness the board, that is to plane the other face parallel to the first, mark the required thickness along all four edges with a gauge then plane to the marks, checking straightness as before. Similarly, to plane the second edge to the exact board width required, mark with a gauge on the sides and ends, and plane the edge straight.

The final step is to trim and square the ends. Mark one end first about 25mm from the end, and cut off to the line with a crosscut or panel saw.

Plane off the cut end in the shooting board, or if it is too bulky, hold it in the vice. Finally mark the exact length with a tape measure or ruler. Saw the other end about 1mm outside the line to allow final planing in the shooting board, exactly to the line.

Of course, with a table saw you can trim the ends quickly and accurately. You can also rip the board to width, but remember that sawn edges will require final planing before they can be glued together in edge to edge joints.

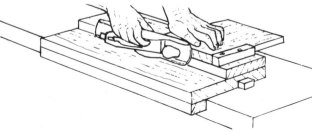

PLANING UP

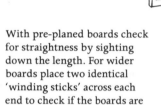

With pre-planed boards check for straightness by sighting down the length. For wider boards place two identical 'winding sticks' across each end to check if the boards are warped.

Planing many boards by hand is tedious work so it may be worthwhile taking the boards to a nearby supplier or woodworking shop to have them machine planed.

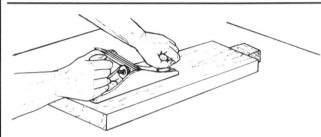

Select the best face, place it on the bench against the bench stop and use a try or a jack plane to plane up the board. Work along the board with the grain. Constantly check for straightness with the straight edge along and across the board and check for twisting with the 'winding sticks'.

with a try or jack plane. The board is usually straight when the plane removes a long, even shaving, but make a final check with a straight edge. Also check that the edge is square to the face by checking with the try square at several points along the length.

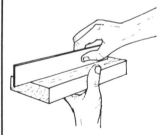

With a bit of practice you can usually tell how straight the wood is by the evenness of the plane shavings. Always mark the prepared best face with a pencilled loop called a 'face mark'.

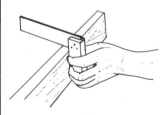

Correct any bevels, not by tilting the plane in the other direction, but by planing along the edge while supporting the plane with your fingers to keep it square. Finally, mark the face edge with a pencilled mark, as shown left.

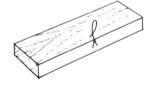

Prepare the best edge by planing along the length, again

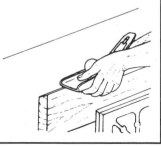

edge to edge joints

Edge joints are used to glue up boards into a larger surface such as a table top. The boards can be held together with glue alone or they can be reinforced with dowels or tongues set in grooves.

First prepare the pieces to make the edges straight and the thickness constant. After you have planed the edges straight it is a good idea on long boards to take off a thin shaving or two from the edge along the middle of the board starting about 75mm in from the end. This keeps the ends,

which are the weakest part, pressed tightly together during clamping.

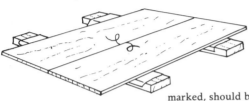

After preparing the boards, lay them out on a couple of battens on the bench. All the best faces, which have been

marked, should be up but it may be necessary to turn one or two over, alternating the grain pattern to minimize warping.

REINFORCED JOINTS
To strengthen edge to edge joints and also to help align them during gluing up, you can reinforce them with dowels or tongues-and-grooves.

Edge joints with dowels
After laying out and marking the boards, hold them on edge in pairs to square lines across and align the dowel holes. Then use a marking gauge, always working from the

marked face, to mark the hole centres which should be centre punched before drilling.

Refer to dowel joints on page 232 for instructions on drilling with or without a dowelling jig.

Tongue-and-groove edge joints
This joint is more cumbersome to make by hand than the dowel joint. The grooves are easily cut by machine with a table saw or a router. To cut by hand, use a plough plane or a combination plane, working from the marked face.

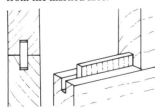

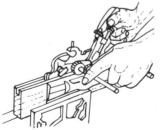

Cut the tongues to fit snugly in the grooves. The easiest way is to make the tongues first out of 4 or 6.5mm plywood and cut the grooves to match. If you don't want the ends of the tongues to show, stop them a few centimetres from the end of the boards.

GLUED JOINTS

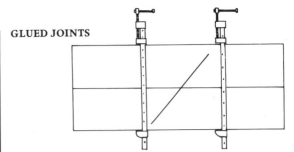

If the boards are thick enough and if the wood is not oily or resinous, like teak or pitch pine, the boards can simply be glued together with a woodworking adhesive. White woodworking glue is quite strong and sets quickly, but resin glue is waterproof, gap filling and stronger.

First check the joints by clamping lightly across to see if there are any gaps. Also mark the top with a diagonal pencil line so that you can re-position the boards during gluing. Undo the clamps, stand the boards on edge and apply the glue evenly with a brush or stick. For frequent gluing, you can buy a glue roller which applies glue quickly and evenly (page 225).

Bring the boards together to the marks and clamp across, using a long batten on each side to prevent the clamps from marking the wood and also to spread the pressure of the clamps.

You shouldn't have to use too many clamps, nor tighten them too much. If badly made joints are pulled together the strain will eventually cause the joints to open up. Place one clamp at each end then alternate clamps over and under the work to keep the surface straight.

To keep the surfaces lined up, apply clamping pressure gradually and tap the boards with a rubber-faced hammer. Or, clamp the ends together until the glue starts to set.

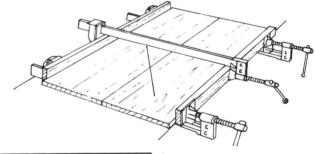

Check with a straight edge across the surface and release the clamps to take out any arching or to align the boards.

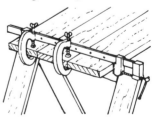

Make sure to make the groove a touch deeper than the tongue so that it doesn't prevent the joint from closing up, and don't make the tongue too thick or the wood will split when the joint is assembled.

Also remember to wipe off excess glue at this stage with a damp cloth. It is much less work than cleaning it off with a plane after it has set.

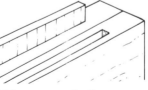

dowel joints

The dowel joint is used extensively in the furniture industry principally as a mortise and tenon substitute because it is quick, efficient and strong. It is a perfect joint for the home workshop as it requires very little equipment and is quite easy to make accurately, even for the beginner. A dowelling jig makes the drilling easy and accurate and is a worthwhile device for anyone planning to make several pieces of furniture using dowel joints.

DOWEL PEGS

Ready-made dowel pegs are available in several diameters: 6, 10 and 12mm but most craftsmen prefer to make their own from lengths of dowel. The pegs must fit tightly in the hole and extend a minimum of 19mm into each piece of wood. The flutings or grooves allow the trapped air and excess glue to escape as the dowel is driven in with a mallet. Notice that the ends of the pegs are

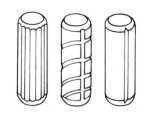

chamfered. This serves to guide them more easily into the hole and to prevent them from splitting when being driven in.

MARKING THE HOLES

The dowel holes in the pieces to be joined must line up exactly. To get this right, the marking must be accurate. The easiest and most foolproof method is to use a dowelling jig which clamps on the wood and centres the holes the set distance from the edge of the wood on both pieces. Use common sense in spacing the holes and centre them on rail ends as far apart as possible leaving enough strength above and below. A minimum of two dowels is required, but for heavy work, three or even four staggered holes are necessary.

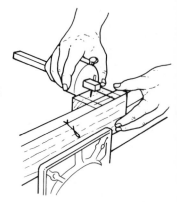

To mark the hole centres, start by marking the rail location on the stile or leg with two square lines. Then clamp the rail and leg together in the vice, face sides out, and use a try square to mark the hole centre lines straight across both pieces. Then use a marking gauge set to half the rail thickness to locate the centres from the face sides.

MAKING YOUR OWN DOWEL PEGS

Dowels are available in diameters of 6mm to about 38mm. For dowel pegs, you will need three sizes: 6, 10 and 12mm diameter. Be sure to use straight dowels. Keep a few lengths of each diameter in a dry place to use for pegs. As dowels may vary slightly in diameter, check the size in a drilled hole. Reject dowels which are too small, but those which are slightly oversized can be sanded down or driven through a homemade metal dowel pop A, after cutting each peg to length on a bench hook. Make sure to test one of the pegs for snug fit before cutting the rest. To make the grooves, carefully run each dowel peg back and forth over a saw clamped in a vice. Then chamfer the ends slightly using

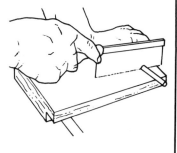

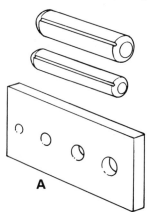

A

a pen knife, rasp or a special tool called a dowel sharpener. These jobs become almost automatic with a little practice and it is worthwhile making a batch of common lengths in the three sizes and keeping them on hand in the workshop.

MAKING A MARKING TEMPLATE

Make a template the exact size of the end of the board. Make the top piece out of 4mm plywood or metal plate and screw it to a piece of 12mm wood. Carefully mark, punch and drill hole centres to accept the top of the marking tool.

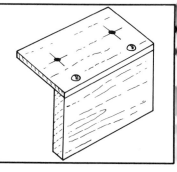

along the length. Marking for the pegs is made easy by clamping the pair of boards together face sides out, centre marking both boards with the gauge and then squaring across.

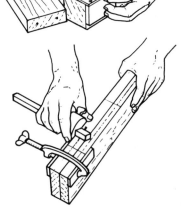

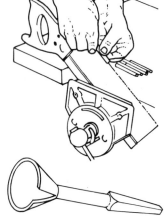

Another method is to use a homemade marking template. Always use the template from the face side to first mark the rail and then the leg or stile.

Use a marking awl to mark the centres. It is best to make up a new template for each size rail and you will soon build up a collection of templates to match common wood sizes. To strengthen edge joints in boards for table tops, a few short dowel pegs are added

dowel joints

DRILLING THE HOLES

In order to locate the drill bit before drilling the hole, always use a centre punch to make a centre mark. Use a homemade depth stop (page 214) made from a length of 25 × 25mm to make the holes just slightly deeper than the dowel pegs. It is best to use a drill with a special dowel bit or, alternatively, a brace and auger bit. The holes should be straight and true in both directions, but it is better that any slight slant be along the board rather than across it. Therefore it is best to stand near the end of the board to drill the hole, standing a try square on the bench to serve as a vertical guide. To make drilling easier and more accurate, use a dowelling jig

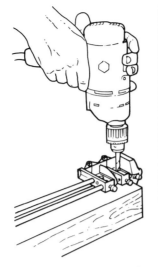

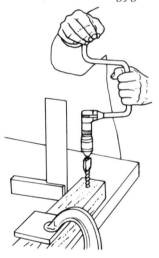

which can be used with 6mm or 10mm diameter dowels. The holes are adjusted and set the required distance in and no marking is necessary. The jig is clamped along the guide marks and you just drill the holes to the correct depth. The jig also prevents you from leaning the drill over, enabling you to drill accurate vertical holes.

The manufacturer includes complete instructions with each dowelling jig for making several types of joint including edge to edge and mitre joints.

After drilling, countersink the holes slightly. This makes it easier to locate the dowel pegs and also collects any overflow of glue.

ASSEMBLING THE JOINT

For the final assembly, the pegs are driven into the rail ends first, then the rail is immediately joined to the leg. Apply glue to the holes only to prevent swelling the dowel peg, and tap the pegs in with a mallet, not a hammer. Use light taps to prevent splitting the ends. If possible, use a block of wood next to the peg when tapping it in so that you will leave identical lengths of peg exposed. It is not usually

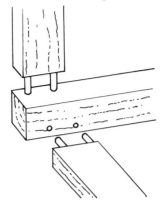

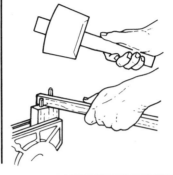

necessary to clamp the work. The pieces are tapped home with a mallet and the glue allowed to set.

If the holes are out of line so that the dowels cannot be pushed in, fill the faulty hole with another dowel of the correct diameter, cut it off flush and re-drill a new hole in the correct location.

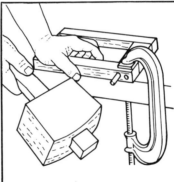

A quick and effective way to make joints is to use a through dowel. Clamp the two pieces to be joined and drill straight through one piece into the end of the other. Then tap a dowel peg in place and cut the end off flush. However the exposed dowel end can be used as a decorative feature especially if it is left slightly proud of the surface.

USES OF DOWEL JOINTS

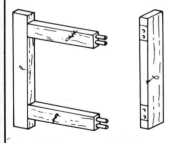

Dowel joints are used in all types of work. They are ideal for light work such as cabinet frameworks and doors, and for table legs and rails. The closet doors on page 70 and the table on page 12 were joined with dowels. Notice that the ends of the rails are rounded to fit round legs. In this case it

is best to drill the dowel holes first before shaping the ends of the rails.

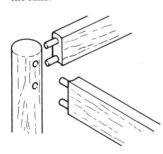

Short dowel pegs are also used extensively in inexpensive chipboard furniture instead of screws which split the brittle chipboard. They are often used to strengthen joints such as mitres where two short dowel

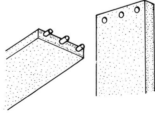

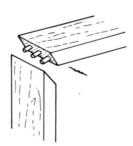

pegs are added instead of nails to reinforce the corner. Dowel pegs are also important in

reinforcing edge to edge joints, for example in a table top. The pegs not only strengthen the joint, but they also serve to keep the edges of the boards lined up as they are clamped together. This saves considerable hard work in planing and then sanding the top smooth afterwards.

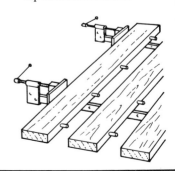

mortise and tenon joints

The mortise and tenon joint is frequently used in woodwork because of its strength. It is used in furniture such as tables, chairs and cabinets and in making door frames of all types.

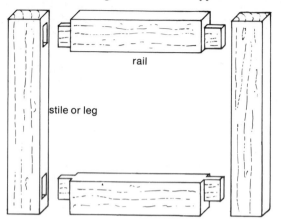

stile or leg

rail

Basically the joint consists of a tongue cut in the horizontal piece, called the rail, which fits into a matching slot in the vertical member, called the stile or leg. But there are many variations depending on whether the tenon is haunched or not, whether the mortise goes straight through the wood or is stopped or 'blind', and whether the tenon is wedged through, called 'fox wedged'.

For most furniture applications however, there are only a few variations on the basic joint which is quite straightforward.

CUTTING THE BASIC MORTISE AND TENON

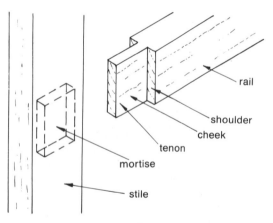

rail

shoulder

cheek

tenon

mortise

stile

The basic tenon, used in this example for making a cabinet door, is a blind tenon, that is it does not go all the way through the stile.

When preparing the wood, it's always best to leave an extra 25mm of wood at the end of the stiles to be cut off later. Having more wood at the end prevents the wood from splitting while you are chiselling out the mortise. Also remember to make all measurements and mark all gauge lines from the marked face and edge.

First mark the position of the rail end and the mortise on the stile, leaving the 25mm waste at the end and squaring across with a try square.

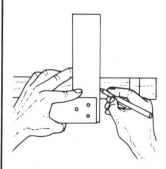

Set the mortise gauge to the exact width of the chisel. The

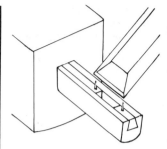

mortise should be about one third the width of the wood so a 6mm chisel is used for 19mm thick wood and a 10mm chisel is about right for 25mm thick wood.

Using the gauge, mark the mortise on the stile and the tenons on the rail at the same

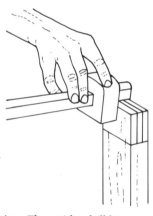

time. Then with a drill bit slightly smaller than the mortise width, drill out most of the waste. If possible use a drill stand as shown on page 214, so that you can set the depth accurately. Alternatively use a depth stop on the drill.

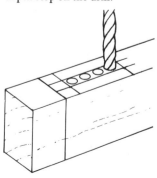

Clamp the board to the bench to chisel out the waste. It's a good idea to place a small C-clamp or thumbscrew across the end as shown to prevent the wood from splitting during chiselling.

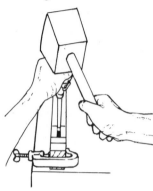

Use a mortise chisel if you have one, but an ordinary bevel edge chisel, although it isn't as robust, will do just as well.

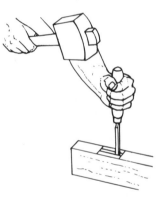

Remove the wood in the centre of the mortise first. Turn the chisel one way then the other to remove chips. Work with a mallet until you get within about 1mm of the mark, then pare away the waste vertically in one shaving.

To mark the shoulders of the tenon, always use a utility knife or a sharp chisel to score lines around on all four faces. This leaves a clean edge and forms a starting groove for the saw.

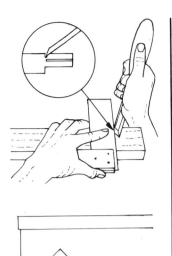

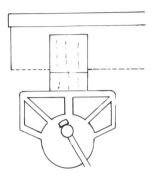

Saw the cheeks before the shoulders. For the first cut, place the rail at an angle and saw with the tenon saw to the scribed line. Then turn the rail around and place it upright to finish the cut.

Finally, place the rail flat in the bench hook to cut off the waste at the shoulders. The V-shaped groove, made with the chisel, forms a guide for the saw.

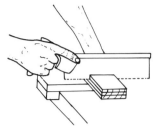

To size up the width of the tenon, offer it up to the mortise, and mark the width of the slot before cutting off the waste with the saw. When trying the joint for fit, you may

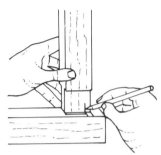

want to clamp across the mortise again in case the tenon is too large. For final fitting, you can also bevel the ends of the tenon slightly to make it easier to fit. The pieces should fit moderately tightly.

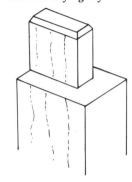

When gluing up, don't tap the joint together with a mallet as this will mark the work. It is better to add the glue to both tenon and mortise, then gradually tighten the joint with a clamp.

OTHER TYPES OF MORTISE AND TENON JOINTS

Haunched tenon

In most good quality work, the basic tenon shown would have a haunch with a corresponding stop cut in the mortise, to make the joint more rigid. The haunch can be 'ordinary' or it can be cut slanted as a 'secret haunch'.

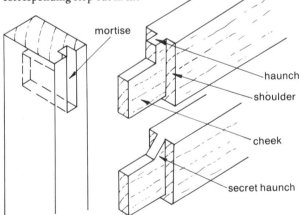

mortise

haunch

shoulder

cheek

secret haunch

Through tenons

Where the appearance isn't so important the tenon can go straight through the stile. The joint can be held as usual by glue alone, or it can be wedged for strength. For a decorative effect, the wedges can be made from a contrasting wood.

Notice that the mortise is sloped out on the other side to make room for the wedges,

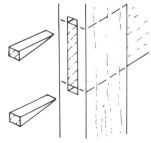

which should be cut to match the shape cut in the mortise.

Loose tenon

Another clever variation of tenons used for knock-down furniture is the loose tenon. The tenon is cut slightly small to fit loosely. It is locked in position from the other side with a tapered wedge. This joint is frequently used to connect the cross rails on refectory tables, for example.

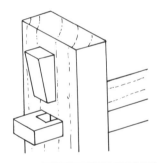

Fox wedging

To strengthen a stub tenon, cut the mortise wide at the bottom. Start the sloping sides 6mm down from the top. Insert the wedges in the saw cuts and clamp the joint tight, forcing the wood apart for a rigid joint.

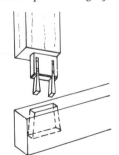

The wedges must be of the right length and the mortise should be about 12mm deeper for clearance. Once the joint is assembled, it is almost impossible to get it apart.

Draw bore tenon

Tapered dowel pegs can be used to lock tenons in position.

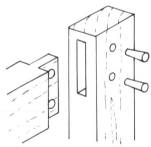

Slide a waste piece into the mortise to drill the peg holes. Take out the waste piece, slide the tenon in, then use the drill to mark the centre on the tenon. Remove the tenon and drill the holes about 1mm in toward the cheek from the mark. The joint will be pulled tight by the tapered peg during assembly.

dovetail joints

Dovetail joints are shaped so that the component pieces cannot pull apart. This makes them ideal for frameworks where strong and immoveable joints are required. Drawer fronts, for example, are pulled constantly but a dovetail joint prevents the front from being pulled away from the sides.

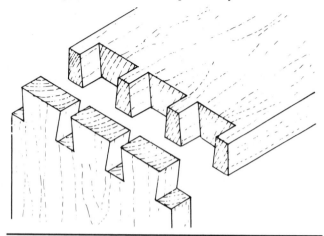

Dovetails are ideal for connecting two sides of a cabinet rigidly. By dovetailing the corners of bookcases the sides remain fixed and the shelves between, which are usually housed in grooves, will stay in place.

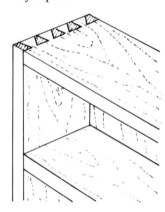

Dovetails are usually cut across the width of the board, as for a bookcase, but in many applications a narrow rail is connected to the carcass sides with a single or double dovetail for greater rigidity. The front and back of the roll top desk on page 128 were dovetailed to the sides to keep the sides absolutely parallel for the successful operation of the sliding tambour.

There are many variations of the dovetail joint. The most common is the through dovetail in which the joint is visible on both faces. This is used when the joint is a decorative feature.

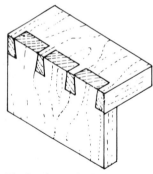

The lap dovetail is hidden from one face and is therefore often used for drawer work to connect the front of the drawer so that the joint will be hidden when it is assembled.

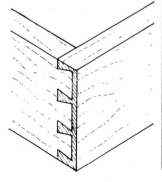

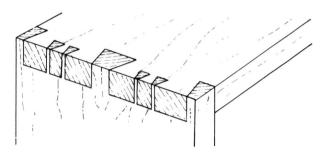

However, in many applications, the dovetail is used as a decorative feature, visible from both faces. In that case the plain through dovetail is used or it can be made more interesting by varying the sizes and shapes of the pins in the joint.

On the roll top desk for example, notice that the dovetails of the top are left exposed to enhance the appearance of the desk.

Dovetails were traditionally cut by hand using a chisel, fretsaw and a dovetail saw, which is a fine-toothed version of the tenon saw (page 196). Today almost all the dovetails which are used on manufactured furniture are cut all at once by machine.

To cut dovetails, either use a dovetail attachment on the router, or cut them in the traditional way, by hand, using a chisel and mallet.

CUTTING DOVETAILS BY HAND

Setting out

First make sure the ends of the boards are square. Plane them if necessary in the shooting board. Then gauge a line in from the end equal to the thickness plus 1mm to allow for trimming later. Set out the tails so that they are wider than the pins. There are no exact rules for the size of the tails but generally, in structural work, make them about as wide as the thickness of the boards. In fine work they can be as thin as you like.

The slope of the tail can vary from about 1 in 5 where strength is required to about 1 in 8 for very delicate work. A slope of 1 in 6 is usually about right.

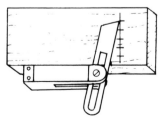

Set the sliding bevel by setting out five divisions in and one over on a piece of wood, as shown.

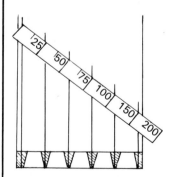

If you plan to do a lot of dovetailing by hand make a template out of a piece of hardwood cut to a shape to simplify the job.

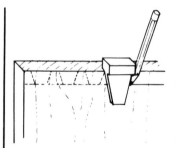

Decide on the number or size of tails making the width of the pins equal at their widest part. Draw lines through the middle of each end pin, then divide the distance between the two end lines into equal spaces by laying the ruler at an angle. Then draw in the tails with the sliding bevel.

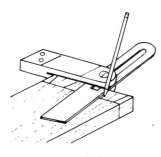

Finally, square the lines across the end with a try square as a guide for the saw and be sure to mark the waste with pencil marks so that you don't make the classic mistake of cutting away the wrong pieces.

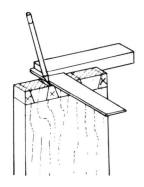

Cutting the tails

Hold the wood at an angle in the vice so that the saw is cutting vertically. Saw on the line square across, down to the gauged line, then tilt the wood the other way to cut the opposite sides.

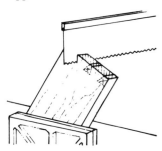

Some woodworkers prefer to mark the pins by scribing through the saw cuts with the saw onto the other piece at this

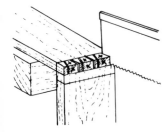

stage, before the tails are cut. However, in the method shown here, the tails are cut out before the pins are marked.

Remove most of the waste with a coping saw, but don't saw to the line. Leave the last 1mm or so of waste to be cleaned out with a chisel.

Clamp the work down to the bench with a piece of waste wood underneath, then pare down to the gauged line using a bevel edged chisel. Turn the wood over and make the final cut from the other side.

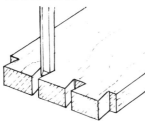

Marking and cutting the pins

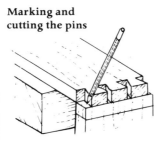

Hold the other piece in the vice while you place the tails over it and mark the pins with a knife or a fine sharp pencil. Take the wood out of the vice and square the lines down to the gauged line.

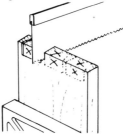

Before cutting out the pins, mark the waste with X marks. When cutting, hold the wood

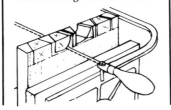

DOVETAILING WITH THE ROUTER

Choose the finger template to match the wood thickness, then clamp both pieces of the joint perpendicular to one another in the jig.

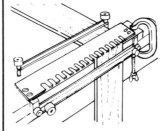

Check to make sure the two pieces match up perfectly, then add the finger template and set the depth of the cutter and cut

each slot separately. The dovetails will fit perfectly since both sides of the joint are cut at the same time. For more detailed instructions on how this is done, refer to the booklet included by the manufacturer.

BOX JOINTS

The box joint or finger joint, like the dovetail joint, can be cut by hand but is most often made by machine. It is frequently used in drawer work. The pine kitchen drawers on page 16 were cut with a jig on the table saw.

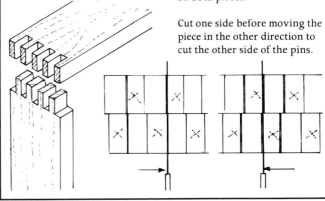

To make the joints by hand, clamp the two pieces together in the vice and mark both pieces across with a try square. Make the fingers about 8mm wide. To make it easy to cut, keep both pieces in the vice but move one sideways so that you can cut in the waste area on both pieces.

Cut one side before moving the piece in the other direction to cut the other side of the pins.

vertically in the vice and make sure to saw on the waste side of the line, otherwise the pins will be too small. After sawing to the line, cut out most of the waste with a coping saw in the same way as for the tails, then pare away the final waste with a chisel.

Assembling

Dovetail joints should only be fully assembled once, ensuring that the fit is tight. But to check that the joint will go together, push the joint

partially home, cutting down any over-sized pieces if necessary. To assemble, glue both pins and tails lightly, then tap them together with a hammer on a piece of waste wood.

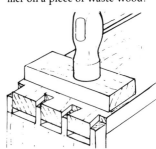

mitre joints

The mitre joint is used to connect two pieces at right angles. Each piece is cut to 45° so that when they are fitted together they form a 90° corner. Mitres can also be cut at other angles, but the most common is the 90° joint.

This is used most frequently to connect mouldings for picture frames and for decorative infills on panels and doors. But reinforced mitre joints can also be used in light framework for doors. For example, the glass panelled door for the corner cupboard on page 155 was mitred and reinforced with dowel pegs.

CUTTING MITRES

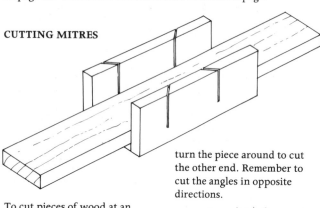

To cut pieces of wood at an accurate 45° angle use a tenon saw and a mitre box. Mitre boxes are quite inexpensive so it is not really worth making one especially as it is difficult to make one really accurately.

Before using the mitre box, screw a long piece of waste wood to the inside from underneath to prevent marking the base of the mitre box itself. Place the piece to be cut in the box and saw with light, even strokes through the slots in the mitre box. Then

turn the piece around to cut the other end. Remember to cut the angles in opposite directions.

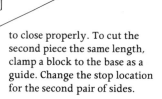

To make frames, you will have to cut mitres on all four ends. Keep in mind that the opposite sides of the frame must be identical in length for the joint

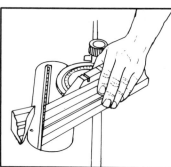

to close properly. To cut the second piece the same length, clamp a block to the base as a guide. Change the stop location for the second pair of sides.

Mitre joints must be reinforced since the end grain connection has virtually no holding power when it is just glued. The simplest way is to pin the corners by skew nailing finishing nails or pins from both sides. Drill the pin holes first to avoid splitting the wood when the nails are driven in.

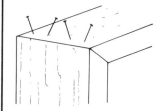

The splined mitre joint is most easily cut on the table saw as shown on page 210. The plywood spline is glued into both pieces to hold the joint firmly in place.

Dowel reinforcements on larger joints are best drilled using a dowelling jig. Use two to three short dowel pegs per joint, spacing them evenly along the end.

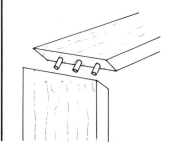

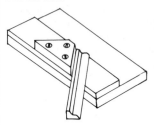

USING THE MITRE SHOOTING BOARD

For most work, the cut made by the tenon saw is good enough to give a smooth surface for gluing up. For very fine work, trim the ends on a mitre shooting board made by screwing an accurate block to a base. Hold the piece against the block and run the plane sideways against it to trim the end.

GLUING UP

Use mitre clamps, either singly to do one corner at a time, or in sets of four to glue the whole framework in one operation.

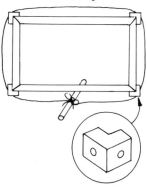

A far simpler and cheaper method of gluing up mitre joints is to fix a cord tightly around the frame with small wooden blocks at each corner. First tie a stick to the cord ends and tighten the cord by turning the stick round and round. Then hold the stick firmly against the frame while the glue sets.

There are several other ways to cut mitres. Using the table saw it is simply a matter of setting the mitre guide at 45°. Refer to page 210 for full instructions on using the saw.

Another easy way to cut

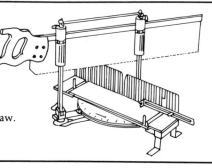

mitres is on the radial saw as shown on page 213. Alternatively use a professional mitre saw with fine teeth for a very smooth cut. This saw is rather expensive but it is very useful since it can be set at any angle to make square as well as angled cuts such as mitres.

halving and bridle joints

Halving joints are very common both in rough carpentry work and in cabinet-making where they are mostly

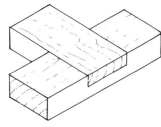

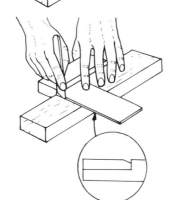

used to joint light frames such as the cabinet doors on page 16. They are easy to make either by hand or with a table saw (page 210).

When the two pieces are of equal thickness, make the cut grooves of equal depth. Mark the pieces first with a knife or chisel as a guide for the saw, then with a marking gauge to set off half the thickness. Always mark the waste area with a pencilled X.

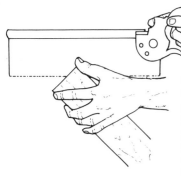

To cut away the waste, first saw away the shoulder in a V-shaped groove. Saw exactly to the gauge mark, then place the piece in the vice in the same way as for cutting tenons and saw on the waste side of the gauge line to remove the waste.

For cross joints, where the halving occurs in the middle of the piece, make the two saw cuts on either side, then pare away the waste as shown below.

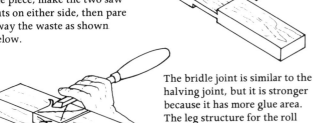

Halving joints are usually used with the pieces joined flat as shown in these drawings, but they can also be used with the pieces held vertically, particularly in plywood which doesn't have the same tendency to break along the grain as solid wood.

The plywood children's high chair on page 96, for example, is made entirely with halving joints and the pieces are held together without nails or screws.

The bridle joint is similar to the halving joint, but it is stronger because it has more glue area. The leg structure for the roll top desk on page 128 uses bridle joints both for strength and as a decorative feature.

housing joints

Housing joints are wide grooves, usually cut across the grain to hold boards to a vertical. The groove can be cut right across the board, called a through housing, or it can be stopped short of the front with a matching step in the shelf, called a stopped housing.

Although the groove is usually only 5mm deep, the housing joint relies on tight fit to hold the pieces together firmly. The joint is glued up in assembly, but it is the tightness of the joint which provides strength.

The groove is easily cut with a router fitted with a straight cutter. Run the router against a square straight edge guide as shown on page 216. For a stopped housing, fix a block to the straight edge to stop the router at the appropriate point, then square off the end of the groove with a chisel.

Mark the setback on the stopped housing with a marking gauge and use it at the same time to mark the notch in the end of the shelf, which should be cut slightly smaller.

Cut the housing groove by hand using a saw, chisel and hand router as shown. First score two lines the width of the housings, then use a chisel to form a V-groove against the scored line for the saw. Saw down to the required depth with a tenon saw, then clean out the waste with a chisel and, if possible, a hand router which is set to the required depth and run back and forth to remove the waste. To make a stopped housing, first cut a small notch at the front with a chisel, then proceed in exactly the same way.

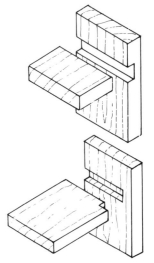

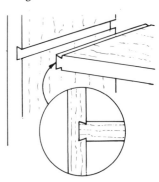

For a more rigid joint, use a dovetailed housing joint. The groove and shelf end are cut using a dovetail cutter fitted to

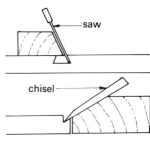

a router. They are then slotted together for a permanent joint. To cut by hand use separate bevelled battens as guides.

working with sheet materials

Traditional woodworking joints are not often used for joining sheet materials. Plywood, blockboard and chipboard each have properties which differ from solid wood so that joints like mortise and tenons are unsuitable. Sheet materials are thin, planar surfaces whereas wood is linear. This means that most sheet joints are along narrow edges which must be reinforced with screwed brackets or nailed battens.

The strength of sheet materials also differs from that of wood which tends to split along the grain. Plywood with its alternating layers of glued veneers is strong in both directions so that a groove can be cut near the end without splitting the material.

Blockboard is strong in one direction but weak in the other so, depending on the direction, it can be joined by traditional woodworking joints. It is possible for example to cut dovetails in blockboard. Chipboard has no grain at all and tends to break easily and must therefore be well supported along the edges with battens, for example, to give it strength. Screws driven into the end grain of chipboard have almost no holding power unless fibre or special plastic plugs are first inserted in the holes to give the screw thread something to grip.

The details shown below give a few examples of joints used in the book for projects made with sheet materials.

CORNER JOINTS OR T-JOINTS

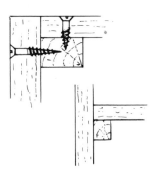

The easiest corner connection for joining sheet materials uses a reinforcing batten which is glued and pinned or screwed to both pieces (captain's bed page 60).

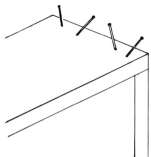

Joining the corners with pins at alternating angles is surprisingly strong. Hide the pins by punching them below the surface and filling the holes (wall unit page 124).

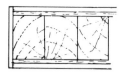

A groove and rabbet joint for plywood and blockboard is stronger than ordinary butt joints (cabinet page 118).

Screws don't hold very well by themselves in the end grain of chipboard or plywood. To strengthen the joint use a fibre wall plug or a special plastic plug inserted in a drilled hole

Plywood edges can be left exposed as a decorative feature (kitchen page 44).

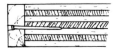

Use iron-on veneer edging to match the surface veneer (bookcase page 114).

Solid wood lipping is either glued on and held with clamps until the glue sets or just glued

in the end grain. The plug expands when the screw is applied (bookcase page 114).

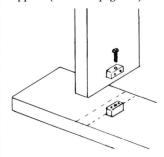

Special plastic block connectors are quick and easy to use. The block halves are screwed to the pieces separately, then joined (wall unit page 110).

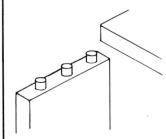

Traditional dowel pegs are often used as a method to reinforce chipboard joints. They require accurate setting out and drilling as shown on

and pinned in place with the pins punched below the surface and the holes filled (kitchen cabinets page 16).

Chipboard edges are often covered with plastic laminate for kitchen counters. Notice the bevelled top edge (kitchen page 44).

Strips of moulding pinned to the edge have many decorative uses such as shelf edging or as decoration for drawers as on the chest of drawers shown on page 64.

page 232. Use two or three 10mm diameter pegs per joint (corner cupboard page 155).

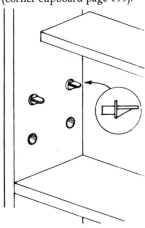

For adjustable shelving there are several systems to use. You can drill holes at regular intervals using a homemade drilling jig as shown on page 112. Then insert either plastic or brass cups into the holes to take small moveable brackets which support the shelves (kitchen page 44).

Metal brackets are old-fashioned but still very useful. The L-brackets are used for inside corners. The flat L- and T-shapes are fixed on the front face. Metal brackets are

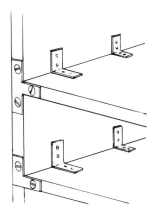

available in ordinary steel or in decorative finishes such as chrome and brass (see example shown on page 242).

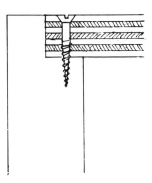

The splined mitre requires a table saw for accurate cutting. See page 210 for instructions.

GROOVED AND RABBETED PANELS

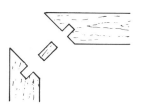

Thin plywood is often used for drawer bottoms. Hold it in place by fitting it into a groove cut in all four drawer sides. See page 216 for instructions on using a router to cut the groove to hold the bottom.

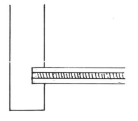

Alternatively glue and screw a batten to the sides of the drawer to support the bottom (captain's bed page 60).

Cabinet and bookcase backs are usually cut from plywood 4 or 6.5mm thick. For solid or veneered bookcases use a plywood veneered to match (bookcase page 114). Standard sheets in various veneers are available from large suppliers. For kitchen cabinets use white hardboard for the backs to match the cabinet. The backs are either screwed or pinned into a rabbet cut in the edge of the cabinet.

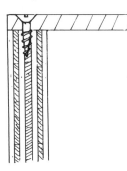

A plywood back panel can also be simply nailed or screwed into the back edges. But notice that the edge can be seen from the side (wall unit page 124).

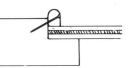

Plywood door panels are usually held in a rabbet by a strip of thin beading which is pinned in place. Use fine veneer pins to avoid splitting the beading and set the pins below the surface to hide them (closets page 70).

Alternatively the door panels can be held in grooves (kitchen page 16).

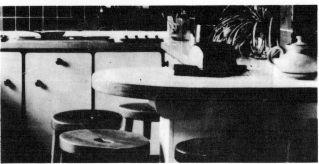

The alternating bands of light and dark veneer in plywood end grain can be used as an attractive feature, as in the sofa with storage, page 148, and kitchen worktop, page 44.

HARDWARE

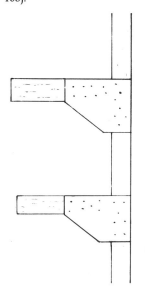

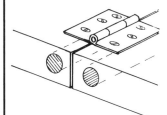

in chipboard which doesn't take screws well (trestles page 108).

Plywood and blockboard take screws well but to strengthen the screw fixings in chipboard for hinges for example, either use fibre plugs or glue dowels into the end first and then drive the screw into this so that it has something to grip into.

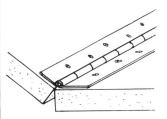

Continuous hinges are very easy to fix. The large number of screws means that no reinforcement is required even

Plywood gussets can be used to make quick and sturdy joints in construction work. Glue and nail the thin plywood gussets on both sides. For heavy work such as the wood racks on page 206, use 12 or 19mm plywood and hammer in the nails at an angle to strengthen the fixing.

241

BASIC FURNITURE CONSTRUCTION

The most important consideration with any piece of furniture is that it be attractive and suited for its purpose. This usually means that it should be strong, square and rigid. But there are other factors such as lightness, durability of finish and choice of material. Most of the planning involved in making a piece of furniture becomes fairly intuitive with experience, but it is a process of learning by mistakes. Sagging shelves, swaying cabinets and split table tops are either the result of bad design or bad workmanship and both usually improve after a few minor disasters. As a guide to good construction, refer to the many standard joints which have been developed over centuries. For quicker, less traditional but equally sturdy joining methods, modern connectors should be used, particularly when working with sheet materials.

There are also many standard construction procedures and hints dealing with problems which are very useful to study as examples for your own work.

It is fine to learn all about cutting perfect joints, but it is no use having good joints unless the assembly procedure is also well thought out and the construction is designed for squareness and stability.

Many of the standard procedures used in furniture construction are shown in detail in the various projects in this book. However, no written instructions can ever be as informative as actually solving the problems as they arise in making your own furniture.

decorative touches

ROUNDING CORNERS
On doors or table tops and many other pieces of work, rounding the corners helps to take away the square, clumsy appearance. It not only makes work look more graceful but it is also nicer to touch. Refer to the kitchen doors on page 44 and the baby's bed on page 88 for good examples.

CUTTING OUT SHAPES
A sabre saw or coping saw is easy to use to cut out many different decorative shapes such as the heart shaped cut-outs on the plant container on page 178 or the arches on the Welsh dresser on page 36.

MOULDED EDGES
You can cut many shapes on the edges of shelves, drawer fronts and table tops with a router. Refer to page 216 for instructions on how to use the router and to see the great variety of profiles available.

Alternatively apply moulded sections by gluing and pinning them to the edges. Set the nails and fill the holes with filler,

sanding smooth when dry. This is a useful way to cover the edges of plywood as in the wall unit on page 124).

EXPOSING THE WOOD JOINTS
Instead of hiding the joints in a piece of furniture, make a decorative feature of them. The exposed dovetails in the cabinet of the roll top desk for example, give the desk a nice, handmade look.

HARDWARE

Hinges, handles and pulls can add decorative final touches to a piece. The brass drawer pulls on the chest of drawers (page 64) for example make the whole piece of furniture sparkle.

bookcases

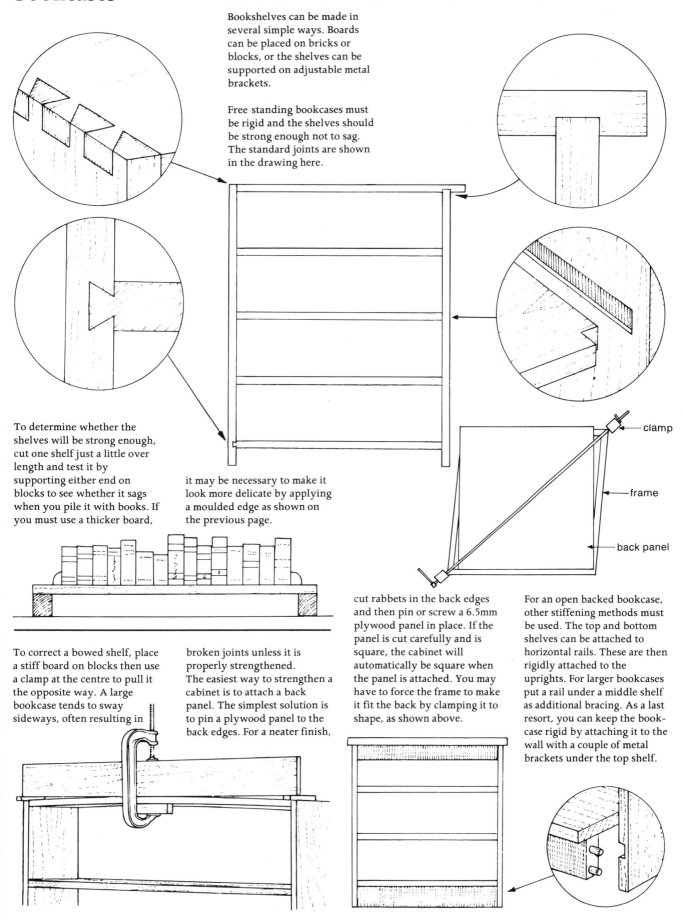

Bookshelves can be made in several simple ways. Boards can be placed on bricks or blocks, or the shelves can be supported on adjustable metal brackets.

Free standing bookcases must be rigid and the shelves should be strong enough not to sag. The standard joints are shown in the drawing here.

To determine whether the shelves will be strong enough, cut one shelf just a little over length and test it by supporting either end on blocks to see whether it sags when you pile it with books. If you must use a thicker board, it may be necessary to make it look more delicate by applying a moulded edge as shown on the previous page.

clamp

frame

back panel

To correct a bowed shelf, place a stiff board on blocks then use a clamp at the centre to pull it the opposite way. A large bookcase tends to sway sideways, often resulting in broken joints unless it is properly strengthened. The easiest way to strengthen a cabinet is to attach a back panel. The simplest solution is to pin a plywood panel to the back edges. For a neater finish, cut rabbets in the back edges and then pin or screw a 6.5mm plywood panel in place. If the panel is cut carefully and is square, the cabinet will automatically be square when the panel is attached. You may have to force the frame to make it fit the back by clamping it to shape, as shown above.

For an open backed bookcase, other stiffening methods must be used. The top and bottom shelves can be attached to horizontal rails. These are then rigidly attached to the uprights. For larger bookcases put a rail under a middle shelf as additional bracing. As a last resort, you can keep the book-case rigid by attaching it to the wall with a couple of metal brackets under the top shelf.

cabinets and doors

There are many different ways of making cabinets such as chests of drawers, desks and wall-hung units. In traditional construction, the basic

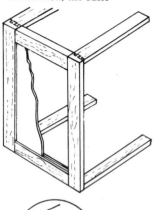

framework is made from lengths of wood joined by dowelling, mortise and tenon or other woodworking joints. The framework is enclosed with infill panels of either solid wood or plywood set into grooves or rabbets in the frame. Modern construction techniques use sheet materials to do both jobs of framing and covering with one panel. The panels are usually connected by a combination of traditional and mechanical joints.

Cabinets are similar in construction to bookcases. The

shelves must not sag and the whole structure must be rigid. Squareness is particularly important so that the doors will fit properly. Strengthening methods are also similar to those shown for bookcases. The back and side panels usually make the cabinet rigid.

Another method often used is to attach side pilasters both for strengthening and for aesthetic effect. The traditional oak veneer corner cupboard shown on page 155 is strengthened by this method.

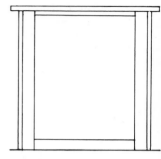

A pilaster is a vertical version of the horizontal braces shown for the bookcases. This idea is often incorporated into the design of the cabinet in the form of plinths and cornices, as for the chest of drawers page 64.

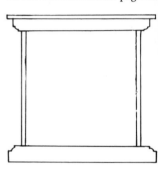

The plinth can be projecting as in most traditional work or recessed as in much modern furniture.

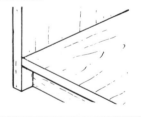

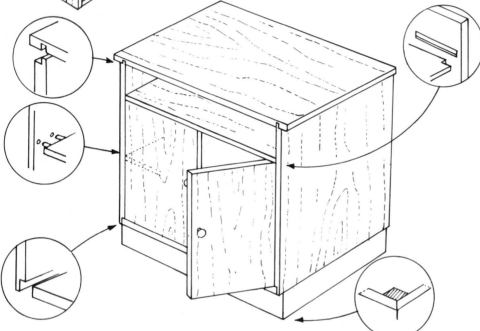

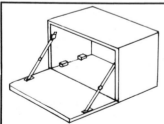

MAKING SIMPLE BOXES
Boxes, which are very easy to make, can be used in a number of ways to make wall units such as on page 124 or toy bins on castors, or any number of small and large cabinets. Various methods of connecting the sides are shown on page 226.

1. To make a box, cut the sides accurately, and check with a try square.

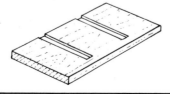

2. Make sure to cut any grooves or rabbets and to drill any holes, as for adjustable shelves, before assembly.

3. Assemble the four sides. Then before adding the back, attach any dividers.

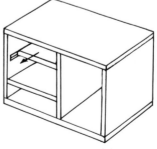

4. Use the back panel to pull the box square, attaching it with pins or screws.

For larger boxes, it is a good idea to connect the shelves to

one side and the back before attaching the last side.

Finally add any hardware to the box such as hinges or stays or plastic channels to hold the doors. Refer to the details on page 242 for decorating the edges of the box to make it look more finished.

cabinets and doors

Cabinets must also be designed to hold together so that the uprights don't tend to move apart, resulting in loose joints and a wobbly structure.

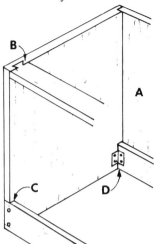

The back panel helps to tie the whole framework together (A) but the horizontal rails and shelves must do most of the work. Dovetailed joints such as those used on the roll top desk

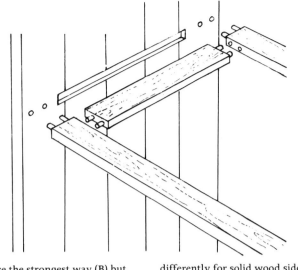

are the strongest way (B) but the rails can also be screwed and plugged to the front and back edges in less fine work (C). Alternatively, use metal brackets in unobtrusive places to hold the rails (D).

In cabinets with drawers, the drawer runners are treated

differently for solid wood sides than for sides made of sheet materials which have no tendency to expand and contract. For solid wood sides, place the runner in a groove without attaching it and keep it in place by dowelling or grooving it into the front and back rails which are rigidly

joined to the cabinet sides. For sides which are made of plywood, blockboard or chipboard, the drawer runner can be glued and screwed since there are no problems with movement of the materials. This was done for the chest of drawers on page 64.

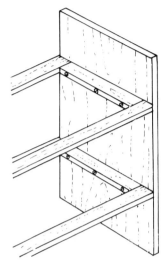

DOORS

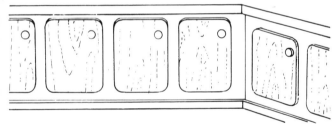

Cabinet doors can be made very simply out of pieces of plywood with rounded corners as in the town kitchen on page 44. Or, they can be made in the traditional way with a frame and infill panel as in the country kitchen on page 16 or the bedroom closets on page 70.

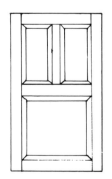

Traditional door construction uses mortise and tenon (A), dowel (B) or halving joints (C). The panel is held either in a

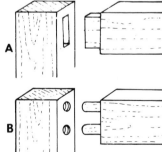

groove (A) or rabbet. The rabbet can be cut at the back or front and the panel held in place with a small bead (B) or decorative moulding (C) using small pins or fine veneer pins.

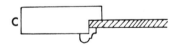

Plan corner joints so that any grooves or rabbets do not show. They can be stopped short of the joint, or the joint

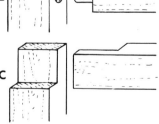

can be cut to accommodate them, such as the haunched mortise and tenon joint.

Light sliding doors made out of plywood, hardboard or glass can run in plastic channels. These are available in matching pairs to suit different thicknesses of material in single or double track versions. They can be screwed in place or just glued down with contact adhesive.

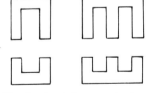

Heavier closet doors are best suspended from rolling hardware available in a variety of types and grades.

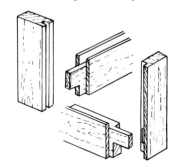

245

tables

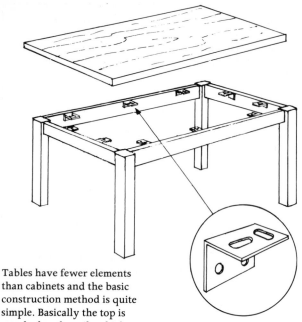

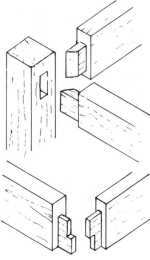

Tables have fewer elements than cabinets and the basic construction method is quite simple. Basically the top is attached to the rails which are fixed to the legs at the corners. There are, of course, variations. The table can have rails near the bottom, the ends can be solid or trestle-shaped with bracing rails fitted at mid-height, or if the table is

circular, it will usually have a central pedestal base.

Basically, the stability of a table comes from the rail to leg connection which must therefore be solidly made.

Trestle tables rely on a wide central rail for rigidity. The two end trestles, which are dowelled or joined by a

mortise and tenon, support the top. The connection between the trestles and the cross rails is usually made so that the table can be dismantled for easy moving.

The traditional joint used is the pegged through tenon which is strong and easily taken apart. A modern substitute uses the bolt and cross dowel shown on page 226. The flat brass bolt heads are decorative but the short cross dowels are hidden in holes drilled in the top and bottom of the rail.

Tops made from plywood or chipboard can be attached from underneath by screwing

CORNER JOINTS

The traditional mortise and tenon joint can be made with tenons that just meet inside the mortise, or the tenons can be mitred or stopped.

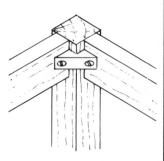

Wood or metal corner blocks or brackets are easy to fix and hold very well. See the kitchen work island on page 24 for instructions on how to fix the metal brackets. This or the traditional wood bracket is particularly handy because the legs can easily be removed.

Dowel joints must be well made with at least two, preferably three, 10 or 12mm diameter dowel pins.

For fixing rails to round legs use dowel joints and shape the ends of the rails to match the shape of the leg.

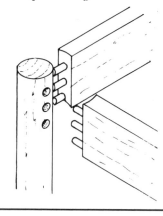

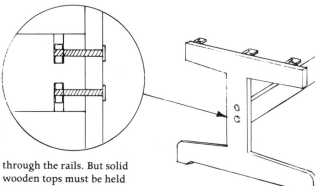

through the rails. But solid wooden tops must be held down with slotted shrinkage brackets to allow the wood to expand and contract according to changes in the seasons or in the moisture content of the room.

The angle type of shrinkage bracket screws directly to the inside of the rail but the flat

brackets must be set in recesses in the tops of the rails. Always attach them so that the round head screw is free to move back and forth across the width of the table, perpendicular to the grain as the wood expands and contracts.

drawers

In fine work, drawers are made from hardwearing hardwoods such as oak or maple, but in modern work most drawers are made from plywood or blockboard. The bottoms can be solid wood, in which case they must be loose in the grooves to allow them to shrink. But usually the bottoms are made from 6.5mm plywood which is stable and therefore can be rigidly attached to the sides to help strengthen the drawer.

The joining methods vary according to the material and the type of project. In fine cabinetmaking dovetails are required but for ordinary work screwed corners may be sufficient.

CORNER JOINTS
Traditional dovetails are the strongest and best looking joint for drawers.

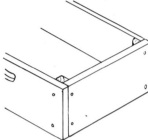

The groove and rabbet joint is convenient for plywood sides.

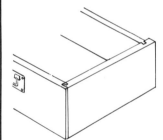

The simplest corner joint is the butt joint reinforced by a batten or a more attractive

quadrant moulding glued and pinned in place.

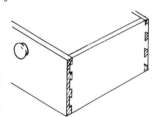

Screws do not hold well in the end grain of plywood but by inserting fibre wall plugs into the end grain the screwed joint is strong and permanent.

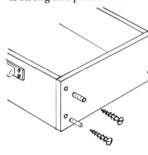

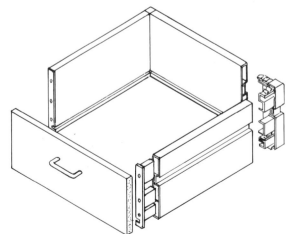

A simple alternative is to use plastic drawer kits. The side section comes in long lengths and is cut off to length with a saw according to instructions. Corner joints simply clip on with hand pressure and lock

tight. Grooves for the plywood bottoms and the drawer runners are part of the moulded section. These drawers were used for the work table on page 120 and the night table on page 56.

Plywood bottoms can be held in grooves which are usually stopped to avoid showing at the ends, by screwing a batten underneath or simply by gluing and screwing them directly to the bottom edges of the drawer sides.

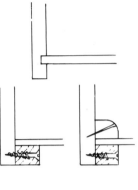

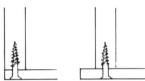

It's easy to attach a separate piece to the drawer to serve as the front, screwing it on from the inside. This technique is useful for drawer fronts which overlap the opening, such as the drawer in the kitchen work island on page 24.

Alternatively, the drawer fronts can be an integral part of the drawer with the front side exposed. Since the joints will show, use dovetails or perhaps finger joints for a decorative effect, as on the country kitchen drawers on page 16.

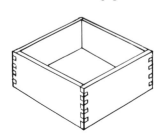

DRAWER RUNNERS
The drawers can run on battens screwed to the cabinet sides as in the bins for the closets on page 70.

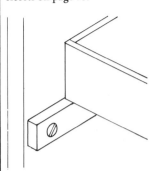

The oversized drawer bottom can run in plastic or metal channels screwed to the sides.

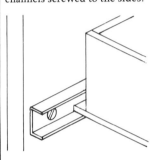

The traditional method is to put a groove in the drawer side which runs on small battens screwed to the side of the cabinet as in the kitchen work island (page 24).

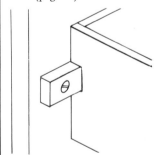

Metal drawer runners with rollers are easy to fix and very smooth running. As examples, see the kitchen on page 44, or the captain's bed on page 60.

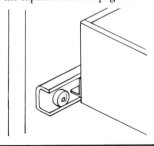

wood finishing

The fashion in wood finishing changes periodically. During the last decade, most people preferred a shiny, gloss finish on furniture, whereas today the trend is for the wood to look as natural as possible with no heavy build-up of lacquers.

Wood doesn't necessarily have to be finished at all. In Scandinavia, beautiful hardwood furniture is sold unfinished.

So long as the furniture is kept in a dry environment and any marks are removed by scrubbing or rubbing with steel wool or very fine sandpaper, it is not necessary to apply a finish.

But generally, finishes are applied both to enhance the beauty of the wood and to protect it from moisture which causes it to warp and creates unsightly stains. If the wood is attractively grained, the finish should enhance the pattern. Lighten or darken the tone of the wood by bleaching or staining to match existing furniture.

You can protect the wood by sealing the surface with a variety of finishes such as oil, wax, shellac, lacquer or paint. The finish you choose will of course depend on the type of wood used and the kind of effect you want the finish to have.

No matter which finish or technique is used, the secret to a beautiful finish is in the preparation.

PREPARATION FOR FINISHING

First the wood must be made smooth by planing, scraping or sanding. Any noticeable nicks or bruises must be removed by careful planing. In order not to create a hollow in the damaged spot, plane over a larger area with a fine set plane until the mark is removed.

Scraping produces a very fine finish on hardwoods which will require little or no sanding. Use a sharp cabinet scraper as shown on page 205 to remove a fine, even shaving of wood. Sharpen the scraper often to keep it sharp.

Sanding is the best method of getting a really smooth finish. There are different types of abrasive papers available, glass or sandpaper, garnet paper and aluminous oxide paper. Garnet paper is preferred by woodworkers because it is harder than glass or sandpaper and therefore cuts more quickly and cleanly. Aluminous oxide, also used for woodworking is even harder.

The size of particles or grit governs the roughness of the paper. Although most people buy papers by the general terms rough, medium and smooth, the abrasives are technically graded by grit size – 60 or 80 grit is equivalent to coarse grade, 100 is medium, 120 to 150 is fine and 180 to 240 is very fine or flour grade.

When sanding, start with the finest paper appropriate for the particular surface. For a rough, open-grained wood like oak you may have to start sanding with 80 grit, but birch plywood, for example, is already quite smooth and a rubbing with 150 or 240 grit may be all that is required.

Hold the work firmly on the bench or in a vice, use a sanding block to hold the paper and sand with short even strokes, with the grain.

On fine work, it is a good idea to brush off the dust as you work since loose grits from the abrasive paper may mar it.

Work from coarse to medium to fine paper until the surface is very smooth. Remember that the smoother it is at this stage, the better the finish will be.

POWER SANDERS

To make the work easier, use an orbital sander (page 215). Never use a disk sander on furniture as it leaves marks which are very difficult to remove. Don't use a belt sander unless you are experienced in using it.

An orbital sander works in a circular motion. Bear down gently on the sander as you work. Be careful to examine the surface periodically by eye and also by touch to find any imperfections.

Brush away the dust from time to time so that loose grit does not imbed in the sanding belt and mar the surface. Always finish sanding by hand, working along the grain to remove any marks.

To get a really smooth finish, adopt a method used by furniture makers. Brush off the sanded surface and then wipe it with a damp cloth to raise the grain slightly. Let the wood dry and then sand again with very fine flour grade paper. This will prevent the grain from being raised when you apply the finish.

FILLING AND PATCHING

Small holes and scratches can be filled either with store-bought or homemade wood filler. Fillers or stoppers can be bought in a variety of shades to match various woods, but keep in mind that they will never match the wood perfectly and it may be just as well to leave a slight mark rather than to draw attention to it by filling it.

Another method is to carefully drill a hole, removing the mark, then fill the hole with a wood plug (page 214).

Painted and stained work is easy to fill as the finish will cover or mask the filler.

To make a filler which matches the wood perfectly, spread a small amount of white woodworking glue on a scrap of the same wood and then produce fine sawdust with a scraper or chisel and mix it with the glue. Make it into a paste and apply to the hole immediately. Sand smooth when dry.

GRAIN FILLING

For a really glossy finish, the wood surface must be very smooth before the finish is applied. Coarse grained woods like oak, ash or mahogany have fairly rough surfaces even after careful sanding and it is a good idea to fill the grain before the final finish is applied but after any stain is applied.

Fillers are sold in either liquid or paste form to match the type of finish you will be using, whether oil or lacquer.

Rub the filler into the grain with a stiff brush, then rub it off with a coarse cloth before it is completely dry. The aim is to fill the pores leaving no filler on top of the grain to cloud the finish.

If in doubt about the type of filler to use, ask a specialist supplier who will recommend the right one to go with the sealer you intend to use. Try it out before you proceed.

STAINS

Most woods look good left natural. Even the most ordinary species such as pine, Douglas fir and beech have their own warmth and beauty even if the grain figuring is not dramatic.

When you want to tone the colour slightly or even darken it dramatically, use a water or oil based wood stain. Water based stains are the easiest type to apply, and they tend to penetrate more deeply into the wood to yield a more even and clear tone than the oil stains. Raise the grain with a damp cloth and sand smooth before applying a water based stain.

Apply the stain with a sponge, cloth or brush, testing the colour first.

Brush the colour on liberally and evenly and when the surface is finished, wipe the stain with a clean cloth to get an overall even tone. Remember it is always better to put on two or three diluted coats of stain than one heavy coat which may go blotchy.

Oil stains don't raise the grain as much so there is no need to dampen the wood before application. Apply the stain with a cloth, working it over the whole surface and then wiping it with a clean cloth to even out the colour while the stain is still wet. Unlike water based stains, oil based stains dry slowly so there is plenty of time to work in the colour. Don't use oil stains under lacquer finishing coats; use water based stains which will not react with the lacquer.

BLEACHING
To lighten the tone of woods you can apply special wood bleach to the boards. You can make a homemade mixture using oxalic acid, but it is safer to use a commercial bleach sold at hardware stores. Bleach is dangerous to use as it will burn skin and clothing so wear rubber gloves and an apron and use the liquid carefully avoiding any contact with the skin.

Bleaches are usually sold in two parts; the bleach itself which is applied with a fibre brush or a sponge and the neutralizer which is applied to stop the action of the bleach.

Follow the manufacturer's instructions carefully and after bleaching, sand the work lightly before applying finish. Never put bleaches into metal containers; keep them in the plastic bottles in which they are sold. If you mix your own, use glass, earthenware, or plastic containers.

VARNISH
Varnishes consist of copal gums and linseed oil mixed with turpentine.

Varnishing is the traditional technique for producing a clear finish, though it is often used with pigments for toning or staining at the same time. Today, varnish has been largely replaced by synthetic lacquers like polyurethane which dry more quickly and are more water and stain resistant.

SHELLAC
Shellac is also a traditional finishing material long favoured by craftsmen because it is easy to apply and is quick drying. Unlike varnishes and synthetic lacquers, it penetrates into the wood surface, filling the pores so that it creates a beautiful deep polish. It is often used as a combination sealer and filler. One or two thin coats applied under a coat of wax produces a beautiful and natural finish.

Shellac is also used in French polishing but because it stains easily and has little resistance to water or alcohol, it too has been replaced by synthetic lacquers.

LACQUERS
Modern synthetic lacquers produce an extremely hard, clear finish which resists heat, water and other stains very well. Lacquers are therefore ideal for surfaces like table tops and children's furniture which must withstand a lot of hard wear. It is non-toxic, and easy to apply making it a perfect all-purpose finish for many types of furniture.

Non-synthetic nitro cellulose lacquers are still widely used in industry but for home and small workshop use, polyurethane lacquers are unrivalled for their ease of application and durability of finish.

Rubbing with pumice powder

As a final touch to varnished surfaces, rub them down with a fine abrasive to take away the glossy look and to give the surface a deep, lustrous and smooth finish.

You can buy various rubbing compounds, but the easiest method is to rub the surface with a mixture of pumice powder and oil. Teak oil is suitable, or you can buy a special polishing oil for the purpose.

Pumice powder is available in different grades and only the finest should be used for finishing. Either mix the powder and oil together to make a liquid the consistency of cream or dip a cloth first in oil and then in the pumice powder. Rub it in really well, working with the grain. Renew the oil and pumice finish from time to time.

The pumice acts as an abrasive to remove any imperfections on the surface. Once the surface is well rubbed, go over it again with oil alone, buffing well to make it really shiny and smooth.

APPLYING POLYURETHANE LACQUER
The best finish is produced by spraying but for finishing an occasional piece of furniture, a brush is the best applicator. It is recommended that you apply a sealing coat first with the lacquer thinned down. Let this dry completely and then rub with flour grade sandpaper or with fine 000 grade steel wool before applying the first full coat. You can also buy a special sanding sealer which dries in minutes and forms an ideal base for the final coats of lacquer.

Rub down the surface between each coat with flour grade paper or grade 000 steel wool and wipe off all dust carefully with a clean cloth before applying the next coat of polyurethane.

Polyurethane lacquer is widely available for home use from most hardware and paint stores. It is available in matt, satin or gloss finish. To get a matt or semi-gloss finish, apply a thinned sealing coat, then one or two coats of gloss before applying the final matt coat.

First brush against the grain, then with the grain, finishing off with fine, feather-like strokes to even the surface.

For a more natural finish, apply only one coat of lacquer over the sealer coat or use a special penetrating sealer, available for finishing floors, and finish off with wax.

WAX FINISH
Wax can be used either on the bare wood or on top of a sealer for a deep, matt finish which is beautiful, natural looking and which can be renewed easily. Buy a good quality commercial paste wax, not a spray or liquid, or better yet, make your own wax paste.

The standard craftsman's recipe is to mix about 400g of pure beeswax, available from specialist stores, with 0.25 litre of turpentine. Mix these together in a metal container placed in hot water until it forms a paste. To make the wax finish harder, add a little carnauba wax to the beeswax before melting it with the turpentine. Store the wax in a container leaving the applicator pad on top and the lid tightly closed.

This formula produces a wax ⟶

wood finishing

continued from page 249

which is harder than commercial preparations and which is therefore better for applying straight onto bare wood.

Apply the wax as a paste, thinning it with turpentine if necessary. Use a clean lint free cloth to apply the paste and allow it to harden for about ten minutes. Then buff with a soft cloth to achieve a really fine sheen. The more buffing you do, the more lustrous the finish. Build up two or three thin coats of wax, buffing well between coats with a soft cloth for a really beautiful finish.

To make the wood more resistant to stains, first finish with a thin sealer coat of lacquer and then apply the layers of wax, rubbing them in well.

OIL FINISH
Some fine grained woods like walnut, sycamore and maple look good with a natural oil finish. The traditional linseed oil requires many coats and is not very resistant to heat and water. Modern oils such as teak oil and Danish oil contain oxidizing agents which make the finish more durable and only two or three coats are necessary. Be sure to buff well, using a soft cloth between coats.

Like wax finishes, the advantage of an oil finish is that it can be renewed. A scratch in a table top for example can be rubbed out easily with fine sandpaper or steel wool and then the bare wood can be refinished with oil to match the rest of the surface.

Apply teak oil with a cloth, rubbing it into the grain. Let it stand for about 30 minutes, then wipe the surface with a clean soft cloth to remove any oil which has not dried. Buff the surface to polish it and then repeat this two or three times for a deep and beautiful finish.

SPRAY FINISHING
Spray finishing with a pressure-fed spray gun is quick and simple and produces the best finish. You can buy small and relatively inexpensive guns and compressors such as the one shown here for applying lacquers, water based paint, oil paint, varnish and even stains. Its use isn't limited to furniture. Household jobs such as painting rooms, door and window frames and spray work on a car are easily done with a spray gun.

Applying paint with a gun takes a little practice so it is important to try the gun out on a sheet of hardboard or plywood so that you develop the right touch before you spray a piece of work.

The most important part of spray painting is the preparation of the material.

Preparation for spraying
Most finishing materials are suitable for spray application but if you are in doubt, ask the paint supplier or the manufacturer of the spray equipment for advice. Before you fill the gun, you must follow certain steps to prepare the liquid you are spraying.

First stir the paint or lacquer thoroughly to be sure that the colour is well mixed. Check the viscosity of the liquid before you fill the gun. This is an important consideration as liquids that are too thick will spray a blotchy surface and if the liquid is too thin, the paint will run.

Use a viscosity cup supplied by the spray gun manufacturer to check that the liquid is the right consistency. The cup is filled with paint and the time that the liquid takes to run out is timed. Thin the liquid with the appropriate solvent if it is too thick.

In the absence of a viscosity cup add a small quantity of the recommended thinner and stir thoroughly to mix with a clean stick. Withdraw the stick and hold it at a 45° angle. When the paint runs from the end of the stick in a continuous stream, it should be at roughly the right consistency for spraying.

It is also good practice to strain the paint before use and remove all impurities to minimize wear of the moving parts of the spray gun as well as helping to achieve a better surface finish. You can strain the liquid by pouring it through a single layer of nylon stocking mounted over the top of a container. As with all finishes, the surface to be sprayed should be clean, dry and free from dust.

Spraying should be done in a large, clean, well ventilated area with good lighting. Cover everything which is not being sprayed. It's also important for your own safety to wear a mask to cover your mouth and nose when using spray equipment.

If you are spraying outdoors, do it on a still, dry day and do the work early in the morning to minimize insects settling on the surface. Cover the area around the work with a plastic sheet or newspapers secured with adhesive tape.

Using the spray gun

Make sure that the fluid control adjustment on the gun is correctly set. While practicing, experiment with the adjustment, starting from an almost closed position to create a small pattern. Adjust the spray gradually to widen the pattern created. Notice that the more liquid which is sprayed through, the more the spray tends to break up or atomize into large particles.

Practice spraying both vertically and horizontally with the adjustment set to a fine spray in a flat fan pattern until you are satisfied with the result. When spraying, it is important to use the correct techniques. The gun should be held at right angles to the work with the distance between the surface and face of the gun maintained at 150 to 200mm. The best idea is to practise on an old piece of furniture which will allow you to make mistakes.

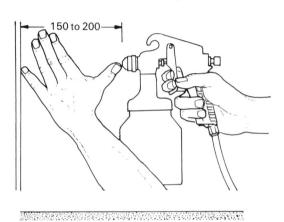

150 to 200

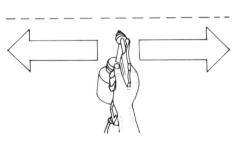

Each stroke is made with a free arm motion across the face of the work surface with the wrist kept flexible so that the gun is kept at right angles to the surface and at the correct distance from it at all times. Keep the speed on each stroke constant to maintain a uniform thickness of coating. To

prevent the building up of paint at the beginning and end of each stroke, the movement of the gun should be started before you pull the trigger and the trigger should be released again before the movement of the gun is finished at the end of the stroke. Do not jerk the gun or move it abruptly.

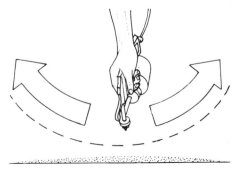

Overlapping strokes

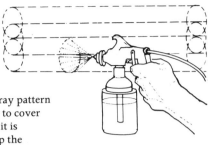

The edges of the spray pattern taper off slightly so to cover the surface evenly, it is necessary to overlap the previous stroke by about 50 per cent. To do this, aim the

gun at the edge of the previous stroke to get the right overlap. Then finish off the ends with one cross stroke.

To cover a large area, spray with a series of straight overlapping strokes and also overlap the ends as shown.

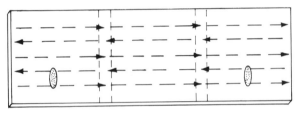

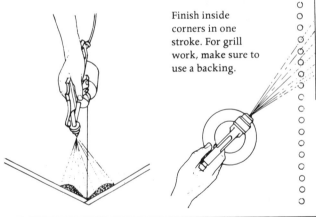

Finish inside corners in one stroke. For grill work, make sure to use a backing.

Cleaning the equipment

It is essential to clean the spray equipment after each use and the sooner you clean it, the easier the job.

Use the correct cleaning fluid to match the finishing material.

When spraying is completed, stop the compressor and pull the trigger to relieve air pressure. Unscrew the paint cup and allow excess paint to drain out. Empty the paint cup and clean thoroughly with solvent.

Pour some thinner into the paint cup, reassemble the gun and spray until pure thinner is passed out. Switch off and take the paint cup off again. Dry all the pieces well. Remove the air cap and soak in thinner, cleaning the slot with a wood toothpick.

Wipe all the pieces with a soft rag and keep in a dry, dust free place when not in use. Be sure to keep the compressor clean and clean the air inlet filters and inside the air hose each time.

Index

Index

Index

The publishers would like to thank the following for generously supplying the tools, equipment and accessories used to make the projects in this book.

Black & Decker Ltd
Power Tools
Cannon Lane
Maidenhead
Berkshire

DeVilbiss Company Ltd
Ringwood Road
Bournemouth

Dormer Tools (Sheffield) Ltd
Summerfield Street
Sheffield

Record Ridgway Tools Ltd
Parkway Works
Sheffield

Sandvik (UK) Ltd
Saws and Tools Division
Manor Way
Halesowen
West Midlands

Stanley Tools Ltd
Woodside
Sheffield

Stanley Power Tools Ltd
Nelson Way
Cramlington
Northumberland

The following kindly supplied the materials used to make and finish the projects and to complete the locations in which they were photographed.

J D Beardmore and Co Ltd
Field End Road
Ruislip
Middlesex

Burmah Industrial Products Ltd
147 London Road
Kingston-upon-Thames
Surrey

Eaton Bag Company
16 Manette Street
London W1

Evode Ltd
Common Road
Stafford

**Finnish Plywood
Development Association**
21 Panton Street
London W1

Formica Ltd
Coast Road
North Shields
Tyne + Wear

Laura Ashley
London and New York

ICI Ltd
Paints Division
Imperial Chemical House
Millbank
London SW1

Arthur Sanderson and Sons Ltd
53 Berners Street
London W1

Sterling-Roncraft Ltd
Chapeltown
Sheffield

Swales-Sofadi Ltd
Dock Road
North Shields

Special thanks are due to
Liberty & Company Ltd, Regent Street, London W1 for loaning props for photography and to **21 Antiques**, Chalk Farm Road, London N1 for assistance with props.